A HISTORY OF
RUGBY IN LEINSTER

Dr David Doolin is Lecturer Above the Bar at the University of Galway, developing innovative inter- and trans-disciplinary classes, as part of a project titled Designing Futures. He teaches Public History, History of Technology, Navigating the Digital World and Intercultural Encounters. Prior to this, Dr Doolin taught in the School of History at University College Dublin, holding posts as Teaching Fellow in American History and subsequently the Postdoctoral Newman Fellowship, allowing him to research and write *A History of Rugby in Leinster*. With an eclectic research and teaching background, he also teaches the history of Digital Technology, the history of Irish America, US global issues, and the immigrant experience in the United States more broadly. His first book, released in 2016 to coincide with the 150th year anniversary, was titled, *Transnational Revolutionaries: The Fenian Invasion of Canada, 1866*, offering a fresh perspective on a largely forgotten past.

A HISTORY OF
RUGBY IN LEINSTER

David Doolin

MERRION
PRESS

First published in 2023 by
Merrion Press
10 George's Street
Newbridge
Co. Kildare
Ireland
www.merrionpress.ie

978 1 78537 478 4 (Hardback)
978 1 78537 479 1 (Ebook)

A CIP catalogue record for this book is available from the British Library.

Typeset in Minion Pro 11/15 pt

Front cover images, clockwise from top: A loose ball during the 1949 Leinster Senior Cup final in which Lansdowne were victorious over Old Belvedere. Courtesy of Des Daly's private collection; Brian O'Driscoll during Leinster's Heineken Cup final clash with Leicester Tigers at Murrayfield, Scotland on 23 May 2009. © Brendan Moran/Sportsfile; Leinster captain Leo Cullen and Chris Whitaker lift the Heineken Cup after victory over Leicester. © Brendan Moran/Sportsfile
Back cover image: Dan Sheehan scores for Leinster in the Champions Cup final against La Rochelle at the Aviva Stadium on 20 May 2023. © Ramsey Cardy/Sportsfile

Merrion Press is a member of Publishing Ireland.

CONTENTS

Acknowledgements

This book would not have been possible without the Kevin Brabazon Newman Fellowship in the History of Rugby in Leinster. I am greatly indebted to Ruth and David Brabazon, and the Brabazon family, for their support. In addition, the idea of tracing the origins and evolution of rugby in Leinster was initially formulated by Professor Paul Rouse. I will be forever grateful to Prof. Rouse for allowing me to pick this idea up and run with it, taking my own path, while always being supportive and generous with insights, direction and feedback. I also acknowledge and offer much thanks to UCD's Newman Fellowship staff, with special thanks to Órfhlaith Ford, as well the School of History at UCD, who provided me with support, help and encouragement.

The backing of Leinster Rugby has also been pivotal, through the generous access allowed to all of their records, going back to the Branch's foundations. The vast majority of these records have subsequently been digitized for posterity and are housed in the UCD Archives for anyone curious to examine the history of rugby in Leinster. Additionally, thank you to the staff at the UCD Archives for allowing me access to the Leinster Rugby material. What's more, Leinster Rugby – especially Marketing Head, Kevin Quinn and CEO Michael Dawson – backed the project from the outset, and I thank them for their support and enabling us to produce not just the history in text but to share some of the countless images that help us visualise that story. Without Leinster's backing to reproduce and share these images, the book would have remained text only.

This research project faced an initial, significant challenge when the Covid pandemic closed down much of Ireland for well over a year (starting March 2020), including access to all public archives and libraries. However, I owe a massive thank you to Helen Daly and her family for allowing me to access the extensive records and masses of documents, a veritable private archive, that were kept by her late husband and the honorary statistician of Leinster rugby, Des Daly. Des was obviously a dedicated rugby man, as his records showed the attention and detail he paid to the game in Ireland and in Leinster especially. He was interested not just in the provincial Leinster side, as well as in the Leinster clubs, but kept records for all four provinces; for teams in the All-Ireland League once it commenced; the universities, especially UCD; and the Irish rugby teams – senior, women's, schools and underage. Des Daly clearly dedicated much of his time to rugby, a diehard fan no doubt, and maintained a detailed interest in so many of the various players, clubs, game results, records and statistics. His archive allowed the project to continue during so much disruption, during multiple Covid lockdowns. Thank you to Des and thank you to Helen and the Daly family; without your generosity, this book would not have progressed and your permission to access Des' records is hugely appreciated.

In addition to Des' records, I also owe much thanks to Pat Fitzgerald, former IRFU president. Pat also supplied a great archive of material to access for this research and was especially generous with images and photographs to choose from. Pat additionally offered personal insights of his time in rugby and Leinster Branch material to aid the process, helping to bring about the final draft. A very special thank you to Ollie Campbell, who spoke to me at length over coffee about Belvedere, Old Belvedere and Leinster rugby, and for his generosity in offering me material on the history of Leinster rugby in books and DVD format. I also want to say thank you to radio documentarian and sports journalist (and near neighbour) David Coughlan for the many, many chats and listening to my deliberations about the material I was uncovering and the direction the study was taking during two years of Covid lockdown also. Thank you especially for directing me to Brendan Behan's *Borstal Boy*, which became a brilliant conduit for my thoughts on Leinster rugby's evolution.

There are too many people to name individually, but to everyone I spoke to on the phone, in person or via email across so many clubs in Leinster, as well as several schools, who so generously shared the histories of their clubs, I can't thank you enough for your generosity. Detailed club histories that came my way included those for: Emerald Warriors (Nick Costello and Richie Fagan), Dublin Dogos (Gonzalo Saenz), Tallaght RFC (Emma Louise Doyle and Jim O'Connor), Longford (Derick Turner and Pat Fitzgerald), Enniscorthy (Rory Fanning), Edenderry (Sean O'Donnell), Gorey (Trysh Sullivan), Tullow (Cora Brown), Clontarf (Brendan Smith), CYM (Bernard Murray), Ashbourne (Bill Duggan),

Mullingar (Terry Short), West Offaly Lions (Audrey Guinan), Seapoint (Mick O'Toole), Roscrea (Terry Farrelly), Newbridge (Oliver Delaney), Blackrock (Colm Jenkison), Tullamore (Tony Doolin), Birr (Padraig Burns), Balbriggan (Caroline and David McFadden), Portarlington (David Hainsworth), Wexford Wanderers (Debbie Carty and Brendan Culliton), Naas (John Walsh), Ardee (Ian Stewart), North Meath (Jack Kenny), Navan and Dundalk (Gerald Williamson), as well as more specific insights from the High School and Blackrock College too. I must also mention and thank the archivists at TCD Archive, National Library of Ireland and the National Archive for their help and service during my research at their repositories.

Thank you, of course, to Merrion Press for taking on this project, for all the advice and feedback and for navigating the book to its final version. Thank you to Conor, Patrick and Wendy for your expertise, guidance and patience. To all of the staff who produced this final version of the text and the designers who organised the format for the final product, thank you sincerely.

I must offer my thanks and huge appreciation to my family – my parents, Martin and Brigid, and siblings Mark and Niamh – for showing interest in, supporting and encouraging my academic journey for many years. Without their help, curiosity and generosity along the way, projects such as this one would not have been possible for me to pursue in the first place. Finally, I dedicate this work to three very special people, who keep me going with their love and encouragement. To my ever-patient wife, Rebecca, who has been my greatest supporter, especially when challenges arose and I needed an ear to bend about certain frustrations; thank you as always. And to two wonderful boys, Cillian and Pearse, whose curiosity, inquisitive minds and hunger to know more inspire me and spur me on in everything I do. Thank you and I dedicate this book, with all of my love, to Rebecca, Cillian and Pearse.

Introduction

The recognisable codes of the various types of football (soccer, GAA, rugby) that command huge popularity in Leinster today all have their origins in versions that had been played in Ireland for centuries. Originally 'folk football' was associated with festivals, with a religious calendar or with a simple yearning for recreational play in rural and urban areas.[1] Indeed, '[p]erhaps the earliest surviving written reference [in English] to the playing of [football] in Ireland is one from 1308 when a man was accidentally stabbed while "playing ball" in County Dublin'.[2] A few hundred years later, in a book printed in 1699, Englishman John Dunton recorded a football match in Fingal, while other sources show that a ball-kicking game was played at Trinity College Dublin (TCD) as early as the 1780s. A poem by a Trinity alumnus, Edward Lysaght, published in 1811, is regularly cited to prove that a form of football was played among students at the university's College Park.[3]

It was during the increasingly industrialised nineteenth century, in conjunction with increasing urbanisation, technological change and imperialism on a global scale, that the reorganisation of sporting pastimes began to shape the modern world. But the organised game of rugby, when it came to Leinster, did not arrive into a vacuum. Codified football had reached the province via its initial configuration within English public schools, and TCD was prominent in the development of a modernised game in the province. More specifically, in 1854, 'former schoolboys of Cheltenham and Rugby established a football club at Trinity and hence initiated an incipient process of modernisation that would eventually see rugby football become a properly codified sport with a national governing body in Ireland by 1879'.[4] It was within the walls of the university that a group of young men playing a game of 'football' first devised a club for contests that involved trying to score points using an oval-shaped ball. It was, in essence, the dawn of a modern era in the organising and playing of rugby football in Ireland. In the decades that followed, the spread

1

▲ Early depiction of a ball-kicking game in Britain, 1839: Thomas George Webster painting titled 'Football'.

of this sport soon transformed the lives of generations of people who lived in the province of Leinster.

The centrality of institutions of learning to rugby's development is stark. Across the decades, education and Leinster rugby became inseparably intertwined. In the years after 1854, when educated students from Trinity, or the private secondary schools of England and Ireland, graduated into professions such as doctors, solicitors, headmasters, businessmen and local government agents, their work often brought them outside Dublin. With that in mind, what emerges from an exploration of the history of Leinster rugby is an evolution, not just of the game and how it was administered, but also of the meaning and significance of rugby in the province. It was by no means a smooth progression, nor always an advancing trajectory, as the changes that occurred in Leinster rugby reflected the various challenges and struggles within the broader social and cultural history of Ireland.

This work seeks to provide a comprehensive explanation of the place of rugby in Leinster. In order to highlight the most pivotal developments in Leinster rugby between 1854 and 2020, it will look at the history of individual clubs and schools, women's rugby and youth rugby, utilising financial, administrative and administrators' records, along with the records of interprovincial Leinster squads, teams and games. The social and cultural history of Ireland will also be examined through the lens of Leinster rugby. The very fact that rugby evolved along provincial lines in Ireland, for example, reflected a peculiarity that was unique to this island and its relationship with Britain. The provincial branches emerged because of the politics of Ireland and the country's contested identity, which drove the desire of those who were central to rugby in Ulster to act independently of the other provinces.

But divides over political and national identity are only one aspect of this story; class mattered more prominently. In Dublin's urban centre, where Leinster rugby evolved, the lives of the working classes and those of the elites were clearly demarcated and Dublin's senior clubs retained a stubborn exclusivity. However, a more socially diverse rugby following could be found in smaller towns around Leinster, where interaction between and among professional and landed classes and the client and labouring groups was more common. When junior and rural clubs began to appear, they were reliant on social, cultural and religious intermixing to maintain teams. With these social and cultural realities in mind, Leinster rugby developed a particular infrastructure along with some geographical idiosyncrasies across the twelve counties that gave the game particular meanings to different groups within Leinster, although that understanding was malleable and shifting.

Nothing in Irish sport can really be viewed as neutral or apolitical, and rugby reflected the complexities of politics and identity in Ireland. It was one of the sports that was understood within the British Empire to be part of its civilising mission – 'a blending of muscular Christianity and cultural imperialism in which the cooperation, discipline and healthful aspects of sport would supposedly enhance the civilizing process and create common ground between coloniser and colonised'.[5] When the Lord Lieutenant of Ireland, the Duke of Abercorn, was declared president of the IFU in 1875 and invited to the first Leinster rugby contests, where British military bands would entertain a crowd with the best of British ditties after their

▲ Sketch of College Park and rugby posts, Trinity College Dublin, 1879.

▲ Sketch of an early game of rugby football from the late 1800s, unnamed school but probably Rugby.

rendition of 'God Save the Queen' under the Union Jack, rugby was one element of colonial incursion and imperial celebration that, by design, ignored any alternative identity or political viewpoint.

As it became one of the first properly organised sports in Ireland in the middle of the nineteenth century, rugby represented 'an imperial culture ... that manifest itself in certain customs, symbols and tendencies'.[6] But it would be entirely wrong to assume that *all* of those who attended matches to watch or to play endorsed the Empire or embraced the sense of Britishness that was on display. Indeed, for so many who embraced sport, the idea of a game being a marker of identity never entered their consciousness, at least not in a decisive way.

Those who chose to pursue rugby across Leinster were far more diverse than sometimes presumed, because of the ever-shifting social and cultural landscape in Ireland. Although there were elements of privilege, snobbery and southern Irish unionism present in Leinster rugby clubs, nevertheless '[t]hose who played sport did not necessarily belong to the tribe they were said to belong to by virtue of their sporting choice'.[7] The reasons for selecting rugby as one's sport of preference varied greatly. Some found themselves playing the sport by virtue of having a particular skill or not having the right skills for other sports. Other reasons included school or college preference, peer pressure, professional aspirations, commonality in work, a sign of solidarity and loyalty, or a pastime that many partook in for plain, ordinary enjoyment or even just curiosity about this new game. The rugby world bred an inordinate love for this version of football, whether watching or playing, and the elements of sociability and friendship or, more pertinently, the networking opportunities that it offered. As Paul Rouse has said,

> While it is true that the alumni of certain British public schools and of Trinity College were instrumental in the initial spread of rugby across Ireland, rugby was not simply an imperial game and the preserve of unionists … By the end of the nineteenth century many of those who filled the expanding clubs … were nationalists and the idea that they were identifying with the British Empire by dint of the game they played was simply wrong.[8]

What the history of rugby in Leinster reflects was that the new world of organised sports became central to Irish society for myriad reasons, primarily to do with recreation, fraternity, exercise and fun. Simply put, 'there was a tremendous upsurge of interest in sport generally throughout Britain and Ireland during this period, a factor due in no small measure to the immense amount of social reform that was then taking place.'[9]

Of course, when it comes to the history of rugby in Leinster, it is, primarily, a story about men. For decades, sport in Ireland was a profoundly male experience and women have had to fight to make inroads into that world. 'Muscular Christians saw sport as a promoter of manliness, a check on effeminacy, and an alternative to sexual expenditures of energy. Moral men would earn their manhood on the playing fields … Sport would enable sedentary middle-class men to maintain such "manly" physical characteristics as ruggedness, robustness, strength, and vigour rather than degenerating into foolish fops.'[10]

Rugby, as it was set out in the beginning, was always a game that had massively gendered connotations, and it was viewed and presented in the context of what it was to 'be a man' in a specifically Anglo-European, imperialist context. Rugby union was a game that sought to forge masculinity, and gender segregation was from its earliest days one of its most appealing aspects for the men who played and watched it. 'We have no dealings with women here,' declared one rugby union enthusiast in 1889.[11] However, given the growth and success of twenty-first-century women's rugby in Leinster, we can see that sport is far from stationary; despite the presence of purists who disdain such change, it is fluid and transformative. In what was once promoted as an exclusively upper-class, male domain, women's rugby across Leinster is evidence of the barriers that have been broken down in rugby circles, although contemporary controversies are raising new questions about inclusivity, especially when it comes to gender identification.

Leinster rugby traditionalists, those die-hard advocates of amateurism in the 1890s who fretted desperately about the prospect of professional sports, often mirrored attitudes in England and scorned the growing popularity of rugby. These men from the upper classes talked of either stamping out the participation of unwelcome lower-class players or, alternatively, altogether abandoning rugby to the working classes.[12] In contrast, there were progressive rugby visionaries and also commercially motivated entrepreneurs who wanted to widen the pool of players and spectators, and those who held onto a narrowly restricted vision for rugby were always under pressure from these more broad-minded forces. Nonetheless, to understand the history of rugby in Leinster, an examination of class dynamics is needed.

Prior to the mid-1990s, among much of the population encompassing the twelve counties of Leinster, the perception of rugby might have been best reflected in something Brendan Behan wrote back in the 1950s. Rugby 'was a game for the Protestant and shop-keeping Catholic, and I never thought it had anything to do with me.'[13] As Behan explained:

> Rugby was a game I always connected with the English or the upper classes. There was a rugby pitch on the grounds of the huge Gaelic football and hurling stadium of Croke Park, separated from it by a concrete wall, at the bottom of our street. We used to see the boys from Belvedere Jesuit School, and from Mountjoy Protestant School, going down there on Wednesdays. We persecuted them without distinction of religion … We only knew they were rich kids … They were toffs, college boys, and toffs' sons. I certainly never thought of Rugby football as having anything to do with Ireland or with Dublin.[14]

While that perception, depending on one's social and cultural experiences, has not yet changed for everyone, for a great many others there has been the same kind of awakening to rugby that Behan expounded in his novel *Borstal Boy*, perhaps the unlikeliest of places to find rugby as an important narrative trope. While in an English prison, the character 'Brendan' reads a former rugby international's description of what it felt like to play rugby for Ireland. 'Brendan' explained: 'Reading Collis' book

▲ Early photograph of a Leinster team, dated 1884.

was like meeting someone from home, and I could see Rugby football not as a winter meeting of cricketers, but as a battle fought in the churning mud and myself in the forward line charging for Ireland.'[15] The arc in *Borstal Boy* that traces the evolving relationship 'Brendan' has with the game seems almost impeccably analogous to the trajectory of Leinster rugby's history, from an exclusive minority interest to a sport of mass appeal. As such, the proceeding exploration will follow the story of rugby's development in Ireland's easternmost province, what it stood for, how and why it evolved as it did, and what it came to mean for those involved.

The success of rugby in the province, firstly in the amateur game, but also in support for the professional outfit, has undoubtedly relied on the sense of community that has been fostered in rugby clubs across Leinster and the ongoing dedication of volunteers within the organisation. With that in mind, this history, ultimately, will trace the growth and development of the game of rugby in Leinster, from an informal recreational pastime – a reserved game at the outset that was altered by those in the province who intended to promote and encourage the sport – to a sport that was increasingly developed to cater for expansion, competency and commitment. It will uncover the highly sophisticated apparatus that helped form a modern professional sport with a unique interconnectedness to the amateur game. In doing so it will consider issues of class, gender, politics and identity, while highlighting Leinster rugby's infrastructure, community, volunteerism and geographical spread via the club game, culminating in the commercial conglomerate that emerged from the original interprovincial set-up that is today's professional Leinster rugby club.

1

Rugby Comes to Ireland

Codified Football's First Years

The Dublin University Football Club (DUFC) was officially founded in 1854 and represents the first appearance of a recognisable rugby football team in the province of Leinster. The rules those first students loosely followed were based upon the game played in England, associated with the private school in the town of Rugby, from where the football code derives its name. At the club's formation, nonetheless, these first contests were an amalgam of footballing styles and practices with no formal set of rules written down. In fact, the Rugby Football Union was not formed until 1871 and it was only at that point that the rules of rugby were properly codified under the auspices of a governing body. Up to that point the tradition was to play a handling football game based on the game associated with Rugby School, and the earliest reports of the games at TCD note that there were always ex-Rugby students who organised and played in the matches.

Those who played rugby, no doubt, played for their own amusement and for exercise, but equally the game they learned was shrouded in the ideological framework of Muscular Christianity. This was an ideology that suggested rugby would train young men in physical health, thereby improving their moral health in line with imagined Protestant Christian virtues that would define them as suitable leaders of the British Empire. Rugby, therefore, was not merely about having fun, but signalled a particular set of beliefs. Trinity, in 1850s Ireland, had a very distinctive make-up: almost entirely wealthy, unionist and Protestant. That the game

▲ College Park, Trinity College Dublin.

in Leinster had its origins there, at this specific time, gave it a very particular social and cultural context, which shaped its peculiarities, prejudices and its subsequent development. Rugby was strongly associated with a specifically upper-class, English, cultural viewpoint; it was intended to shape blue-blooded young men into tough, healthy and rational gentlemen. While people of all backgrounds and traditions had played some type of ball sports for centuries across Leinster, the codification of football at TCD reflected the imperial peculiarity of that institution as a bastion of an English cultural viewpoint among its strongly unionist cohort.

The rise of organised sports, or more specifically organised football, was informed by the consolidation of industrial capitalism and the propagation of Empire. Among the elite of society in the 1850s, the establishment of clubs, organisations and associations to administer these new 'official' forms of recreation, began to take hold. As this happened, efforts to replace folk football revelry with more controlled and 'civilised' pastimes emerged, and rugby sat at the heart of this process. It was consciously promoted from the outset as much more than just a game for mere enjoyment; it was a moral framework to guide 'the best of British' both at home and abroad.

In the context of post-Famine Ireland, the game of rugby football was just one form of daily life that reflected the new world emerging and spoke of novel social and cultural developments taking hold. In Leinster, an associational culture began to emerge and the structured format of clubs for all types of recreation

▲ Earliest image of the DUFC team, 1866, with Charles Barrington (self-proclaimed grandfather of Irish rugby) holding the ball. Barrington was the first person to write down and have published a set of rugby rules for DUFC.

became the norm. Organised sport became important in society as a new form of entertainment, an outlet for finding a sense of belonging and identity, partaking in sanctioned vices such as gambling, as well as a chance to blow off some steam vis-à-vis a sports team to play with or to follow. Cricket clubs, athletic clubs, polo clubs, and yachting and rowing clubs were all being formed from the 1830s and 1840s, for example. Before rugby, cricket had been a model for organised team sports, with a club having formed in Trinity as early as 1840. Most rugby players who joined DUFC partook in the game of cricket too. One of the advantages of formally organising in this way was that the football club was able to lobby successfully for a large area of TCD's College Park for its games. The cricket club donated a section of the green for football, saving DUFC from the expense involved in finding a playing field. Thus, the main initial expenses for DUFC were goalposts, uniforms and some kind of hut for dressing.[1]

Many of the first rugby players in Ireland would have spent their lives journeying back and forth across the Irish sea to the schools and universities that the children of the elite frequented, which gives us a sense of the very first mechanisms behind the growth of the game here. Indeed, 'the spread of rugby to Ireland – and then around Ireland – was facilitated by the fact that up to 1,000 boys from Irish families went annually to English public schools in the 1870s.'[2] Within the walls of Trinity, rugby emerged in much the same way as it would have at Rugby School, with DUFC rugby players using the game to 'self-consciously' express and promote 'the

11

spirit of Mid-Victorian England.[3] These beginnings offer a glimpse of where some of the long-held stereotypes about rugby in Leinster originated. Its proponents and participants identified it as a unionist sport, associated almost entirely with the professional and upper classes.

Informal Rugby on TCD's College Park

The earliest rugby matches demonstrate how the creation of the modern game was a process rather than an event. They would often be played over several days, rather than within a defined time frame in an afternoon. One 1856 newspaper reporting on a DUFC rugby game, for example, stated that the 'club will finish their match of the two freshman classes against rest of club',[4] one week after the initial kick-off. Another game, advertised on 5 December 1856 for College Park, was for a match where 'those whose names begin with a letter of the first half of the alphabet, will play the rest of the club'.[5]

The emerging popularity of newspapers was central to the promotion of popular sports. Without their advertisement of fixtures and game reports, and the later lionising of sport 'stars', the game would not have been as quick to embed itself into the everyday lives of the population. From the early days, newspapers promoted rugby, which reflected the kinds of trends and attitudes that were seeping into Ireland in the later 1800s. As for DUFC as an organisation, reports gushed that, 'these young gentlemen are making very praiseworthy efforts to encourage manly exercises and sports, and it is to be hoped that their example will be generally followed in the university'.[6]

While these early newspaper reports show us that there was an evident interest in the game of rugby,[7] details of the sport's history can also be ascertained from players who recorded their memories of the game's earliest days. Letters fill in some of the gaps about what rugby looked like and who was playing it. Arnold Graves, writing in the 1930s, recalled that a cousin of Anthony Traill, a man by the name of Robert Traill, was Trinity captain for two years in the 1860s. 'He was about 6ft 2, and 14 or 15 stone weight – A very Hercules. He was not a fast runner, but he had a marvellous swerve, and when collared around the body, he would give his body a sudden swing which would send the holder flying.'[8] Graves wrote that the version of rugby played in Trinity had characteristics peculiar to Leinster when compared with the rules in England – for example, hacking was not allowed. He recalled that the line-up would usually comprise two half-backs, two quarter-backs,

▲ Late 1800s drawing of a rugby scrum, depicting the large numbers of players on each side.

one full-back and ten forwards. The aim was to get the ball and run with swerves and dodges to get to the try line.

Graves' letters leave a fascinating record of the game as it appeared in the 1860s. For example, one of his recollections, dated to November 1929, gave a glimmering insight into the earliest days of Leinster rugby:

> Some of the rules I remember, hacking was barred but tripping was allowed. Passing was against the rules and was called hand ball. We played without a referee. There was off side of course. The scrummages were interminable, and lasted until the man holding the ball expressed his readiness to put it down, and that was only when his side were losing ground. I have seen a scrummage travel half way down the ground. I don't think that the ground was any particular length or breadth, our ground extended more or less the whole length of the ground between the cricket ground and the trees on the Nassau Street side … We played fifteen a side and not twenty which was more usual in England. As regards the Play or the distribution of players, it depended very much on who was playing …[9]

Because there was no passing, and with the lack of a measured pitch in mind, he explained that scrums were welcomed, as they gave the players built for the scrum a rest from chasing runners around the field. The backs would be apt to make very long runs with the ball, Graves explained, sometimes half or three-quarters the entire length of the ground, involving swerves and dodges. It might be fairly assumed that speed and swerve were necessary if there were to be any score at all, and so in the 1876–77 season the teams were universally reduced from twenty to fifteen players in order to facilitate more of a running game and less of the tedium of endless scrums. It was not until 1886–87 that a points system was introduced to award a numerical amount to each type of score, which included the introduction of the penalty in the 1880s.

Graves went on to write: 'In every respect the game was more individual than it is today … The ball we played with was distinctly a Rugger ball but not so narrow as the ball in use today … There was no pavilion, and only on the occasion of a big match was a tent erected, and refreshments provided.'[10] In order to enjoy the game, the players who embraced rugby would gather in Trinity and throw together a 'pick-up game every day at 3 o'clock', recalled Graves. It was at these scrimmages that the DUFC committee would scout out new talent to sign up. We can clearly see the roots of rugby in Leinster were very much tied to Trinity College and to a young, male proclivity and indeed privilege of having such leisure time, conferred on those in third-level studies during this period in Irish history.

Re-formalising the Rules

As football developed in Leinster, DUFC players Charles Barrington and Richard Wall wrote down a version of rugby's rules in 1868. These were published in *Lawrence's Handbook of Cricket* with an eye to promoting the game and encouraging schools and clubs to follow a standard set of rules. The publication of these rules signalled a path towards expanding interest in the game. The reminiscences of Barrington shed light on Leinster rugby's roots:

> I came from Rugby to T.C.D. … and found there was nothing to do there during the winter term. There were no cycles, no golf, no hockey, no anything – cards, billiards and whiskey and the more social dressed smartly and paraded up and down Grafton Street … A poor time indeed. There was a little … football with no particular rules to speak of … a good little chap called Wall was trying this show. I started away and pulled things together, made a good club of it, with the rules of Rugby School and we were very successful for it caught on at once.[11]

Despite the fact the rugby club at TCD was some ten years old when Barrington arrived, it was he and Wall who helped organise a clear and consistent set of rules in a Leinster context, which in turn encouraged a regular season of games, bringing a more clearly defined organisation for the game of rugby. While still mostly played internally in TCD, within two years of the rugby rules being published in Leinster, the first official 'outside' clubs were formed.

Barrington recalled the earliest days of playing at DUFC:

> I have a photo of our first XV by me, and we are a queer-looking lot judged by modern ideas. We had 'caps' made in Rugby too, but there was no one in those far off times to play against. The match of the year was against the medical school. Sometimes too the Dublin garrison boiled up a team to play us. We played matches against ourselves, 'pick ups,' twice or three times a week … The Club was really a great success and did introduce the Rugger game into Ireland.[12]

He also suggested that, back in the 1860s, the rules of rugby were, 'Like the old Brehon laws, unwritten and strictly obeyed and enforced', until he and Wall wrote down their set of codes. Their system involved a try, a touchdown and a goal, but only a goal was counted as a score. The touchdown was a defensive move, when a player could touch the ball down behind their own line, while a try gave a team the opportunity to kick at goal. 'A goal off a try and a goal dropped were the only two kinds of goals we had. There was no such thing as a penalty goal. When a misdemeanour was committed the ball was brought back to the spot of the crime, placed on the ground and a scrum formed around it and on again.'[13] The rules were, more or less, the same as the Rugby School's rules, 'with the important difference that the DUFC rules outlawed what was known as hacking'.[14] These, then, were the codes forwarded to other rugby enthusiasts across Leinster, in the hope of spreading uniformity within the game.

In the 1868–69 season of *Lawrence's Handbook of Cricket* (an almanac of several different sports), a new team appeared in the guise of the DUFC second fifteen, which signalled the game's growing popularity. In that season the recorded number of rugby matches played by DUFC's first and second teams combined was twenty-five. 'The first 15 played against "The Gentlemen of Ireland", "rowing club", and "the club" … The second 15 played against St. Columba, Hume Street School, Dungannon and The Engineering School.'[15] *The Irish Times*, the *Dublin*

FIRST LAWS OF FOOTBALL

1. The kick-off from the middle must be a place-kick.

2. Kick out must be from 25 yards out of goal, not a place-kick.

3. Charging is fair in case of a place kick, as soon as the ball has touched the ground; in case of a kick from a catch, as soon as the player offers to kick, but he may always draw back, unless he has touched the ball with his foot.

4. If a player makes a Fair Catch, he shall be entitled to a free kick, provided he claims it, by making a mark with his heel at once; and In order to take such a kick he may go back as far as he pleases, and no player on the opposite side shall advance beyond his mark until he has kicked.

5. A Fair Catch cannot be made from Touch.

6. A player is off side when the ball has been kicked, or thrown or knocked on, or is being run with by one of his own side behind him.

7. A player off side may impede the game by standing close to the ball; but he may not, in any case kick or touch it, charge or put over.

8. A player is on side when the ball has been kicked or thrown or knocked on, or when it has rebounded from the body of any player of the opposite side.

9. It is not lawful to take up the ball when not in touch, except in an evident hop. Lifting the ball is strictly prohibited.

10. Running in is allowed to any player on side, provided he does not run through touch.

11. If in case of a run, the ball is held in a maul, it shall not be lawful for any other player on his own side to take from the runner and run with it.

12. It shall be lawful for any player to call upon any other player, hold the ball in a maul, to put it down, when evidently unable to get away.

13. A player, if he wishes to enter a maul, must do so on side.

14. No player, out of a maul, may be held or pulled over, unless he himself is holding the ball.

15. No hacking, as distinct from Tripping, is fair.

16. Try at Goal. A ball touched between the goal posts, may be brought up to either of them, but not between.

17. When the ball has been touched down behind the goal the player who touched it down is entitled to walk out straight 25 yards, and any one of his side may take a place-kick, but as soon as the ball has been placed, the opposition side may charge.

18. It shall be a goal if the ball be dropped, but not if punted, hit or thrown, between the post or posts produced at any height over horizontal bar, whether it touch it or not.

A Ball in Touch is dead; consequently, the first player on his side must, in any case, touch it down, bring it to the side of touch, and throw it straight on.

19. Holding and throttling is disallowed.

20. The Captains of sides, or any two deputed by them, shall be the sole arbiters of all disputes.

"No law may be altered or made unless a week's notice be given of a meeting, and such meeting shall consist of at least 20 members or more."

Drawn up by C. B. Barrington and R. M. Wall.

▲ First rules of rugby at DUFC, thus the first rules of the game in Leinster written down.

Evening Packet and the *Dublin Evening Mail* all carried reports about rugby in the last decades of the nineteenth century and began to add further details to address rugby followers' growing interests. Thus, not only the results of the games, but the players and scorers' names became an important reporting appendage.[16]

One motivation behind the promotion of the game of rugby by private school and university educators, military officers, religious and political figures, and its upper-class players, fans and promoters was to try to create a sense of commonality among Britain's colonies and a connection to the 'mother country'. This became more apparent when the rugby union in England conceived the idea of 'international' games, starting in 1871, initially among the so-called 'home nations' of England, Scotland, Wales and Ireland, and subsequently incorporating Canada, Australia, New Zealand and South Africa. The internationals, then, were simultaneously and somewhat contradictorily about solidifying Ireland's place in the UK while at the same time promoting a separate national pride. Primarily, rugby was understood as a game that would highlight a common strand, a link to the British Crown and an acceptance of the Empire.

Not surprisingly, given the game's origins, it was the education system that was central to the process of rugby's popularity in Leinster. Within a couple of decades of the first recorded club games played by DUFC against teams from private Protestant schools, British military fifteens or hospital teams, Leinster's 'elite

Catholic schools where prosperous merchants and professionals sent their sons in the hopes that they would there develop contacts and networks that would aid their future careers,' became rugby schools.[17] A penchant for rugby among school-goers was often reflected in their later lives, where successful political, professional, business and merchant classes maintained a network of contacts through rugby participation. The origin and organisation of rugby in Leinster by 1870 had:

> brought together a small number of clubs (eight), all of whom had close links with Trinity or else involved college graduates. But what does one sport, an avowedly Protestant dominated sport, with close links to northern unionism, tell us more generally about Irish sport? Given the context of Trinity in the late nineteenth century as a bastion of unionism and Protestantism, it tells us that the athleticism process, so far as it existed, was essentially self-replicating … Rugby emerged as a minority pastime … a significant marker of an all-Irish unionist identity to those who played it … This was not diffusion but social separatism played out on the playing field.[18]

This observation was true of Leinster senior rugby for many decades. It would take the emergence of an educated Catholic middle class, and of province-wide junior and provincial town rugby, to begin to change that reality. While those making up the 'elite' in Ireland clearly shifted, beginning with the outcome of the Land War in the 1870s–80s, through to the establishment of the Irish Free State in the 1920s, the identification of rugby as an exclusive game for the privileged in Leinster society remained unimpeded for some decades.

Rugby Beyond the Walls: Leinster's First Clubs

In the 1870s rugby reporting expanded, reflecting an obvious interest in and an editorial penchant for promoting sports for which there was a personal preference and/or an economic imperative in terms of identifying what sells papers. In that decade, what was noticeable was that the listing of team selections and the date and time of the game, as well as those of future fixtures, were all included. From these sources the emergence of a more fully developed proto-league system can be seen. Once enough graduates from TCD, from the Queen's Universities across Ireland and from the private school system had moved on from their education, they began to set up or to join new clubs, and rugby evolved again. While Leinster rugby started in Dublin's centre, by the end of the 1870s more concrete expansion was taking hold in other areas of the province.[19]

The first provincial rugby clubs that emerged were connected in various ways and degrees with Trinity, and its graduates were central to the diffusion of rugby across Leinster. For example, in schools in Westmeath, 'the two headmasters who promoted sport in the schools, T.C. Foster and Robert Bailie, were both Trinity graduates … The first recorded rugby game in Westmeath was played between the two schools at Farra, on 25 February 1879 … This game came a year after both Bailie and Foster were appointed headmasters at Ranelagh and Farra schools respectively.'[20] All of the earliest clubs, logically, contained former TCD students, bolstered by others who had been educated in private schools across Britain and Ireland. Additionally, British Army officers, British civil servants and those qualified to work in the legal system, the banks and the professions – notably lots of qualified doctors – found their way into rugby clubs.[21]

It was with the foundation in 1870 of Dublin's Wanderers FC, the second oldest rugby club in Leinster, that former DUFC players came together with the express purpose of challenging the dominance of Trinity. According to a history of Wanderers, 'Richard Milliken Peter was one of a number of Trinity students who formed Wanderers FC in 1870 to provide rugby players with the opportunity to play on graduation from Trinity – and to provide the initial sole opposition in rugby football for Trinity College at the time.'[22] As a player Peter was good enough to make the first ever Leinster team that played Ulster in Belfast during the 1875–76 season.

When Wanderers were founded, DUFC decided that they would not allow their first fifteen to play against the new club until Wanderers beat their seconds; only then could the challengers play Trinity's firsts. Since the only score to count at this stage was a kicked goal, it was almost impossible to gain a win, because place- and drop-kicking skills were far from being perfected, and so many games ended in nil–nil draws. It was not until November 1875, when it was decided that the rule should be changed to count tries (i.e. touching the ball down behind the endline of the goal one's team was attacking) as a score, that Wanderers were victorious against Trinity's seconds. When DUFC's firsts played Wanderers, in the same month, this was, in some ways, the inaugural official Leinster senior rugby club match.[23]

The next Dublin club to be established, Lansdowne FC, was formed in 1872 by Henry W.D. Dunlop, after he had secured a lease for athletic fields from Lord Pembroke at Lansdowne Road. Dunlop is historically important for Leinster sports

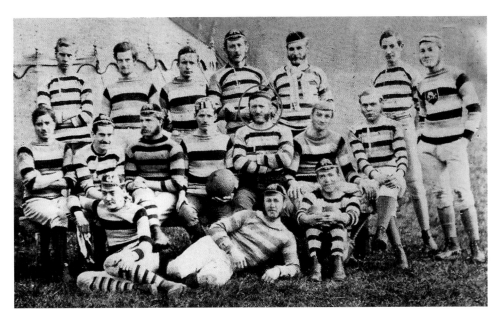

▲ R.M. Peter and Wanderers FC, the 1877–8 team.

in general, as he organised the Irish Champion Athletic Club (ICAC) at the same address. He was keen on promoting the ideology of Muscular Christianity in Leinster through sports, and as part of that project he worked to establish a rugby team alongside the promotion of athletics more broadly. Dunlop espoused a romantic vision, claiming he had 'a dream of an enclosed arena which would provide facilities for athletics meetings and healthful games such as football, cricket, lawn tennis and so forth … In due course the necessary land was leased from the Pembroke estate and the money was raised to develop a cinder track, football pitches, tennis courts and archery butts.'[24] Lansdowne FC recruited ex-schoolboy players from academies like Walker's and Scott's and welcomed an

▲ H.W.D. Dunlop, an ardent rugby and all-round sports advocate, credited with establishing the Lansdowne Road playing fields.

influx of ex-Trinity students as well. The need for these new clubs can be explained by the desire of many ex-DUFC players, along with ex-schools' rugby players, to continue playing a sport they had grown to love.

Another major development in Leinster rugby at this stage was the evolution of refereeing. At the outset in Leinster rugby 'refereeing was carried out by an umpiring system, whereby the 2 Captains or their nominees adjudicated on

▲ Lansdowne FC, Leinster Senior Cup winners, 1891, with cup.

disagreements during the game'.[25] It is not entirely clear when a neutral referee was initially introduced, although there are references to single umpires in the first Leinster Senior Cup in 1882 and of a single referee overseeing internationals games as early as 1875. In the last quarter of the nineteenth century, this practice of nominating one referee seems to have become the norm, unless it was impossible. This would allow that person to concentrate on officiating the rules and, in theory, reduced the hold-ups that often occurred if there was a disputed decision where the two captains had to negotiate their way out of the impasse. At first the nominee often came from the host club for a match, but over time the need for a neutral arbiter was agreed to by all.

With the expansion of teams and games, it soon became clear that there was a need for a central rugby organisation to oversee and organise the entirety of the rugby game in Ireland.

IFU, IRFU & the Leinster Branch

After DUFC had played against the Dingle Club of Liverpool in 1874, the question of a governing body to oversee rugby in Ireland was raised. In response, the Irish Football Union (IFU) was formed that year, instigated mainly by DUFC and ex-

Trinity men. One of them was Richard Milliken Peter, who, as well as being the honorary secretary of Wanderers, became treasurer of the IFU during its short life. The IFU was ostensibly set up to manage the organisation of Ireland's first international match, which was against England, to be played on 15 January 1875 at the Kensington Oval.[26] It was Leinster rugby men, therefore, who established the foundations for a broader organisation to regulate Irish rugby into the future.

However, on its formation, the IFU immediately became a contentious organisation and led to division within Irish rugby. When the Leinster rugby group that established the IFU failed to properly inform in a timely manner their northern rugby brethren of their intention to form a national organisation, the Ulstermen went their separate way and formed their own association. The issue for Ulster rugby, it seems, was about control over any entity that had the temerity to suggest itself a representative body for all of Ireland. That it had been a Dublin-centred meeting which had taken the lead in its formation invoked Ulster unionist outrage in the guise of its rugby representatives. It was due to this split that the provincial branches ultimately came into being in Irish rugby.

To reunite Irish rugby, Leinster's rugby men suggested forming a kind of federalised association, under which the independent provincial branches would affiliate to one Irish Rugby Football Union (IRFU) for the sake of the international team. The union would function to 'promote and foster the game of rugby in Ireland and to arrange international and interprovincial matches',[27] while the branches would have autonomy over their own local rugby affairs. In meetings in 1878, after a lot of placation towards Ulster, the sides discussed the formation of three branches, 'Leinster, Ulster and Munster, to manage the affairs of the clubs in these provinces belonging to the union'. The arrangement was consecrated in January 1879, when interprovincial games were organised to be played in Lansdowne Road. After those games 'the papers of the day heralded ... the formation of the Irish Rugby Football Union'.[28] The Leinster branch of Irish rugby, therefore, arose from the earliest signs of political fractiousness on the island vis-à-vis the province of Ulster. The Dublin men, especially those of DUFC, had reassured their brethren that they were as staunchly unionist as their northern counterparts and that the formation of a football union initiated in the south was not some nationalist, cultural usurpation.

Dr William Cox Neville, who was pivotal in the mid-1870s to the organisation of the United Hospitals' team in Dublin, helped amalgamate the IFU and the Ulster rugby association.[29] Richard Milliken Peter was also given much credit for reuniting

Irish rugby after the north–south split, diplomatically cajoling the Ulster men into a singular Irish rugby organisation, and he subsequently served as the IRFU's first honorary secretary. An obvious enthusiast, he even wrote a book on the history of football in Ireland. Nonetheless, Peter was, allegedly, forced out of Wanderers in 1882 for what we might call today 'un-sportsman-like behaviour', after he was accused of jeering an opposing team when they missed scoring a try at some point during the game. At the next general meeting, the Wanderers' administration asked him to resign, believing that the good name of the club should not be tarnished by such boorish behaviour. In disgust, Peter stepped down and severed all ties with the game of rugby, instead turning his organisational skills and love of sports to the setting up of swimming, rowing and sailing organisations in Dublin.[30]

One of the first Leinster Branch meetings was held on 31 October 1879, and representatives from the Wanderers, Lansdowne, Arlington School, DUFC, Dundalk, Phoenix FC and Steevens' Hospital clubs were all present. The Branch's job was to oversee the progression of the game in the province, in terms of standardising the rules around the game itself; keeping records of players, clubs, fixtures, referees and later the schools and leagues; and also the organisation of a representative provincial team, which was one if its primary responsibilities. The provincial games were undertaken partly to assuage Ulster rugby's umbrage, but more importantly to facilitate trial matches in order to select the best fifteen for the international team. The provincial rivalries that emerged from this competition were really a boost and a boon to the game of rugby across Leinster. The rivalry of interprovincial games and competition focused the minds of rugby lovers to reassess their organisation in such a way as to make their teams, both at club and at provincial level, the best in the country.

▲ Col. Horace Rochford, a central founder of the County Carlow Football Club in 1873.

Expanding the Game to Small Towns

Following the establishment of Wanderers and Lansdowne in Dublin in the early 1870s, County Carlow FC became the oldest provincial club in Leinster, initiated by Colonel Horace Rochford in 1873. The club was founded in George Wilson's hotel, the same venue providing the Co. Carlow Cricket Club with regular and favourite recreational and meeting rooms. Horace Rochford was the occupier of a 'big house' on the family estate at Clogrennane, Co. Carlow, and held lands in Carlow, Dublin and Laois of over 3,000 acres. Rochford, with the input of those within his social circle, organised rugby in order to replace the folk football usually played on the site known as the football meadow, a vast area in front of another Carlow country estate at Oak Park owned by Sir Henry Bruen, MP. It was here that Carlow organised a field and a pavilion for playing its games and it was to here that Rochford managed to bring the rugby football club.[31]

What emerged was later described by one Carlow rugby player, writing in the 1920s:

> The ball used was a kind of leather bladder which looked more like a misshapen circle, sometimes blown up by the stem of a clay pipe. The footballers made up their own boots by fitting leather bars across the soles of old ordinary boots. The players came from the nearby towns and counties to play. A big number played in each game as there was a large number allowed on teams at that time. This apart from the size of the ground made it very difficult to score. They played on this huge field which had no lines or markings but there were two trees as one set of goalposts. They had no referee and the teams agreed the rules as they went along. Play was stopped by agreement when the players got tired, and sometimes the game continued into the next day. It was an unwritten rule that spectators could have the use of the ball when the players were resting or injured, and after this period the ball had to be retrieved from the crowd, and this almost always ended up in a game in itself. The rules for tackling were different too, as you could stop a man from running with the ball by kicking him below the knees, but this was not an easy thing to do.[32]

Rural rugby, as this example suggests, retained many elements of the folk football that had gone before. Apart from the persistence of some of the more rough and dangerous elements of play, the lack of a bounded playing area with proper goals or a set time for play were elements that codification was meant to control. It was in the schools and the cities, where things like a lack of wide-open fields for play, as well as a need to temper some of the more injurious elements of the game to keep the younger players safe, that the rules of rugby became continually refined.

The game would become safer and easier to join when 'the new football knowledge filtered down to Carlow and the provinces from the families of the

◁ Images from Clontarf FC minute books, 1890s, courtesy of Brendan Smith.

▲ Early depiction of a game of rugby, from 1880 (artist and picture name unknown).

local gentry, almost all of whom had members who were educated in the English Public Schools and later in Trinity College, Dublin'.[33] However, rugby was not a game that was opened up to the 'natives' in an effort to promote a sense of commonality between loyal subjects and the peasantry. This exclusivity emerges within the context of the British–Irish colonial relationship, and Leinster rugby often fell into an 'us' and 'them' binary. The game was to be played by those whose allegiances and identity were more clearly a British–Irishness and by those who had the appropriate wealth, political outlook and 'proper' social standing.

Because it was the landlords, the elites of a local town recognisable to all in the locality, who had taken up this peculiar version of football, these games became spectacles for those not involved. Thus, 'It is not surprising then that when word went around … that "d'lords are playing their fierce football again" it was the signal for the local tenantry to gather and watch, in puzzled wonderment, the propertied gentlemen engaged in mortal combat over a piece of inflated leather'.[34] Of course, there would have been versions of folk football that the Carlow tenantry knew of and partook in. Perhaps they turned out to watch the rugby games in wonder at the way these men had seemingly appropriated the folk game for themselves.

Back in Dublin, in one of the capital's emerging suburbs of choice, a fifth club (following DUFC, Wanderers, Lansdowne and County Carlow) was created. Clontarf Football Club was founded in 1876 and the rugby code was the preference when it came to choosing what type of football game to play. The local yacht club provided facilities for Clontarf before and after matches, and membership crossed over between the two clubs: 'The Yacht Club and the Clontarf Rugby Club worked in unison in the early days; the Rugby Club playing their games in a field near … and using the Yacht Club premises as dressing rooms.'[35] Clontarf's original ground was on Vernon Avenue, rented for £3 per annum from a Monsieur George, who was a horse buyer for the French Army.[36] Early meeting minutes show that goalposts were erected each Saturday morning and taken down after the match, giving us a flavour of the era and the work involved to run a club and organise games. While the club's official establishment was 1876, it was not until the 1886–87 season that it joined the Leinster Branch of the IRFU.[37]

Following Carlow, the trend of rugby spreading beyond the city continued with the founding of a club in the town of Dundalk. Dundalk RFC came into existence in 1877 with a Mr Graves Leech the strongest advocate for the club's establishment and its first captain. Although Dundalk initially had representatives at the foundation of the Leinster rugby organisation, they opted to play with a group called the Provincial Towns Union, which included Armagh, Bessbrook, Derry and Dungannon, and later merged with the Northern Union, remaining a participant in Ulster rugby until 1892.[38]

By the late 1880s, the emergence of new clubs, despite the fact they were still mostly based in Dublin, enabled country clubs to organise more regular games. In Carlow's case it was Bective Rangers (formed in 1881 by past pupils of Bective House College, Rutland Square, Dublin) and Lansdowne that were regular travelling sides to the town. In the 1890s, Clontarf and Monkstown gave the provincial town more games to look forward to. While the suggestion was that these games would help improve rugby in the countryside, the sentiment seemed to backfire somewhat when teams from Dublin sent their strongest outfit. These games would often result in something of a cricket score on the rugby field. The fact that the Dublin sides seemed to win so easily turned some of the young rugby players away from the county club. It was moments like these that helped rugby recalibrate with proposals to grade teams and competitions for parity, which gave Leinster rugby its particular shape.

However, even before such refinements, these matches were important, for the more games that were being played outside Dublin, the more aware people became of this new sport and interest was incrementally sown in the local news of the day.

Depiction of a game of rugby at Rugby School, dated 1845. Off-the-ball clashes, albeit connected to a scrum, were a common feature of earliest football games. ▶

When a Baltinglass team played Carlow in 1884, the match was described in the *Carlow Sentinel* as 'being the first football match played in Carlow under the new rugby rules and so excited considerable spectator interest – a very large number assembled to see the play which they appeared to thoroughly appreciate'.[39] The crowds, the papers claimed, were large and enthusiastic at these contests, especially when local rivalries came to the fore, which assuaged the hammerings that Dublin clubs sometimes brought to bear. Indeed, perhaps one of the saving graces for the rural game in Carlow was the establishment of Athy, as well as school teams at Portarlington and Carlow College, which offered new countryside fixtures from the 1880s onwards. While teams came and went, it would be teams such as Carlow and Athy that would become a mainstay for Leinster in the provincial towns.

By the early 1890s, the Leinster Branch boasted thirteen rugby football clubs and had weathered the storms that might have potentially scuppered the game's popularity. Importantly, interest in schools also continued unabated, and when Catholic secondary schools began to adopt the game, the playing cohort in Leinster was expanded once more. Leinster rugby was planting deep roots that would continue to allow it to thrive in the face of other codes and challenges to come.

SMYTH.

2

Leinster Rugby and the Centrality of the Schools

The Sporting Turn in Irish Education

When sport became something to be organised, with the founding of clubs and associations to oversee teams and games, it made sense that these would flourish in schools and colleges. Educational institutions offered a life that included substantial periods of free time, with populations of young males of an appropriate age for games, as well as having access to or being located in a physical space with suitable grassy fields. The secondary school system was foremost in this regard and the pedagogical turn of the era encouraged boys to partake in sports, so educational establishments became the lifeblood for rugby in the province. Historically, the exclusive, fee-paying schools of Leinster were the 'institutions that … implemented … ideas of "muscular" Christianity and tried to train outstanding civic leaders by exposing them to organized sports. In their view, all the requisite civic virtues could best be inculcated in a physical education program that made cricket, soccer, rugby, and rowing almost essential features of the … curriculum.'[1]

A popular approach to education in the late nineteenth century, then, was to emphasise the centrality of physical and moral health, with both achievable through an adherence to sport within the school system. Indeed, '[b]y the early twentieth century, elite Irish schools had embraced an ethos of athleticism, heavily promoting team sports as a means of developing a child's ethical character. For both

Catholic- and Protestant-run establishments, the encouragement of such games was also a valuable means of demarcating the exclusivity of their institutions.'[2] To have a successful rugby team, in particular, was an indicator that all of the right kinds of credentials were achievable at a particular school, and that in turn would open many more doors in a boy's future.

Although Ireland's social elite often chose to send their children to schools in England, in the nineteenth century it was recognised that there was an opportunity to open similar fee-paying institutions in Ireland. What's more, the demand in the age of industry for more practical schooling beyond religious studies, Greek, Latin and Hebrew required new courses in engineering, architecture, science and modern languages. As a result, Dublin began to see a preponderance of fee-paying schools emerge that followed the structures and ethos of similar institutions in England, including the prioritising of rugby. One example was Wesley College, Dublin, which was modelled on the English college of the same name, set up to educate the sons of the laity in the Methodist faith.[3] The Irish school opened in October 1845, and by the 1860s it seems that 'some kind of football' was played, with St Stephen's Green, beside which the first school building was located, used for games.[4] With a clear and well-defined Christian ethos, Wesley College built a philosophy around sports, aiming to provide a stimulating and challenging programme geared towards participation, self-improvement, commitment, community, discipline and structure via rugby.

Existing Protestant Ascendancy schools also enthusiastically embraced rugby.[5] For example, the Church of Ireland-run King's Hospital school undertook to expand its curriculum in the 1850s, which included making room for outdoor activities and plans for the future installation of a gymnasium in what was then their city-centre campus location. In 1878 King's hired a young headmaster, Rev. Thomas Brownell Gibson, who was credited with allowing the boys independence specifically through the encouragement of school games.[6] That Gibson was a TCD graduate undoubtedly informed the choice of rugby at the school, and the headmaster himself joined in the boys' games.

Following Gibson's retirement, Rev. Thomas Richards, a Welshman, served as headmaster from 1896 to 1922. A history of the school reports:

Within a few years of his arrival he had ... secured the erection of a gymnasium and relaid the playing field at the rear of the school. Richards believed that sport was an integral part of a boy's education; that it built the body and improved the spirit. Accordingly, during his time, sport played an increasingly important part in school life. In the decade and a half leading up to World War One, there seems to have been a great deal of sporting interest and advancement in Leinster, which inspired rugby enthusiasts both in and then beyond their school days.[7]

It is a matter of record that Richards brought his Welsh passion for the game of rugby to King's. Indeed, 'Before long, The King's Hospital began to establish itself as a leading rugby school and in 1907 the final of the Leinster senior schools' cup was reached.'[8] In the early years of the twentieth century, then, rugby was ensconced as the 'traditional' sport for boys at the school.

Not every educational institution immediately bought into the idea of Muscular Christianity. William Wilkins, the headmaster of another of Dublin's Church of Ireland institutions, The High School, saw games as an impediment to study and a distraction from the Intermediate Examinations that he had so focused on as the best method to ensure a successful institute. The Intermediate Education (Ireland) Act of 1878 had been introduced to improve secondary schooling by bringing in a standardised intermediate examination, and student success in exams carried financial rewards for schools. This was a great incentive for schools to do well and improve their graduating outcome. Under the new scheme, 'In 1881 High School boys won more awards than any other Dublin school. These successes produced an influx of new pupils.'[9] Wilkins boasted to his governors that students from rival schools were joining the institution from every quarter, and was one of the few schoolmasters in the late nineteenth century who was *not* convinced by the argument that organised sports would develop 'the virtues of manliness and team spirit [as] part of the training of the boys who were destined to lead armies and provide the governors of empire'.[10] Nonetheless, given the pedagogical influences of the era, the school requested a gym and, although it was never built, gymnastics was introduced as mandatory exercise for the boys.

Despite Wilkins' dislike of sports, rugby still became part of the school's programme when the boys started a rugby team for themselves. This most likely happened in 1875, the same year that they successfully petitioned their governors to be allowed to start a cricket team. Two rugby teams were organised and The High School enthusiastically signed up for the first season of the Leinster Senior Schools Cup when it was inaugurated in 1887. One ex-student, Godfrey Ferguson, who played in the 1890s, became a founding member of the Palmerston Rugby Club in 1898. The club utilised the link to recruit players after graduation, although

▲ The High School Senior Cup team 1933–4.

it seems as though the Lansdowne Club was also a popular venue for ex-High Schoolers. Regardless of the initial wariness, sports soon became important, and rugby was the game of choice. Indeed, when a couple of ex-High Schoolers became star soccer players, playing for Bohemians and Ireland in the 1890s, the school paper ran an article under the headline 'Is not a soccer team in the school treason?' In time there were rugby teams for several age groups, as rugby football became the school's premier game.

Another 'traditional' Dublin rugby school was St Andrew's College. It won the Leinster Senior Schools Cup on four occasions: in 1906, 1911, 1921 and 1922. The college aimed to instruct Presbyterian youth primarily with moral, social, spiritual, cultural and academic learning, focused on the physical and mental well-being of the student. From the school's foundation in 1894, rugby became part and parcel of education at St Andrews, defined as the core sport for young boys' personal development and for honing loyalty. One of the more famous rugby players who emerged from St Andrews' in the early days (although Jewish and not Presbyterian) was Bethel Solomons:

> who later became … Master of the Rotunda Lying-in Hospital, immortalised by James Joyce in *Finnegans Wake*. He was taken at the age of eleven to St. Andrews and studied there from 1897 to 1902, later recalling that there was no bullying, like at other schools, and that he felt he was learning something worth learning, such was the quality of the teachers.[11]

Solomons himself wrote:

> I did fairly well at lessons but I am afraid rugby was my real joy. When I was
> about thirteen it was discovered I might have possibilities and I was picked
> for an under-fourteen team. When I went home delighted with myself, my
> father dumbfounded me by saying I could not practice as the match was on a
> Saturday, the Sabbath. My mother was really a far more religious person than
> my father, but in spite of this she reasoned with him, saying: 'We are living
> in a Christian country, wait until we get to Palestine, then we shall not allow
> games on Saturday. But he can play.' And I did.[12]

The Solomons, a Jewish-Irish family, remained in Ireland and Bethel went on to
earn ten Irish caps between 1908 and 1910, becoming the only Jewish-Irish player
ever to earn rugby international honours.

A further standout Protestant institute in Leinster was Kilkenny College. With
a prestigious reputation, 'Kilkenny College past pupils wielded a great deal of
power in Ireland. Their influence was not restricted to Ireland, for some became
governors or senior judicial figures in the colonies.'[13] The school taught boys
from the highest echelons of society from its foundation in *circa* 1666. In efforts
to recruit students throughout the nineteenth century, like most of the private
schools, Kilkenny College extolled its virtues as a place of education to prepare
'boys "for the universities, army and navy, the civil service, the banks, intermediate
examinations, etc." and offered as enticement eight house scholarships, four
of which were reserved for clergy sons'.[14] It was a new principal of the school,
Reverend George Baile, who encouraged a focus on rugby in the 1890s. A son of
the headmaster of the Ranelagh school of Athlone, where he himself had studied,
Baile was also a TCD graduate. Kilkenny College persevered with the game of
rugby at junior level even after financial trouble saw it have to close its senior
school. There was an understandable sense of frustration among Kilkenny's rugby
enthusiasts at seeing the school's former pupils attending the Mountjoy School in
Dublin, where several played senior rugby with some success.

St Columba's College further added to the numbers of 'traditional' rugby schools
in the province. The school was originally set up to proselytise and convert Gaelic-
speaking Catholics to the Anglican Church. Its primary focus was on religion, and
it made sure always to have higher fees so as to attract 'pupils from a different class',
ideally those from the gentry and nobility. The school made a conscious effort to

attract the children of the families who were ordinarily sent to the private schools in England. To this end, it defiantly rejected the idea that it was an 'Irish' school and emphasised its Englishness, appointing only English tutors. The Columbans made a rule that rugby matches should be played exclusively internally amongst themselves, or occasionally against DUFC, Lansdowne or Wanderers, unabashedly professing their preference not to mix with the 'natives'. It was not until 1892 that a new warden, Percy Whelan, granted the pupils 'permission to play football and cricket matches against other schools. This had been long wished for by the boys …'[15]

At the beginning of the twentieth century, rugby football was the game of choice at all of these institutes, installing a particular connection and culture between fee-paying secondary schools in Leinster and the lauded game of rugby. Rugby schools and rugby promoters often self-consciously expressed and promoted the spirit of mid-Victorian England by following the lead of the imperial centre. Building on this momentum, the Leinster Branch soon introduced cup competitions for both clubs and schools. The onset of these cup competitions enticed a wider array of schools to affiliate to the Branch and to improve rugby standards, now that there was a prize to be gained in competitive fixtures.

Leinster's Catholic Ascendancy, Education and Rugby

As Ireland's Catholics began to assert themselves, thanks to campaigns in the nineteenth century for more social equality, the democratic franchise and a fairer system of governance in general, they began to infiltrate and mimic the favoured cultural practices of the Protestant Ascendancy, at least among the middle and upper classes. As Protestant political power faded in the face of a Catholic political consolidation, Irish Catholics, by and large, embraced British popular cultural practices. This allowed the old-world Ascendancy to maintain a sense of cultural belonging in a religiously and politically changing Ireland. The world of schools' rugby became one area of common ground between the old world and the new world's privileged set. The appeal of the schools' game was self-evident given that, apart from the senior internationals, it drew the biggest crowds to rugby matches prior to the professional era. Rugby emerged in Leinster with a strong following among the province's most advantaged and powerful population.

Irish Catholic secondary schools mirrored their Protestant counterparts, hoping to create institutes that focused on the same subject matter and, to a large extent, the same social and cultural mores. Thus, Catholic secondary schools also

▲ Engraving of Kilkenny College and grounds from the 1700s.

embraced a version of Muscular Christianity, instituting the same sporting biases. An 'estimated 1500 Irish boys who travelled annually to receive education in English public schools … were exposed to the prevailing ethos of sport and took this knowledge back with them across the Irish Sea'.[16] Many of these returning students would subsequently become teachers in Ireland's exclusive Catholic-run boys' schools, and inevitably rugby was the game of choice advocated by the masters. The connection between both Protestant and Catholic fee-paying colleges and the game of rugby has been quite profound and, without the popularity of Muscular Christianity as an educational mantra, Leinster rugby would not have developed along the distinctive lines, so tightly tied to the schools, that it has.

One of Ireland's oldest Catholic Colleges is the County Kildare-based Clongowes Wood. In Clongowes it seems that a version of football closer to soccer was played regularly in the nineteenth century. This initially developed into a very particular, and school-exclusive, sport called gravel football. It was not until either the 1880s or 1890s that rugby was introduced, when the mission at the school was seen as one to develop leaders in a rapidly changing Ireland. Clongowes took some time to get to grips with the game of rugby, and only entered the Senior Schools Cup for the first time in the 1922–23 season.

▲ Depiction of St Columba's College Dublin, taken from *The Times*, printed in 1949.

Around the same time that Clongowes was turning to rugby, so too was Belvedere College. An old Belvedere student recalled a story from his school days that explained how, some time in the early 1890s, there was an unofficial team comprised of Belvederians that played rugby under a different team name, because 'uncouth field-pastimes were out of favour at the Jesuits' Day College in Dublin'.[17] Regardless of this initial discouragement, the Belvedere students played soccer in the Phoenix Park, organised by a pupil who happened to play rugby for Monkstown as well. What's more, one of the junior teachers at Belvedere, 'Pa' Cahill, was a rugby player with Bective, and he volunteered to act as the referee during the students' soccer gatherings. This reflects the trend of the times when there was a desire among young men to play some form of football. Belvedere's students, the story suggests, were not very good at soccer, so they turned to rugby over the Christmas and New Year period in 1898/99 and started playing friendly matches in the 1899/1900 season. They played St Mary's, the Marists on Leeson Street and The High School, all of whom gave them their first home and away fixtures. With rugby now adopted as the school game, since the end of 1898, Fr Tomkin and Pa Cahill advised all the Belvedere boys to keep up their rugby playing after they left school. The best place to do that, they were told, was with Louis Magee at Bective Rangers. This convenient farm system for Bective lasted for about

▲ Early sketch of Belvedere College, Dublin.

eight or nine seasons, but thinned out after that as many students abandoned the game on leaving school.[18]

At Castleknock College (est. 1835), they similarly searched for a sport to help train their boys in the ways of Victorian propriety. At first, soccer was the game of choice, and the school also had a hurling team. However, by 1909 the sporting preference at the school had become rugby. The motivation for pursuing rugby is explained in the school's ethos as still set out today for incoming students. 'Rugby is seen as vitally important to the development of the college students and its key values such as teamwork, leadership, determination, sportsmanship, and humility are actively encouraged. As well as providing physical education to your son it is an integral part of the social bonding process.'[19] The roots of Muscular Christianity run deep in the ways that rugby was, and still is, promoted and understood by those Leinster elite schools that not only encouraged the game but, like Castleknock, made it mandatory.

At the Catholic University School (CUS, est. 1836) the encoding of rugby as the premier sporting activity underscored a persistent Muscular Christianity ideology at both their primary and secondary school levels. As the Irish Catholic hierarchy began concentrating on the central importance of developing Catholic secondary schools (in the face of the British government's intention to create

▲ St Columba's College in the news, celebrating its centenary. *The Times*, 5 June 1949.

'mixed' schools), it was as part of the desire to train the toughest and brightest young men that the adoption of rugby became important. The push to open Catholic-specific secondary schools was also down to the founding of the Catholic University (later UCD), which would need a perpetual influx of secondary school students in order to ensure it was a success. CUS was one of the first institutes earmarked for that function.

It is not definitively clear how early the push towards the importance of rugby within the curriculum at CUS became manifest, but the record shows that the boys played 'football' on St Stephen's Green throughout the 1860s and later in the grounds of the Royal Hospital for Incurables.[20] One CUS alumnus and Irish rugby international recalled 'the old playground in Leeson Street with its clay and gravel surface where in winter we enjoyed a kind of Rugby of our own during the half-hour's lunch time'.[21] The teams would score a try at one end by touching the ball against the school wall within an imaginary goal area and at the other by touching it against a big wooden gate at that end of the schoolyard.

The penchant for rugby among the exclusive schools of Leinster did not differ hugely between Catholic or Protestant schools, although arguably in the latter's case the sport was much more closely tied to both a unionist as well as a religious identity. For Catholic schools, however, it was the pursuit of a sense of social and socioeconomic elitism, tinged with a version of Muscular Christianity, that led to rugby becoming the game of choice. Alongside the aforementioned Clongowes Wood, Belvedere, Castleknock College and CUS, the other fee-paying Catholic institutes of education that were organised for those who could afford to pay all embraced the game of rugby to shore up their bona fides as establishments of learning and privilege.[22] As J.C. Conroy explained:

▲ Castleknock College.

As the years went by more and more schools entered the Schools Cup. Some [of these] private schools … lasted only as long as the headmaster owner lived or retained an interest in the school. …. Thus St. Stephen's Green School, often referred to as Strangeways, appeared first in 1895 and played until the school was disbanded in the 1920s … one of the founder members – Corrig School – ceased to exist about 1909 … Some Schools which have been prominent in more recent [memory] … were late entrants in the Schools Cup. In 1908 Terenure entered; in 1910 … Roscrea; in 1913 Castleknock; in 1923 Clongowes and Presentation College Bray and in 1929 … Newbridge.[23]

For future 'gentlemen' who were destined to pursue important roles in Leinster society, as envisioned for them by their parents and social cohorts, rugby became an increasingly important sport to be associated with. To be on a winning rugby team, especially once there were organised competitions in which to compete, grew in significance. Thus, the ethos of all these rugby-playing schools began to sound very similar, as prospectuses explained that while academics were important, their approach was to also build students' characters with 'the spiritual, the social, the moral, the aesthetic and the physical', which were integral to students' training.[24] And rugby came ready-packaged to fulfil those suggested aims.

RUGBY FOOTBALL.

LEINSTER SCHOOLS CUP.

BLACKRO CK COLLEGE v. WESLEY COLLEGE

The final tie of the Schools Cup competition was played at Lansdowne road yesterday between the above schools, and a game which was productive of some capital football ended in the " Rock " representatives retaining possession of the trophy for the third successive time. There was a good attendance, mostly of juveniles, who were not wanting in the lung power usually associated with these matches. The weather was fine, and the ground, too, was all that could be desired for a good display. Blackrock were much the heavier team, and to this is mainly due their victory; for their opponents showed equal science, and fought their corner exceedingly well. The following were the teams—

Blackrock College—Full, J Leenihan; three-quarters, A Briscoe (captain); J O'Sullivan, W Smith; halves, J M'Guinness and M Neary; forwards, R Britton, G Griffin, J Keogh, M Kelly, P M'Kendry, J Murphy, J Murty, G O'Brien, J Toohey.

Wesley College—Bere, full; H Brown (captain), A Brown, Atkinson, three-quarters; White, Cooke, half-backs; Monahan, Thorpe, Lee, Burgess, Holmes, Coe, Forbes, Mullins, Williams, forwards.

Referee—Mr. R S Montgomery.

Blackrock won the toss, and after Monaghan's kick off they were penalised frequently in rapid succession, with the result that the Wesleyans gained the upper hand for a time, but then the weight of the Blackrock boys told, and they succeeded in carrying play to the Wesley end, where they granted a free off, which Briscoe kicked a fine goal, but it was, however, disallowed, as the ball had touched one of their opponents in transit. Soon after, however, a nice bout of passing on the "Rock" side let Briscoe in, and he was cleverly followed across the line by his schoolmate, MacGuinness. Neither try, however, was converted, and at half time the score was—

Blackrock ... ... 2 tries
Wesley ... ... niker.

On changing ends Blackrock attacked strongly, but sound kicking by the Wesley backs alterní

▲ Leinster Schools Cup rugby in the news, *The Freeman's Journal*, 1895.

▶ Rush v. the Grammar School, Past and Present report, *The Cork Examiner*, 1893.

RUGBY FOOTBALL.

RUSH RS v GRAMMAR SCHOOL (PAST AND PRESENT).

This match was played in the Camp Field on Saturday. The weather and ground were dry, but there was a bitter, cold wind blowing, which was anything but pleasant for the spectators, and even the players complained. The game was a very one sided affair from the start to the call of no time, the Rushers having it all their own way, their backs, as usual, making a very good display. Grammar, though three or four of their team played very well, were unable to put in any score, and they suffered defeat by a goal and three tries to nothing. From the strength of the fifteen they had on the field Grammar should certainly have made a better show than they did, as they were totally unable to get a look-in the whole time, even when they had the high wind in their favour. Nothing could be better than the play of the Rushers' backs, which was neat, sure, and fast but the goal that was given to them by the referee was scored off a forward pass by Nicholson to Pratt.

Establishing the Senior Schools Cup

One of the most important mechanisms that gave all early codes of football their real sense of purpose and rootedness, alongside the codification of basic rules, was the possibility of winning newly established competitions. This was most obvious when it came to schools' rugby. The formulation of a schools-only competition was envisioned as an opportunity to allow boys to compete in their own age bracket, creating an exciting spectacle of youthful sporting endeavour. At the same time, a schools-only competition could widen the pool of rugby interest, enticing more and more educational institutions to pit their athletic prowess against one another. Indeed, 'The conscious effort to foster sports was also another means of defining the superiority of these institutions as the preferred training grounds for the future ruling class of Ireland.'[25] Thus, the fee-paying schools began to embrace rugby to suggest their credentials as elite academies, equal to institutes that were already considered prestigious.

The reputation of the Schools Cup attracted parents' attention when they were considering the schools to which they might send their sons. Blackrock College was one of the foundational teams that entered the first iteration of the Schools Cup competition in 1887, winning it in its inaugural year, beating the now defunct Farra School. Blackrock won the cup six times before 1900 and then competed in eleven consecutive finals from 1900 to 1910, with only one loss. The school continues to hold the record in Schools Cup victories, having won an impressive sixty-nine times from the very first championship through to the twenty-first century.[26] A growth in schools' competitiveness as a result of such competitions helped create a ready-made pool of talented players for senior Leinster clubs, in the pupils of fee-paying institutes such as St Columba's, Clongowes Wood, Blackrock College, St Mary's, Gonzaga, Castleknock, Newbridge, The King's Hospital, The High School, Wesley and Portarlington, to name just a few.

Participation in the Schools Cup was also a way of gaining some free publicity to encourage new enrolments impressed by rugby success. As mainstream newspaper coverage of sports increased, it included ample coverage of school as well as the club matches, helping to feed a growing sports-specific press. 'The rise of modern … sports journalism is really an important manifestation of the increasing significance of sport to Victorian society … Cartoons and paintings depicted men at play with increasing frequency, while novelists and poets also devoted considerable thought to sporting heroes and events.'[27] With that knowledge, wily headmasters did not

▲ A Leinster Senior Schools Cup medal, called a Maltese Cross.

want to miss out on having their school's name brandished in the papers, or indeed appearing in a novel, for positive reasons of athletic success.

As one of the oldest private Catholic schools in Leinster, and with its unmatched success in the Schools Cup competitions, Blackrock became a model which others sought to follow. The story of its development as a rugby power is central to the story of Leinster rugby. Arguably one of the unusual things about Blackrock's path was the fact that, initially, rugby was primarily played by Protestant schools. This meant that 'in the [eighteen-]seventies rugby as it was in Blackrock was a matter of internal competition … usually between the various houses or categories: boarders, day boys, scholastics and the Castle.' However, '[t]hese internal encounters were no mere parlour games by all accounts … "The usual sides were Leinster and Ulster versus Munster and Connacht, and the fierce rivalry in these Interprovincial contests often divided the school into two camps."'[28] The French Catholic priests who founded the college had brought with them from France a pedagogical outlook that ensconced the ideal that a healthy body bred a healthy mind. It was gymnastics that was the exercise of choice initially, which the French Fathers promoted in their school, but they also encouraged boys to play 'Irish sports' as they recognised them: namely cricket and rugby. Just as rugby playing became symbolic for the type of persistent, conquering, masculinity required for future leaders of the British Empire, that symbolism was equally suited to the model of the ideal Catholic missionary that the French teachers at Blackrock advocated.

Within a couple of decades of rugby's growth across Leinster, 'elite Catholic schools where prosperous merchants and professionals sent their sons in the hopes that they would there develop contacts and networks that would aid their future careers'[29] had become known as rugby schools. As with their Protestant counterparts, a penchant for rugby among these school-goers continued to be reflected in their later lives, where the successful professional and merchant classes maintained a network through rugby participation. From the 1880s onwards, rugby became a popular sport among a wider cohort of Irish life, even among some of the staunchest Irish nationalists. However, what was clearly prominent from the very foundations of rugby in Leinster was that status and wealth were generally a common denominator of those involved. In the closing decades of the nineteenth and into the opening decades of the twentieth century, the game in Leinster was controlled and played by, on the one hand, those most threatened by the major social and political transitions of the era and, on the other, by those who would most benefit from the changing of the guard.

The Junior Schools Cup

The massive success of the Leinster Schools Senior Cup soon inspired the idea of the Leinster Schools Junior Cup, which was subsequently introduced to generate interest and competitiveness at an earlier age. Although it took some years to come about, the call for a junior schools cup was advocated by a former student and rugby enthusiast at Blackrock in the 1890s. Credit for advocating for the junior competition goes to one John O'Reilly, a Longford man who, as a seventeen-year-old, enrolled in Blackrock College in 1887, the same year that the Leinster schools' senior rugby competition started. The senior tournament clearly left an indelible impression on O'Reilly. When he started as a junior teacher in St Mary's (in 1893), O'Reilly was playing rugby for Bective and was a regular first-team member. A well-respected rugby man by his mid-twenties, many of his colleagues backed him to become an executive on the Leinster Branch board at an early stage. It was at

▲ The Blackrock College team that won the first Leinster Schools Cup, 1887–8.

43

St Mary's that O'Reilly began to campaign for an under-fifteens Leinster school competition, to complement the Senior Schools Cup.

Nonetheless, it took almost two decades from the Senior Schools Cup's debut for the idea of the Junior Schools Cup to come to fruition, perhaps due to the fact that its main cheerleader was in France in the early 1900s, training for the priesthood. It was not until November 1908, at a meeting of the representatives of the schools' section of the Leinster Branch, that it was decided to petition the Branch for a competition for under-fifteens schoolboys' rugby. The Leinster Branch approved and presented a Junior Cup as a trophy for a knockout competition. The first iteration was in the 1908–09 season, getting under way in December 1908, with fifteen schools entering teams.[30] St Andrews College beat Belvedere in the final to win the first Junior Schools Cup.

Schools Cups were an important addition to the Leinster Branch for the promotion and continuation of the game of rugby. What is interesting is that, for

▶ 9 February 2023. Bank of Ireland Leinster Rugby Schools Junior Cup, first-round match between St Mary's College and Gonzaga College at Energia Park in Dublin. © Daire Brennan/Sportsfile

▲ Mark Hernan of St Michael's College leads his side out for the Leinster Schools Senior Cup final v. Gonzaga, 2019.
© Ramsey Cardy/Sportsfile

many at least, there was a recognition as early as the 1890s that establishing a youth competition and getting boys playing competitively at an early age could only benefit the game in terms of retention and of honing rugby skills early. The centrality of schools' rugby in Leinster was important, therefore, for producing future star players and rugby men excited about the prospect of disseminating the rugby football gospel across the province. While rugby was envisioned as a game for those within similar and delimited social and cultural circles at the outset, nonetheless it was being played and extended across Leinster, with the inevitable outcome of accessibility for more and more newcomers over time. The Senior and Junior Schools Cup competitions, no doubt, aided the game's dissemination as more and more schools turned to the game when they realised that athletic accomplishments in the Victorian and Edwardian-era education system were considered to reflect a school's overall acumen. Moreover, Leinster's rugby schools' alumni continued to search out those youthful sporting glory days, helping to establish clubs across the province as players, administrators and supporting members.

3

Steady Progress: Leinster Rugby, 1880–1900

Forging the Leinster Senior Cup

The last two decades of the nineteenth century saw increasing interest in rugby across the county, with a total of fourteen clubs being established by 1900. With this upswing in interest, there was a need to consolidate the growing support. Part of this involved rule changes to make the game more enjoyable to play and watch for its principal social group of young, mainly urban-dwelling, professionals. Support was also encouraged by promotion of the game in the press by clubs, who were willing, despite the strict rule of amateurism, to spend money on this, as well as on bigger things, such as the creation of rugby-specific venues. One sure-fire way to maintain player and spectator focus was the creation of prizes to stimulate players and the spectating public. At Leinster Branch level, there was investment in the purchasing of cups and awards for new competitions. In a meeting held on Halloween 1881, the Branch agreed to provide a Challenge Cup for which the affiliated clubs could compete, and the Leinster Senior Challenge Cup (LSC) competition was born. A subcommittee was put in place at this same meeting to oversee the competition and met for the first time at 63 Grafton Street.[1]

The clubs agreed on a ten-shilling entry fee and the proposal that all the cup games would be played at Lansdowne Road to ensure the income of a gate was approved. This income was to be kept as part of the Cup Fund, to go towards payment for the cup itself, as well as fifteen 'Maltese cross' medals commissioned for the winning side. At the outset, then, the following guidelines were agreed:

(1) Entries for the competition should be sent to the Honorary Secretary of the Branch on or before November 30th, 1881, and the Cup ties should be drawn on December 1st, 1881. (2) Any Club entering the competition should guarantee the payment of £5 to the Cup Purchase Fund and should pay an entrance fee of ten shillings. (3) All matches should be played at Lansdowne Road and the ground should be engaged for the matches (4) The proceeds of the gate should be added to the Cup funds and (5) The Cup winning team should be presented with 15 medals, or in 1882 parlance, fifteen 'crosses.' Five teams entered the first competition in the season 1881–82 ...[2]

The first final was scheduled for 18 March 1882. Played in front of approximately 2,000 spectators, it saw DUFC defeat Kingstown to win the first ever LSC.[3] *The Freeman's Journal* described the festivities at Trinity after the win: 'In the evening there were tar barrels, blazing rockets, squibs and fireworks let off and all sorts of jollification among the students in the College Square in celebration of the victory.'[4] Between the years 1881 and 1900 Trinity won twelve of their nineteen appearances in the Senior Cup, including a four-in-a-row streak from 1895 to 1898.

The LSC competition continued to grow with the addition of new senior teams. In the 1882–83 season Monkstown and Bective joined, and a team called North Suburban entered in 1887 and 1888, but that club eventually folded. In 1896 Old Wesley became senior and entered; in 1897 Carlow College became an addition; and when Blackrock College went senior in 1899 the competition began to heat up, added to by Clontarf, which entered in 1902, the same year the team was graded as senior. During this period, when clubs initially formed, they were graded as junior. As Edmund Van Esbeck pointed out, 'with the arrogance that comes from a superiority that is total, Trinity decided that any team that wished to play their First XV must first prove their worth by defeating their second string.'[5] Prior to the establishment of a junior cup in 1888, defeating DUFC's second team in order to play their first team essentially made these emerging clubs senior. For the very first clubs that had more than one team (i.e. a first and second XV), the firsts were the senior team and the seconds were the junior. Later, as more clubs emerged, usually with only one team of fifteen, at least at the outset, they were given junior status until they had proven themselves to be well-established and successful (i.e. by winning the junior cup) and they had to apply for senior status through the Branch. New and young clubs' hopes were, therefore, at the behest of Branch executive committee members, who continued to vote on whether or not to allow a club to become senior into the 1960s, at which time rules were changed to try to create a fairer system.

The growth of Leinster senior rugby was accelerated by the inauguration of its premier cup competition, the LSC. This competition incentivised players in junior clubs to strive for the honour of bringing their team up to senior standard to compete for the cup. When the Branch rules were changed to limit the number of senior clubs, the best players at junior clubs transferred to senior clubs so they could play

▲ The Leinster Schools Senior trophy.
© Pat Murphy/Sportsfile
▽ DUFC/Trinity College, the first winners of the Leinster Senior Cup, 1882.

at the higher standard. For clubs like Wanderers and Lansdowne, whose team members also often played for DUFC, one of the important outcomes of this new competition was that the rules stipulated a player could only tog out for one club during the cup season. This brought consistency to teams like Wanderers and Lansdowne when ex-DUFC players joined these new clubs, and a new sense of loyalty and pride in the stand-alone clubs among players, administrators and fans.

Dublin Club Dominance

The new clubs that formed in Leinster contributed to the continued growth of rugby there, but some of these clubs were short-lived. So, at the outset of organised rugby, to ensure a regularity of games, school teams played against both club and university teams, and university teams also played the club teams. But it was not quite the 'men against boys' image that this may conjure up. The schools' teams would not only have had some of the masters togging out with their pupils, but more often than not included a few 'old boys' as well. With that in mind, one can see the perhaps natural progression to the establishment of more club teams, where teachers and ex-pupils could find a common social, as well as sporting, interest away from their workplace or their old seat of learning. This is evident in the establishment of Bective FC (1881), Blackrock College P&P (Past & Present, 1882), Old Wesley (1891), St Mary's College (1900), Old Belvedere (1918) and, eventually, Terenure College (1940). All of these clubs were organised by and for, or associated with, alumni of their constituent schools.

By the end of 1881, Bective FC had played a number of games against various opponents in the Phoenix Park before establishing their own home ground, and records show that the club had established a second fifteen. Indeed, in their second ever annual general meeting, Bective reported having played nineteen games, winning ten, losing four and drawing five. They had joined the IRFU and had, on advice, decided to alter their name to Bective Rangers.[6] Their honorary secretary was industrialist Harvey Du Cros, who lived at Cullenswood in Ranelagh, where he secured a field for the club to move to, thus leaving the Phoenix Park. Du Cros was said to be a guiding light for the club and is credited with choosing the location, close to the Clonskeagh tram line – a clever proposition considering the need to get players to and from matches with as much ease and convenience as possible.[7] The expansion of rugby's popularity in Leinster was helped by the expansion of the tram system in Dublin and the rail system across the province. Indeed, south

Dublin clubs deliberately positioned themselves close to the suburban tram stops, and, province-wide, many clubs were located in the towns that boasted a train line connected to the capital.

The attraction of players to clubs like Bective reflected the success of rugby in Dublin, as did the ever-present reportage in the newspapers. By the end of the 1800s, rugby coverage not only included detailed game reports but, more significantly, punditry had become a regular feature.[8] Rugby correspondents reported the nature of play and, from their reports, it would appear that, on the field, rugby still required a little refinement. One newspaper report of a Leinster club game between Bective and Wanderers in 1890 argued, 'the practice of trying to pull the head off a man when he is not only tackled but is in touch should be sat on at once'.[9] In spite of that reporter's admonition of such violent acts, reports of the day claimed that a crowd of about 2,500 turned out in December 1890 for Bective's game against DUFC, and the intrepid rugby writer Jacques McCarthy offered some fascinating lines – a snippet of the world of rugby at this moment in Leinster's history: 'The match was a long way the best ever played in Ireland. The arrangements were excellent. There was a sixpenny gate to keep out the roughs with sixpence extra for seats on the cricket ground side and pavilion.'[10] Quite clearly, the institution of a gate had as much to do with ensuring class exclusivity at rugby matches as it did with fundraising. Nonetheless the regularity of reporting in the papers, including claims of crowds between 2,000 and 5,000 attending games in the 1890s, confirmed rugby's popularity.

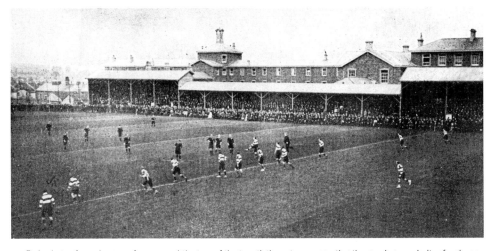

▲ Early photo of a rugby game from around the turn of the twentieth century, suggesting the growing popularity of rugby as a spectator sport.

▲ Various photos of rugby being played in the early 1900s against a New Zealand team on tour, showing how the game had developed from its earliest incarnation in schools.

The attention being paid by newspaper reports to the emerging rugby powerhouse that was Blackrock College P&P demonstrated the important links between schools and new clubs, as well as showing from where the popularity of rugby was first derived. The club team was quick to establish itself, winning the very first, newly inaugurated, Leinster Junior Cup competition in 1889. The team's success continued for the rest of the 1890s and it won the Junior Cup four more times in 1892, 1893, 1898 and 1899. Blackrock, therefore, exemplified the trajectory of Leinster rugby in that, as a newly established junior club eager to compete, they helped lead the way in advocating for a junior cup competition. They excelled at junior club level and proved their worth in the eyes of the rugby establishment.

With the team's credentials firmly established, Blackrock College applied for and earned its senior club status for the 1899–1900 season. This was despite the fact that the team had been cautioned by the Leinster Branch on numerous occasions in the 1890s for rough play – a manifestation of the tough masculinity that was expected from the game of rugby. Bective's John Sheridan provides another example of this rough play, when he intimated the danger to his spine that teammate Billy Collopy posed during one practice match. Sheridan whimsically recalled, 'I made no impression on Billy Collopy, but Billy Collopy made a considerable impression on me. It was like running up against a stone wall, and then and there I abandoned my dream of hooking for Ireland someday. I had only one spine, and it had to last me the rest of my life.'[11] It was an ongoing process, over the years, for rugby officials

▶ Rugby action in the early 1900s against a New Zealand team on tour.

▲ Blackrock P&P Senior Cup winning team 1887.

to develop the game into something that retained its competitive edge yet did not devolve into a dangerous and contemptible game to play or watch.

Despite misgivings relating to the physical risks associated with the game, rugby remained popular in schools and clubs, which inevitably helped new clubs to form. The Monkstown club, established in 1882–83, continued the growth of the game in Leinster. The team, it was written, was 'really an off-shoot of the old Kingstown Club, which we find mentioned in the very earliest records of Irish rugby history. For several years Monkstown depended for players largely on the old boys of the … Corrig School, which, in its time, produced many a player who later achieved [rugby] fame.'[12] Monkstown was known for its connection to the British Army officers who, at the time of the club's formation, were stationed in south Dublin and remained there until the arrival of the Free State. Thus, it was a link to those within the province and the society of the era who had British credentials. It was clear among the Branch's executive that such connections to the Empire were important, as regular toasts to the monarchy and the Union were part and parcel of their sport. The team could also rely on a steady supply of Trinity players. The club first competed in the 1883–84 season, playing for approximately sixteen seasons in the Dún Laoghaire area, and then moving in 1901 to new grounds leased from the Earl of Pembroke, who had been generous with his land when it came to the burgeoning interest in rugby in the south Dublin environs. What is interesting is that Monkstown, once a paragon for the image of rugby as a garrison game, with officers of the British Army long forming the backbone of the club, continued to see an influx of soldiers into the club after the War of Independence, but this time Irish rugby-playing soldiers from the Free State Army.[13]

Leinster Junior Competitions

Rugby union continued to grow in popularity among elite Leinster society, a fact reflected and abetted by the decision to create the LSC competition and to continue in that vein by adding competitions for all adult rugby interests. With the LSC gaining momentum, it made sense that a junior cup competition should come up for discussion at a Leinster Branch meeting in October 1883. On that occasion it was agreed that the £75 credit balance in the Branch accounts should pay for a challenge cup for junior clubs, and a subcommittee was organised to investigate the matter. Santry School, Blackrock College, Carlow College, Clontarf, Claremont and University College (St Stephen's Green) were the clubs represented on this subcommittee. The Branch agreed that the best way to run the Leinster Junior Cup competition was on a knockout basis, but it took the best part of five years to get the go-ahead from the Branch's executive committee. The Junior Cup was finally sanctioned at a meeting in 1888, with the first competition run during the 1888–89 season. Nine clubs took part in the initial cup – Athy, Cabra, Claremont, Blackrock College P&P, Clontarf, Bective Rangers, Farra, National FC and Santry – and it was won by Blackrock.[14] The cup itself was christened the 'Leinster Junior Challenge Trophy'. Initially, medals were presented to the winners, and it was not until the cup's fourth rendition, in 1892, that a winner's trophy was presented, as it took the Branch the guts of three years to manage to purchase it.[15] Somewhat fortuitously, it was once again Blackrock College who won that year, for the second time in the cup's short history.

While it is evident that the establishment of new clubs reflected a healthy interest province-wide, those at the top table of the Branch were interested in the quality of the game, as well as general growth. As rugby evolved, the Leinster Branch honorary secretary's report for the 1894–95 season worried somewhat about the standard of rugby being played, citing too many scoreless draws, although conceding that the weather over the season had been particularly bad. Nonetheless, the game was as popular as ever in the province and four new clubs had affiliated – Sandymount, Royal Irish Constabulary (RIC), Stephen's School and St Andrew's College – all of which would compete at the junior level. With new teams being added to already established clubs, there was soon a push for more sanctioned competitions, starting with the demand by senior seconds to be allowed to compete in the Junior Cup. Thus, 'the second teams of Senior Clubs brought pressure on the Leinster Branch' and at

the Annual General Meeting … in October 1895 it was proposed that the Second XVs of the Clubs competing in the Leinster Senior Challenge Cup should be entitled to compete in the Junior Cup. This motion was supported by the representatives of the Senior Clubs, but it was opposed by the Junior Clubs. The resolution was beaten, but as a compromise a Sub-Committee consisting of representatives of three Senior Clubs and of three Junior Clubs was set up.[16]

▲ Leinster Junior Schools Cup. © Ben McShane/ Sportsfile

The purpose of this committee was to draw up some sort of plan with the view to having second fifteens of senior teams in a junior cup competition and to see how that might work and please everyone involved.

There was no satisfactory compromise to be found, however, and the subcommittee instead recommended that, 'a [separate] Cup be presented by the Leinster Branch for competitions between the Junior Clubs and the Second XVs of Senior Clubs on the League principle'.[17] From discussions and negotiations about this potential new cup emerged the format of the Junior League. The Branch decided to organise a subcommittee to establish the rules for this league, in which the first XVs of junior clubs would play against the second XVs of senior clubs on a home-and-away basis, except for the inaugural season of 1895–96, where teams only played each other once to ensure that the system got up and running. With two points awarded for every game won, the Junior League winners would be the team with the most points at the end of the league season. The Branch approved the Junior League format rules and they agreed to order a new trophy for this third adult rugby competition.[18]

▲ Lansdowne FC, winners of the Leinster Senior Cup 1891.

▶ 1880s team sheet, Clontarf FC records, courtesy of Brendan Smith.

As the nineteenth century came to a close, Leinster's senior rugby clubs continued to expand internally, introducing much-needed membership to bolster their revenues to meet overheads by creating second and third fifteens, and sometimes more. The gate money at games was the biggest earner for the Branch and it was the LSC that was bringing in the largest gates at the turn of the century, followed by the interprovincials and then the schools, Junior League and Junior Cup.[19] Competitions, therefore, became the important sustenance that fed the Leinster rugby organisation in its earliest iteration. Significantly, the popularity of the Junior Cup and Junior League confirmed rugby as a sport that was sowing roots and reaping the rewards of competitive action beyond the well-defined exclusivity of the senior game.

▲ Leinster Metropolitan Cup 2022. © Seb Daly/ Sportsfile

Rugby in Leinster Towns

In October 1883, a group of local men from what was then called Parsonstown (Birr, Co. Offaly) came together to discuss the idea of forming a football club. The local newspaper reported that there was a large attendance at Dooley's Hotel in the town, comprising the well-heeled of the area, including the Rev. Dr Ewing, the headmaster of the local Chesterfield School, Mr Waring of the Provincial Bank and Mr Crooke of the Third Leinster Regiment, who became the founders of the new rugby club. The men charged a subscription fee of five shillings and were adamant that anyone wishing to play on their newly formed team must have the appropriate attire, otherwise they were not welcome. Records of the meeting explained:

> An animated discussion took place, with the result that a club was formally initiated, Mr. Waring, Provincial Bank, undertaking the hon. secretaryship, Dr. Ewing the less onerous, but equally important post of treasurer, and pending the trial matches, the first of which is fixed for Thursday next, the 25th Oct., the appointment of a captain was left an open question. A convenient ground has been secured in the enclosure known as Hanks' field, on the railway road … and it is hoped that a large attendance on the opening day will prove what a warm interest is felt in this manly game.[20]

After this initial meeting, there were another couple of get-togethers recorded in the papers that illustrate the efforts to get the team up and running. The Midland Counties Advertiser revealed that a good number turned up at the first official meeting, which was a positive given this was the first time of asking, but there was a complaint about the tardiness of the majority of potential members, some of whom arrived thirty minutes late. Regardless, the men interested in playing for the new team assembled and '[u]nder the supervision of Mr Crooke and Dr Ewing, both enthusiasts for the success of the club, the ground was prepared during the forenoon, goal posts erected … so that little remained but to strip to the work. A couple of scratch sides were picked … Waring and Crooke as Captains … and a rattling hour's play resulted.'[21] The 'rough material' for a team was evident, but with a bit more practice, the reporter believed, there would not only be a good side, but they would attract spectators to come to watch as long as the weather co-operated. Interestingly, the paper admits 'that the rugby game was a perfect novelty' for a number of the farm labourers and local peasantry who turned up to witness games in Birr.

In their inaugural 1883–84 season, the organisers made a decision to amalgamate the football and cricket teams under the name Parsonstown Athletic Club in order to assure there were enough players for the team to go ahead. However, contemporaneous reports from the midlands reveal that Birr struggled to retain a team for any great length of time and the rugby element to the Parsonstown Athletic Club came and went, perhaps due to the comings and goings of particular men involved in the game. For instance, when Rev. Ewing left the town and his position as headmaster of the Chesterfield School, from where he had promoted the game, this coincided with the disappearance of the Birr rugby team. Nonetheless, rugby in the province's rural towns at the end of the nineteenth century endured, laying pivotal roots for the future of rugby union in Leinster.

When both the metropolitan and provincial town clubs are considered, there seemed to be enough momentum to allow the steady development of Leinster rugby and improvements in play year-on-year. To compete locally with the County Carlow FC rugby team, a team was formed 'by the students at Carlow College. It is worth recording here the influence the College had in promoting rugby in the area. The College was the seminary in the Diocese of Kildare and Leighlin for the training of young men in the priesthood.'[22] These young men would have been from well-to-do Irish families and were being trained for the priesthood abroad. As a seminary college that hoped to train priests for future missionary work, one can understand the rationale for the introduction of the game to the college, given rugby's overt imperialist connotations via the philosophy of Muscular Christianity. Carlow College brought many of the leading Dublin clubs down to play, with teams travelling for double-headers to play both County Carlow FC and Carlow College. The two Carlow teams played each other regularly, of course, as many as five games throughout a season and with the rules on membership still relatively lackadaisical, and teams swapped players for games if needed, often according to the strength of the opposition coming to visit. Despite this, the College club only existed on an active note until around 1900.

These difficulties did not discourage other provincial towns from forming their own clubs. Adding to the growth of rural Leinster rugby, Kilkenny County Football Club came into existence in the late 1880s to offer opposition in the region. Rivalries were cultivated and Kilkenny and Carlow tested each other on occasion, keeping a local attentiveness on rugby. Adding to the regularity of the games was Wexford FC, which appeared in 1887, and there were reports of a team in Rosslare as well at this time. The game in the countryside more broadly, was predominantly played by the gentry until about the 1890s when the expansion of trading and commercial life in towns like Carlow, Wexford and Kilkenny saw the influx of new blood and, more to the point, a new cohort of socially acceptable players for the game, allowing it to grow and embed. The Carlow *Sentinel* reported on all the local games giving scores and scorers, presented with great excitement to the readers. These reports, alongside the establishment of local rivalries, such as Carlow's games against Kilkenny, Athy and Wexford, fed a sense of pride in one's club, town and no doubt one's county, which helped to promote rugby clubs and recruit players from the locality. Some international success in the 1890s also helped raise the game's profile. Ireland won the Triple Crown in 1894, with thirteen of the fifteen starters coming from Leinster clubs (6 DUFC, 5 Bective, 2 Wanderers). Ireland won the championship again in 1896 and then another Triple Crown in 1899. Prestige is always part of

ATHY RUGBY FOOTBALL CLUB.

A meeting for the purpose of starting the club for the season was held in the Town Commis-sioners room on Tuesday evening. Mr J. A. Spillane presided, and there were also present— Messrs L. Heffernan, T. Heffernan, M. Doyle, S. Dunne, R. J. Clandillon, R. Wilson, M Haugh, J. Doyle, J. Orford, M. W. Whelan, W. Taylor, R. Frame, T. Orford, R. Large.

Mr J. A. Duncan, J.P., was elected President, Mr W. Taylor, Hon. Sec., and Mr M. W. Whelan, Treasurer of the Club; Mr Pennycuik, Vice-President.

Messrs W. Taylor and L. Heffernan were appointed Captain and Vice-Captain, and the following as a committee to act with the officers— Messrs J. Orford, R. Wilson, P. Lalor.

On the motion of Mr Clandillon, seconded by Mr Whelan, a vote of condolence was passed to Mr J. Crampton in a recent bereavement he had suffered.

Messrs L. Heffernan, Taylor, and Whelan, were appointed a committee to obtain a suitable field for the season, and it was arranged that practices should be held on Mondays and Fridays.

▲ Athy Rugby Club in the *Nationalist and Leinster Times*, 1894. With the backing of newspaper reportage, rugby (and other sports) began to attract more spectators.

sport's attraction, and winning international games brought a new sense of distinction to rugby.

The Early Interprovincials

Interprovincial games had been inaugurated in 1875 and carried on annually since. The Leinster team continued to progress in its matches against Ulster and Munster. Leinster had originally proposed the provincial branch system to help placate a defiant Ulster rugby contingent who were unhappy with the establishment of an Irish Football Union dominated by a southern rugby cohort. As part of that plan, the proposal included the inception of an interprovincial competition, which was ostensibly formed as a way to organise trials for the selection of an Ireland team. The first match, played in the Ormeau Ground in Belfast in November 1875, attracted the attention of the newspapers, and a crowd of spectators of about 1,000 and saw Ulster defeat Leinster by a try and a conversion to nil. The second took place on 16 December 1876 in Lansdowne Road, where the home province balanced the record with a Leinster win. The first Leinster versus Munster tie took place in March 1877, at TCD's College Park, with Leinster winning by a goal to nil. Over the next century of fixtures (excluding those during the Second World War), Leinster dominated Munster, losing only twenty games, drawing eight and winning sixty-three.

Leinster had advocated for fixtures between all three provinces in March 1878, but Ulster at first refused to play against Munster. While Leinster and Ulster's game went ahead, the Ulstermen declined to respond to the issue of including Munster in the process. They would rather cancel the forthcoming international against Scotland, a fixture that had been placed in the care of the Northern Union and was scheduled for Belfast in March 1878, than play a Munster team in a 'trial' match. In spite of Ulster's recalcitrance, given the argument for an interprovincial system being the mechanism for choosing an Irish international team, Ulster were finally persuaded to embrace an interprovincial Munster fixture, which, initially, was to be played at Lansdowne Road. Once the branch system came into existence in 1879, the interprovincial schedule generally progressed accordingly, with regular matches between all three provinces becoming annual fixtures. However, Connacht, which had yet to be fully affiliated to the IRFU, not having the minimum requisite of clubs to be allowed to join, was still missing from the system. Nonetheless, Leinster tried to facilitate games with a representative Connacht team, first playing them some time in December 1885 in Dublin.

The Leinster–Connacht games, in the nineteenth century at least, were not the easiest fixtures to bring about. When a second Connacht–Leinster match was organised for the following year, again in December but this time to be played in Galway, to the Leinster Branch's annoyance, the Dublin players showed a distinct lack of interest in playing: 'Leinster found great difficulty in getting fifteen players to travel to Galway, and were it not for Monkstown F.C., who provided ten members of the Leinster team, the match would have had to be cancelled.'[23] Prophetically, on the night before and throughout the day of the 1886 match, a terrible storm raged up across Galway as the teams took to the field. *The Irish Times* reported, 'the gale raged with undiminished violence and was accompanied by cutting showers of hail and sleet … after a short time it was agreed to abandon the game.'[24] As Connacht remained the outlier in terms of its struggles to maintain a strong interest and any kind of success in rugby, Leinster resorted to playing a 'B' team against the westerners.[25]

From 1879 onwards, the centrality of the interprovincial game was tantamount to the ongoing growth and improvement of the game, for several reasons. It was the mechanism to reunite rugby in Ireland after Ulster obduracy early on; it fuelled competition, which became an incentive to improve play in each of the four provinces; it provided the imperative 'trial' matches for an international team; and it helped to popularise rugby, as the increasing numbers who were turning out to watch interprovincials suggest. Between 1875 and 1900, Leinster played Ulster twenty-five times, with only the game scheduled for the 1881–82 season cancelled due to impossible weather conditions. Of those, Leinster won eight, drew six and lost eleven. In the 1900–01 season, the report from the Leinster Branch honorary secretary revealed a proposal for caps to be awarded to all Leinster players who travelled for interprovincial games. Up to then players had only earned a cap for a win, but administrators thought that players should now be rewarded for selection and participation, regardless of the result.[26]

Leinster players had a fair representation on the Irish squad in the nineteenth century, with the interprovincial talent often the equal or better of Ulster and generally having an advantage over Munster at that stage in rugby history. Among the internationals who were capped by Leinster were the Bulger brothers, Larry and Michael. They attended Blackrock and TCD and, along with their brother Daniel, were outstanding athletes, winning track and field events, and getting involved in the Olympics; first and foremost, however, they were ardent rugby enthusiasts. As such, the 'careers of the three Bulger brothers are indicative of the aspirations and achievements of the rising Irish catholic middle class'.[27] All three brothers played for Lansdowne, and Larry and Michael won Ireland caps in the 1890s, including Larry's cap in 1896 on the team that brought home Ireland's first ever championship title. Larry was one of five men who were the first ever Irish players to be selected to join a Great Britain (later the British and Irish Lions) tour to South Africa.

Another example of the family connections among Leinster's rugby fraternity were the Magee brothers. Louis Magee, a notable Leinster player educated at CUS, Clongowes and at third level in Edinburgh University, was an 'ever-present in the Irish side at half-back, he became the first Irish player to win twenty caps for Ireland … Widely regarded as one of Ireland's greatest-ever rugby players, Magee was a master of the sidestep, swerve, and dummy, and was capable of winning games on his own …'[28] Two of Magee's brothers, Joseph and James, were also rugby players, with Joseph also playing at international level. Leinster players, then, were making a significant mark in helping to raise interest in rugby across the province. Elsewhere, there were sets of three brothers that excelled to national note, including the Collopy brothers of Bective Rangers, the Dorans for Lansdowne, the Forrests for Wanderers, and the Harvey brothers, Johnstone brothers and Moore brothers of DUFC and Wanderers. There were also two Galbraiths, Gwynns, Kennedys, Stokers and Wallises, all brothers with noted rugby names, who played to the highest level towards the end of the nineteenth century.

As clubs came and went in the 1890s and early 1900s, the 'traditional' clubs that demonstrated staying power, accounting for the first generation of senior Leinster

▲ The 1884 Leinster team that played Ulster on 6 December that year.

rugby, were DUFC, Wanderers, Lansdowne, Monkstown and Bective. When Old Wesley became senior in 1897, then Blackrock in 1899 and Clontarf in 1902, this gave Leinster eight of its ever-present powerhouses of club rugby. But there was a dichotomy appearing between city and rural rugby, which coalesced into senior and junior rankings and gave Leinster rugby a particular administrative and cultural distinction, with a geographic idiosyncrasy to boot. The dominance of a handful of senior clubs specific to the environs of Dublin 4 dictated much of the direction of the Leinster Branch for several decades. It became increasingly clear to junior rugby clubs, especially those established outside Dublin, or at least south Dublin, that there was a particular favouritism emerging, reinforced by the emergence of the division of forthcoming competitions. The organisation of the Branch's executive and the decisions around new competitions perhaps best reveal the peculiar divergence that emerged between junior and senior Leinster rugby.

All of the Leinster clubs picked representatives to attend a mandated AGM to be held at least once a year, in order to select the executive that oversaw the main organisation of rugby in the province. At this AGM, the representatives would elect an honorary secretary and treasurer to oversee the running of the Branch, as well as nominating representatives to speak for the province at the IRFU's general meetings, known as the 'big five'. In terms of the names put forward for the executive positions, the senior clubs dominated by selecting their own members for these positions. So, regardless of the voting system, the choice was always to vote for an executive that was only ever derived from the senior clubs. However, the Branch did revise its constitution in order to better administer to the game's needs in the province in 1885. The new provisions revolved around rules for elections of officers, plus guidelines for the honorary secretary and treasurer roles, alongside any other officers. New byelaws also allowed for the appointment of subcommittees, the first one being the committee that ran the Leinster Challenge Cup. Between 1886 and 1920, there were very few changes to the structure of the Branch, although the introduction of a Junior

TO-DAY'S FOOTBALL

RUGBY.

LEINSTER v. ULSTER.

Really grand weather favours the Rugby inter-provincial match between Leinster and Ulster at Balmoral to-day. The sun shines from a clear blue sky, and the breeze is of the very lightest kind. The ground is, too, in first-class order. At the time of wiring (2 o'clock) a great number of people are wending their way to Balmoral, and there is every likelihood of a record crowd for an inter-provincial contest. Of course, the launching of the great ship Oceanic drew a large number of people to the northern capital, and when the big White Star Liner was put afloat the visitors naturally turned their attention to the Leinster-Ulster contest. The teams are the same as published in this morning's papers. Of course, Leinster is very much weakened by the defections of Louis Magee and Meldon, but the Ulster side, on the other hand, is as strong as possible.

Ulster won the toss, and J Little kicked off. During the early portion of the game Ulster had the best of matters against the wind, and five minutes before the interval M'Gowan got over, but Little failed to convert. Half-time score:—

Ulster—1 try (5 points).
Leinster—Nil.

▲ Ulster v. Leinster match report in the *Evening Herald*, 1899.

League committee, to oversee the junior section, reflected the growing popularity of the game across the province. Another change was to do with the schools: schools' representatives were appointed to help oversee the smooth running of the school competitions and to select the Leinster Schools interprovincial team. There was also the introduction, in 1902, of the Association of Referees, which helped give the game more structure and conformity province-wide by creating a central committee to ensure referees were in universal agreement about implementing the laws of the game and that those laws were disseminated to the clubs. Furthermore, they could better attend to the increasing fixtures, which required umpiring. The fact that so many rugby players and administrators came from a professional job allowed for a well-managed organisation, which helped ensure Branch finances were maintained and the game put on a secure footing, with regard to competitions, silverware, pitches, facilities and so on.

However, the Branch was still largely controlled by senior club men, and they tended to favour the senior club game. So, it was left to rugby at the emerging junior level to bring the progressive change that was needed to grow rugby across the province, make it more inclusive and change attitudes among the general public, as well as within rugby union circles along the way. The addition of the Junior League, which was initially set up for any junior club affiliated to the Leinster Branch, reflected the growing interest in rugby in Leinster, and by the 1905–6 season it was necessary to divide the league into two sections. At the end of the season there would be a play-off between the winners of each section to determine the ultimate Junior League Cup champions. The honorary secretary's report for 1906–7, stated that 'that the game is popular, progressing, and deeply rooted in our province are facts beyond dispute'. It is surprising then that relatively quickly the Branch decided to limit the Junior *League* to the junior clubs within the Metropolitan area only; ostensibly the second teams of all the senior clubs. This left what was then still the Junior *Cup* (as opposed to the league competition) for provincial town teams that wanted to compete for a trophy. To expand competitions, therefore, to cater to the growing interest in rugby province-wide, new proposals emerged from the Branch. At the October 1906 AGM, a motion was put forward for the establishment of a Minor League for senior thirds, junior seconds and new teams starting out of similar strength. The new Minor League cup competition proved a great success, and new schools signed up for the Leinster 1907–8 season, including Sutton, Kilkenny College, Mount St Joseph's College Roscrea, Terenure College and Drogheda Grammar School.[29] In spite of the ongoing protectionism that persisted around Senior rugby, come the first decade of the twentieth century, Leinster rugby appeared to be on an upward trajectory.

Leinster Rugby in Turbulent Times, 1900–1919

Rugby in a New Century

In the first decades of the twentieth century, in an Ireland still under British rule, improvements in education opened a pathway, at least for some, into professions previously closed off to the majority of Irish people. Those paths often led to jobs facilitating the Empire, in the police force, the military and, for a few who could access secondary education (about 6 per cent of the population), in industry, the civil services, law and other professions. Despite rising nationalist sentiment and calls for political separation, little changed in terms of social class structures. 'Amongst the educated Catholic elite, class distinction was based on Victorian English norms ... [I]t was less a new world these people wanted than to dominate the old and despite the vigour of the Gaelic movement Irish audiences showed little inclination to shun English popular culture.'[1] As this new century dawned there was a continuation of the retreat from parts of Dublin city centre by the wealthiest class, primarily to the south suburbs, while at the same time, '[i]n 1911, 22.9 per cent of Dublin's population lived in one-room tenements.'[2] Slums, penury, disease and death filled the city's core. 'There was no shortage of outrage expressed at such conditions in the opening years of the twentieth century and, indeed, there was much analysis ...'[3] But little was done about the situation, in terms of implementing real change, at national or local governmental level.

▲ Donnybrook village in the 1920s (note the important tram lines), an exemplar of South Dublin suburbia, from where the wealthy elite formed the 'traditional' Leinster rugby clubs.

▼ In stark contrast, inner-city Dublin slums, created by wealthy landlords often fleeing to the aforementioned suburbs, saw some of the direst living conditions in all of Europe.

Away from the city-centre slums and rural impoverishment across the rest of Leinster's small farming communities, the further south one went in the Pembroke township, the area now known as Dublin 4, the wealthier the inhabitants became, with grand houses all through Ballsbridge, Sandymount, Sydney Parade, Park Avenue, Merrion, Pembroke and Ailesbury Roads. 'In this township, middle-class families sent their sons to schools in England, where they played cricket and rugby. Others sent them to Irish schools like Wesley or Bective College or, if they were Catholics, to Belvedere or Blackrock College, all of which are still famous for their rugby teams.'[4] There is no hiding from this reality of Irish life, which developed along entrenched, class-divided lines, and the geographical particularities that saw south Dublin suburbs become bastions of the upper class at the turn of the century.

These realities informed people's cultural choices and entertainment preferences. The wealthiest parts of Irish society – whether Catholic or Protestant, nationalist or unionist – embraced the games that had pre-existing considerations of social capital. For example, a growing alliance between rugby and more prosperous Irish nationalists, presented that code of football as having been 'adapted to the genius of the Irishman … [R]ugby provided a culture of sporting success, masculinity and heroism, and national distinctiveness, which allied neatly with wider ideas of national identity and affiliation.'[5] For Ireland's elites, then, playing rugby could reinforce pride in one's sense of Irishness, while for others it confirmed their sense of superior Britishness within Ireland. Culturally and politically, rugby playing in Ireland meant different things to different people but within Leinster, by and large, it was the common denominator as the sport of the wealthy and privileged. Nonetheless, it was also never a game that was incompatible with nationalism, nor with nationalist views on politics, despite being a game of choice of southern Protestantism in particular.

Rugby offered a network of friends and acquaintances within the professional and business world, regardless of religion or political outlook. For some, it overtly signalled an attachment to the crown, to the union with Britain and with Protestantism. While these latter designations might have been viewed as the ideal identity for a rugby player among a particular cohort, in an Irish context it would not remain that way for very long. Senior rugby, up to the middle of the twentieth century, remained stubbornly elitist, but in the junior ranks in Leinster, attitudes within and towards rugby became more nuanced. The earliest murmurings of criticism from within Leinster rugby complained that the senior rugby people dominating the Branch were averse to change, retaining the sense of rugby being a niche sport, while among the junior clubs there was a push towards openness.[6]

As Irish people looked to 'get on' in their careers and lives, the networking possibilities that rugby offered were quickly understood. In Leinster, just as in England and elsewhere, 'rugby was the passport that demonstrated one's bona fides for entry to and progress within the appropriate social networks. Rugby itself was also one of those networks, and thanks to its matches, tours, committees and dinners, offered considerable opportunities for the creation and cultivation of social and business contacts.'[7] What's more, there was a heavily bureaucratised structure to rugby clubs, with all affairs managed by a president, vice-presidents, team captains and vice-captains, honorary secretary, treasurer, committee members and selectors. In addition, subcommittees were established to look after the particulars of the club, like specific financial matters, grounds and maintenance, pavilion, social activities and general advocacy for clubs, amongst other things. By default, these structures required some administrative and executive acumen. There was, therefore, a very specific unit around which rugby in Leinster developed, resulting in the oldest clubs with the strongest networks holding sway over the Leinster Branch structures.

However, with the development of the junior rugby scene, newer clubs began to emerge, and those of a less Protestant and less unionist outlook became part and parcel of the Leinster rugby scene as the decades proceeded. That rugby began to reveal some inner tensions and divergences at this particular time reflected the ruptures happening across broader Irish society. It was an era where Ireland's contradictions and tensions were prominent, and it was in that context that Irish sports, including Leinster rugby, developed. The sporting world in Ireland, then, emerged from

> a moment of great political, social, and economic upheaval; this played a major role in shaping modern Irish sport and in ensuring that sport in Ireland held characteristics shared by no other country. What was apparent in this new sporting world was that love of sport, in itself, did not adequately explain why certain people played certain games in certain places. Usually there was a complex of factors involved … of class, gender, religion, geography, political allegiance, and much else, including personality.[8]

When it comes to deciphering the history of rugby in Leinster, there was a particular set of circumstances that helped rugby thrive. Of the fourteen Leinster rugby clubs created up to the outbreak of war in 1914, for instance, six were established in the

Pembroke township and another five a stone's throw away.[9] It was the progression of these established Leinster clubs that became important for the maintenance of rugby in the province during the turbulent years that followed.

An example of the strong presence and the establishment of solid foundations, built on traditions tied to rugby during the pre-First World War years is the story of St Mary's College, Rathmines. This is, today, one of the most recognisable rugby clubs in Leinster. Rugby was a popular team sport at St Mary's secondary school in Rathmines, and senior pupils, ex-students and teachers had been mulling over the possibility of a setting up an external rugby club, as an addendum to the school's teams, since the late 1890s.[10] The president of St Mary's College, Rev. Dr Crean, agreed to facilitate the first proper meeting to help establish this, at which it was agreed that the 'Old St Mary's FC' rugby club would enter the Junior League and Junior Cup within a year. The team was allowed to use the facilities at the college and, although the founding members were alumni, it was to be an open club, welcoming anyone who desired to join. In its first two official seasons, the club made it all the way to the Junior Cup final, only to be beaten by the RIC team in both finals. It was an impressive start for a fledging club and St Mary's went on to a whirlwind of success in the first thirteen seasons of its existence (from 1901–2 to 1913–14), appearing annually in cup finals and winning several trophies.[11] Other teams that officially affiliated with the Leinster Branch in the years 1900 to 1920 included Kilkenny (1900), Railway Union (1905), Carlisle (1908), UCD (1910) and Enniscorthy (1912). While these clubs had staying power, several others that affiliated folded soon after, although a few would reform and re-affiliate in the future.[12]

In the first decade of the 1900s, Leinster rugby's evolution was minimal, in the sense that not very much changed in terms of the kinds of cultural and social capital that went with being involved in the game. However, the addition of Railway Union RFC marked the beginnings of change. While the various football codes elicited teams connected to businesses and factories all across Britain, in Leinster, prior to Railway, the clubs were almost all closely affiliated with secondary and third-level institutions. The RIC, General Post Office (GPO) and Monkstown clubs' connection to the military were examples of clubs not tied to provincial towns or educational institutions, but, somewhat unique in Leinster, Railway Union echoed mainland Britain's pattern of sports' clubs connected to transportation networks and their employees. This was not a club merely for the elitist schools' old boys, the landed gentry, or the aristocratic and professional classes. The Railway and Steampacket Companies' Irish Athletic and Social Union 'held its first general meeting in June

1904 … "to promote and encourage sport and games and other forms of social and athletic activities among the staffs of the Railway and Steampacket Companies represented in Ireland, the Irish Railway Clearing House (IRCH), the Dublin United Tramway Co., and the Grand Canal Company".[13]

Although founded in the summer of 1904, Railway Union didn't play in any official competitions until the 1905–6 season. They competed first as a junior club and then applied for senior status after winning the Leinster Junior Cup in the 1920–21 season, only to be controversially turned down.[14] The Leinster Branch's refusal to allow Railway to turn senior exposed for Harry Gale, a long-time Railway Union and rugby advocate, a cynical and 'ruthless opposition' to junior rugby teams from the top brass in Leinster rugby. The result was that the best junior players either left to go and play with senior clubs or, worse, quit the game altogether. Gale felt that the system had created a kind of monopoly on talent for the senior clubs. Fuller details of Gale's accusations would come later in his rugby career, but it was in the 1920s that he first identified a need to address the inequitable structure of Leinster rugby, which favoured the senior teams to the detriment of junior clubs, and more to the point, the detriment of Irish rugby more generally.

Another club that did not arise from the usual sources was Carlisle RFC (associated with today's Parkmore RFC), which was founded in 1908. The team was drawn together from a number of young men from within the Dublin Jewish Community. With a familiar refrain from the era, the rugby team was associated with the Carlisle Cricket Committee, which got its name from the addresses of its founding members, many of whom resided on Carlisle Street in Dublin. The club faltered around the time of the First World War, struggling to re-establish numbers after 1918, but reappeared 'in 1926, sometimes referred to as the "Dublin Jewish Rugby XV". However, in 1927 the club [was] formally re-established and affiliated to the IRFU as Carlisle RFC. The man behind this development was Maurice Stein who was elected captain.'[15] The old club's archive claims that Bethel Solomons, who played in the 1900s, was one of their most noted players. More substantial records definitively show he was a Leinster and Ireland player, winning his representative caps while playing with DUFC and then Wanderers, so it is unclear when he played with Carlisle exactly. But as an outspoken critic of anti-Semitism and a proud Dublin Jew, it is not unlikely that he lined out for Carlisle in some capacity.

The story of Bethel, and his brother Edwin, gives us a glimpse of a part of Irish society that is, perhaps, not often considered. Edwin, a successful international businessman and the first member of the Dublin Stock Exchange, sat on Leinster

▲ Some Railway Union RFC representatives, probably taken in the 1970s or 1980s.

Branch committees and helped look after the finances of the Trinity College rugby team. Bethel, who records claim was close friends with some of the men involved in the Easter Rising and came out as a supporter of that insurrection,[16] became synonymous with a prominent rugby anecdote about a taxi ride into Dublin city on a rugby international game day. He enquired of his driver, who was ignorant of his passenger's identity, what he thought about the Irish rugby team. The driver's disaffected and incredulous reply, to loosely summarise Solomons, was: 'Irish team? Playing an English game, with fourteen Protestants and a bleedin' Jew. I'd hardly call that an Irish team!' Although perhaps apocryphal, this anecdote reflects entrenched ideas of a more extreme Irish nationalism; that the 'true' Irish were Catholics, who were culturally opposed to at least an overt English culture (excepting the language of course), especially a game like rugby. Less ideologically, the cabby's response to Solomons echoes the sentiments of working-class Dublin, if not the wider Leinster population outside of the upper-middle classes, in terms of the exclusivity of the rugby game. The Solomons' yarn is reproduced with a wry tone when it appears in rugby records, but it reveals the challenges Leinster rugby was faced with when it came to public perception throughout the twentieth century.

73

To keep interest alive in the game, Leinster rugby's authorities debated how best to structure new competitions in the first decades of the new century. While the Junior Cup competition was available to each of the junior clubs, not all registered every year to partake.[17] Outside Dublin, the *Carlow Sentinel* offered a criticism of the way the Branch treated the provincial towns, as it was seemingly unwilling to expand and popularise rugby outside the capital. The *Sentinel*'s editor, Mr Langran, was annoyed by the lack of interest from Branch leaders over the 1912 Junior Cup win by Carlow (their second). 'Incidentally, neither the cup nor the medals were forthcoming after the game,' he wrote, 'which reflects anything but credit on the powers that be whom we innocently presume to be managing rugby for the Metropolitans – one can but suppose that if the Provincials were considered good enough to play in Lansdowne Road it might have had a better ending.'[18] Voices like Carlow's Langran and Railway Union's Gale are not just prescient examples of discontent, but are signs of the grassroots push for change within the structures of Leinster rugby.

Outside Dublin, County Carlow was the most successful Leinster junior team in the first twenty-five years of the twentieth century and won the Junior Cup in 1904, 1912, 1913 and again in 1921 and 1922. Examples of players who togged out for Carlow included O'Callaghan, the son of the local surgeon; Heffernan, an employee at the Bank of Ireland; Barney Hennessy, who came to rugby after playing GAA first; and Patrick 'Pa' Bergin, who learned rugby at the Knockbeg College before joining County Carlow RFC and playing in the 1912 and 1913 cup-winning sides. Having amongst one's ranks a local newspaper editor (the *Sentinel*'s Langran), who was a consistent booster of the rugby game and his home club, also helped. Carlow's first Junior Cup win in 1904 brought the team some kudos, and more visiting teams from Dublin came to play – Blackrock, Clontarf, Palmerstown, Monkstown, St Mary's – all of which helped raise the standard of football, as well as interest in the game. It was a lesson in how to build success for other junior clubs to try to emulate, and no doubt a lesson for the Branch as well, seeing the positive results of a cup-winning side from the countryside in raising rugby's profile. Emulating the success of Carlow in the Junior Cup in the pre-First World War period were another provincial team, Dundalk, who won the competition in 1909. After the war, Kilkenny won it in 1920 and County Kildare RFC (based in Naas) in 1924, with Enniscorthy winning in 1923 and 1925, and runners-up in 1924.

It was a further sign of progress, when, in order to build upon momentum within the game, the Branch broadened the annual competitive fixture list,

▲ The County Carlow FC winners of the 1913 Junior Cup.

introducing the Minor League for the third fifteens of clubs in Dublin, plus any new club that wanted to start up across the province.[19] The league was inaugurated in the 1907–08 season, and the teams played on a home-and-away basis in a league structure. The top two teams at the end of the league from each of two sections played each other in a final to decide the ultimate winner.[20] In addition, new rules were introduced, largely due to the persistence of low scores and dull nil-all draws, which are replete in the earliest years' match statistics. Some of the new rules were to do with changing the points allocated for scoring; some had to do with the rules around kicking, tackling and the scrum. The Branch was not the only organisation effecting change. UCD RFC, set up in 1910, would be pivotal in trying to change the game over the years.[21] The subtle changes evident within UCD rugby came through administrative experiments and the open style of rugby the club advocated. In the former regard, UCD had a club-wide, as opposed to the traditional first fifteen, captain, two distinct positions of accountability. A first fifteen captain's remit was to oversee the exploits of the first team only, but greater responsibility was given to the UCD captain, appointed to oversee the interests of the club more broadly.[22] The new distinction took the focus off prioritising the first team above all else in the club; debatably, this marks a cultural shift in how the game of rugby was now evolving in Leinster.

Leinster Rugby and the First World War

Regardless of any undercurrents of divergence, Leinster rugby was content with its own progress in the first decade of the twentieth century and there was much self-congratulation in the midst of competition from other sports.[23] But just as confidence was on the up, the global crisis of 1914 brought progress to a shuddering halt. Once the First World War broke out, rugby was inevitably caught up in the realities of its ideological background. For those from the Leinster rugby world, the motivation to fight in the First World War was tied to an imperialist ideal, although ideas about adventure no doubt also partly informed the choice. For most men tied to rugby, it was certainly not about economic needs, which it would have been for the far greater number of Irish men from the working classes and, in sporting terms, from a GAA background, who signed up. Apart from the motivations of wartime adventure, and perhaps military and/or political career ambitions, there was clearly a sense of duty for those who signed up for a 'pals' regiment.[24] Rugby rhetoric of the era was 'centred on the theme of sport promoting imperial cohesion and sympathy'.[25]

It is hard to disavow the motivation to fight for king and country among Leinster rugby circles. As Neal Garnham has noted, 'the reality and the rhetoric that surrounded the visits of British colonial touring teams to Ireland … offer some conclusions as to what they tell us of both rugby and politics in Ireland before 1914'.[26] Between 1888 and 1912 five teams from the British Empire visited Ireland to play rugby, which included games against Leinster. These visits were a part of the mechanism that aimed, through the British imperial ideas and ideals reflected in rugby, at placing Ireland within a 'wider imperial context'. Undoubtedly, '[b]efore the Great War rugby union was ascribed an important role in developing and strengthening good relations between Britain and her imperial dominions by helping cultivate shared values …'[27] The accounts of the Leinster games against these touring sides were lauded in the language of imperial greatness, the pre-eminence and spread of the colonial project and the apparent conviviality between the British outposts, exemplified by the very fact of the tours themselves.

Of course, not all Leinster rugby players signed up to play for loyalist reasons or accepted the connection between rugby and empire. Nonetheless, when it comes to understanding those rugby players who signed up for the war, among that group there was a prominent theme that emerged of duty to king and country. In the midst of the bloodlust that the declaration of war sparked in late August 1914, rugby's advocates in Ireland boldly proclaimed that their sport 'provided a shining

light of unison which rose above the sectarian divide and marked it out from the
… Nationalist sports.[28] That is, rugby was understood to represent a shining light of
unionism in a fractious Ireland and, to prove it, rugby men would be called upon
to sign up for combat. Indeed,

> as early as 1880 an article in the *Irish Football Annual* had noted that 'the
> rugby game had forged a link between the various colonies and dependencies
> of our Empire.' Once in the colonies rugby could provide an entrée to local
> society, and a sense of cohesion for the natives abroad. The rugby club was the
> social focus for both the newly arrived and the established émigré community.
> For their fellows at home who envisaged themselves as the coming masters
> of Ireland under the imminent Home Rule regime, rugby football provided a
> tangible means of demonstrating their superiority over the representatives of
> the existing powers.[29]

At the same time, on the urging of political leader John Redmond, many Irish
nationalists also signed up during the First World War, believing that it would help
secure Home Rule.

When the war broke out in 1914, it was the Leinster Branch executive's decision
to unanimously endorse Leinster rugby players' participation. The executive called
a meeting on 9 October to discuss halting all rugby games. The final word from
the debate reflecting the thoughts of the Branch stated that 'men have gone away
to risk their lives and in England, Wales and Scotland they've given the game up
and so we in Ireland would look very bad to be seen playing football.'[30] A show of
hands confirmed that Leinster rugby would support the war by halting all official
games except for schools' rugby.

As mentioned previously, the centrality of the public school model to the sport
of rugby was vital to the development of the game in Leinster. As such, 'Rugby union
saw itself as the very embodiment of the public school imperial ideal: vigorous,
masculine, militaristic and patriotic.'[31] From the perspective of Leinster rugby,
this becomes observable through the number of ex-students from several private
schools around Ireland commemorated for their service in the First World War. For
example, St Andrews in Dublin was one school that had an Officer Training Corps
(OTC) for the British military from around 1912 onwards. The school instituted
a romanticism around the British military specifically, which helped persuade
ex-students to sign up in 1914. What's more, '[a]t least 19 St. Andrew's alumni

▲ Two university rugby teams in the 1910s pose together for pre-game picture.

responded ... by joining the first 300 ... [rugby] footballers to gather at Lansdowne Road to become the "Pals" Company'.[32] Of these 300 'Pals' deployed in 1915, only seventy-nine were still alive after three months in the quagmire of Gallipoli, and only two of the nineteen St Andrew's contingent came home.

Aside from the pressure to join the fight itself, senior students in these schools were called upon to maintain the game of rugby. The Branch had decided to continue running a schools' league to keep up rugby interests. There were seven teams in the first iteration of a new Schools' League competition, and all the matches were played on Wednesdays and Saturdays at Lansdowne Road during the war. There was a recognisably strong link, then, between Leinster rugby and the First World War, exemplified post-1918 when senior clubs and rugby-playing schools erected memorials to the fallen British Army soldiers, who had been members of their teams.

In relation to the fallen, many of their personal stories are available to us. For example, twenty-one-year-old Jasper Brett was a second lieutenant in the Seventh Battalion of the Royal Dublin Fusiliers. Brett was born in Kingstown (Dún Laoghaire) and attended Monkstown Park before being sent to the Royal School in Armagh. Back in Dublin, he became a solicitor and was apprenticed at his father's

▲ The Irish 'pals' rugby players at Lansdowne Road who were recruited into the British Army for the First World War. They were among the troops that were sent to Gallipoli.

business, all the while playing centre for Monkstown RFC. Brett heeded the call of Frank H. Browning, President of the IRFU, and joined one of the special 'pals' companies with fellow Monkstown rugby players. The company was made up of barristers, doctors, solicitors, stockbrokers, bankers and civil servants, all from the upper echelons of Dublin's social and business classes. Indeed, they were given the nickname the 'toffs among the toughs'.[33] Brett landed in Gallipoli in August 1915 and saw severe combat, writing graphic letters home of the horror he was witnessing on a daily basis. By June 1916 he had been sent to a military hospital in Malta, and was then shipped back home to Richmond Hospital, having been diagnosed with severe shellshock. Released in January 1917 a broken man, he returned to Ireland and committed suicide that February by lying on the train rails at Dalkey tunnel where he was decapitated by the 10 p.m. train to Bray.

From the moment the war commenced there was a concerted effort to link Leinster rugby to the British efforts. *The Irish Times* was quick to demand that young rugby players enrol and began documenting the names and numbers of rugby players who joined the British forces. Frank Browning inaugurated the IRFU Volunteer Corps (VC), with recruits generally taken from the professional

▲ First World War recruitment propaganda aimed at rugby players in Britain and Ireland.

and commercial classes and connected to rugby football. Browning placed an advertisement in *The Irish Times* in August 1914, urging all Irish rugby club members to join the 'Irish Rugby Football Volunteer Corps'.[34] This corps eventually 'separated into two outfits: D Company of the 7th RDF, who served in Gallipoli with the 10th Irish Division; and a group of older men who stayed behind in Dublin as a home defence corps'.[35]

Liam O'Callaghan has tabulated that '[o]f the 60 players who lined out for Wanderers FC in 1913–14, 35 (58%) served in the War. Of the 39 players who played for Dublin University, 30 (77%) served. Of 46 men who played for Clontarf in the final pre-war season, 24 (52%) joined up'.[36] In total, 336 past and present members of the DUFC joined His Majesty's forces. Of the Wanderers' players mentioned by O'Callaghan, thirty-three were killed in the war. Of the 239 D Company Irish men who went to war, only seventy-nine came back, with 160 killed, wounded or taken prisoner. Lansdowne FC lost thirty-nine men with D Company and had a total of 250 members who fought at Gallipoli, with seventy-two killed.[37] Those first group of 'pals' sent abroad were cannon fodder in the Gallipoli campaign in 1915.

However, those who consciously defined themselves as a part of the 'rugby pals' regiments, in order to claim an identity tied to the Union, were only a part of the story of this period. This is due to the fact that rugby at school's level, since the 1880s, had been dominated by Catholic institutions. The Leinster Schools Senior Cup had, by 1914, only been won four times by Protestant schools since its 1887 inauguration. Schools, in turn, were key rugby nurseries in Dublin. There were plenty of young Catholic men playing rugby in Dublin and many of these joined the colours, but they didn't join 'pals' units. For the 'pals', there was a clear line of connection between their identity as rugby players and the cause of the British Empire, but clearly not all those from Catholic backgrounds bought into, or were conditioned by, this concept. Moreover, in complete divergence, the sympathies of some Leinster-based rugby players lay with the growing opposition to the imperial ideal and, rather than sign up for a war with Europe, they chose instead to support the fight going on at home for freedom from British rule.[38]

Interprovincials, 1900–19

A recurring theme in Leinster Branch deliberations in the early 1900s was the need to create a vast improvement in rugby standards across the country. As previously suggested, the need for the interprovincials was largely defined by their usefulness for selecting the national team. Interprovincials themselves ostensibly served as trial matches, and so matches to get on to the interprovincial squad in Leinster became a popular topic in the sports pages. For example, in January 1906, one report revealed:

> The value of the annual Hospitals match at Lansdowne road as a trial for the purposes of picking a Leinster team, may be gleaned from the fact that of the fifteen chosen to do duty for Leinster against Munster only seven played in Saturday's [trial] game at Lansdowne road … On the run of the play there were some players who merited favourable notice from the Selecting Five … All that needs to be said about Saturday's event at Lansdowne Road is that Wright's try was a brilliant individual effort and that he and De Courcy gained a six point's victory for the Hospitals that was well deserved.[39]

Apart from criticism of the poor standards of play in the report, Leinster interprovincial selection trials, when the so-called 'big five' selectors came out to watch potential representative players, were anything but province-wide. Trial matches were generally populated by Dublin players only. The presumption was that any player good enough would naturally leave a junior or provincial town club to seek out a senior club to ply their trade. But that leaves out the inability of, or the refusal to allow, a successful junior team to become a senior club, not to mention the fact that some of the best, but unselected, players resided in particular

▲ Lansdowne FC teammates, with Ernie Crawford in the middle.

locales because of work, or perhaps family, where there was no senior team available on which to play. There was, then, an institutionalised bias in the Leinster representative selection process, which was difficult to overcome.

To address some of the criticisms being increasingly highlighted by some within rugby, including Ernie Crawford and Sarsfield Hogan and some rugby journalists, the Branch focused on promoting the junior interprovincial series. Yet the attitude towards this was somewhat condescending. For example, at a Leinster 'big five' meeting in November 1902, the issue of caps for the junior interprovincials was raised for the second time in a year, and the response was that the committee had already agreed to give caps to senior interprovincial

G.P.S. Hogan, who had a big impact on 'democratising' and progressing Leinster (and indeed Irish) rugby.

players and didn't see any reason why they should do this for the juniors.[40] The point exposed the inherent inbuilt bias within Leinster senior rugby that privileged senior clubs and players,[41] often to the deep frustration of the rugby men at the junior level, who were promoting rugby in provincial towns for the benefit of the game as a whole.

Away from the club scene, the revamping of the schools interprovincials was recognised as a positive way to keep the game of rugby competitive by instilling the incentive for representative honours on a more consistent basis at a younger age. The revamp was required because of the structure and schedule that had been in place since 1888, when Leinster had first begun to take on Ulster at school level. With matches played around Easter time, none of the Catholic school students was allowed to compete in games that landed on those holy days. At other times, there seemed to be favouritism when standout cup-winning players were omitted from the Leinster squad in favour of players from schools that had not even entered the Schools Cup. It was when the Branch moved the fixture to ensure it was kept clear from Easter holidays, and when the Leinster selectors were supplemented in the late 1890s in the selecting of a schools' interprovincial side by a representative from each school that had competed in the Schools Cup, that the interprovincial schools fixture became an exciting prospect for all schoolboy players.

▲ One of the Leinster teams that played Ulster in the interwar years.

The Leinster junior interprovincials also went some way towards helping ensure rugby's popularity and survival outside of Dublin by creating rivalry between the junior players across all the provinces. The junior interprovincials provided a bigger prize for young rugby players to aspire to and drove clubs at all levels onwards, so that the changes the Branch was making inspired not just schoolboy and junior, but also senior, players to be successful, in the hopes they might be noticed by the various Leinster selection committees. Interprovincial success offered bragging rights on the one hand, but also that sense of competitive edge needed to spur on any sport at all levels, from schools and juniors up through the senior game. Provincial rugby was further motivated by service to the national team, again at school, university, junior and senior levels, once those competitions were sanctioned. All of this fed into the motivation to improve skills and rugby acumen, which in turn fuelled greater spectator interest and, ideally, club membership.[42] The goal of winning an interprovincial cap helped ensure that a constant flow of players would emerge, enticed by the prospect of representative honours and the potential appurtenances that came with reaching such heights among one's peer group. The central hope was to create a vast improvement in rugby standards across the country.

In terms of evaluating the health and status of Leinster rugby, on-field success is one measure of how the game in the province progressed. Of the official senior interprovincial matches played against Ulster from 1900 to 1920, Leinster won six, drew one and lost eight (there were no games played during the First World War). The record against Munster was twelve wins, two draws and one loss. So, Leinster rugby was certainly in good health given these outcomes. Junior interprovincials against Ulster officially started in 1901 and in the period up to 1920 the Leinster juniors won eight, lost five and drew one. There were only two games against Connacht at this point, one in 1911 and one in 1919, with Leinster victorious on both occasions. Leinster players were also regularly selected for Ireland in the new century. Pre-eminent Leinster players on the international team were coming to the attention of the public at large as notable rugby stars. And with sporting celebrities emerging in the new media of the era, being mentioned on radio, recorded on cinema reels and caricatured on things like cigarette cards, the game of rugby got a boost in Leinster, attracting more and more players and spectators, as well as demands for improvements in play and entertainment value.

2 March 1985, Michael Bradley of Ireland dives with the ball in the Ireland v. France match at Lansdowne Road. The final score was Ireland 15, France 15. © Sportsfile

Leinster Rugby and a New Ireland

Leinster Rugby and Irish Revolution

The story of Éamon de Valera's penchant for rugby is one that demonstrates the nuances of the game in Leinster, in that while he associated with a Gaelic nationalism politically, in sports his first preference was rugby. As a pupil of Blackrock College, it is not a surprise that he should have become a rugby aficionado. Yet, his political leanings may have fed into a perception of extreme cultural nationalism where it did not exist. Indeed, de Valera was a critic of essentialists who tried to preclude sports in their definition of Irishness.[1] But of course, as with all cultural practices, sport is not apolitical. Irish and Leinster rugby was replete with tension and contradictions, no different than Irish society writ large. Nevertheless, in the prevailing cultural atmosphere of Free State Ireland, a 'discursive line between Gael and West Briton was drawn, and for a significant and vocal body of opinion rugby was on the wrong side'.[2] Not that the ordinary rugby player necessarily thought much about that reality. However, the rugby world did become caught up in the conflicts of the era pertaining to the Irish struggle for independence, especially in the guise of the IRFU's president, Frank Browning.

As the First World Word continued, Browning himself did not go to Europe to join the conflict but was killed during the 1916 Easter Rising, the effort by Irish nationalists to overturn British rule and establish a republic. Browning was enlisted in the home defence corps, 'consisting mainly of men who were too old for military service … though the Army could find little for them to do.'[3] Browning's group regularly marched up and down the leafy suburbs of south Dublin, from Lansdowne to the foothills of the mountains, wearing armbands with the letters G.R., designating *Georgius Rex*, on their uniform sleeve to confirm their loyalism and support for King George. In the quick-wittedness of the Dublin streets, these men were conferred with the nickname the 'Gorgeous Wrecks'. Browning's demise occurred on Easter Monday 1916, not long after his return from a faux-military exercise in the Dublin Mountains. On that day, of all days, the home defence corps:

> marched back to their base in Beggars Bush Barracks in Ballsbridge, most of them in a uniform similar to that of the Army; they carried rifles, but had no ammunition … Frank Browning, leading about forty of them, came under fire from No. 25, Northumberland Road, which was occupied by Lieut. Michael Malone and Volunteer Séamus Grace, members of the Irish Volunteers who were under the command of Commdt. Éamon de Valera, based in Boland's Bakery. Frank Browning sustained a head wound and was taken to Baggot Street Hospital, where he died two days later.[4]

De Valera was not the only rugby enthusiast, who exalted in the fight for Irish freedom in 1916 and through the subsequent Irish War of Independence. Many rugby players, like Bethel Solomons and Kevin Barry, supported the Irish cause. The story of Kevin Barry supports the conclusion that rugby was played without any regard to unionism or empire by at least some young men in Leinster. As Edmund Van Esbeck wrote on the occasion of Old Belvedere's golden jubilee in 1980,[5] 'boys who had got their formal education at Belvedere College, were among those who paid for [Irish freedom] in full'.[6] Barry played rugby as a schoolboy with Belvedere College and was on Old Belvedere's seconds in their first season. He also had a strong connection to UCD, where he enrolled as a scholarship student in 1919 to study medicine. A member of the IRA, allegedly from the age of fifteen, Barry was active in Dublin early in the War of Independence. During an IRA ambush on British soldiers in an attempt to acquire arms, he was captured by British forces and executed at the age of eighteen on 1 November 1920. As his legacy evolved in Irish nationalist culture, his association with rugby in Leinster became a common focal point. From Old Belvedere's perspective, his arrest and execution seemingly brought about something of a crisis at the club, since there

▲ The shell of the GPO on Dublin's O'Connell Street after the Easter Rising, 1916.

were other players who had similar nationalist leanings and the club was now on the radar for further scrutiny. A few weeks after Barry's death, the club captain, Michael O'Brien, 'and another member of the senior team, M. McGowan were taken to Arbour Hill en route to the military detention centre at Ballykinlar Camp in Co. Down. The fullback, James O'Brien had decided to set sail for the U.S.A',[7] presumably to escape a similar fate.[8]

By the close of the First World War, domestic events in Ireland had changed the entire reality of life on the island in profound and contested ways, as an appetite for independence swept over the country. When the leading officials of Leinster rugby continued to celebrate their British military connections, that link put them in a category of disapproval among the Irish public. 'The objective diversity of the game's adherents did not … prevent its pejorative labelling as a "foreign" sport.'[9] As cultural and political nationalism prevailed in Ireland, the top

▲ Frank Browning in the uniform of the Irish Rugby Football Volunteer Corps. Browning, as president of the IRFU at the time, demanded that Irish rugby players join the British Army in the First World War. He was shot and killed by Irish rebels during the 1916 Rising.

▲ Éamon de Valera in his Blackrock Rugby days, from the *Evening Herald*, 6 May 1939.

representatives of rugby seemed to firmly define themselves as intransigently unionist through actions such as funding First World War memorials and retaining the Union Jack and 'God Save the King' as the anthem at games and rugby functions, even after the Free State was established in 1923.[10] This fed into a perception that those associated with the game were defining themselves as British first. In the 1920s, such actions understandably seemed provocative given the desire of the majority of Irish people to sever links with Britain. Thus, 'the perception that the Irish rugby team did not truly represent Ireland … was a potent one.'[11] This perception neatly fitted into the campaign to reclaim Gaelic Ireland for everyday people, in that rugby, as well as other overt 'English' practices, represented a kind of British culture that should be rejected if Ireland were truly to regain national selfhood. The perception of Leinster rugby, then, in an Ireland that had largely embraced nationalist sentiment in the 1920s, was one of foreignness, especially given the perpetuation of a socioeconomic exclusiveness for some decades to come. It was a game that seemed out of touch and out of reach for the ordinary Leinster public.

Nonetheless, rural Leinster town clubs continued to play rugby throughout the 1920s and the game even expanded. For example, rugby had been played in the earlier 1900s around Mullingar, although there was no organised club, with locals organising matches against the military barracks' sides prior to the War of Independence, and some scratch games among Mullingar's rugby enthusiasts were also often played. However, the foundations of a club were being figured out, and Mullingar RFC's records show that 'a meeting [was] held at the Central Hotel in 1925 and [organised by] J.E. Wallace, Solicitor; S.K. Brabazon, Dr J.J. O'Sullivan, J. Doyle, Sergt. Brophy (Garda) and J.M. Winckworth' to form a club.[12] They received permission to play at the Mullingar Showgrounds and remained there until the club faltered in the late 1930s due to a shortage of players.

During the Civil War period, some country town clubs had struggled due to arrests, emigration and at times difficulties posed by travelling to fulfil fixtures. But when things began to settle down and a relative peace was reached, Leinster rugby would grow exponentially. While there were still the problems among the rural clubs of Leinster around the rule not to play games on a Sunday, which at times made it more difficult to organise fixtures or field a team, as well as an issue with senior clubs from Dublin being reluctant to travel to country towns, voices of progress like Ernie Crawford and G.P.S. Hogan (referred to more generally as Sarsfield Hogan) in the late 1920s began to push for a province-wide approach at the higher levels of Leinster rugby.

The Aftermath of War

While Leinster's rugby hierarchy in the 1920s and 1930s remained stubbornly unionist, ordinary players within the rugby world often held a very different point of view. For example, when senior metropolitan clubs in Leinster advocated memorials to those who had died fighting for the British in the First World War, UCD RFC 'decided to send a subscription of £3–3–0 to the Kevin Barry Memorial Committee'. Indeed, within a few years of the IRA man's death, UCD RFC chose to memorialise their connection to Irish nationalism by organising a Kevin Barry commemoration. A committee was formed to appeal to graduates of the college for funds to create the memorial. Through the collection of subscriptions and the sale of mortuary cards, the Kevin Barry Memorial Fund gathered £100 to pay for the project.[13] A Kevin Barry memorial committee included Kevin Mangan, John Kent and Patrick Donovan, all members of the UCD rugby team with apparent nationalist proclivities.[14] Sarsfield Hogan, another member of the Barry memorial committee, was UCD's representative on the Leinster Branch committee.

In the actions of Leinster rugby clubs and the provincial administrators, then, some of the tensions and contradictions that were inherent in 1920s Ireland can be distinguished. There were plenty of people who watched sport for sport's sake,

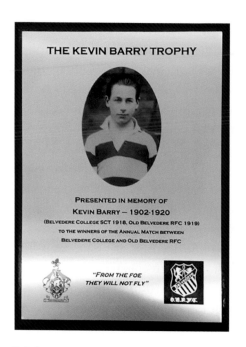

THE KEVIN BARRY TROPHY

PRESENTED IN MEMORY OF
KEVIN BARRY – 1902-1920
(BELVEDERE COLLEGE SCT 1918, OLD BELVEDERE RFC 1919)
TO THE WINNERS OF THE ANNUAL MATCH BETWEEN
BELVEDERE COLLEGE AND OLD BELVEDERE RFC

*"FROM THE FOE
THEY WILL NOT FLY"*

▲ Kevin Barry played rugby for Belvedere College and UCD, before being executed as an IRA member by the British authorities during Ireland's War of Independence, aged just 18.

and rejected added political meanings, ignoring the ideological foundations of rugby. There was no incompatibility for people like Éamon de Valera or Kevin Barry in playing rugby while embracing and campaigning for an independent Ireland, nor for someone like Bethel Solomons, the Jewish TCD alumnus, DUFC and Ireland rugby player who was a supporter of the 1916 Rising. Yet, as late as the 1940s, Solomons was also openly raising toasts to the King of England in his capacity as the Dublin University Central Athletic Club (DUCAC) chairman. His view of sports was quite clearly that it should not be defined by politics. Jim J. White, a former Bective player, writing in the 1970s about playing in the 1920s, said:

I recall my good friend, the late Jack Callanan, a stout-hearted, loyal member of Bective, both as player and administrator, and active member of the IRA in the Black and Tan War (1918–21) and afterwards on the Anti-Treaty side in the Civil War telling me that opponents in the field of war, known to each other, laid aside their arms in the dressing rooms of the Club house before going out on the field of play to engage in a friendly Rugby combat, and resumed them after the match to go on their different ways of war. Jack, who was a Bank Manager, was President of Bective in 1947–48.[15]

A similar story is recalled by Sean Diffley about Blackrock rugby, of two teammates who togged out together one Saturday but were firmly on opposite sides of the Anglo-Irish Treaty question that sparked Ireland's Civil War. Allegedly these two men were on the field of play when the pro-Treaty player spotted an undercover policeman entering the grounds. He quickly tipped off his teammate, an active anti-Treaty fighter during the Civil War, alerting him to the presence of the undercover agent. Thus, the teammate made his escape unseen by vaulting a nearby wall and taking to his heels. These are the kinds of extraordinary anecdotes that inform and complicate the Irish Civil War and, more to the point, reassert the shades of grey when it comes to who played rugby in Leinster.

Where a more obvious disjuncture between wider Irish society and rugby was apparent, however, was in terms of socioeconomics and privilege. For example, Jim White admitted the clubs he came up against were far from welcoming and far from democratic in how they viewed the ordinary rugby player based on class and creed. When criticism was needed and change required, it was from within the Leinster rugby world itself that alterations were elicited. White maintained that Bective Rangers

> was in the very forefront, actively supporting any action or movement, to bring about reforms in the Leinster Branch of the Irish Rugby Union, and the Union itself. They were there as far back as 1919 at a meeting in Bewley's Café to initiate a reform to the Leinster Branch to take control out of the hands of the Initial 'Big Five' Clubs, and extend the franchise to all Leinster Senior Clubs, Junior Clubs and Schools. That was known as the 'Bective Revolution' and it paved the way for the bigger Revolution in 1934, which swept the old minority which held Office for so long out of power, and paved still further the way for the bigger Revolution later which effected big and sweeping Reforms in the whole Constitution ... I may mention that the chief forces in those Revolutions and in effecting those reforms were: Messrs Sarsfield Hogan, Larry McMahon and Father Walter Finn (Blackrock College) ably assisted by such as Peter Dunn, Ned Powell and Billy Fallon of Bective and Paul Murray of Wanderers.[16]

New clubs reflected the societal changes in Ireland during the emergence of the Free State in the late 1920s and throughout the 1930s. Those from a nationalist-leaning background who had always promoted and played the game began to come more to the fore in terms of rugby's administration. Whatever divisive politics seeped into the sporting world generally, rugby continued to gain in popularity in a post-partition Ireland:

> [By] 1929 there were 160 clubs and fifty-nine schools affiliated with the IRFU. Every province in the country saw its playing numbers increase ... This growth had been driven in the 1920s by the establishment of new competitions –

particularly ones for junior clubs – and was most noted in country towns; rugby was spreading into areas where it had never previously enjoyed any favour … a growth driven by members of the Catholic clergy across the Irish Free State – was crucial to all of this.[17]

To put it more plainly, when Free State, post-First World War Ireland came into existence, Leinster rugby became more 'Irish'.

The one common factor with the game's past that did remain was that rugby retained an overabundance of society's most privileged, with its network still connected to the fee-paying schools, universities, colleges and those at the top of the socioeconomic ladder. This gave the game a surfeit of the old Ascendency, working professionals, establishment political conservatives, wealthy businessmen and the well-connected. Regardless, room was made in rugby for a wider cohort of Irish sportsmen. When it came to junior rugby in particular, those involved were less concerned about social status and more focused only on the promotion of the game and the survival of their clubs. Another change was that the newer clubs and

▲ Bective Junior Team, 1920s.

▲ Eugene Davy with the ball, supported by Jammie Clinch and Ned Lightfoot, Leinster v. Ulster game, late 1920s.

younger players did not embrace the same colonial or political associations when they engaged in the game of rugby. It was played for pleasure, for its networking opportunities, its health benefits and the idea of upstanding gentlemanliness associated with the game. For many Irish players, far from any association with Britishness, the game of rugby exemplified the ambitions of the new Irish Free State. These were sentiments that 'trickled up' as the old guard of Leinster rugby began to be replaced, but change was painfully slow.

Leinster-wide Growth

Up to 1914, just six of Leinster's nineteen rugby clubs were located outside of Dublin. While these six provincial teams cried out for games with the best clubs from the metropolis area, rather than organising matches against their provincial brethren, the Dublin senior sides generally favoured the English tour. As late as October 1934, at the Leinster Branch AGM, 'Mr. P.J. Power expressed the opinion that the Dublin clubs were not treating the country clubs fairly in the matter of fixtures and suggested a recommendation to the Dublin clubs to facilitate the country clubs by giving more fixtures', sentiments seconded by Skerries RFC.[18] It took influential senior club figures who empathised with junior rugby voices, such as Sarsfield Hogan and Ernie Crawford, to try to change the outlook. They began the work to try to alter the Leinster Branch's perspective in terms of inclusivity and appeal.

▲▼ Two Enniscorthy rugby football teams. County Wexford was one of the central spots in Leinster outside of Dublin where rugby was popular at an early stage.

It would require robust efforts to facilitate the game outside Dublin, as provincial town junior clubs demanded more of a voice within the Branch itself and worked to help create competitiveness between clubs of equal ability. When it came to rugby, 'in towns where the game had little in the way of tradition or cultural resonance [it] required the enthusiasm of individuals who had experienced the game either at school or while training for professions in cities ... [For example,] those who worked in the banking sector were ideally poised to bring rugby from the centre to the periphery.'[19] It was qualified professionals (doctors, lawyers, etc.) arriving in provincial towns that continually bolstered rugby clubs in more rural areas. But it took local buy-in and enthusiasm to sustain them, as the game of rugby negotiated more inclusion. This inclusion was easier at the provincial and junior level, as the senior clubs worked to retain an exclusivity.

The role of the schools remained important and the expansion of secondary education helped spread the game of rugby in the first half of the twentieth century.[20] An improving educational system for Irish youth allowed for a larger middle-class to emerge. That had the corollary outcome of increasing the numbers of potential rugby players, given that more young men would be in school for longer, becoming eligible for more advanced jobs, finding further opportunities for social elevation. As well as this improving education system, several other factors also saw young Leinster men taking up the game of rugby. Anecdotes about recruiting players in rural towns included stories of rugby men delivering impassioned pleas to boys and teens, who were spotted hanging around on a match day, to come and help a team when they were a one or two players short. Once recruited, these lads often remained in the game. Additionally, for Leinster's rural towns where GAA was more ingrained, rugby was often a game to play on a Saturday or in the winter, when GAA matches were on a Sunday or curtailed during the off-season. Similarly, there are copious anecdotes of rugby men training and sometimes playing with soccer or GAA teams in the summer when rugby was on hiatus. The crossover among football codes in Leinster was more widespread than is perhaps acknowledged. Despite the GAA's rule 27, which banned its members from playing or even watching rugby, in reality the divide was porous. Ultimately, for many, rugby was just another game for those pursuing sporting pastimes.

Unquestionably, rugby began to grow in Ireland, particularly after daily life settled down in the late 1920s, at least comparatively speaking, after so much conflict. The period 1922 to 1930 saw something of a surge when eleven clubs were added to the records in Leinster, mostly from beyond Dublin. This expansion in

Leinster rugby was due to a growth in interest among ordinary Irish people and the prospect of joining newly created town clubs. In north County Dublin, Malahide rugby club was founded in 1922 at Malahide Castle. The team was given a field on Lord Talbot's estate to use, unsurprisingly alongside the town's cricket club. The rugby club later disbanded in the midst of the 'Emergency' (as the Second World War period is known in Ireland) but was one of those revived in the late 1970s. This north Dublin trend of clubs continued when Suttonians mustered a team in 1924, followed by Balbriggan in 1925 and Skerries in 1926. While both Suttonians and Skerries have gone from strength to strength over the years, Balbriggan was defunct by the end of the 1930s, but was reconstituted in the late 1960s. Meanwhile, clubs also emerged in County Wexford (Wexford Wanderers, 1924), County Westmeath (Mullingar, 1924), County Meath (Navan, 1925) and County Kildare – there was a North Kildare RFC at Kilcock in 1928. Two additional Dublin metropolitan clubs were the Terenure-based Catholic Young Men's Society (CYM), formed in 1924, and Old Belvedere, which re-emerged in 1930. At this stage, what is interesting is that so many of the new clubs materialised from areas beyond Dublin 4. The other team was the Curragh RFC, comprising players in the Irish Army stationed at the military camp there. Founded in 1923 they merged with the Old Kilcullen rugby team in 1996 to form Newbridge RFC.

Further evidence of the winds of change came in February 1923, when the junior committee requested regular junior interprovincials be fixed with Munster (they had only played annually against Ulster up to then), and reprimanded the executive of the Leinster Branch for not yet having purchased a trophy for the winners of the Junior Cup competition, stating that it was hard to keep 'the interest amongst teams playing for a cup which did not exist'. Additionally, the new Metropolitan (Metro) Cup, inaugurated in 1921, catered to junior teams and the second fifteens of senior clubs that were situated inside an 18-mile radius of Dublin's General Post Office (GPO). The conditions of the Junior Cup competition were then changed for the 1925–26 season, and a clear demarcation between a Dublin city-based cup and a competition for clubs from the rest of Leinster, the Provincial Towns Cup, was established. The Metro Cup became Dublin specific for Junior One teams within an 18-mile radius of the GPO in O'Connell Street (i.e. any Metropolitan junior clubs and any second fifteens of Metropolitan senior clubs), rather than a competition for all junior clubs. This new cup format underscored the work being done to ensure rugby catered for a wider body of interested players, in terms of abilities and opportunities, giving them something tangible to compete for when playing

▲ County Carlow and Wanderers FC teams photographed together from an encounter in 1922.

each weekend. Financially, the Branch was making large returns it seems, with over £2,000 taken in from Lansdowne Road gates alone in the 1922–23 season, and the growth of junior rugby in the 1920s gave it something of a confidence boost.[21]

Junior Rugby Expands

Interestingly, the new momentum within the Leinster Branch coincided with criticism aimed at the IRFU from Branch members, who labelled the national union an undemocratic cabal that ignored the wishes of the four branches by allowing 'self-appointed gentlemen assisted by ex-presidents' to outvote progressive amendments to develop Irish rugby. The Leinster Branch blamed the IRFU for the fact that rugby was excluded from the Tailteann games (an Olympics-style state-organised sporting and cultural festival held in 1924 to celebrate the establishment of the Free State) because of an apparently out-of-touch attitude among the old guard in charge. Some of Leinster's administrators concluded that rugby did not deserve inclusion 'because the present control [of the IRFU] was undemocratic, unsympathetic and almost un-Irish'.[22] The internal struggles and changes being sought in the rugby world, which were somewhat reflective of social and political change of the era, were displayed in such frustrations.

Notwithstanding such exasperation, the success of clubs outside Dublin in official competitions underscored the growing level of play and the positive status of 1920s rugby in the province. For example, Enniscorthy and Carlow were two of the strongest sides in Leinster junior rugby and were regularly bringing home silverware. This decade 'also saw the emergence of Athy, Enniscorthy and Kilkenny as very strong opposition ... All this increased rugby activity and the strength of players involved had the effect of reviving enthusiasm for the code throughout the province. The provincial clubs soon became the dominant teams in the Leinster Junior Cup which in 1926 had the result of this trophy being renamed the Provincial Towns Cup ...'[23] During this period one of Carlow's staunchest supporters, a Mr Bergin, brought the game to the local Christian Brother's School (CBS). He was eager to pick from the pool of young athletic boys and turn them towards rugby. Bergin was credited with the innovative approach of bringing in these local boys to Carlow rugby club, aiding the team's cup wins in 1929, 1931 and 1933, with several players having attended the CBS. This reflected how playing interest in Leinster had diversified into a playing fraternity that would become future administrators.

It would largely take new leadership at the Leinster Branch to help push through change, with people like Sarsfield Hogan and Cahir Davitt taking positions of power within Leinster rugby. Their playing years were in the 1920s, while their administrative influence extended across almost four decades, from the 1930s to the 1970s. However, in 1920, at a special general meeting, the administration of the Branch was newly ordered as follows:

> (1) the management of the business of the Branch be entrusted to an Executive Committee consisting of one representative from each Senior Club, two persons (one from the City and one from the Country) representative of all Junior Clubs and one person representing all the Schools. (2) a Special Rules Committee consisting of one representative from each Senior Club be appointed to revise the Branch Rules and in this revision provision should be made for the Executive Committee mentioned above.[24]

The committee now consisted of a representative from each of the eleven senior clubs, although it still only allowed two to speak for all of junior rugby. The amended bylaws were passed at the end of the October 1920 AGM, with a rule citing the power to appoint subcommittees becoming perhaps the most important to help elicit change.

In 1924 another amendment allowed a representative from the Branch's Association of Referees to be nominated to the executive committee, although without voting power. The founders of the referee's association were, of course, by and large active referees, 'sportsmen all and all loyal subjects of His Majesty King Edward VII'.[25] The latter revelation betrays the fact that although rugby had progressed within an independent Free State, among the upper echelons of the administration there was still a particular political coterie in charge within both Leinster and Irish rugby.

Historically, it is generally accepted that the introduction of the singular referee, a man of authority to enforce a game's rules and oversee any disputes, was ultimately secured with the introduction of the whistle into sports, first dated as having appeared in rugby in 1885. Initially the top referees were themselves mainly former top-rung players.[26] However, as rugby grew in popularity, there was an increasing strain to find 'good' referees and the practicalities of organising referees needed an association to function effectively. It was on 12 October 1902 that eight rugby men congregated in the Royal Hibernian Hotel to organise the Association of Referees to cover the Branch's demands.[27] They were H.W. Jones of Monkstown, Burke of Blackrock College, Clayton of Wanderers, Crawford of Clontarf, George from DUFC, Henley from Bective, Monahan of Old Wesley and Studdart from Lansdowne. The men utilised the guidelines of the organisation of referees already established in London on which to model the new society. It, of course, required funding and so every established club was asked to pay a subscription of 10/- per annum, later adjusted for junior (2/6-) and senior clubs (5/-). The Association of Referees' worked in tandem with the Leinster Branch, with a committee independently appointing referees for all junior and senior domestic club games, although the Branch executive reserved the right to appoint its preferred referee for interprovincial and Senior Cup games. This would change in due course, but in general the Branch followed the lead of the association when it came to shortlists and recommendations about suitable men to oversee matches.

In 1920 the Association of Referees set out a clear set of rules for the organisation, which were 'to provide competent referees, to stimulate and develop interest among former players and others [to referee], and generally to further the best interests of the game'.[28] Regular meetings were held to ensure a full understanding and a uniform implementation of the rules and laws of the game, with club captains, committee personnel and representatives from the schools in attendance to make sure everyone was on the same page. In the 1920s and 1930s there were never more than twenty-five affiliated referees. This was a problem due to the ongoing establishment of new clubs and new club teams in Leinster, leading to an ever-increasing number of fixtures. The association even considered a proposal to make it mandatory for every senior club to supply two referees and junior clubs one referee annually to the association. Free entrance to all rugby grounds for Leinster referees to watch club games was one perk aimed at helping to keep referees involved in interwar rugby, but dwindling numbers of referees became a perpetual concern for the game. Only five former Irish internationals became post-First World War adjudicators, and after the Emergency this was reduced to a mere two. But while referee numbers dwindled, the overall numbers of those involved in rugby soon began to soar.

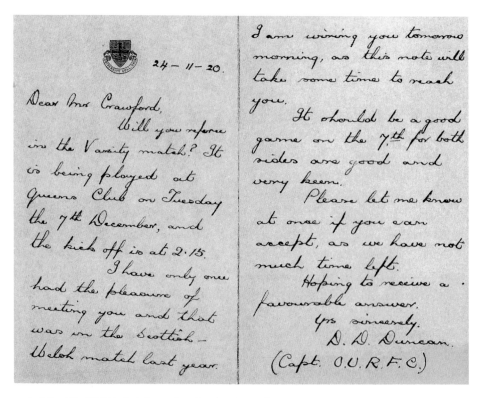

▲ Invitation letter (1920) to the Leinster referee Sam Crawford to officiate a match between Queen's, Belfast, and Oxford University RFC.

LEINSTER BRANCH:
IRISH RUGBY FOOTBALL UNION.

all clubs affiliated to branch including Schools & Referees

12 Westmoreland Street,

Dublin,

1st January, 1929.

MEMORANDUM.

The Executive Committee of the Leinster Branch desires to draw the attention of the Committees of affiliated clubs to Law 34 of the Game and to Bye-Law VII. of the Branch, and request that the same be brought to the notice of playing members.

Law 34 deals with:—

(a) Foul play. The following are prohibited:—Wilful hacking, tripping or striking, or wilfully holding a player not in possession of the ball, or illegal tackling, charging or obstruction. (b) Misconduct. (c) Persistent infringement of the laws.

The personal penalty for (a) and (b) is:—The Referee on the first offence shall either caution the player or order him off the ground. For the second offence he must order him off. The personal penalty for (c) is:—The Referee must order the player off the ground.

If ordered off the player shall take no further part in the game in progress, and must be reported to the Executive Committee by the Referee.

Bye-Law VII. is as follows:—

Suspension of Player or Club.

(1) The Executive Committee shall be empowered, after due investigation, to suspend for such period as may be considered desirable any player belonging to an affiliated Club who has been reported to that Committee by a Referee or authorised person for rough play or other misconduct.

After a player has been reported to the Executive Committee by a Referee he shall not be entitled to take part in any game until his case has been considered by that Committee.

(2) The Executive Committee shall also be empowered to suspend an affiliated Club for misconduct.

(3) Any player or Club so suspended shall have the right of appeal in the first instance to the General Committee of the Branch, and finally to the Committee of the Council of the Union.

The Executive Committee is prepared and anxious to support Referees in the enforcement of the law against Foul Play and Misconduct, and appeals to Committees of Clubs to deal severely with any member of their Club who violates the true spirit of the game by any breach of Law 34.

VICTOR V. DRENNAN,

Hon. Secretary.

A 1929 Leinster Branch circular to all clubs on laws against violent conduct.

6

An Interwar Rugby Surge

The Senior and Junior Committees

As the 1920s edged towards the 1930s, the Leinster Branch put together the requisite subcommittees needed to oversee the running of rugby around the province: Selection committee, Finance committee, Schools committee and a Junior League committee. Crucial to the overall expansion of the sport in the 1920s was the continuous growth of the game at school level, and it was also greatly aided by a raft of new competitions introduced at county and provincial level to cater for junior clubs, which helped spread the game to many country towns.[1] With the growth of rugby on the one hand, and the need for a stronger voice to address the needs of newer clubs on the other, in 1925 the Junior League committee was set up. Elected committee executives were also the selectors for the junior Leinster squad for interprovincial games. This required the committee to have its own junior section honorary president and five junior committee members, who were elected at a stand-alone junior committee AGM. The junior honorary secretary was required to attend the Branch's executive committee meetings and report on the workings of the junior section in order to ensure a clear line of communication between all the Branch members. The expansion reflects the gradual increase in general popularity of rugby in Leinster.

However, when this space was separated out for the junior rugby scene it highlighted the clear dichotomy in the game between the attitude and ideals of the senior and junior players. In the interwar years, 'internally the game was … in fact deeply divided. [In spite of a] range of political views accommodated within the game ... a decisive strain of unionist sentiment persevered among those in powerful positions ...'[2] When advocates of the GAA's infamous ban on their members from playing or watching foreign games talked about rugby, they clearly delineated that their actions were 'not launched against rugby but against the atmosphere that surrounds the present Rugby Union'. GAA representatives even suggested that the game of rugby could and should find a home under its banner, so that '[i]n this way we might sow the seed of a truly national Rugby Union: and who knows but at a no far date we could boast of a rugby team representing all Ireland – not a very small portion of it!'[3]

An awareness of the prejudices that were part of rugby in Ireland during the first decade of the nascent Free State were summed up by a piece in the *Irish Independent* some time later. Nationalist Ireland made the argument that 'there were decent men playing rugby, but those at the head of the game never were Irish, and never would be Irish. At their annual dinner in Dublin, the principal toast drunk was that of "The King" and as long as such men were at the head of it, there would be no national spirit in rugby in Ireland.' One thing that was clear, therefore, was that 'rugby at an administrative level was certainly emblematic of the old regime and therefore presented something of a soft target for the Gaelic purists'.[4] Indeed, the record books reveal that, up to the outbreak of the Second World War, a significant number of rugby's most influential voices were still advocating Leinster rugby's unionist connections as well as socioeconomic exclusivity.

There was a struggle, albeit gradual, beginning to take shape, as Irish people from slightly different social, political and cultural standpoints began to take control of rugby's reins of power. This happened most noticeably post-Second World War, but in the meantime Leinster rugby's insularity meant that senior club fraternities were less inclined to reach out beyond their own confines. It was undeniably an old boys' network drawn together by kindred members of the elite.[5] Thus, without a surge of junior clubs coming to the fore in the 1920s, especially those beyond the 'Pale', rugby would most likely not have seen the kind of incremental changes that helped the game expand. The Junior Cup competition, so long dominated by Dublin clubs in its first twenty-six years (1889–1914), when only four provincial clubs won, reflected that positive shift when it was resumed in 1920. The provincial-based clubs came to dominate, winning six consecutive finals (Carlow, Kilkenny, Carlow, Enniscorthy, Kildare, Enniscorthy) in the opening years of the 1920s. Perhaps frustratingly, it was at this stage of provincial club success that the Branch instigated two new competitions, the Provincial Towns Cup (PTC) and the Metropolitan Cup, with the result that rugby became segregated.

Creating a Rural–Urban Divide

All the cups are important, but the three historic and standout knockout contests in Leinster have been the LSC, the Metropolitan Cup and the PTC. The Metropolitan Cup, inaugurated in 1921, catered to junior teams and the second fifteens of senior clubs within an 18-mile radius of the GPO in O'Connell Street in Dublin city. This cup, along with the Provincial Towns Cup (PTC), inaugurated in the 1925–26 season for teams who were located beyond an 18-mile radius from the GPO, replaced the original Junior Cup from 1926 on. The PTC trophy the teams competed for was once the trophy that was presented to Junior Cup winners, and it retains a certain mystique in Leinster rugby as one of the oldest rugby trophies still in existence today. Whether consciously or not, with the introduction of these new competitions, Leinster rugby had now manufactured a clear distinction between the rugby clubs of Dublin's oldest, wealthiest and most dominant senior teams, and those of the rest of the province. Once this bifurcation was introduced, it would be several decades before the junior committee again reconfigured the system to induce a Leinster-wide junior competition where all the clubs in the province would regularly meet in competitive rugby. In the interim, Leinster rugby created two separate spaces for rugby within the province.

However, this reorganisation of competitions did help rugby persist in the rural areas of Leinster. Indeed, the idea of playing the PTC final at a neutral venue outside Dublin was proposed in the belief that it 'would tend to awaken a keener interest in the game in the provincial centres', according to the minutes of a junior committee meeting in October 1926. Perhaps surprisingly, therefore, at a vote taken in February 1927, eleven junior clubs declared themselves in favour of holding the final in Dublin, while only seven favoured the country venue idea.[6] When the PTC came online, the finals were initially played in Donnybrook (1926–28) before moving to Lansdowne Road for the next sixteen seasons, then returning to Donnybrook until 1952.[7] It was not until 1953 that the proposal was revisited, and it was again lauded as a pivotal idea for promoting rugby outside Dublin. This time it was agreed to spread the final around the province, where it would be hosted by one of the junior clubs eligible to compete in the competition. Interestingly, despite initial uncertainty among provincial clubs over the proposal, once it was inaugurated any subsequent queries about returning to the capital to play out a final were rejected by the junior clubs, which preferred to maintain the final in a venue outside the capital.

The two cup competitions came about due to specific ideas around standards of play and geographic location for convenience of fixtures, and, quite openly, in order to create a new competition for the strongest second teams in senior Dublin clubs. That it had the unintended consequence of bifurcating rugby in Leinster, however, can be heard echoing down through the decades as junior clubs spoke up in some frustration at the barriers to their progression. For example, a trustee and honorary life member of the Railway Union RFC, Harry Gale, expressed his view of what had happened for three decades of his involvement in Leinster rugby:

> An Iron Curtain was erected against the advancement of Junior Clubs during the 1920s, 1930s and 1940s. In the 1950s that curtain was blown to pieces … Let us hope … that the 'Leinster Rugby Clock will not go back.' It must be obvious to everyone that Rugby in Leinster at the top cannot be world-class unless there is strength, unity and justice all the way up from the bottom.[8]

These few sentences hint at the beginnings of a grassroots rugby effort to shake up the game from below against a stubbornly traditionalist administration controlled by the senior clubs.

Rugby certainly had a new popularity in the 1930s and young men wanted to play the game once they were given the opportunity to do so. One man who was pivotal in at least acting as a negotiator to try to open up the game of rugby in the province was Sarsfield Hogan. After he hung up his playing boots in the 1920s, he became involved in running UCD RFC, as well as being an important figure in the Lansdowne

▲ Provincial Towns Cup 2022 (originally the trophy for the Junior Club Rugby Cup competition). © Seb Daly/ Sportsfile

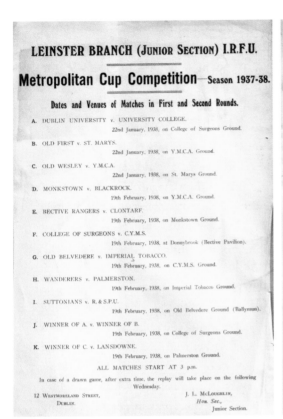

LEINSTER BRANCH (Junior Section) I.R.F.U.

Metropolitan Cup Competition—Season 1937-38.

Dates and Venues of Matches in First and Second Rounds.

A. DUBLIN UNIVERSITY v. UNIVERSITY COLLEGE.
    22nd January, 1938, on College of Surgeons Ground.

B. OLD FIRST v. ST. MARYS.
    22nd January, 1938, on Y.M.C.A. Ground.

C. OLD WESLEY v. Y.M.C.A.
    22nd January, 1938, on St. Marys Ground.

D. MONKSTOWN v. BLACKROCK.
    19th February, 1938, on Y.M.C.A. Ground.

E. BECTIVE RANGERS v. CLONTARF.
    19th February, 1938, on Monkstown Ground.

F. COLLEGE OF SURGEONS v. C.Y.M.S.
    19th February, 1938, at Donnybrook (Bective Pavilion).

G. OLD BELVEDERE v. IMPERIAL TOBACCO.
    19th February, 1938, on C.Y.M.S. Ground.

H. WANDERERS v. PALMERSTON.
    19th February, 1938, on Imperial Tobacco Ground.

I. SUTTONIANS v. R. & S.P.U.
    19th February, 1938, on Old Belvedere Ground (Ballymun).

J. WINNER OF A. v. WINNER OF B.
    19th February, 1938, on College of Surgeons Ground.

K. WINNER OF C. v. LANSDOWNE.
    19th February, 1938, on Palmerston Ground.

ALL MATCHES START AT 3 p.m.

In case of a drawn game, after extra time, the replay will take place on the following Wednesday.

12 WESTMORELAND STREET,
  DUBLIN.

J. L. McLOUGHLIN,
Hon. Sec.,
Junior Section.

LEINSTER BRANCH (JUNIOR SECTION) I.R.F.U.

Provincial Towns Cup Competition—Season 1937-38.

Dates and Venues of Matches in First Round.

NORTH-WEST ZONE.

LONGORD v. TULLAMORE ... ... On Ground of Longford R.F.C.; Saturday, 19th February, 1938.
    If replay necessary—On Ground of Tullamore R.F.C. on Thursday, 24th February, 1938.

CENTRAL ZONE.

CARLOW v. ATHY ... ... On Ground of Carlow R.F.C.; Saturday, 19th February, 1938.
    If replay necessary—On Ground of Athy R.F.C. on Saturday, 26th February, 1938.

SOUTH ZONE.

GREYSTONES v. WEXFORD WANDERERS ... On Ground of Greystones R.F.C.; Thursday, 17th February, 1938.
    If replay necessary—On Ground of Wexford R.F.C. on Saturday, 26th February, 1938.

NEW ROSS v. KILKENNY ... ... On Ground of New Ross R.F.C.; Saturday, 19th February, 1938.
    If replay necessary—On Ground of Kilkenny R.F.C. on Wednesday, 23rd February, 1938.

ROSSLARE HARBOUR v. ENNISCORTHY ... On Ground of Rosslare Harbour R.F.C.; Thursday, 17th February, 1938.
    If replay necessary—On Ground of Enniscorthy R.F.C. on Saturday, 26th February, 1938.

All Matches to start at 3 o'clock p.m. *sharp.* Should a Match be drawn at the expiration of eighty minutes an extra twenty minutes shall be played.

J. L. McLOUGHLIN,
Hon. Sec.,
L.B.; I.R.F.U. (Junior Section.)

DUBLIN,
12 WESTMORELAND STREET,

▲ The Metropolitan Cup competition was inaugurated at the same time as the Provincial Towns Cup, initiating a perceived split between 'traditional' Dublin clubs and rest of Leinster clubs.

▲ Leinster Branch Junior Section crcular, Provincial Town Cup fixtures, first round matches for the 1937-8 season.

club. Hogan implored Dublin's senior clubs and their star players to respond to the requests from the provincial town clubs for friendly games, to benefit Leinster rugby. The idea that rugby in Leinster really was just a game for the privileged D4 set was being perpetuated by the refusal of senior clubs to entertain the idea of sending their best players to play in country towns. All fixtures outside the cup competition at this time were challenges, and the clubs in more rural parts of Leinster felt that they were being ignored. This was exacerbated when the Dublin clubs proved themselves quick and eager to play English, Welsh and Scottish sides at home or away, but not to travel to the rest of the province for a match. Outlining these criticisms to the Branch, members of junior rugby clubs argued that senior clubs agreeing to games in other parts of Leinster would not only make them feel less ignored, but that good-quality rugby would increase interest among the general population and ideally attract new members, especially if there were high-quality games against senior clubs on a regular basis. Furthermore, the all-round standards of play would improve for everyone if provincial clubs got to test their mettle against the Dublin senior sides. Their argument was for a broader view to be taken of improving rugby province-wide.

Hogan spread himself as widely as possible to help the world of rugby, not just in Leinster but globally. As Jim White wrote in 1981, 'No man in our time has played a bigger and more significant part on the administrative side of Leinster and Irish Rugby in bringing about the great reforms – one could say, Revolutions – in the game in this Country. And indeed, on the wider stage of World Rugby.'[9] After Hogan finished playing rugby in the 1920s, he not only represented UCD as a member of that club on the Leinster Branch committee, but later advocated on behalf of Irish rugby more broadly when appointed to the International Rugby Board. As such, Hogan kept abreast of all the latest insights in rugby across the globe and shared the more progressive visions with his colleagues in Ireland. This advocacy for improving the game of rugby as a sport, both in terms of play on the field as well as in terms of increasing its popularity among the public, was central to Hogan's work. Indeed, spreading the rugby gospel in Leinster had always been part of his purview. When clubs like Bective Rangers were trying to make the Leinster Branch a broader church and wrestle control away from a cohort of unionist elites still holding court, it was acknowledged that one of the chief forces in effecting reforms at branch level in 1934 was Sarsfield Hogan.[10]

Hogan pushed through a change in rules that limited the power of ex-branch presidents, for instance, when it came to branch decision-making.[11] One of the most obvious impacts in that regard was his work to overturn Sabbatarianism. When in September 1929, the Leinster Branch executive issued a circular enforcing Sabbatarianism,[12] Hogan, was one of the strongest proponents for reviewing its position on Sunday games.[13] In addition, he was widely read on the skills of the game and commented often on the standard of play in Leinster, advocating for a faster and more open game. He advocated for the universities to be on-field exemplars and helped organise the combined universities selections, as well as encouraging intervarsity games. Hogan's dedication to ensuring the growth and improvement of the game speaks for itself, but importantly he helped ensure that Leinster rugby was more inclusive while encouraging the latest innovations, so as to foster more entertaining and competitive rugby in Ireland.

Rugby in the Southeast

In the 1920s the Enniscorthy club excelled in junior rugby to such a degree that they applied for and were granted senior status in 1928 (after three-in-a-row PTC wins), paving the way for the club's participation in the Leinster Senior Cup between 1928 and 1931. It seems ex-Irish international and president of Enniscorthy RFC in 1926–27, Rev. Robert Knox Lyle, was central to lobbying the Leinster Branch to allow Enniscorthy senior status and to compete in the Leinster Senior Cup. Lyle is a good illustration of Ian d'Alton and Ida Milne's study of southern Protestants in Free State Ireland, in which they explained that 'adult Protestant interest in sport in Wexford undoubtedly centred on rugby, with equine sports (mostly racing and hunting) a close second'.[14] They go on to explain how, in the cultural sphere, one of the avenues for adjusting to the new reality of a Free State Ireland for southern Protestants was the game of rugby. There Protestants (with a strong

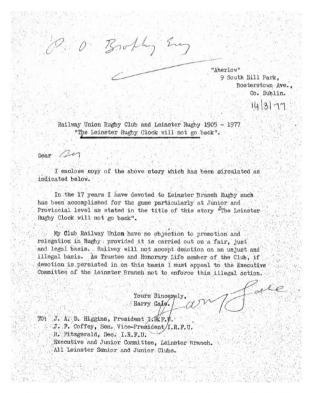

▲ Railway Union's Harry Gale's introduction letter to his essay indicating his criticism towards Leinster rugby and the plight of Junior Rugby. Courtesy of John Walsh, Naas RFC.

▲ Enniscorthy RFC members on the steps of the Hibernian Hotel, Dublin, after winning the Provincial Town Cup.

sympathy towards unionism) could interact with Catholic and nationalist Ireland's prosperous constituency, while avoiding larger questions and debates about politics and sovereignty. Rugby, therefore, to borrow from d'Alton's explanation of the role of *The Irish Times*, 'helped to supply an essential narrative of continuity, easing the ex-unionists into a tolerance – albeit often grudging – of the new Ireland'.[15] As a space to retreat into social exclusivity, the rugby world afforded room in which to deal with this new non-unionist Ireland by, on the one hand, providing a commonality with fellow loyalists and, on the other, supplying a place to find a common socioeconomic camaraderie, regardless of political leanings or religious differences.

As for developments in the rest of Leinster, after Enniscorthy moved to senior status, this allowed Carlow to return to winning ways between 1927 and 1933. Carlow's return to success, in turn, bred enough interest that the club soon had the membership to field a second fifteen on a regular basis. According to a history of the club, 'Carlow was also getting the benefit of young players who emerged from the Carlow CBS schoolboy teams … Another feature of the club was that playing ranks included some sons of former players.'[16] As well as this, you had examples of players like Willie Fanning from Coolkenno, County Carlow, returning to the club after playing at scrumhalf on two of Blackrock College's Senior Schools Cup-winning sides, and Sean Prendergast, who had played for UCD's first fifteen and came to play for Carlow in the 1932 season, featuring prominently in their 1933 cup win. From the beginning of the PTC in 1926 to the 1932–33 season, Carlow won three times (1929, 1931, 1933), building on five previous wins of the Junior Challenge Cup (1904, 1912, 1913, 1920, 1922). It seems, however, that despite the success, the players had begun to lose interest, as records show turnout for training beginning to drop off and players not showing up for games throughout the 1930s. One of the reasons that the proverbial 'rot' set in may have been the lack of competition outside of the PTC for the more rural junior clubs. The Junior League was, at that time, 'limited to all affiliated Junior Clubs whose ground was situated in the Metropolitan area'.[17] Moreover, the ongoing reluctance of Dublin's senior clubs to travel to play Leinster's country teams hurt the game across the province. Indeed, one of the most common refrains from meeting minutes of the Branch's junior committee all throughout the 1930s, 1940s and 1950s was the pleading for senior clubs to fulfil fixtures with county clubs beyond Dublin's suburbs.

That these friendlies often failed to come off reflected the need for a different structure in organising the game if it was to grow in all corners of the province. These were problems that the Leinster Branch would later address with the introduction of the Towns Plate and eventually the Provincial Town Clubs' League in the 1960s. In the interim, to keep interest in rugby alive, it was left to the junior committee to try to come up with innovative solutions. Thus, in a December 1927 meeting, a questionnaire was developed and given out to all the countryside clubs to gauge reactions to the idea of creating 'four zones and to designate them North-East, North-West, South-West and South-East', assigning clubs to each zone based on geographic location, so they could more easily organise fixtures amongst themselves. The idea was approved and junior rugby forged ahead, although one year later, Mr Clinch of the Leinster executive accusingly questioned whether the junior clubs were playing the game for the love of it or just to acquire medals and cups, a signal perhaps of some underlying tensions between the junior and senior administrators' different visions of Leinster rugby's future.[18] Regardless, some (though not all) of the provincial town clubs grew in confidence, the game came to the attention of more people and junior rugby got a kick start that would set it up to demand more Branch support. By the 1930s new rugby clubs had emerged across Leinster in towns like Wexford, Tullow, Naas, Navan, North Kildare, Greystones, Arklow and Tullamore.

▲ Rugby action, Carlow v. Balbriggan at Lansdowne Road in the 1931 Provincial Towns Cup final.

The Sunday Rugby Relic

As the Irish Free State tried to piece together some sort of society after the upheavals of war and revolution, Leinster rugby evolved along lines that separated out 'traditional' senior and newer provincial town and junior clubs and competitions. The former offered an atmosphere of:

> merriment, self-congratulation, and mutual back-slapping among old chums … [offering] a forum for airing the political views of a minority whose formal avenues for political expression were circumscribed. [Rugby in the interwar years, then], was still firmly bound culturally to Britain … In this situation the game was set firmly on the road to conflict between its Protestant ex-unionist establishment and its [growing] Catholic grassroots.[19]

One example of that sentiment, which many of the new and junior clubs across Leinster would expose, was rugby's bizarre insistence on maintaining the practice of Sabbatarianism.

In September 1929 the Leinster Branch executive issued a circular enforcing Sabbatarianism, warning clubs that it did not recognise or adjudicate over any Sunday matches and reprimanding clubs and individuals for deliberately flouting that precedent.[20] Leinster rugby's bizarre insistence on maintaining the practice of Sabbatarianism finally came to a head when there was controversy

> around a provincial competition in Leinster, the Midland League. The union refused to allow any games under its jurisdiction on Sunday and several times reiterated that stand ... and in October 1929 a deputation ... met the union and explained their difficulties. The union refused to review their attitude and ... offered one of the reasons for forbidding Sunday play ... that according to reports that had reached them, the behaviour of players and spectators at games ... strengthened them in their resolve to oppose such games.[21]

These men in control of Leinster rugby accused those who watched and played Sunday rugby of being undesirables and they aimed to keep them out of the game. While Sabbatarianism was a specifically Protestant cultural trope, it was replete with elements of class snobbery. For those in the upper echelons of Leinster and Irish rugby, gentlemen players did not play rugby on a Sunday, end of story. Nonetheless, in the 1930s personalities like Ernie Crawford persistently aired criticism at the administrators of rugby in his drive to see Sunday football become the norm. A man not to rest on his laurels, Crawford put together scratch sides from anyone he could round up to take rugby outside of Dublin and play Sunday games in the provincial towns, an action for which he was reprimanded and threatened with suspension.

While sectarian elements were part of the position taken by the Branch, this motivation was not as strong as that of the socioeconomic exclusivity that Sabbatarianism was essentially set up to maintain. Correspondence throughout the 1930s underscored the difficulty of fulfilling fixtures that were scheduled for Saturdays or mid-week for those from the lower socioeconomic brackets due to work commitments. This didn't apply just to the players – even referees were struggling to commit to matches.[22] Yet, despite the fact that the demographics of rugby were changing, the governing authority's resistance in this regard was unshakeable. Their ideological convictions meant that they held firm in their views – and their view of rugby came from a position that was at 'a significant social and cultural remove from much of the game's constituency and Irish society in general'. The ban on Sunday games was espoused by *The Irish Times*, toeing the line of the rugby elite, and the paper began 'referring to the practice of Sunday rugby ... [as] "this growing evil," while making suggestive comments about how it drew "an undesirable class of player" into the game'.[23] Some among Irish rugby officialdom

▲ Provincial Towns Cup Final 1927. Team photo taken in Donnybrook in front of the Bective Club House. Photo courtesy of Hugh Cumisky.

▲ Carlow FC Provincial Town Cup winners in 1929.

even went so far as to suggest that the game should not be allowed to become popular, that the uneducated should not be enticed to the game as the wrong kinds of players and spectators would not understand the 'true' or 'right' spirit of rugby. As the game of rugby became popular among the 'ordinary' Irish sports enthusiast in Leinster, one IRFU old boy exclaimed, 'I am sure … nobody wants to see the headquarters at Lansdowne turned into Jones's Road of a Gaelic Sunday afternoon: so that there is a danger of rugby becoming too popular.'[24]

It took energetic contributions towards systematic change from figures like Harry Gale, Ernie Crawford, Sarsfield Hogan and Cahir Davitt to diminish some of these old exclusivities. Standing up to the outdated idea of banning Sunday rugby and those who peddled it, Hogan in particular admonished rugby union's administrators for imposing upon the players what he deemed were the views of a minority in Leinster's upper rugby circles. At a November 1929 Leinster Branch meeting, the outdated attitude and the elitism that coursed through the veins of its ranks was challenged by a request from Hogan, as the voice of UCD RFC, about overturning the Sunday play rules.[25]

Eventually, at a meeting in January 1930, a simple compromise, implemented via a mechanism of bureaucracy, solved the Sunday game issue by suggesting that if all possible fixture dates were exhausted, and only Sunday remained an option, then once permission was sought, which would inevitably be granted, Sunday games could go ahead. 'Change was needed within the union and the clamour for it came … notably from Leinster, where once again the UCD club were the architects of the dramatic changes that took place within the Leinster executive in the mid-thirties, and subsequently the wind of change blew, with beneficial results, through the IRFU …'[26] Another augury of transformation appeared in the same year, in the form of a reorganisation of both the executive and selection committees of the Leinster Branch. Two men credited with instigating these changes were Paul Murray and, once again, Sarsfield Hogan. The October 1930 Branch AGM delivered Cahir Davitt as president, alongside Hogan taking a lead role in the executive committee. Proposals for change began to be delivered immediately. Tellingly, one of the first rule changes proposed by Hogan and resolved by the committee was that Leinster Branch past presidents could no longer have a vote during executive meetings.[27] Those ex-presidents were from an older, much more elitist and unionist-orientated background, and had a disdain for the ordinary Irish population that was eager to embrace the game. These men could now no longer stand in the way of change and progress.

The Growth of Rugby Clubs

In the interwar years (1919–39), the popularity of spectator sports was on the rise and regular commentary of sporting events was broadcast on the wireless and filmed for newsreels. In Leinster daily life, radio and cinema, new forms of music and dancing, public baths and ballrooms informed the kinds of recreation appearing across Ireland. In the 1930s one of the things that appeared in Branch committee meeting minutes were requests to broadcast interprovincial games (at no cost to the Branch), permission for which was granted. Radio broadcasts, then, of rugby matches became the norm and were popular throughout the 1930s.[28] Popular entertainments of the epoch also became an aide to Leinster rugby, as clubs organised various social nights beyond the field of play. In May 1934 the perpetual Lorcan Sherlock Cup for golf was established, an extra-curricular activity in which Leinster's rugby members could compete. Of course, the pressing motivation for such activities was the need to revitalise finances, either directly through match gates or by running dances, dinners, hosting bands and entertainment nights with music, magicians and even the odd comic, and charging for tickets to help swell the bank accounts of rugby clubs.[29]

As invitations widened to women to participate in rugby socials, they included an undercurrent of exploitation, where wives and partners were roped into providing voluntary work at the club. Whether recruited for fundraising efforts, mending jerseys or providing cooking and serving refreshments during and/ or after a game, women were allowed 'in' as long as they worked *gratis*. While one can, of course, suggest that in the hypermasculine world of rugby there was obvious patriarchal exploitation, there is also an argument to made about a sense of independence, resistance and indeed infiltration when it comes to the roles women played in rugby. In the 1930s they became more visible as supporters, and clubs begat a particular female social space, community and camaraderie within that very male universe. For instance, during the 1931–32 season the ladies committee at Balbriggan RFC, run by Mrs W.E. Cox, looked after the catering for the annual dance at the town hall.[30] Mrs Cox procured help from her friends and female associates throughout the world of rugby. Women became the backbone of many a club in organising such annual events in the 1930s and beyond, getting fully behind teams and earning an invaluable place through their volunteerism and fundraising efforts. That this was free labour should not be glossed over, of course, yet labelling women's roles as simple exploitation denies agency and perhaps misses the covert acts of resistance to the restricted and restrictive world women were subjected to in ultra-conservative Ireland. For example, being out at a rugby club allowed women to be in the company of their male counterparts outside of heteronormative Irish expectations, fraternising with men who were not their husbands and enjoying time away from maternal obligations. They could drink, smoke and admire the opposite sex in what was a public space sanctioned to do so. Rugby offered a social outlet via participation in club activities and was a way for women to find a modicum of independence, albeit usually at a cost of being assigned roles as unpaid volunteers.

The rugby world also shines a light on the social life of an era, reflecting Irish cultural trends, and helps detail the evolution of entertainment and popular culture. The arrival of the big band era and dance nights in the 1920s, 1930s and 1940s enabled sports clubs to organise various fundraising nights and entertainment-centred revenue streams. For example, Balbriggan RFC's annual dance was regularly held in

▲ Judge Cahir Davitt, son of Land League agitator Michael Davitt, was a keen rugby enthusiast, a Leinster Branch president and member of the board of the IRFU during his lifetime.

▼ Mrs Davitt, wife of Leinster Branch President Cahir Davitt, presents the Towns Cup to the Carlow captain W.J. Duggan.

the town hall with music from the Melrose State Dance Band.[31] Showbands in the late 1950s and through the 1960s, and then the disco revolution in the 1970s into the early 1980s, reflected an evolution of the fundraiser for the rugby club, while giving a little insight into the cultural changes that were seeping into Ireland, not least when it came to music, as Irish society matured and grew in confidence. Arguably, Irish economic improvements reflected and engendered these changes, at least among the growing middle classes committed to the world of club rugby.

Speaking to, as well as writing reports in newspapers and to the Branch officials, clubs and their players, characters like Sarsfield Hogan and Ernie Crawford were promoting a fast, open and exciting brand of rugby on the field, involving themselves in the politics of the game. They continued to advocate for change, like they had done as players, and it was recorded how they both were 'frequently at daggers drawn with … most of the [rugby] Alickadoos, particularly for [their] military zeal on behalf of Sunday football … [Crawford bore their wrath for] taking scratch sides all over the place to encourage rugby outside Dublin, and … for a reduction in the *ex-officio* influence of past presidents of the I.R.F.U.'[32] The activities of these two men somewhat exemplify elements of the struggle that rugby irrefutably had between exclusivity and inclusivity, not just in Leinster but universally.

To those with a longer-term outlook for the health of the game in general and their clubs more specifically, keeping a close eye on growing membership in clubs was not to be neglected. The growth of rugby presented new challenges, with more teams needing more space and bringing more expense, but at the end of the day this meant that the game was more popular, had more loyal volunteers, more players to select from, more competition, more potential income and more spectators, all leading to better standards in play. The development and evolution of Leinster rugby was tied in to changes in society, to which the clubs adapted, and this helped steer the sport in a positive direction. More players meant more teams, and as youth blended with experienced players, the standard of the game inevitably improved. When the playing standards improved, more people were attracted to the game both as participants and spectators.

In this respect, it is worth noting the influence of UCD more broadly in the 1930s. In that decade UCD RFC, still a relatively young club, began to improve in leaps and bounds. On the playing field, what it brought to the mix was an important farm system, being fed a plethora of players from schools like Blackrock, CUS and later St Michael's, not to mention the other elite rugby-playing Catholic schools. But perhaps more importantly, a cohort of athletes arriving from across the island to study in UCD, who may never have had an opportunity to partake in rugby before, was now exposed and introduced to rugby as players or spectators, often for the first time. What's more, they had Sarsfield Hogan in their administration, which arguably connected the culture within UCD to changes at the Branch. As Trevor West wrote, 'Sarsfield Hogan was a man at the heart of affairs when the UCD Club was in its early years … In the mid-thirties, he did much to

At a Rugby football match in the Navan Show Grounds last Sunday, Mr Thomas Duffy a local solicitor's assistant, was accidentally injured— sustaining a double fracture of the right leg. He was conveyed to the County Hospital and subsequently discharged to his own home. At the same match the Rev Father Kil martin, C.C., a Rugby player, got a kick over the eye—high kicking—as the circus people say.

An early example of a rugby injury story in the *Leinster Leader*, 1930s (exact date unknown).

reorganize the Leinster Branch at a time when it needed such reorganization and was president of the branch in 1937–38 …'[33] In addition, UCD RFC became an important feeder club, not just to the provincial team, but also to the senior clubs in the province, as well as offering lifeblood to the junior game.[34] While during the 1920s the clubs emerging in Leinster seemed to spread the game northward and westward from the city centre, into the 1930s the pendulum swung firmly back to the southeast, with new clubs established in Greystones (1930), Seapoint (1934) and Arklow (1935), and a geographic outlier coming with the formation of Tullamore RFC.

The present-day Tullamore club traces its history to April 1937, although there had been Tullamore teams prior to that, which came and went depending on interest and numbers, or rather lack thereof. Tullamore is said to have had a club as far back as 1879, but it was not sufficiently organised to affiliate to the Leinster Branch of the IRFU. When the club did find some rootedness, the story of its foundation from among the professional and business class of the midlands town is very familiar. The impetus came from the local doctor, John O'Meara, alongside Steve Morrison of the Hibernian Bank and Pat V. Egan, chairman of a well-known local family business, P. & H. Egan Ltd.[35] They first organised a team to play Edenderry, interestingly on a Sunday, 16 January 1927, only to be beaten. Nonetheless, with that game under their belt, the rugby club was formed at a meeting on Saturday 5 February 1927, when a Danny Williams was elected president. Although the club were attracting a good following, the 1927–28 season turned out to be a solitary experiment, as the club

▲ Homemade flyer for a cake sale to raise money for St Mary's RFC; Leinster trial teams 'Whites XV versus Blues XV', early photo of club rugby on tour.

couldn't muster a team for 1928–29. Tullamore was without a permanent club until 1937, when new blood saw to it that the lacuna was filled. It was another local doctor, J.M. Prior Kennedy, who was elected first president of the club on 19 April 1937. Tullamore has maintained a strong and proud presence in the midlands ever since and has become particularly expansive since the professional era of Leinster rugby.[36]

As for rugby in County Wicklow, Arklow RFC and Greystones RFC set themselves up in the 1930s to reflect a growing rugby interest. According to Greystones' lore, it was at the beginning of the 1930s that a group of young men organised a game among themselves over the Easter school holidays. The chief engineers of the get-together called on the privately schooled local boys who were home from their rugby-playing boarding schools, mainly from Wesley College, Newbridge College, Presentation College Bray, St Andrews College, Kings Hospital School and the Presentation College at Glasthule.[37] These young men discussed forming a club and decided to identify and approach locals with the idea. They found an ally in the shape of Dr J.J. Hickey, who had come to live in Greystones a year or two previously, after living in Malaya for a number of years. He was approached by Billy Dennehy, whose father had seen service in India, and thus, with the imperial link being made, Dennehy ventured to ask Dr Hickey if he would join the venture. Hickey, being a former president of the Malayan RFU, encouraged a larger Greystones following to come and join, which ensured the club's success. The sense of a fruitful start was further enshrined with the arrangement to have Eugene Davy, a well-known international player from the Lansdowne Club, present them with a new ball to mark the occasion of their organisation.[38]

Elsewhere, Seapoint RFC was established in 1934 by a group of young men from the Blackrock and Monkstown areas, who regularly frequented the Seapoint waterfront. The rest of the membership was recruited from among friends of the initial nine enthusiasts. Initially, the club was not affiliated with the Leinster Branch, but it played several friendlies for about a year against teams from the Dún Laoghaire area. 'Seapoint was a motley team, that first year, playing in Joseph's coat of many colours – all the old school jerseys' of the former boys from Blackrock College, Monkstown and elsewhere.[39] There was also a Dún Laoghaire team in the 1930s and the group decided to pool their resources with Seapoint and unite to become a club affiliated with the Leinster Branch. However, they lost their playing field at the outbreak of the Second World War, becoming a nomadic outfit without a permanent home for a time.[40] Land was at a premium, and while the areas south of Terenure, for instance, were largely green belts, those fields were jealously hoarded by their owners as the lack of common space for playing rugby attested.

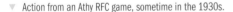
▼ Action from an Athy RFC game, sometime in the 1930s.

123

▲ UCD RFC beating London University, 1932.

The problem of a lack of real estate and stories of clubs trying to find a home speak to issues around clubs' efforts to survive in the developing 1930s Ireland.

Junior rugby teams in the metropole, alongside those in the countryside, had, nonetheless, managed to establish some roots and garner support, and the Leinster rugby game would continue to meet challenges and grow throughout the latter half of the twentieth century. But they often came up against their own organisation as senior clubs consolidated and regularly voted down progressive proposals, such as a league system that might have seen junior clubs gain promotion through merit. The Leinster story continued to be one of grassroots progressiveness versus old guard conservatism.[41] At the Branch AGM in September 1932, new byelaws that included adding two representatives from junior and minor clubs to be included at Branch meetings and be allowed to vote were introduced, helping to consolidate changes by giving more voices to the newer Irish clubs. By February 1934 the growth of rugby was such that a full-time assistant secretary job had been created in the Branch, with an annual salary of £170, which signalled in many ways the success of the Leinster rugby fraternity and the game's successful growth over the previous decades.[42]

Interprovincial Progress, 1925–39

The interprovincial team of the interwar years had a number of standout rugby names, players of remarkable quality who are credited with helping popularise rugby in the province and indeed nationally because of their skills and/or personalities. Jack Arigho was one such player. He had an impressive record, as well as being regarded as one of Leinster's most jovial personalities. He played schools' rugby with CUS, Belvedere and Castleknock, and, after school, joined Lansdowne, from where he won nine Leinster caps. Arigho made his Leinster debut aged just twenty in 1927 and within a few months he had won the first of his sixteen Ireland caps. He was an outstanding three-quarter on a Lansdowne team that won five LSC trophies in a row from 1927 to 1931, and was on the team that won it again in 1933. Indeed, as Lansdowne FC are proud to recall, in 1931 they supplied the entire Irish three-quarter line (Arigho, Eugene Davy, Morgan Crowe and Ned Lightfoot).[43]

One other noteworthy name of the era was that of James 'Jammie' Clinch, the son of Andrew ('Coo') Clinch, who was an Irish rugby international himself.[44] Jammie, it has been widely accepted, was one of the finest wing-forwards ever to play the game as it was at the time. He was apparently something of a wild character, which his father indulged because of his boy's rugby success. Clinch had gone to the CUS, St Andrew's College and TCD, where he spent seven years playing rugby but never graduated. His father famously said that he had sent his son to Trinity for the rugby, not the education. Clinch earned twenty Leinster caps between 1920 and 1932 on the road to reaching thirty Ireland caps. 'Fun-loving and gregarious', Clinch was remembered for the

> many colourful anecdotes attached to his playing career … One such story involves the veteran English forward A. F. Blakiston ('Blakey'), who informed him during the Lions tour that he was not tackling the South Africans hard enough … Several months later when Ireland were playing England in Twickenham, Clinch strongly tackled Blakey and as the Englishman lay stretched out on the ground asked if he had hit him hard enough.[45]

Jammie was the second of four generations of Clinches to play rugby at a high level, all having lined out and, indeed, all winning rugby colours playing for DUFC.

PICTORIAL PAGE   MONDAY, *Irish Independent*   JANUARY 29, 1934.

RUGBY INTERNATIONAL TRIAL.   HOSPITAL'S CENTENARY

▲ International trial match report from the *Irish Independent* of 29 January 1924.

▶ Leinster Branch Junior Section circular of December 1930 inviting clubs to select players for a junior interprovincial trial match in 1931.

Irish Rugby Football Union: Leinster Branch (Junior Section)

12 Westmoreland Street,
Dublin,
20th December, 1930.

Junior Interprovincial: LEINSTER *v.* MUNSTER, 27th February, 1931.

TRIAL MATCH.

Dear Sir,

In connection with the above Junior Interprovincial Match, it has been decided to hold a Trial Match between two fifteens—Probables v. Possibles—on Thursday, 5th February, 1931, at Donnybrook, Dublin, kick-off 2.30 o'clock p.m.

My Committee have decided again to invite the assistance of the Committees of the various clubs in selecting the players to represent the respective sides in this game. Will you, therefore, please bring this communication before the Committee of your club at an early date, with a request that they will forward on the enclosed form, to reach me not later than 10th January, 1931, the names and addresses of the players whom they would suggest should be considered for selection. My Committee desire it to be distinctly understood that club Committees are not to confine their consideration of the merits of players solely to members of their own club, but to include players from all clubs affiliated to the Branch, and particularly to those who, met with as opponents, were noticeable by their display.

This method of seeking the advice and co-operation of the clubs has been decided upon by the Junior Committee to ensure that each club will have an opportunity of expressing an opinion as to the composition of the teams to take part in the Trial Match, and accordingly they trust that your Committee will give the matter careful consideration.

Yours faithfully,

W. H. ACTON,

The Hon. Sec.   Hon. Sec.

_____Rugby F.C.

These men are just two of Leinster's best-remembered, high-calibre players from the interwar years, when the interprovincial team was consistently top of the pile. Leinster officially played Ulster fifteen times from 1924–25 through to the 1938–39 season, winning ten, drawing one and losing four. Significantly, between 1927 and 1937, Leinster remained unbeaten against Ulster, with nine wins, seven of them consecutive, and one draw. As for their meetings with Munster over the same time frame, there was a total of twelve wins, just one draw and two losses. Importantly, the first official interprovincial games versus Connacht began in the 1931–32 season, with seven matches played up to the 1939–40 season, Leinster winning all seven.[46] As a reflection of Leinster rugby more broadly in the 1930s, the Branch Honorary Secretary E.C. Powell, writing in 1934–35, urged everyone involved to celebrate rugby and to listen to the needs of clubs across the province:

> No one here will deny that Rugby Football is second to none as a game and perhaps it is that enthusiasm which is sometimes responsible for losing sight of what should be our main object, namely, the furtherance of the game along proper lines … It should be remembered that the aim and object of your Executive and its Sub-committees, of all clubs, both players and non-players, is to further the interests of Rugby Football … May I also appeal to all city clubs to remember the not so fortunate Country Clubs and to facilitate them as far as possible by the granting of fixtures. Many of these Country Clubs are carrying on under most grave difficulties and any help they may receive is as desirable as it is deserved.[47]

The echoes of change and an acknowledgement of the wider province in rugby was thus embedded in the 1930s. Alas, in 1939 another global threat, momentarily at least, threw up a serious challenge to what had been significant rugby progress in Leinster.

7

The Second World War, the Irish Republic and Leinster Rugby, 1939–69

The Emergency Years

Unsurprisingly the Second World War era was a hinderance to the growth of the game of rugby, with only two new clubs founded during the 1940s after the boom of clubs between 1925 and 1939. However, unlike the First World War, official Leinster rugby came to the decision to maintain rugby competitions during the war years. Nonetheless, there was still disruption to the game. Even Ireland's stance of neutrality could not interrupt the traditional connection between Irish people and British wars. An estimated 200,000 Irish people migrated to Britain during the war years, with about 50,000 southern Irish signing up to one or other branch of the British military, while another 41,000 joined Ireland's own defence forces.[1] Second World War-era challenges for sports, then, had to do with the loss of athletes, the loss of playing fields and the economic challenges due to 'the Emergency'.

In November 1941 Drogheda folded, citing the ongoing Emergency conditions; Navan folded in July 1942 due to travel restrictions; and there were ancillary stories like that of a rugby team made up of employees from the Imperial Tobacco company[2] that ceased playing in November 1942 because so many of their players had gone to join the forces.[3] Furthermore, by the time of the Leinster Branch's October 1941 AGM, it was conceded that several provincial town clubs had had to suspend activities until 'conditions again become normal'.[4] Luckily, with the expansion of interest in rugby during the 1920s and 1930s, there was at least a larger playing pool that helped the game to continue. As the war raged on, Irish newspapers reported on cuts in national transport due to the shortage in petrol, and transport companies operating out of Dublin had to curtail their services because of fuel pressures. The tram companies cut non-essential services, including special buses for race meetings and dances. National train services were also disrupted. Nonetheless, rugby matches continued to be recorded at all levels: schools senior and junior, provincial, hospitals, and senior, junior and minor leagues, as well as charity matches. What's more, Irish and Leinster rugby teams regularly played matches against the British armed forces in the midst of the war, games which were orchestrated to boost British Army morale while signalling somewhat friendly relations between the Free State and the UK.

It was schools' rugby that remained a perennial favourite in the sports reports of the era. For example, the *Sunday Independent* in 1941 waxed lyrical about the 'Magnetism of the Schools' Cup' in an enthusiastic report that described Leinster

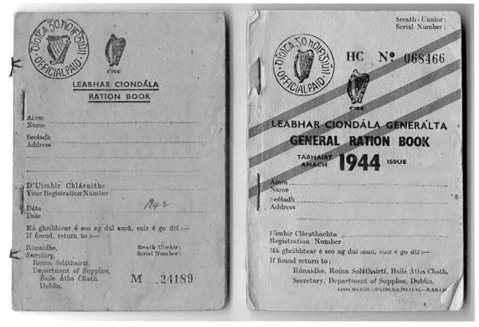

▲ Examples of 'Emergency'-era ration books from the Second World War. These were used for the duration of the war and a few years afterwards, when food, fuel and other goods were in short supply in Ireland.

▲ In 1945 Leinster played a touring 'Kiwi' rugby side, which included New Zealand Second World War veterans. Matches in Britain and Ireland were organised to promote rugby, while underscoring rugby's connection to the British Commonwealth.

schools-cup excitement: 'Arms that ache from waving banners; throats that are hoarse from high-pitched shouting; the loss of caps in the wild scuffles which follow a score – all these will be endured gladly by hundreds of schoolboys at Donnybrook this week when … the eight first-round ties in the Leinster Senior Schools' Cup are played.'[5] Despite several challenges, provincial sides, according to the junior section's honorary secretary Frank Conroy, were doing stellar work in keeping the game alive in their towns and country districts. Conroy submitted:

> Being a country man myself I have more than a fair idea of the apparently insurmountable difficulties which they have at times to overcome, particularly in these days of financial stringency, uncertain rail timetables, and priceless petrol coupons. If there is anything at all that those other Clubs more favourably placed can do to lighten their load, I would ask them to do so, particularly in the matter of facilitating them with fixtures etc.[6]

Still, the war hindered momentum that had been built up over the previous two decades. Conroy asked fellow members to brainstorm ideas about promoting the game through competitions, proposing a cup for 'minor clubs, second XVs of junior clubs, and third XVs of Senior clubs'.[7] However, under the circumstances it was considered an inopportune time to make a definite decision on that request.

The cost of everything was rising according to the Leinster Branch, including postage, stationery and travel. Indeed, it was necessary for the Branch to write to the Great Northern, Western and Southern Railway companies lobbying for 'concessions for large parties' for rugby teams and their entourages in order to fulfil fixtures.[8]

The Branch aimed to continue to bring games to the public, especially since international fixtures were cancelled for the duration. Rugby in Leinster pursued various initiatives to keep a playing and spectating public entertained. For example, in September 1940 there were newspaper ads for a seven-a-side competition for all senior teams, which was the season opener tournament to be held at Lansdowne Road. The seven-a-side became an event that the Branch thought would be a positive pre-season opener, although not everyone agreed. Some reports of the 1941 seven-a-side competition bemoaned the strains that were put on out-of-shape players. The city newspapers were also utilised to recruit and entice anyone looking for a team to play with during the disruptions. As the Emergency continued there were newspaper ads for 'open practice', an effort to recruit players which suggested that the exclusivity associated with the game was being somewhat rethought. No doubt an open-door policy, which some clubs had previously resisted but now accepted, was emblematic of a slow cultural shift in rugby circles.

We can adjudge that rugby remained an important and popular sport during the war, with people continuing to pay club subscriptions and paying in to watch games. Indeed, in the autumn of 1940 the Leinster Branch reported a profit, which was a positive sign given the realities of the Emergency. Excess income over expenditure was put down partly to the fact that the Branch had cut their travel grants. Leinster clubs weren't heading to England for their normal tours, nor very far within Ireland due to fuel shortages and rationing. But perhaps more interestingly, Leinster gate receipts were up. More people were attending games in 1940 than ever before. Indeed, the popularity of rugby can be attested to by the fact that not only were senior and junior matches reported on in the newspapers, but the Minor League results were printed also. The fact that in Leinster there was no need to halt sporting gatherings resulted in a growth in interest in the game of rugby as a live, spectator sporting day out.

That there was a need to promote the game outside the city was echoed in the newspapers in the 1940s writing of the 'missionary work' the Leinster Branch undertook to spread the game across the province:

The Leinster branch are continuing the missionary work they started last season by sending a useful Dublin XV to Tullamore to-day to oppose a Provincial team. The Dublin side is strong in the back division with two of our leading centres in G.J. Quinn and L. O'Brien, fast wings in K. Doyle and N. McNelis, and a powerful half-back combination of T.D. Brophy and C. Fox – these six would almost be entitled to represent the province.[9]

Leinster hoped these games, and these newspaper reports, would give rugby some much-needed propaganda outside the capital.

As for the junior rugby clubs in the other eleven counties, and indeed, beyond the metropole region of Dublin city, there were still discontented rumblings pointing out that junior clubs had plenty of good players who never got a look in when it came to interprovincial selection. From the provincial town clubs' perspective, it seemed like Leinster rugby's bias even trickled down into the representative junior selections, where the second fifteens of Dublin's senior clubs had players disproportionately picked for the junior interprovincial side. For example, for one 1941 junior trial match, the teams selected were divided into players from the metropolitan clubs versus players from the other clubs.[10] The match ended with an easy win for the Dublin-based selection, but the fact that the teams were chosen in this way suggested a preordained outcome. Indeed, 'The winning side included several men who are frequently seen in senior club matches and two of these … had a big part in the easy win of the team.'[11] It was not until several decades later that the junior interprovincial selection saw a rule change where it was decided that only players from junior clubs, and not players on the second fifteens of senior clubs, should be selected for junior interprovincials, even though those second fifteens of senior clubs were designated junior teams.[12]

In the meantime, concerns for rugby continued to be focused on the level of play and the desire to improve the quality of matches for players and spectators. There were grumblings about too many players in Leinster being past their prime but unwilling to give up the game. Rugby was a young man's game, which interprovincial matches were exposing, with an aging Leinster side struggling against a very youthful-looking Ulster team in their 1941 interprovincial. Then, in October 1942, the IRFU committee circulated two letters via the Leinster Branch to all its affiliated clubs, and the general gist was that the game was deteriorating in Ireland. The complaint was the killing of open football and the tendency for all teams to be overly defensive, kicking too much, with not enough emphasis

▲ A 1946 poster advertising a Dublin v. Wexford selection, a match organised to help reawaken rugby across the province after the Second World War.

▲ Leinster Senior Cup final 1949 action shot. The by-line evokes the Lansdowne players' determination – 'Leo Gibson, Jack Dawson, Bill Moynan, Tom McNally, Ken O'Brien, John Flood and Jack Coffey, in concerted pursuit of a loose ball characterize the determination that beat Old Belvedere' – to win the final, 11–9.

on either the handling game or on improving attacking movements. The negative tactics needed to change, and all of the provincial branches called on club captains to address the level of poor and overly defensive rugby. The Leinster Branch emphasised that school and university teams had a special duty and should lead by example, having the courage to pursue constructive methods of play, instilling an attacking mentality at a young age.

Another challenge that arrived out of the Emergency constraints to confront Leinster rugby was an apparent shortage of referees. A piece in *The Irish Field*, subsequently reproduced in *The Irish Times* in February 1943, highlighted the continued problem of attracting referees. In hopes of remedying the situation, sports journalists appealed to retired players to take up the responsibility.[13]

The longer the conflict went on, the more pressure it brought to bear on all aspects of Irish life. Clubs were finding it harder to travel and players were being urged to remain committed. *The Irish Press* came up with one solution to overcome the 'Rugby Travel Crux', by suggesting that the Leinster Branch should host a rugby carnival in Dublin, starting in December 1941, where the provinces would send their teams to the capital for a knockout tournament of rugby; semi-finals on Friday, final on Saturday.[14] It would not be a replacement for the interprovincial games but a supplement to help fill the fixture card.

In the midst of the struggle to keep the fixture lists fulfilled, the rugby world had its lighter moments as well during the 1940s. The image of the modern man of the 1940s, the well-groomed urbanite, perhaps influenced by the Hollywood screen star, led to accusations of 'Football Foppery' on the rugby field. As an incredulous reporter explained, with tongue firmly in cheek:

> During half-time at a recent senior Rugby match I noticed one of the players – his team, by the way, has a reputation for toughness – trying to improve his shining hair by combing it back off his forehead, afterwards returning the bare comb to the side pocket of his shorts. In a few minutes he was in the thick of scrums, mauls, line-outs and what-not, while my blood pressure and I went up and down along the touch line. Apart from the fact that nobody expects a Rugby he-man to be impeccably groomed in the middle of a game, I feel that now, at the start of the season, this care-for-the-hair business on the field of play should be discouraged among our up-and-coming footballers. To run a comb through one's hair may be all right; to have a comb run at speed through, say, one's liver is, of course, quite different and cannot be considered good football. At best, it tends to slow down the game.[15]

Despite wartime's challenges, or perhaps due to them, sports in Ireland were gaining more and more attention, and rugby was reaching province-wide weekly columns as a spectacle for good entertainment.

Rugby commentators came into their own during the 1940s it seems, with regular writers pontificating under pseudonyms like 'Crito' and 'Rugger', for example. As is the wont of the sporting critic, opinions differed and contradicted. Thus, in contrast to the earlier observations of the IRFU about the over-defensiveness of Leinster club rugby, *The Field* newspaper somewhat counterintuitively worried about the size of the rugby player in Ireland. They were much too underweight and there were no heavy men in the Leinster pack. 'The point we are coming at is that hefty forwards, with sufficient speed and mobility to make them of international class, have been extremely scarce in Ireland, and especially in Leinster, for a good many years.'[16] 'Crito' admonished the team for its lack of teamwork. However, far from bemoaning negative rugby, the papers were congratulating Leinster senior clubs on the numbers turning out at pre-season training, which they suggested boded well for the 1942–43 season ahead.

Standards of Play

From the 1940s through to the 1990s and into the professional era, constant anxieties about how best to improve rugby in Leinster were aired. During the Emergency, the standard and quality of the game in Ireland was, at times, of grave concern to a certain cohort of fans, sportswriters and administrators. Sarsfield Hogan weighed in on the debate:

> Mr. G. P. S. Hogan, the outgoing Hon. Secretary, at the annual general meeting of the Council of the Leinster Branch, I.R.F.U. last night said that the standard of play in the province was not satisfactory. This, he said, was due to the lack of efficient first-class backs in recent years rather than to any deliberate failure of the clubs to attempt the open handling game, which is the basis of modern Rugby.[17]

Concern over the quality of play in rugby continued, with an *Irish Independent* piece from November 1943 providing some advice about the situation, under the headline: 'Better and Brighter Rugby: A Few Suggestions'. Its rugby pundit proposed that the time 'for experiments in the Rugby game is becoming more and more clear. There is a general demand on the part of both players and followers of the game for better and brighter football … and an equally general consent that it cannot be obtained without altering or modifying the present rules.'[18] The public push for change suggested not merely a great interest in rugby, but a change in mindset that demanded a break from tradition. There was a strong public demand for more open and exciting rugby on the pitch.

A willingness to alter the game's rules illustrated an awareness of public interest and a recognition of the need to make the game more entertaining. Some rule-change suggestions brought forward at Branch meetings were that the option of taking a scrum in place of lineout should be scrapped – a lineout is a lineout; a player should not be penalised for charging down a defensive punt; the technical knock-on issue should be defined as only applicable when a player fumbles the ball in the action of a pass, but if he regains control of the ball before it hits the ground, he should not be penalised and the game should play on; if the full-back didn't catch a ball cleanly, but managed to hold the ball before it hit the ground, no matter the way it was fumbled, then play would go on and he should not be penalised; and, of course, the deliberate knock-on would be illegal in all of this.[19] If these changes were allowed, it was suggested, it would speed up the game and cut down on excessive scrummaging.

However, those of the more conservative rugby viewpoint were generally non-plussed. One scribe wrote:

> Rugby football is an amateur game, played at week-ends by men who work in offices through the week. To speed up rugby to such a degree that it becomes a game only for athletes trained to the last degree of fitness, would be unfair to these men, and only result in the game being played by few outside the schools and universities.[20]

However, the Leinster public's influence in asking for better and more entertaining games began to shape the evolution of rugby rules. Often, when there are shifting winds of change, there comes a doubling down among the old guard and a retreat into the old excuses of tradition as a way to express resistance to transformation. As the player pool was enlarged, bringing a variety of new people from new backgrounds into the fold, it upset some of the mainstays, who despaired over the new inclusivity of Leinster rugby. Nonetheless, hints of approaching change lingered.

Two Leinster clubs that emerged in the 1940s were Terenure and Guinness RFC. The Guinness company's sports initiative echoed the earlier emergence of Railway Union, in that the firm sought to promote a positive culture in the company through the social outlet of various sport clubs. Thus, when it became clear that there were several employees eager and willing to set up clubs, the Guinness management recognised an opportunity. It had been a common feature since the late nineteenth century for industries to support and encourage their employees in the pursuit of sports, as a way of supplying much-needed recreation and, indeed, distraction from the grind of their workaday lives. Indeed, it also could lead to a closer sense of loyalty to one's work when an employee was representing the company's football or rugby team on any given weekend. Guinness, then, acquired land at the Iveagh Grounds, Crumlin, from where their employees could organise football clubs in any code of their choice. There had been records of rugby played by Guinness employees from the 1920s, but a more permanent RFC was not established until 1943, when they affiliated with the Branch.[21]

The other club that garnered great attention was Terenure College rugby club, which was more standard in the story of how it evolved. When Rev. Fr Jackie

Corbett worried that past pupils of Terenure College were not continuing to play rugby upon graduation, he called a meeting of former students. Following the meeting, a new rugby team, the Terenure Collegians, was formed. Straight away the club ran into some conflict with the Leinster Branch, as senior clubs expressed unhappiness at the prospect of another Dublin team with, for all intents and purposes, a farm system of young talent coming from Terenure College. Notwithstanding this, Terenure RFC drew up documents for affiliation and played in the Minor League during the 1943/44 season, their first 'official' season.[22] The club went from strength to strength, opening the first club pavilion in April 1947 and winning the Minor League and Metropolitan Cup in 1949. As the number of teams joining the Junior League increased, the Branch managed the expansion by subdividing the league into sections, initially labelling them Junior, Minor, Third A, Third B and so on. This system was subsequently renamed around the late 1960s to Junior One (J1), Junior Two (J2), J3, etc., and often these designations have been retrospectively used in the record books when designating clubs' successes.

The 1950s saw Terenure's first fifteen win the J1 League five times, but, controversially, the team failed to secure senior status.[23] Terenure had won the J1 League and Metropolitan Cup double, the only junior club to do so, yet they were refused senior status each time they applied. Eventually the persistence of Terenure's members, alongside the backing of the other junior clubs in Leinster, pushed them over the line, but the saga of Terenure's treatment by the Branch and the senior club representatives who sought to obstruct them, which is discussed in detail later in this chapter, was one that the wider Leinster rugby world viewed with bitterness.[24]

After the Emergency, 1945–49

In April 1943, the Leinster Branch organised a subcommittee to reassess some of its byelaws and to make recommendations for change. It would take until the beginning of the 1946–47 season, with the prospect of a full restoration of rugby games across Ireland, for this committee's suggestions to be adopted. The new provisions gave more voice and power to the junior and the schools section, as well as to the referees, who were finally given a voting seat. Some things had not changed, however, and there continued in this era to be countless calls to expand the game beyond Dublin, while the junior clubs outside the capital continued to lobby for games against senior teams. The fielding of multiple teams in various clubs was noted in Branch meetings at this time, as was the beginning of some juvenile squads in both senior and junior clubs. It was important to seize the moment, with growth in the popularity of sports recreation emerging more generally in the postwar society.

At the end of 1945 things seemed to be looking rosy for rugby in Leinster, given the quality of the side evidenced by a 10–10 draw with a post-Second World War touring New Zealand team. The positive state of the finances was evident as well and complaints about poor rugby seemed to have been silenced by the end of the year. From the AGM of October 1945 came a request to the press 'to restore as soon as possible the pre-war amount of space to Junior, Minor and Provincial football activities in Leinster', while the Branch also put out a general appeal to 'all players to restore the former standard of football'.[25] The papers promised 'holiday treats in store' over the 1945–46 Christmas period, as a full rugby schedule returned for the festive season.

Four more clubs were added to the roster of Leinster rugby between 1948 and 1957: Swords RFC (1948), Roscrea RFC (1950), Edenderry RFC (1951) and the Unidare rugby club, established for the 1957–58 season. Unidare, renamed in 2014 to Ballymun, Glasnevin and Finglas Ravens Rugby Football Club (BGF Ravens RFC), originally comprised a team organised from the now-defunct Unidare factory in Finglas. Swords RFC's origins were actually in Aer Lingus RFC, founded in 1948, which foundered in the 1950s but rallied again in the 1960s. It was later renamed ALSAA RFC for a time, before rebranding as the Swords club in 2005. The village of Swords saw exponential growth that mirrored the rise of the global airline industry and of Dublin airport itself. Between Aer Lingus, ALSAA and Swords, there was rugby played on the town's perimeter from the moment the airfield arrived. The growing numbers of airport employees and an expanding Swords population saw the club affiliate to the junior section of the Leinster Branch in 1962.[26] As the area around north County Dublin already had several rugby clubs (Balbriggan, Skerries, Malahide, Clontarf, Sutton), and with the airport developing as it did, the growth of a club at Swords makes sense given the fraternal network that Leinster rugby fostered.

Outside Dublin, Roscrea and Edenderry were the two provincial town teams that affiliated in the 1960s, bringing the number of Leinster clubs to almost forty. Roscrea it seems, was initially quite exclusive, as suggested by a former player and clubman:

▲▼ Two Gorey RFC teams: top image is a 1954 team; bottom image is the 1954 cup team that defeated Wexford.

> Looking back at the members and players in the early decades of the club's existence, the players nearly all came from rugby-playing schools. Many young men and their families from poorer or deprived backgrounds felt they were unwelcome at rugby and that it was elitist … I never thought that at the time but in hindsight … it was true.[27]

The club started about 1950, and at the beginning most of the games were friendlies. As for Edenderry RFC, founded in 1951 in County Offaly, they first started playing 'in Clarke's field when it was sometimes difficult to find fifteen bodies to wear the white shirt on a Sunday'.[28] The fact that the games were conducted on a Sunday perhaps suggests that the playing personnel were more diverse than Roscrea's. From 1954, Edenderry RFC was running an annual dance, held for the first few years at the town hall.

The spread of rugby football to Edenderry can be explained by examining the backgrounds of some of the men involved. It is almost axiomatic that the local doctor became Edenderry's first chairman, and local bankers were central to the establishment of the team. Bob Clarke, who joined in 1959, had previously played with Garryowen in Limerick, while Michael Best was a British Army officer, and his accent, when he urged 'come on chaps', stood out in every game among the midlanders' intonations. These men reached out to the local youth to help supplement their teams, of course, and one of the 'clueless natives', who had to learn the game as he went, was Joe Brereton, the youngest player to tog out, at the age of just fifteen. Young Brereton played in the late 1950s and into the early 1960s, and he was on the 1969 Provincial Cup-winning team. Peter Moore was a GAA player from Meath who crossed the border into Offaly to play rugby to avoid being sanctioned by the GAA for ignoring the infamous ban. Even with the experience evident in Edenderry's ranks, Charlie Owen insisted that what really kept the club alive was not the few good players it had, but the five or six local lads – farmers such as John Bermingham, who might have to be called on and who would inevitably rope the caller into helping feed the cows before he could leave the farm. This became a ritual that saw Bermingham turn up, week in, week out.[29]

While there was a need for and invitation to the locals to come out and play, there were also the necessary devotees who had not just played the game but brought their economic and social capital to bear as well. But the rural clubs of Leinster rugby did not maintain the pretensions that were so clearly ingrained in the more traditional clubs of senior Dublin rugby. Edenderry's claim was that 'From the first day of the club's existence one of its great strengths was that it crossed all barriers and it was up to each to decide if they wanted to be part of our adventure … In the 1950s it took no little courage to form a rugby club in a small Irish town.'[30] By the 1960s Edenderry was one of the emerging clubs in Leinster and started to improve performances year-on-year, winning three Midland Leagues and reaching the semi-finals of the PTC twice before eventually winning it in 1969.[31]

Leinster rugby was forging ahead, and through Harry Gale we learn that the period from 1947 to 1958 was pivotal thanks to the work done by the Leinster Branch junior section to try to elevate junior and minor clubs across the province. One of the first steps taken to reinvigorate Leinster rugby was at the 1948 AGM, when it was highlighted that without a cup competition for those on the lower rungs of clubs, potentially these players would drop away, halt their dues and leave the club. Membership fees, lest we forget, are the lifeblood of any voluntary sporting organisation. The remedy, it was agreed, was the inauguration of the Moran Cup competition, which was presented by Fred Moran during his year of holding office as president of the Branch during the 1948–49 season. Before then there was no competition that catered for teams lower down the pecking order, which were the fourth teams of senior clubs, the third teams of junior clubs, the second teams of minor clubs or the first teams of clubs that had not yet been graded. 'The success of this Competition was immediate. It provided an incentive for players at this level to build up their team so as to gain some success at the end of the season.'[32] Importantly, it also worked to maintain interest in rugby at the very end of the season, since this was the last competition to be competed for by clubs. This new competition 'was an outstanding success and was the first competition to be added to Leinster rugby since the Minor League was started in 1906.'[33] Change was clearly happening in Leinster rugby.

Further change was brought about by the campaign by junior rugby proponents who viewed the exclusivity and conservativism of senior rugby as not just a hinderance to those who enjoyed and wished to play the sport, but an obstruction to the progression of Irish rugby. In 1950 the junior section of the Branch made a pitch and recommended the idea of a Minor Cup, although it took another six years before this was up and running, the first season of the cup happening in 1956–57; it was won by Terenure College's J2 team.[34] This was another important trophy added to the Leinster junior competitions, and it encouraged teams to maintain their membership at the lower levels, which ultimately helped to sustain rugby's popularity and expansion. Thankfully for Leinster, this decade also saw more occasions for junior rugby administrators to have their say. In 1952 E.J. Daly of CYM, a junior club, was elected Branch president, suggesting gains were being made to temper the senior clubs' monopoly.

Leinster rugby reports at the beginning of the decade were positive about the progress of the game in the province. Considering the criticisms evident in the 1940s about a lack of skill and lack of open rugby being played, it appears the new decade delivered a significant improvement:

RUGBY FOOTBALL.

Midland Towns Cup.

It will be of great interest to followers of the game in Longford to learn that Mr. Charles F. Ryan, of Dublin, has very kindly put up a handsome cup, to be competed for by Provincial Rugby Clubs in the Midland area. Mr. Ryan had conferred the honour of holding the cup until it is won on the Longford Club. The trophy is at present in Mr. Ryan's offices in Dublin, but will be on show in Longford in the course of a few weeks.

In connection with this cup a Midland Rugby League is being formed, which will embrace all towns eligible to compete for the cup, including Longford. A Midland League Council will also be formed. This latter will be composed of a represenative from each of the clubs concerned. It is expected that the League competition will start in next November, and be finished before the Provincial Towns' Cup competition proper begins.

The following are some of the teams which are likely to take part in the Midland League competition:—Longford, Mullingar, Athlone, Cavan, Meath, Edenderry, Kells, Athy. These are not definitely in the competition yet, but all are probable starters. Among them we recognise many old opponents of Longford, but if the game here is maintained on its present level, we should next year justify our existence in Rugby football, at least where the Midland League is concerned.

The thanks of all Rugby followers are due to Mr. Ryan for voluntary providing the cup. It will undoubtedly give a much needed fillip to Rugby in the Midlands, and viewed from this angle, will be much appreciated by those who are at present struggling to promote its interests to the best of their ability.

The cup will be known as the "Ryan Cup."

▲ Newspaper coverage of the Midland Towns Cup competition, the Ryan Cup, created to promote rugby in Leinster outside of Dublin 4.

The 'Golden Years' of Irish rugby (between 1948 and 1951) … were characterised by the evolution of a new style of play and the development of two world-class players, Jack Kyle (outside-half) and Karl Mullen (hooker and captain). Borrowing from the South African tactic of forwards working in close support of each other, the Irish employed hard, fast, tough, 'devil-may-care' forwards as attacking spearheads. Of course, the 'harrying' qualities of Irish forward play are also connected with other tactical developments in the game, such as 'the Garryowen' …[35]

In the first round of the Senior Cup competition, for the first time UCD wore numbered jerseys because there was a programme produced for the spectators, who could track the players by their jersey. It was a small difference, but again a signal of post-Second World War modernity.

It was not only the game that was gathering new pace in this period. More frequent and extensive references were made to both rugby union and sport in general in the media in the 1950s. 'Throughout the 1940s and 1950s reports on international fixtures were typically restricted to a column approximately six inches in length. By the end of the period whole pages were being

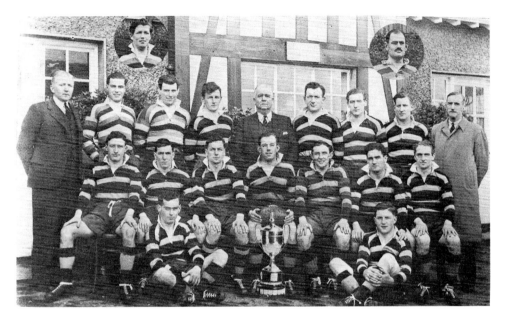

▲ Leinster Senior Cup Winners 1953, Lansdowne FC (insets in the circles above the team are presumably players who contributed during the campaign but were missing on the day of the photo).

devoted to rugby union.'[36] As early as January 1950 the Leinster Branch was trying to find someone to help them out with the question of broadcasting rights and began searching for a public relations person to help with external communication, such was the growing public interest in rugby. Indeed, the Branch, for the first time, had to organise the opening of a female toilet in the Donnybrook venue, which required them to temporarily convert one of the male bathrooms until they got around to building a women's lavatory.[37]

In January 1951 the fixtures subcommittee of the Leinster Branch finally allowed the provincial towns to organise Sunday fixtures without a formal request to the executive. However, the Branch would still not officially sanction such Sunday fixtures. It was not until September 1960 that the rules were changed to officially recognise Sunday matches for the first time in the 1961–62 season.[38] Despite the barriers that seemed to be put in front of grassroots rugby, the junior committee vowed to keep pressure on the papers to ensure coverage of junior, minor and provincial town rugby. It also suggested that the clubs themselves needed to write to the press about their games and self-publicise.[39] But it was the Terenure story, in particular, which would rally the junior section of the Branch from 1958/59 onwards to become more vociferous and observant of the mechanisms of the senior club's administrators, ensuring that they focused on all of Leinster rugby when making decisions at Branch level.

By the early 1950s Terenure College RFC had two teams, with the first team's win rate at 83 per cent over the decade. Despite this, Terenure's first thirteen applications to become a senior club over a period of ten years were all rejected by the Leinster Branch. Several senior clubs, all Dublin-based, continually blocked Terenure from deserved promotion to senior status. Indeed, it took the intervention of the IRFU on Terenure's fourteenth application, in 1959, to force the Branch to promote the club. This came after Terenure themselves had submitted a letter of protest dated

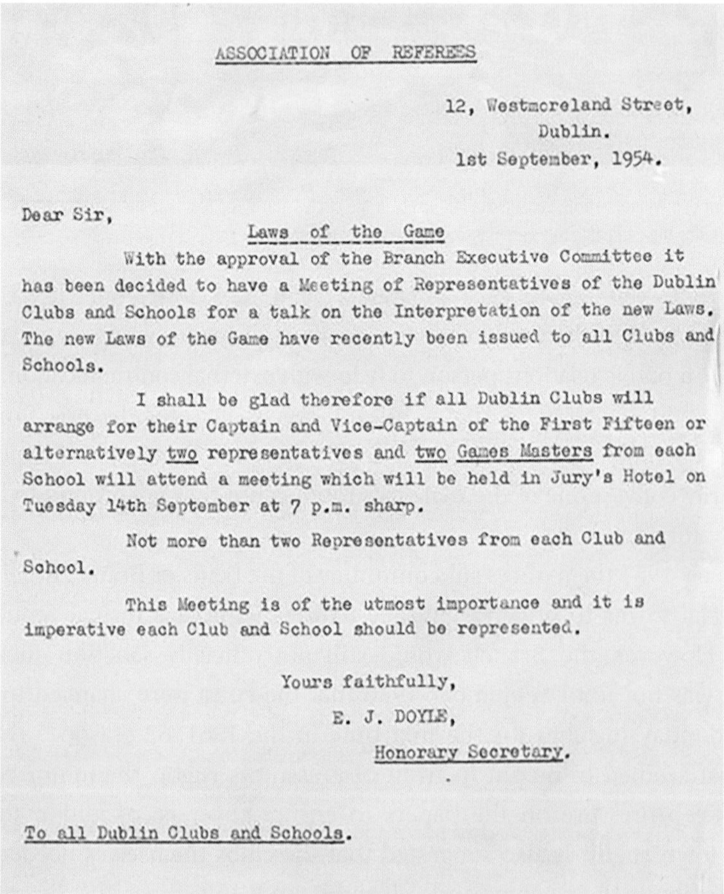

ASSOCIATION OF REFEREES

12, Westmoreland Street,
Dublin.
1st September, 1954.

Dear Sir,

Laws of the Game

With the approval of the Branch Executive Committee it has been decided to have a Meeting of Representatives of the Dublin Clubs and Schools for a talk on the Interpretation of the new Laws. The new Laws of the Game have recently been issued to all Clubs and Schools.

I shall be glad therefore if all Dublin Clubs will arrange for their Captain and Vice-Captain of the First Fifteen or alternatively two representatives and two Games Masters from each School will attend a meeting which will be held in Jury's Hotel on Tuesday 14th September at 7 p.m. sharp.

Not more than two Representatives from each Club and School.

This Meeting is of the utmost importance and it is imperative each Club and School should be represented.

Yours faithfully,

E. J. DOYLE,

Honorary Secretary.

To all Dublin Clubs and Schools.

▲ Invite sent to clubs and schools to a meeting to discuss the rules and laws of the game, prior to the season's start, from the Association of Referees, 1954.

1 May 1956 to the Branch and, one week later, forwarded the same to the IRFU, supported by letters from other junior clubs, notably Railway Union. In their first sixteen years affiliated to the Branch, Terenure reached nineteen official finals. The team did not win much in the 1960s but grew as a club and invested in a new clubhouse and bar. During that decade, they had as many as eight senior players capped on the Leinster senior interprovincial team. Terenure was one of the lead clubs advocating for a Senior League, raising the issue for the first time since 1904 as an official proposal at the 1965 LB AGM.[40] When it was adopted, they donated the first league trophy in 1972.[41] It was Terenure's journey from minor to senior status that exposed the need for further change in the Leinster Branch, where the senior clubs' monopoly was hampering rather than helping rugby's progress across the province. And one of the most vociferous advocates for change was Railway Union's Harry Gale.

Gale had captained Railway Union in the 1936–37 season, was the honorary secretary for ten years (1944–54), the chairman for six (1952–58), the president for three seasons (1958–61) as well as vice-president, a lifetime member and a trustee of Railway Union RFC. He was also on the Leinster Branch junior committee and executive committee, was honorary secretary of the Leinster junior section and chairman of the Leinster under-nineteen committee, and was on the rules committee and the development committee between 1971 and 1974. What's more he was on the IRFU executive assessment committee too. Gale chose the Terenure College controversy to articulate his frustration at the persistence of senior Leinster rugby's lack of care for junior rugby. He celebrated what he saw as 'an Iron curtain' between senior and junior rugby being blown apart in 1959 (when Terenure went senior) but feared what he saw as a new attempt in the mid-1970s by the senior rugby club members of the Branch committee to rebuild the wall and undermine rugby's province-wide progress.[42] But before that concern emerged, the club scene was looking positive in Leinster in the 1950s, 1960s and early 1970s. In these decades the progressive voices in Leinster rugby emphasised the need to revive junior rugby and develop the game in the country districts outside Dublin. For example, Branch reports noted that referees travelled to places including Curragh, Skerries, Greystones, Longford, Athy, Mullingar and Kilkenny, giving us an insight into the extent of provincial rugby interest. The responsibility of those in charge was to build on that positive progress.

▲ The 1949 Leinster team that played Connacht. Senior Dublin rugby club players often refused to play in Connacht, revealing a certain snobbishness in rugby, but enough Leinster players were eager to promote the game and work to be more inclusive.

Interprovincial Progress

One of the standout Irish athletes in the 1940s was Kevin O'Flanagan. O'Flanagan's story is instructive in a couple of ways. A graduate of CBS, Synge Street, he captained the school to an All-Ireland Gaelic football under-16 championship win and was selected for the Dublin GAA minor panel, and clearly had a big future in sport ahead of him. However, when the GAA authorities discovered that O'Flanagan played soccer for Home Farm FC, he was summarily dropped and exiled from Dublin GAA football. Their loss was firstly soccer's and then rugby's gain. O'Flanagan played soccer for one season with Home Farm before being snapped up by Bohemians for the following nine seasons. He held various scoring records, captained them to an Inter-city Cup win against a professional soccer side from Belfast, scored on his international debut for Ireland and was Ireland's youngest international scorer until Robbie Keane broke his record in 1998.[43] O'Flanagan went on to have a distinguished athletic career too, and later was a long-standing presence on the International Olympic Committee (IOC), having previously advocated for and promoted sports medicine in Britain and Ireland.

It was while he was studying medicine at UCD (1937–45) that O'Flanagan took up rugby, appearing in two losing Leinster Senior Cup finals during the war period. He also played for Lansdowne FC, partnering his brother Michael in the centre but mostly playing wing-three-quarter. He earned his first Leinster caps in the 1940s against Ulster and Connacht. The brothers 'achieved the unique distinction of being awarded international caps in both rugby and soccer'.[44] Apart from all that, Kevin played soccer with Arsenal but remained an amateur while he did so, having turned down repeated offers to turn professional from several of the elite English clubs because he wished to focus on his medical career. Playing soccer on the weekends and sailing home to Dublin for Leinster games and even an Ireland rugby match, he insisted rugby was his hobby. Some have suggested that the Leinster and Ireland rugby selectors shunned O'Flanagan because of his interest in so many sports, especially as he played soccer so regularly, and that he should have earned many more caps than he did.

Elsewhere, Seamus Kelly, according to the *Enniscorthy Guardian*, was remembered as 'a great servant of Irish rugby and was capped five times for his country. [He] was one of the best-loved figures on the Wexford rugby scene, having played with his local Wexford Wanderers club, Lansdowne RFC, Leinster and Ireland.' Kelly was the first Irish player to score over 1,000 points in senior and representative rugby but, while a regular player with Leinster, he did not make it to international rugby, competing with the likes of Jackie Kyle and Mick English for the out-half position.[45] Alongside Kelly in the Leinster player statistics was another Wexford native, Bill Tector, from Clonroche. Tector played as a schoolboy at Kilkenny College and later at TCD. He made 'his debut for Leinster while in Trinity in 1952 and, after he joined Wanderers, won the first of three international caps'.[46] In spite of some excellent players, however, Leinster interprovincial rugby from 1940 to 1960 was not as strong as it had been.

After the heights reached in the 1930s, Leinster rugby stumbled slightly in the seasons from 1945 to 1959. While Leinster played Ulster a total of eleven times as the Second World War went on, winning each time, when official games started up again, Ulster dominated in the fourteen games from 1945 to 1959, winning nine and drawing one, with Leinster only managing to come away with four victories. The Munster matches during the Emergency shifted the ground for Leinster also, as they lost four, drew one and won just three out of eight wartime interprovincials with their southern rivals. From 1945 to 1959 Leinster only managed a 50 per cent win ratio, with seven victories from fourteen matches, earning three draws

WHITES XV.

BLUES XV.

	FULL-BACKS	
15. W. J. HEWITT Instonians		**15. F. O'LEARY** St. Mary's College

	THREE-QUARTERS	
14. W. W. BORNEMANN Wanderers	RIGHT WING LEFT WING	**11. R. J. McCARTAN** London Irish
13. A. C. PEDLOW C.I.Y.M.S.	RIGHT CENTRE LEFT CENTRE	**12. J. F. DOOLEY** Galwegians
12. A. J. F. O'REILLY Dolphin	LEFT CENTRE RIGHT CENTRE	**13. J. C. WALSH** University College, Cork
11. F. BYRNE University College, Dublin	LEFT WING RIGHT WING	**14. D. C. GLASS** Collegians

	HALF-BACKS	
10. G. TORMEY University College, Dublin	STAND-OFF	**10. M. A. F. ENGLISH** Bohemians **(CAPTAIN)**
9. A. A. MULLIGAN London Irish	SCRUM	**9. M. PIGOTT** Collegians

	FORWARDS	
1. S. MILLAR Ballymena		**1. S. McEVOY** Galwegians
2. J. S. DICK Queens University, Belfast		**2. B. RIGNEY** Bective Rangers
3. B. G. M. WOOD Lansdowne		**3. M. O'CALLAGHAN** Sunday's Well
4. W. A. MULCAHY University College, Dublin		**4. C. J. DICK** Ballymena
5. M. G. CULLITON Wanderers		**5. B. O'HALLORAN** University College, Dublin
6. J. R. KAVANAGH Wanderers **(CAPTAIN)**		**6. D. SCOTT** Malone
8. P. J. A. O'SULLIVAN Galwegians		**8. T. McGRATH** Garryowen
7. N. A. A. MURPHY Garryowen	**Referee:** Mr. H. Jackson (Ulster Society of Rugby Football Referees)	**7. F. O'ROURKE** Bective Rangers

| Touch Judge: MR. W. J. O'BRIEN (Association of Referees, Leinster Branch I.R.F.U.) | | Touch Judge: MR. S. V. CRAWFORD (Association of Referees, Leinster Branch I.R.F.U.) |

EXIT After Half-time Spectators can leave ground from back of West Stand via Tunnel to Lansdowne Lane and Lansdowne Road thus obviating crossing Railway Line on Lansdowne Road.

▲ Example programme line-up for Ireland trials, whites versus blues, which includes Bill Mulcahy and Tony O'Reilly on the whites, from the early 1960s.

and four losses. The only team Leinster continued to dominate at this stage was Connacht, although the westerners earned victories in one wartime match and two more after the Emergency.

Nonetheless, come the 1960s, Leinster rugby took great leaps forward, embracing the modern era of sports coaching by initiating a new and, at times, controversial approach, insisting on higher standards via dedication to training, the implementation of team and game management, and employing top-class coaches to reach those ideals. Furthermore, after the war the prospect of matches with international touring teams became much more doable and sought-after fixtures for all of the provinces' representative rugby teams. The benefits of playing the best players from around the world in touring sides would be two-fold: firstly, they would improve standards by playing matches against top, tough opposition, especially the southern hemisphere's touring international sides; secondly, in promoting the game of rugby in Ireland more broadly, with the corollary incentive of earning big pay, knowing that spectators would want to come out and see, for example, a Leinster team play New Zealand, South Africa or Australia. Between 1957 and 1966, Leinster played four touring sides, all at Lansdowne Road: Australia ('57 and '66), South Africa ('61), and New Zealand ('64), all resulting in defeats. However, following this the IRFU organised for touring teams to play the other provinces rather than Leinster, in an attempt to increase the game's profile across the rest of the country and in the belief that the game was healthy enough in Leinster. Although this made the Leinster Branch extremely unhappy, they continued to imagine ways to improve and ideally to grow the game of rugby across the province.

▲ Dr Kevin O'Flanagan, the oldest player still living to be capped for Ireland. O'Flanagan played both soccer and rugby to international level.

▲ A 1950s Leinster squad with Ham Lambert (back row on the left) as referee.

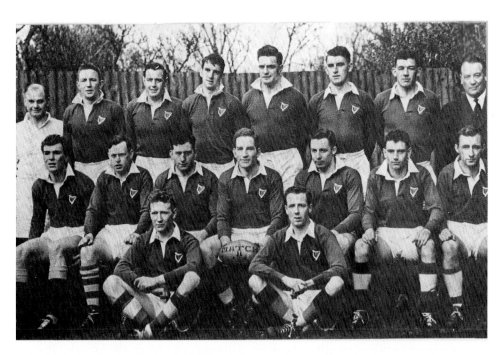

▲ The Leinster team that played Australia in 1957. Securing fixtures against touring international teams not only bestowed prestige, but provided the kind of tough test Leinster rugby teams craved.

▲ Autographed menu after Leinster v. Connacht match, 1948 (with interesting food choices). Rugby's networking was underscored by this kind of post-game shared memorabilia.

8

Rugby's Progress and the Coaching Boom

The Social World of Rugby Clubs

With the demands for better facilities to cater for more teams and larger membership being put on Leinster's rugby clubs as they expanded in the 1960s, the commercial elements of rugby became more prominent, as did the need for sponsorship and fundraising. In the case of the latter, the arrival of showband culture coincided with these imperatives. As ex-Carlow RFC player Dan Carbery recalled:

> 1960 was the beginning of the show band era when the big bands were packing all the public dancehalls all over the country. But obtaining the services of these top line bands was a problem, the best were booked up over three years in advance ... Tom [O'Brien] made contact and arranged regular bookings with the top band managers in the country. The Royal, Clipper Carlton, Capitol, Miami, Cadets, Clancy Brothers ... were all engaged. Tom now had the club members involved in running these dances all over the country ... and to ensure they were a success the club promoted extensive press and poster campaigns ... This was vital work and there were large sums of money involved ...[1]

The dance craze swept the country in the 1960s, which rugby clubs cleverly exploited to help their finances. Rugby pavilions ran weekly dances and discos, which proved popular to the extent that 'the dancing membership increased dramatically and so the functions became another valued source of income to provide the remainder of the money to complete the initial ground development'.[2] The monies raised were ploughed back into club improvements. For instance, taking the Carlow example, ground development included drainage schemes, clearing 200 tree stumps, stone picking and levelling works. During the 1968–69 season the club was able to field three teams every Sunday for the first time in its history.

Aside from fundraising, the junior committee of the Leinster Branch took it upon itself to consider the state of grassroots rugby at the time and push for more reforms. It was noted, for instance, that there was only one trial game for the junior Leinster squad, between a Dublin fifteen selection versus a provincial towns' fifteen. And there were still only two junior interprovincial games, against Munster and Ulster. There were five Dublin-centred cup competitions, but only the PTC for junior teams across the rest of the province outside of Dublin. This needed to be addressed to induce more competitive rugby province-wide. It made sense, then, that more regional leagues and competitions were introduced, to create a greater incentive for clubs at all levels to continue to play, with the promise of glory and silverware at the end of a successful season. It was these alterations, as the 1960s dawned, that suggested a major change in mindset within rugby and indeed among the wider Leinster population when it came to what was, after all, a traditionally exclusive football code.

The addition of approximately seventeen new clubs through the 1950s and 1960s suggests that Leinster rugby was developing steadily. Nevertheless, the Branch's May 1960 AGM did reveal some trepidation about stalling interest in the rugby game, citing twenty-five clubs in the Dublin area but only twenty in the rest of the province, which was worrisome, and questions about financing provincial town clubs were raised. A subcommittee was suggested in order 'to promote and encourage the creation, growth and extension of rugby clubs in towns and areas where none have existed before or where they have gone out of existence'.[3] With the Moran Cup having had such a visible impact on improving the standard of competition at the lower levels, there was a demand for more of the same and, in 1963, the Leinster Executive was first lobbied to officially establish a Junior Three (J3) League. It took some time, but eventually they agreed and any team eligible to compete for the Moran Cup could enter this league competition, which had its first season in 1965–66. Railway Union presented a cup for the new league.[4]

For some of the clubs knocked out of the PTC, they found their competitive season done and dusted by February. To address that problem, the Provincial Towns' Plate was introduced to cater for the teams knocked out by the end of February in the early rounds, as well as to cater for provincial town clubs that had second XVs.[5] Sir William Butlin, who was the founder and driving force behind the Delvin club, based on the southside of Drogheda at Bryanstown after they moved up from pitches located at Mosney, presented the trophy. In addition, the Provincial Towns Seconds' Cup was also inaugurated in 1964, at first as an unofficial competition, but made official in 1968. Throughout the 1960s rugby had a bit of a resurgence and the playing strength of many clubs across the province spiked, with interest ever-expanding.

Inroads Across the Province

The 1960s saw a love of Leinster rugby inculcated in a new generation of Leinster players who embraced rugby with a fervent passion in their youth many of them would go on to blossom as players. As Railway Union's Harry Gale recalled, the executive committee of the Leinster Branch finally began to take the junior game much more seriously and was becoming more conscientious about the undertakings at junior level. Gale credits Judge Conroy, who arrived on the scene as the senior honorary secretary in 1961, with overseeing a decade of improvements when it came to the concerns of Leinster junior clubs. Conroy supervised the implementation of an expanded junior administration, as well as the addition of a junior representative onto the Leinster Branch executive committee in 1963. More to the point, in the 1963–64 season, two more games were added for the Leinster junior team selection: a Leinster provincial junior trial match between north and south Leinster selections, plus a Leinster team selection from the provincial clubs to play a Connacht fifteen.

In this decade, efforts to enlarge the rugby public, if stuttering, were nonetheless driven forward by a tide of grassroots rugby enthusiasts. The province's junior and provincial towns' clubs were working to implement basic on-the-ground changes by pursuing a more inclusive, local-level game of rugby. It was the new connections forged in Leinster between secondary schools, as well as newly emerging third-level colleges, and local rugby clubs across the province that became a boon to the game. The UCD rugby team had five medical students and five law students, for example. That the Trinity team, in 1967, had twelve students who had gone to British secondary schools, with the other three having attended Protestant fee-paying schools was, of course, also quite telling. But change was coming to the rugby world, evident in various events and stories emerging in the 1960s around the game, to the extent that a UCD and TCD collaborative team came together on the rugby field to take on English opposition, reflecting something new in Irish rugby.

▲ Judge J.C. Conroy collated a history of Leinster rugby for the 1979 centenary of the Branch, was very active promoting rugby in the 1960s, and exemplified the professional world of which most of Leinster rugby's organisers were part.

As grassroots rugby expanded, the game was now inviting in players from all walks of life. This was a time when Ireland was undergoing a reinvigoration of the economy, an upsurge in employment and a temporary hiatus in emigration. Additionally, as Trevor West wrote, challenges to the sporting status quo were emanating from an international sports-media growth, especially television coverage and the closer affiliation of spectatorship with revenue generation. 'The media, with television leading the way, have popularized sport to an extent that would have amazed our Victorian forebears. Commercial sponsorship and government intervention have made participation in sport more egalitarian and have assisted in the provision of proper facilities and of qualified coaching …'[6] The other side of that coin, as West concluded, was that 'the old ethos of participation and sportsmanship is soon overtaken by a "winner take all" mentality. Games are subtly professionalized as more and more time is demanded from leading, supposedly amateur performers.'[7] These changing circumstances altered how rugby was developed, leading to new dynamics and pressures as well as opportunities for Leinster rugby.

The obvious opportunity for Leinster clubs was to recruit new players and fans from 'non-traditional' rugby areas and from non-fee-paying, non-rugby-playing schools. However, evidence suggests that throughout the 1960s and into the 1970s not all of the men running the Leinster Branch thought expansion palatable. For example, in an April 1971 Branch executive meeting mentioning the fact that the GAA had lifted the ban on its members playing rugby, one Leinster official explained, 'there might be an influx of GAA players and clubs should think about this matter. Players must opt for one game or the other, otherwise clubs would not know how they stood when selecting teams.'[8] While there was a practical logic to that observation, this was hardly a welcoming, open-minded reaction, rejecting an opportunity to expand and opting instead to maintain a rugby exclusivity; the sentiment was that you are either a rugby player or you are not. Nonetheless, such attitudes were opposed by an increasing number of voices of inclusivity and expansion during the late 1960s and into the 1970s among Leinster rugby enthusiasts, and it was these voices that now began to come to the fore.

A Coaching Revolution

As Ireland's society progressed from the late 1960s especially, more and more people were interested in participating as players or as fans in sports, regardless of the code. One thing that enticed a wider participatory group to play and watch rugby was the vision of a section of Leinster rugby men for 'teaching' the game with authority, science and enthusiasm. It is striking, looking back from today's viewpoint, how little coaching or few training sessions there were prior to the late 1960s. Teams did not have official coaches appointed and generally any kind of organisation was left up to the captain of a particular game-day selection.[9] Indeed, there had long been a reluctance to implement an organised coaching culture in Ireland and Britain, which was tied to the amateurism mantra and driven by underlying desires to maintain rugby's exclusivity. To invite in organised coaching was seen as a slippery slope.

However, with the increasing uptake in rugby across the province, clubs could no longer rely on the sons and grandsons of former players, usually a cohort from an exclusive section of local society who attended private schools or had returned from one of the universities. To survive, they now needed to include boys from all backgrounds and recruit players who had never played before. While this was doable, one of the problems would be the question of coaching and a methodology of teaching the basic skills of rugby to those who had never been acquainted with the game's finer points. Indeed, there had already been a degree of coaching implemented at the schoolboy and university level in Leinster prior to the invitation for junior and senior clubs to participate in a summer academy of rugby coaching that became known as the Mosney coaching scheme, which would signify the most significant coaching transformation in Leinster. The stated emphasis was to train coaches to train newcomers to rugby.

Progress was the standard of the period and the demand for a progressive rugby to improve the game in Ireland was almost universal. As the modern era associated with the 1960s evolved, rugby clubs began to implement the science of the epoch, with tacticians, a focus on fitness, player psychology and new incentives shaping the game more conspicuously. It was the need to have the best rugby knowledge and then to be able to teach that, which was at the top of the agenda in Leinster. As Edmund Van Esbeck has pointed out,

▲ A collage of action shots from schools' rugby in the 1960s.

coaching was gradually becoming an accepted principle within the country, and nowhere more than in Leinster, where since 1964 an annual course had been run at the Butlin's Holiday Camp in Mosney, County Meath. Ronnie Dawson was one of the prime movers in the project and he had a willing and able accomplice in Judge Charles Conroy, the then honorary secretary of the Leinster Branch ...[10]

Several important figures took a modern approach to the amateur game by insisting on improved coaching acumen in order to progress rugby in the province. Ronnie Dawson, Roly Meates and Des Scaife were names credited with bringing in more sustained and specialised coaching. They brought ambition and foresight in terms of the desire to improve the players and coaches involved in the game. The Leinster Branch even looked beyond Ireland to bring in outside perspectives to generate a more well-rounded vision of rugby skills, and they aimed to share that with *all* clubs and players, from schools, colleges, juniors and seniors to representative level. As an example, two French instructors, Julien Saby and René Deleplace, were invited over for the pilot course set up at Mosney in the summer of 1964. Saby was a PE instructor with the French Army, who had developed an introductory methodology for learning the basics of the game of rugby. While the 1964 Mosney project was sanctioned by the Leinster Branch, it was not until 1969 that it produced a pamphlet for its membership highlighting the importance of organised coaching.

The first year of the Mosney experiment was initially set up to cater for a mere twenty people and was greatly oversubscribed. However, utilising the network that the rugby game fosters, the Leinster Branch was lucky to secure extra assistance, for example from Llanelli player Ken Jones. As well as on-the-field coaching, lectures were given by both Sarsfield Hogan and by school's rugby expert Kevin Kelleher. The inaugural year was a huge success, underscoring a clear demand for this kind of instruction. The pilot course and the follow-up in 1965 embarked on an 'ambitious scheme, and we trust that the spirit of the course will be reflected in the beneficial effect on Club and School football'.[11] The day was regimentally itemised with meals, lectures and practical-instruction times laid out to the minute. The meticulousness of the schedule certainly signalled a complete turnaround from the ideas that had been earlier articulated about the amateur, ad hoc, and mere 'fun' that had been the mantra of rugby.[12] Furthermore, in what was a very progressive step, the Branch realised the importance of rugby coaches understanding injuries and their treatment, so 'the course included a lecture from Bob O'Connell on First

▲ Leinster Rugby Coaching Course organisers and participants at Butlin's in Mosney, August 1966. Prior to the 1960s coaching was forbidden in rugby because it was said it undermined the amateur ethos of the game.

Aid and Joe Lennon on the remedial treatment of injuries. Bob O'Connell's lectures were to continue through the years and became one of the "star" attractions.'[13] Clearly, success and proper practice were the new way forward.

The Mosney project provided instruction for senior, junior and schoolboy players, and those coaching at those levels, also catering for schools' games masters and for referees. French, Welsh, Scottish and English coaches were brought in to supplement the Irish perspective on the game. Ken Jones was asked back every year from then to 1974 to coach on the course, as was Gérard Murillo from France, with the explanation that their international perspectives were essential if Leinster was going to keep abreast of the latest trends in rugby. By 1967 the popularity of these courses was reflected in the additional organisation required and the upswing in interest from more and more clubs and individuals, as well as referees and school PE masters. There were seventeen instructors employed for the camp and six and a half fields, with each full field split in two, so there were thirteen different areas on the go. There were 460 participants in total between the coaches and the players attending. The number of clubs and schools with members at the course was much larger too, and not just from Leinster.[14]

The fifth consecutive course run by the Branch at Mosney saw as many as twenty-four instructors, one permanently onsite lecturer and three visiting lecturers. It focused more on tactics, as well as physical training, individual skills, hooking, the ruck and set pieces. Additionally, there were lectures focused on rugby from 'down under'. As early as the 1967 course, there was a lecture titled 'Australasia' and in 1968 there were more specific lectures on 'What we learned from the All Blacks and Springboks in '67 and '68' and on 'South Africa 1968'. In Leinster rugby circles, this seems to reflect an obvious turn towards rugby as it was played in the southern hemisphere.

As well as the coaching courses, the first ever Conference of Referees was organised by the Branch in September 1968, in which the referees' aim was 'to improve our knowledge of the Laws of Rugby Football and so make ourselves better Referees'. Seventy-nine attendees were recorded.[15]

The impact of the coaching courses was self-evident, although the Branch itself seemed a little slow to consider how to expand and add to their success. It wasn't until 1970 that there was a realisation, or perhaps a reluctant acceptance, that even though the course was hugely popular, there were yet more players and coaches in junior rugby who needed to be reached. Subsequently, one of the committees proposed a week-long coaching course for schoolboys' rugby, to be run at various times in different schools that were interested in taking it up throughout the entire year, facilitated by the Branch. Additionally, a special one-day course for schools' sports masters was organised.

Even as coaching became increasingly important and rugby became more technical, with rugby players becoming fitter and more proficient, some rugby devotees doubled down on their views of amateurism. Thus, the then IRFU president wrote in the foreword to Edmund Van Esbeck's 1974 study of Irish rugby:

> Throughout this history there runs one golden thread plain for all to see – the great principle of Amateur Rugby Union Football that 'no one is allowed to seek or to receive payment or other material reward for taking part in the game.' It is one of the great bulwarks of the Rugby Union game and one which, if the Game is to survive in its present form, must be safeguarded at all costs … Amateur rugby union football … is a way of life. In Ireland it has been a way in which the simple virtues of fair play and sportsmanship, of high endeavour and physical contact within the laws of the game predominate.[16]

These sentiments reflected the views of rugby administrators who believed amateurism must be maintained in order for 'the game to survive in its present form' – a hierarchal system where the majority of those controlling the sport came from a position of wealth and affluence. The real-world translation of this view

: Leinster Branch, I.R.F.U. :

12, Westmoreland Street,
Dublin.

Date as per Postmark, 1961.

Dear Sir,

Laws of the Game - Law 1.

Attention is called to Law 1 - plan of field - Laws of the Game and all Clubs are requested to see that the grounds are at once marked accordingly and kept so marked throughout the season.

Players Dress - Laws of the Game - Law 5.

The special attention of all Clubs, Schools, Players and Referees is called to the players wearing dangerous projections - buckles, rings, studs, etc.

The wearing of any kind of harness or protective jacket is absolutely prohibited.

Where the referee is satisfied that a player requires such protection following injury, a protective pad may be attached to the body by plaster tape or temporarily sewn into a Jersey. The pad must always be composed of such material that does not harden in use but remains soft at all times.

Whatever the circumstances, irrespective of any doctor's certificate, the wearing of any kind of harness or protective jacket is absolutely prohibited.

It is in the interests of himself and of other players that any player requiring protective wear which is prohibited under Law 5 should not be playing the game at all.

Inspection of Boots - Law 5.

The Committee of the Association of Referees have been requested to instruct each of their Members officiating at Matches on SATURDAY, 30th SEPTEMBER, to inspect the boots of all players and to disallow any player taking part in a Match if the Referee is satisfied that an injury might occur by reason of the condition of the players boots also that this inspection be carried out from time to time.

A suggestion has been made by the Committee of the Branch that a Notice to this effect should be placed in all Club Pavilions.

FIRST AID EQUIPMENT

I have been asked to urge on all Clubs the importance of First Aid Equipment being provided and available at all times.

Decorum on Field of Play   -   Changing of Knicks

Clubs are urged to impress on their players the importance of strict decorum as to changing of Togs on field of play.

Yours faithfully,

J. C. CONROY,

To:
Hon. Secretary,   Hon. Secretary.
All Dublin Clubs, and
All Referees, All Schools.

▲ Official Leinster Branch circular from 1961 to all clubs and schools, highlighting the laws of the game.

ensured a large element of socioeconomic exclusivity and, more to the point, the unequal dispersal of support and funding for rugby. However, despite this pocket of resistance, change was gathering pace, and the extent and success of coaching from the 1960s and into the 1970s seems to have been a major game changer for the progress of rugby in the province.

Continued Growth of Provincial Clubs

Success, as pointed out earlier, brought with it various challenges. For example, '[t]he growth of the game in the provinces was not matched by a commensurate growth in the number of referees in the two decades after the war. A number of new clubs had started, and some existing ones were able to field additional teams.'[17] With rugby's expansion across Leinster and with established clubs adding more teams, the demands for referees needed to be addressed. One development was the reorganisation of Leinster rugby into regions, which meant that local clubs had to supply their own club referees for games. While the Association of Referees had registered sixty-seven referees by 1966, only nine of those were from provincial town clubs. The Association requested that all sixty-seven make themselves available for matches across the province, which was neither ideal nor necessarily practicable.[18] In 1969, when Tullamore's Oliver McGlinchey was president of the Association of Referees, he, together with Athy's Frank Anderson, outlined a plan dividing the province into four areas, with each referee allocated a geographic section that was preferable to them, to ensure that the game could keep building on the momentum of 1960s rugby growth in Leinster while helping to retain much-needed adjudicators.

One obvious indicator of the expansion and the success of rugby in Leinster was the affiliation of new clubs to the Branch. Two clubs, Longford and Gorey RFCs, both affiliated in 1968. Records show that there had been a Longford rugby team as early as the 1880s, and again in the 1920s and 1940s, with old newspaper accounts recording games against Sligo, Lansdowne and Cavan, for example. In its first iteration, 'the club was formed in 1888 and played games up to the 1914–15 season. The club was only affiliated to the IRFU in 1921 and folded in the 1949–50 season,'[19] but was then restarted in the 1960s, finally managing some permanency for the future. Longford's history highlights the connection between successful teams and university and private school players returning to their rural home towns or others being posted across Leinster. While it was pretty much always those of the professional classes with a third-level degree who started the ball rolling in rural Leinster to form (or revive) a rugby club, the major difference was that over time more and more of the business-world fraternity became involved, with the odd 'ordinary Joe' being recruited into the club. In Longford's example, the second iteration of the club came in the 1920s, when the local doctor, Dr Delaney, organised the committee alongside a Dr Hedley Boyers and George Montgomery, who was the Longford County Registrar.[20] Some of the other players included George Brady of the Northern Bank, Dick Burke of the National Bank, Vincent Mahon of the Bank of Ireland and Jack Prior of Customs and Excise. Dr Delaney supplied two of his own cars as transport for the club and the team must have looked quite the established side, arriving in two limousines for away matches. The doctor's two cars were a Rolls-Royce and an equally large Delage, which was a French-made version of the Rolls-Royce. It was the war years 1939–45 that seemed to bring rugby in Longford to an end until its resumption in the 1960s.[21]

The new Longford club organised itself with the future in mind:

> Another aspect of the foresight that has gone into Longford RFC was the formation in 1974/75 of an under-13 and under-15 youth team under the guidance of a separate Youths Committee. In 1975/76 the under-17 and under-11 sides were formed and in 1977/78 the successful under-19 team was introduced. The vigorous youth policy adopted by the club is now showing dividends as can be seen by the large numbers of young people at weekly training sessions.[22]

This record of innovation and dedication in Longford to Leinster rugby was acknowledged in 2014, with the first ever appointment of an IRFU president from a junior club when Longford clubman Pat Fitzgerald was awarded the honour of heading the Irish union.

Alongside the success illustrated in Longford, Gorey RFC, which celebrated fifty years of rugby in 2018, was another exemplar Leinster club from its founding in 1968. David Bolger was the first president, and he recalled how he had the bare minimum fifteen players in the club when Gorey started out. While there had certainly been some rugby played in the town previously, with records of games there as early as 1947, it took time to establish a permanent set-up. Gorey finally bedded down in 1968, thanks to enthusiasts like Eric Deacon, who was a teacher in Gorey's Vocational School and who played the game for Enniscorthy. When he settled in Gorey for work, he decided that he wanted to bring his beloved game to the town on a more permanent footing. He put the call out to anyone who had played rugby in the Gorey area to come to a meeting in May 1968 at Redmond's Hotel. There were enough people there to form a committee of twenty-five, which included two doctors and a local garda superintendent, and the club began from there.

The first task was to source a ground, and the club captain nominated at that first gathering, Gerry Slattery, happened to be an auctioneer. Slattery sourced ten acres for sale that he believed would be good ground for a pitch and the new secretary of the new club contacted the IRFU, which, rather than lend money to the unknown entity of a fledgling club, instead bought seven acres and gave the club permission to use it as their pitches. In fact, the Leinster Branch junior committee, with a view to expanding the game and an eye on the future, strongly lobbied for the IRFU to buy up land and lease it back to clubs to provide permanency for provincial teams.[23]

Gorey were arguably ahead of the curve when, in 1976, they appointed Sheila Stephens secretary, the first female secretary of a rugby club in all of Ireland. The local paper, *The Echo*, also played an important role, as it was there that the club placed its ads (including a large one for the reorganisation public meeting in 1968) and important notices for social nights that helped raise funds, attract interest and recruit players. By the 1980s Gorey was strong enough to field two teams, and with better facilities, better organisation in terms of fixtures, better training and more interest in rugby more generally, the game in the southeast was quite strong.[24]

Explorations of clubs like Longford and Gorey paint a picture of how provincial rugby in Leinster developed and progressed via the dedication and hard work of community volunteers and rugby enthusiasts. As a game with a reputation in Leinster of being aloof and reserved, these clubs' stories might sound more familiar to anyone who knows what it takes to organise and look after a local club in sport, or any other group leisure activity for that matter.

Several other rugby clubs were established in the 1960s and 1970s, each with a unique foundational story. In the 1960s Portlaoise (1966), Wicklow (1961) and the Garda RFC (1964) were founded. The Garda RFC was apparently the brainchild of some players out of Pearse Street, Dublin, but today the club identifies with their clubhouse's locale as Garda-Westmanstown RFC, scooping up players from the surrounding areas of Lucan, Leixlip, Dunboyne, Clonsilla, Castleknock and Blanchardstown to supplement the police officers who play rugby. As for Portlaoise, the club came together after the Rathdowney RFC had folded and rugby enthusiasts in the area in and around Portlaoise recognised that there was enough of a cohort to

THE PHOENIX RISES FROM ITS ASHES
By Pat Fitzgerald

IT IS generally accepted that Rugby was played in Longford before the start of the present century. Although this is not at all well documented there are still people alive who can remember their fathers being involved in Longford Rugby before the dawn of the 20th century. We have to wait until around 1920 until statistical evidence is available of the rugby life of County Longford. From the early part of this century until the late Sixties Rugby Activities were largely of a "Stop-Go" situation. This will have been written about by people with greater knowledge of that era than this scribe so we shall try and confine ourselves to the present area of "Oval Ball Activities" in and around Longford.

The "Present Era" began in 1967. A number of young Longford Rugby players had played with near neighbours Mullingar and were enjoying their rugby so much that they decided that the Longford Club should be revived. The younger men in question were Warren Turner, Paddy Quinn, Noel Harney and Derick Turner who regularly turned out for the Westmeath Club. They were backed by men of great experience like Pearse McInerney, Syl Higgins, Kevin McNichols and Charles Halligan. Bridging the gap between the old and the young were enthusiasts like David Pearse and Dougie McCormack. So it would seem that in 1967 Longford R.F.C. were very close to having the perfect blend of personnel to once again embark on an adventure into the worthwhile world of rugby.

"3-9-1967' — DAY OF DESTINY

Sunday, the 3rd of September 1967, witnessed the dawn of a new era for Longford. On that auspicious day another saga of rugby in this county commenced. The newly formed Longford played fellow rugby enthusiasts Mullingar in their first game and won 13-0. The *Longford Leader* records this with a graphic account of the game and a picture of that historic first day. The players on that day were: Warren Turner (Capt.), Paddy Fallon, Paddy Quinn, Maurice Battye, Andy McKeon, Ronnie Denniston, Robert Farrell, Dougie McCormack, Chad Farrell, Noel Harney, Frank Quinn, Pat Higgins, David Timlin, Derick Turner and Martin Evans. Paddy Fallon opened the scoring with a penalty. Paddy Quinn and Derick Turner scored a try each with

Fallon converting Turner's try to give Longford their 13 points. So the revived rugby infant was again launched on the rocky road of Leinster Rugby. We shall dwell a little longer on the formative year of this September foundling.

1st SEASON FOR NEW LONGFORD R.F.C.

During that first memorable season Longford played 21 games as well as two local matches — a Colours game between 2 home sides and a St. Stephen's Day Charity Game against the Soccer Club. They won 6, drew 1 and lost the remainder. The first year was a definite struggle for survival and a fight to procure and hold players in the club. This fact is borne out by the changes in personnel in the team from Sunday to Sunday. Each match saw the appearance of new names on the team sheet. The first games were against Mullingar (already mentioned), Navan, Tullamore, Wilson's Hospital, Athy, Athlone, Monkstown, Edenderry, St. Mary's. New players were seen each Sunday — names like R. Flower, R. Cleary, J. Quinn, O. Killian, R. McCann, D. Pearse, M. Mackreal, S. Whyte, L. Farrell, C. Farrell, T. Perm, M. Kennedy, T. Holmes, R. Hackett, D. Ghee, P. Townsend, C. McEvoy, Patrick Quinn (as distinct from Paddy), J. Bradshaw, N. Kennedy.

Longford Cup Team in their first year of the revived Club.
Back Row (left to right): *Pearse McInerney (Coach); Louis Belton; Patrick Quinn; Con Boyle; Noel Harney; Owen Maloney; John Bradshaw; David Timlin.*
Front (left to right): *Derick Turner; Paddy Quinn; Oliver Killian; Warren Turner (Capt.); Raymond Hackett; Harry Smith; Dougie McCormack.*

▲ Revival of Longford Rugby Club story by Pat Fitzgerald (who became the first IRFU president affiliated with a Leinster Junior Club) in the programme for Wolfhounds v. Longford President's XV, printed for the official opening of Longford RFC ground and pavilion in 1979.

enable them to form their own club. By 1971 the club was in a healthy position, to the extent that it was able to purchase almost twenty acres in Togher, organise a couple of pitches and, more importantly, set down permanent roots, which other clubs in Leinster had previously struggled to do, leading to their demise. Portlaoise went from strength to strength, following the zeitgeist during the 1970s of investing in its youth teams and bringing generations of players from underage through to the adult teams.

Records from 1963 document that a 'meeting was held in Wicklow [town] on Friday night for the purpose of forming a rugby club. There was an excellent attendance. The club has applied to the IRFU for membership and it is hoped to participate in the Provincial Towns cup this year.'[25] The new Wicklow RFC secured a friendly match to ascertain its potential against a team from Bray, and an 11–6 win boded well for the nascent club. Wicklow was one of the clubs that began on that shaky platform of not having a ground of its own and it was almost a decade before a field was secured, which was in fact the club's eleventh 'home' venue. It was the security of having a permanent pitch that enabled Leinster rugby clubs to progress, along with the commitment and passion from volunteer groups of enthusiasts to pull the clubs along. When, in 1976, Wicklow managed to build its clubhouse, attention could then be turned to growing the number of teams and improving the facilities as needed. The club swelled the number of the Leinster Branch's affiliated clubs at senior and junior levels to over forty, just the fifth additional club since the end of the Second World War. But, with five more clubs added in the last few years of the 1960s alone, the Branch was in a relatively healthy place.

Interprovincials

While the Leinster club game progressed, the standout stories relating to the interprovincial competition reflect the political realities of the era. Leinster's annual games with Ulster were dominated by questions of player safety at the height of the Northern Ireland Troubles. As early as 1964, there were regular discussions about the safety of traveling north for matches, among both Leinster clubs and the interprovincial sides. One example relates to a letter sent by Leinster requesting from a Belfast hotel a 'personal guarantee of supervision for the Leinster party'. This request was declined, so the booking was cancelled and the Branch was on the lookout for a different hotel. Indeed, the 'new norm' throughout the Troubles was for Leinster teams to travel north on the morning of a match in Belfast, never the

▲ Front cover of the programme for the Wolfhounds v. Longford President's XV match, which marked the official opening of
Longford RFC ground and pavilion in 1979.

night before. Rules stipulated that Leinster club teams and the interprovincial sides should only travel as a party and never leave the party 'under any circumstances', and all teams should return south the evening after a match concluded.[26]

By May 1971 Branch members were bringing up questions of how the rugby world might help influence and dampen down the situation of growing violence that existed in Northern Ireland. Leinster clubs offered their northern counterparts games, and vice versa. However, in the former instance, the Ulster Branch sent a confidential letter to their Leinster counterparts to make sure that any Leinster club traveling north only came by train, had a meeting party organised and left for home the same evening.[27] Then, following Bloody Sunday in January 1972, the Leinster Branch had to carefully consider whether touring British clubs should be advised to stay away, as well as whether to advise Leinster clubs to end fixtures up north. The conclusion was that the Branch should encourage games to continue but make it clear that touring clubs should carefully decide among themselves whether they wanted to take the risk. In the immediate aftermath of Bloody Sunday, the Branch issued a press release to let the media and the public know that they had

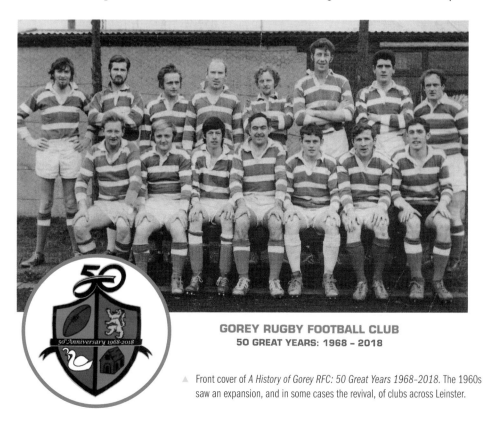

GOREY RUGBY FOOTBALL CLUB
50 GREAT YEARS: 1968 – 2018

▲ Front cover of *A History of Gorey RFC: 50 Great Years 1968-2018*. The 1960s saw an expansion, and in some cases the revival, of clubs across Leinster.

▲ A 1961–2 Leinster squad before a game.

mandated a minute's silence before all rugby games following the events in Derry. Tellingly, the gesture caused outrage among the Ulster rugby contingent.[28] Safety concerns continued throughout the 1970s, as did perpetual efforts not to offend Ulster unionists.[29]

Leinster's records against the other provinces were more easily focused on the field of play, and there were at least fifteen games each against Munster and Connacht from the 1959–60 season up to and including 1973–74. Leinster's return was eight wins and seven losses against Munster, with twelve wins over Connacht. That translated into only thirteen losses in forty-five games. It was with that record in mind that Branch administrators appealed for matches against international touring teams, suggesting that visiting countries would want the toughest tests available, and Leinster was the team to offer that hard examination. The desire for more international opposition was also a reflection of the times. Commercial air travel had a great impact across the globe in the post-Second World War era, and in Ireland's case it was during the 1960s especially that people began to make use of more affordable travel opportunities, spurred by airline growth and competition. This was a technological change that seamlessly became part of the tradition of the rugby tour, which had a big impact on the Irish game. For Leinster rugby it was the prospect of tough, potentially world-class opposition that the 'jet age' seemed to promise.

The first ever Leinster fifteen match (although the team was a County Dublin team, with players from Dublin clubs only) to be played in France was in 1949, enabled thanks to the opportunities of commercial flight. More opportunities to fly allowed teams to undertake tours more easily from the 1950s, and in 1958 Leinster once more flew to France. This time a Leinster selection played in Toulouse. The series lasted a decade, until 1968, with the French team playing in Dublin twice, in 1964 and 1966.[30] The popularity of a French tour was aided by airline travel because it did not burden players by taking up too much of their time in an amateur era where jobs had to be factored in. The particulars of these new tours, however, continued to show that rugby's constituents were, as yet, from a relatively well-to-do socioeconomic elite. For instance, in the 1970s the Terenure College club were raising money to further develop and build onto their facilities. At the same time, they managed a tour to Bermuda in May 1975 – a sign of the rapid development in airline expansion, but one that also speaks to the significant wealth of those involved with that club.[31]

Apart from the opportunities for clubs to travel far and wide for tours, in the 1970s Leinster managed to secure games against international touring sides, with the most excitement aways focused on the southern-hemisphere teams. Leinster played New Zealand twice, losing quite heavily in 1972 but putting up a better performance in 1974, when they were only beaten by eight points to three. Leinster also played Fiji in 1973, winning easily by thirty points to nine, and Argentina in 1978, being comprehensively beaten by the South Americans. Regardless, Leinster rugby was moving with the times, which would give it an important flexibility once the brave new world of professional rugby arose in the mid-1990s.

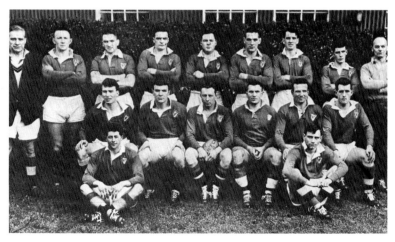

▲ A 1961 Leinster team that played South Africa. From the 1960s to the 1980s, Leinster and the IRFU fiercely defended playing against a boycotted South African rugby team in the midst of anti-apartheid protests, to which the Branch and the IRFU turned a deaf ear.

9

Leinster Rugby, New Foundations

1970s Flourish

To try to modernise the Leinster Branch's approach to rugby, a recommendation was made in the 1960s that the minor and provincial town categories be abolished and that all clubs below senior level should be designated junior clubs and organised into leagues: Junior One (J1), Junior Two (J2), Junior Three (J3) and so on. The 1970s then saw some reinvention. To help prepare for the challenges ahead with the growth of the game across the province, the Branch executive was advised to organise three specialist subcommittees. It was in the details of how the Branch began to restructure, with designated tasks and detailed planning to achieve those tasks being laid out by and for each committee, that the sense of organisation and hard work involved, alongside the commitment to ensure rugby maintained a healthy progression, can be seen.[1] Thus, there was an elaborate organisation mapped out, one that perhaps hints at a developing professionalism for the Branch among the mindset of some of those involved in Leinster rugby.

As well as control of policymaking and management of the Branch, which was designated to the executive committee and the three working subcommittees, the administrators and all members from senior, junior and youth rugby were responsible for working towards the ten objectives of the Branch. These objectives were:

1.   To encourage the playing of Rugby in Leinster.
2.   To ensure that adequate facilities are available for persons willing to play Rugby in the Provinces.
3.   To ensure that the standard of the Game at all levels within the Province should continue to improve.
4.   To make the necessary arrangements for Branch Representative Matches at all levels.
5.   To obtain as much publicity for the game in the Province as is practicable.
6.   To represent the views of the Executive Committee to the I.R.F.U. and vice versa.
7.   To ensure that Leinster shall make a leading contribution to the good of Rugby Football in Ireland.
8.   To work with the other Provinces in Ireland to ensure the growth and success of the I.R.F.U. and Rugby in Ireland.
9.   To liaise and consult with other sporting organizations within the Province in the interests of Rugby and sports in general.
10. To provide an Administrative and Financial Structure capable of realising these objectives.[2]

The efforts to attain these objectives can be traced in various guises, with various levels of failure and success, when studying decisions made and their outcomes recorded in each Leinster Branch end-of-season honorary secretary report throughout the decades.

In the ten years from 1962 to 1972 there had been a vast increase in the numbers of players and in people interested in the rugby game. As of the 1979–80 season, there were sixteen senior clubs, thirty-one J1 clubs, seven J2 clubs, fifteen J3 clubs and forty-four schools officially affiliated to the Leinster Branch.[3] The Branch regularly reviewed its situation and, as of its 1979 centenary year, concluded that there would be an increase in urban populations across Leinster throughout the 1980s, which should translate into even more rugby clubs. It also mentioned the desire to have senior clubs outside of Dublin for two central reasons: to increase the appeal of the game across the province and to give the best players outside the capital an opportunity to reach senior representative level. A Leinster committee suggested that there should be a clear pathway laid out for every club, showing the route they needed to follow to progress to the highest ranking in the Branch structure. With that in mind, the Branch published guidelines for clubs who wanted to be considered for senior status.

▲ Leinster Branch Executive Committee on the occasion of its 100th-year anniversary, 1979.

There was some disagreement in Leinster circles about the issue of senior status. While the representatives of the junior clubs advocated for a clear structure to help determine a pathway to senior status, the old senior clubs jealously guarded that designation and pushed back against most proposals (especially league-format ideas that would include promotion and relegation). Indeed, a clear snobbishness in Leinster rugby circles was demonstrated when some articulated a disdain at the democratisation of the rugby game and the prospect of a 'non-traditional' club being able to achieve senior status. Eventually, the Branch proposed a pathway for a maximum of three junior clubs to gain senior status by winning the J1 League, to join the thirteen senior clubs then in existence, in order to maintain that exclusivity. The intimation and the argument was that there should not be any more than sixteen senior clubs, period.

At the same time the Branch maintained the right to adjudge whether or not any other junior clubs, if they applied, would be allowed senior status. In such a scenario, if it meant that the number of senior clubs would exceed the maximum of sixteen that the Branch had mandated, there would be criteria applied to ascertain if the junior club was eligible for senior rugby. If so, then a judgement would be made about which of the three newest clubs to gain senior status would have to be demoted back to junior status. It was a convoluted approach to ensure that 'traditional' senior clubs retained a level of exclusivity and power. Rather than countenance such a thing as a league-based system, where promotion and relegation was based purely on merit, instead the Branch rolled out subjective criteria, including judgements by the executive about 'the probable benefit to the game in the province as a whole',[4] for allowing a particular club senior status. Critics wondered why a more equitable league system could not be utilised, but the idea of it produced a whole series of denunciations and was avoided at this stage of Leinster rugby's progression.

In the meantime, in an attempt to dispel the criticism of favouritism when defining which clubs could be senior and which should remain junior, the Branch demarcated protocols when adjudging applications for senior status:

(a) Playing strength and record. (b) Membership – playing and non-playing. (c) Facilities, grounds and premises. (d) Financial situation – actual and potential. (e) Club administration – capabilities in terms of Senior status. (f) The needs of rugby in the Province as laid down in the branch objectives. (g) Particular attention should be paid to: (i) growth area of population and their effects on the type of Club required in these areas; (ii) potential increase in playing membership of the Club concerned; (iii) The past and future contributions of the Club to rugby football in general, including its production of referees, coaches and administrators.[5]

The above criteria were to be used to assess clubs on their application for senior status but were also meant to act as a kind of report card, applicable to a newly promoted club's first five years at senior level.

Remembering that prior to 1971 the majority of games outside of knockout cup competitions were 'friendlies', the major change that came about was the decision to run a Senior League, but one without relegation or promotion. The Branch ended up with the somewhat convoluted league structure that ensured the thirteen senior clubs retained their senior status. What's more, Skerries and Greystones had been promised senior club status, largely based on their network of connections to the senior clubs and the Branch itself, it seems. While Skerries, in fairness, had a decent enough record in the PTC to warrant their application (eleven wins in thirteen finals between 1940 and 1980), Greystones had never won the Metropolitan Cup and had only one league win in the same period.

International Meat Packers R.F.C.
Winners of Dublin Business Houses Cup 1971

Standing: P. Moody, J Malone, T. Hayes, T. Martin, J. Barry, F. McDonnell, P. Cremin, R. Fallon, P. Gibbons, T.J. Whelan.
Front: B. Connaughton, J. Whelan, S. O'Byrne, M. Fahy, E. Fitzgerald (Captain), P. Breslin, A. Lyons, P. Lennon,
Absent: P. S. Hession (Chairman), T. Clothier, J. Holbrook, P. Gregan, T. Collins, R. Kinahan, L. Kehoe, D. Byrne and K. Toner

Barnhall's favourite playing memory of the early years came in 1971, just two years after its foundation.

At that stage it was still the IMP team. A hundred per cent were employees of the firm, it was not till decline set in at IMP that the membership profile changed and by the mid-eighties only 10% were employees. "We had enormous loyalty", recalled Eddie Fitzgerald.

The side surprised everyone when it won the Dublin Business Houses competition in 1971. Currently, Kevin Corcoran is planning an anniversary gathering of that team. It scored sixty points in seven games to take that title with kicker Holbrook getting 33 of them, one try, eight penalties and three conversions. IMP dispatched ESB 11-3 at home in the first round. Next round they were away to Brooks Thomas and won 16-5. Guinness proved stouter opposition. After extra time in the third round away the sides were level at fourteen points each. The replay was at home and IMP won 6-3. The side drilled through their next quarry

The 1971 Irish Meatpackers RFC team (today's MU Barnhall RFC).

Regardless, these clubs would not be included in the fixtures until the 1981–82 season, in a proposed Leinster Branch Senior League system revamp. The revamp details proposed the following:

> (1) The League should be divided into three sections – two sections of four teams each, and one section of five teams. (2) Each Club should play one match against each other Club in its section, two league points awarded for a win and one point for a draw. (3) In the event of two or more Clubs in a section having an equal number of League points, ties should be played to ascertain the winner of the section. (4) The winners of the two four teams sections should play a match to decide which team would contest the League Final with the winners of the five team section. (5) To ensure that each Club should have a home match against the other Club in its section, the sections would be redrawn every two years.[6]

The proposal was rejected by the senior clubs, however, who cited their commitments to long-standing UK fixtures and said that there was no room in the calendar for such an extended league. What one can see in all of this was that, alongside the desire and impetus for change, the senior clubs in Leinster were reluctant to alter their ways. Changes in the rugby world, then, threw up perhaps unexpected tensions and resistances that needed careful yet tough negotiation.

Player Welfare

As far back as May 1975, the Leinster Branch had called a special meeting to discuss the findings of a Medical Congress organised to discuss injuries related to the game of rugby. One of the first recommendations was that adequate injury insurance must be arranged by the Branch to cover all potential injury outcomes, and also that insurance be made compulsory for all clubs and players. It was mandated that all grounds across Leinster should have their own small treatment area fully equipped for injured players, and the Branch was advised to organise an education scheme to inform club members of rudimentary first-aid methodologies. It was also hoped that all games would have a medical professional in attendance, although this was a more difficult request to manage. The advice was to work closely with the various ambulance and medical services such as Malta, Red Cross and St John's to supplement Leinster rugby's own medical volunteers.[7] At the beginning of the 1975–76 season, the Branch began to send out letters to encourage teams to sign up for insurance schemes for their players. While this indicates a change in attitudes towards player welfare, it undoubtedly speaks to a change in culture across Ireland too. It was also a tacit admittance that rugby was a very physical and, at times, dangerous game, despite previous deflections about the nature of rugby injuries.[8]

Disconcertingly and somewhat extraordinarily, during the 1979–80 season five players in Leinster club rugby suffered catastrophic injuries and were incapacitated for life. In response it was proposed in July 1980 that a permanent Leinster Branch fund be established as soon as possible, recommended by Mr Heffernan of Skerries, who added that one of those injured and permanently paralysed was an eighteen-year-old Skerries player who would need to be supported for the rest of his life.[9] A central charity was needed to deal with issues like catastrophic injury from playing rugby. Until that central fund was in place, it was incumbent upon rugby clubs to ask their players to donate to drives orchestrated to help severely injured players.[10] In November 1980, the IRFU laid out a plan for a charitable fund into which all clubs would be expected to make a minimum contribution over a two-year period, so that the fund would reach £250,000.[11] As the popularity of rugby continued to increase, player welfare became more and more important for the clubs themselves, as articulated at Branch meetings as well as at the IRFU level, in order to assuage fears about serious injuries, fears that might turn players away, and also to pre-empt potential litigiousness when inevitable injury did occur.

Another signal of the changing face of rugby at this time was evidenced by the introduction of more direct sponsorship of games themselves – a reflection of the times and a reflection of a modernising Ireland. For instance, talks of jersey sponsorship, match-day sponsorship and, indeed, sponsorship for social events became mundane. While advertisements had been around in match-day programmes and tied to announcements of games and game results in newspapers for a long time hence, from the 1970s onwards there is a much more conspicuous infiltration of direct sponsorship of teams or games. Corporate sponsorship was becoming an important factor in all sports, and rugby built up relationships with relative ease. In a forward-thinking initiative, agreement was reached with clubs to allow them accept sponsorship, with Branch pre-approval, as of December 1976.[12]

Rugby's Expansion Endures

The increasing popularity of rugby at junior level, with new clubs and increasing numbers of players joining teams, meant that a restructuring of junior rugby was pressing. Clubs that affiliated to the Branch in the 1970s included New Ross (1970), Tullow (1972), Stillorgan (1973), Clondalkin (1973), Ashbourne (1974), Portarlington (1974), Rathdrum (1975), Cill Dara (1976), Athboy (1978) and the re-affiliation of Malahide (1979). In the 1973–74 season, the Junior League was subdivided yet again, this time into four sections between nineteen teams. The J1 League, which had been reorganised in 1972 initially for the metropolitan-based teams only, invited the J1-level provincial town clubs back in during the 1974–75 season and expanded to a whopping thirty-eight teams from nineteen clubs, divided into six sections. It had reached forty-two teams in eight sections by the 1975–76 season, confirming Leinster rugby's popularity. With this, the Junior League was expanded to become a more inclusive competition than its earlier iteration, which was changed within the first decade of its commencement from a competition to

▲ Leinster Schools Rugby Cup programme, prominently sponsored by Coca-Cola.

▲ The Leinster Branch 'Coca-Cola' Senior Schools Cup trophy. High-profile sponsorships became a common feature in Leinster rugby, from the 1980s especially.

any junior club in Leinster, to become only open to Leinster metropolitan-based junior teams (basically the second teams of senior clubs). The Junior League here became, once again, more inclusive by amalgamating the second XVs of senior clubs, the junior metropolitan clubs and provincial town clubs into an inclusive, province-wide structure. At the same time several new competitions and cups were specifically designed to cater for the metropolitan clubs at the junior level, with at least eleven contests. Indeed, rugby was being played to such an extent in Leinster that the Branch did not quite have the capacity to administer to everyone at all levels, but it was wily enough to at least try and keep an eye on what was happening in the name of rugby in the province. Thus, there was an acknowledgement of unofficial games that were going on, the fifteen-a-side competitions not officially sanctioned by the Branch (e.g. the Hospitals' Cup, the Business Houses Cup and club-based tournaments such as Blackrock FC's Castle Trophy) but, nonetheless, given its blessing.

Some of these competitions had a particularly interesting longevity and/or have long been important to the game of rugby in Leinster in some way or another. The most notable cup competition that came under the 'unofficial' title was the

▲ Leinster club rugby try-scoring action (unidentified teams) from the 1980s.

▲ Leinster club rugby action from the 1980s – getting the pass away.

Hospitals' Cup, which has had a distinctively long history. A Hospitals' Football Union and a cup championship was created in the 1880s so that the various doctors could put together teams to compete against one another, and the games were often played to raise money for charity.[13] The medical community in Dublin had always been central to the popularisation of rugby and was almost as important as the schools. Indeed, the correlation between the medical profession and rugby in the earliest days can be seen by the fact that '[o]f the first 200 players capped for Ireland, 44 were medical students or doctors, many of whom had trained in Dublin hospitals'.[14] When DUFC formed in 1854, their initial internally organised games started a tradition of a medical students team turning out to play some other combination from the club, like teams from other departments (e.g. Physics) and other TCD social clubs (e.g. the boat club). When they qualified, the doctors went to work in various Dublin hospitals and the rugby tradition among medical personnel continued. A Dublin United Hospitals football club was formed, often fielding a team for trial matches to help select the Leinster interprovincial squad up to the 1930s. But it was in 1881 that the Dublin Hospitals Football Union was created and 'organised the running of the Dublin Hospitals Cup competition',[15] which has become one of the longest-running cup competitions and is still played in Leinster today.

Given the socioeconomic realities of the medical professional class in Leinster, the correlation between doctors and rugby often reinforced particular stereotypes about who rugby was open to. To attend medical school in the first place generally required attendance at one of the private Dublin secondary schools and a legacy of inheritance among the Irish medical profession was also replicated in rugby, where sons followed their father's footsteps. What's more, in order to ensure that only those of a 'suitable' background played rugby for the hospitals – i.e. doctors and not porters – the rules for hospitals' rugby stated that, to be allowed play in the Hospitals' Cup, players must be 'resident qualified' and not merely hospital staff. In more recent years, of course, the medical field and those playing hospitals' rugby have become much more diverse, especially in terms of foreign doctors from around the world coming to Leinster to study or to work and being recruited to the rugby team. There has also been a regular crossover of GAA-playing doctors, who took up rugby with their medical peers and colleagues both during their studies and throughout their careers.

The Hospitals' Cup competition retained great interest from rugby fans and was played in the autumn and early winter of each season, occupying the calendar during the period when, prior to the introduction of the first Leinster Branch-organised clubs' proto-league in the 1970s, clubs only had friendly matches. Moreover, the standard was generally of high quality, often attributed to the fact that medical students and young trainee doctors populating the hospital teams were in their prime. What's more, 'full-time students had the freedom to train and work at their sport, not afforded to other players in permanent employment. This gave the medical students an opportunity to impress the all-important rugby selectors with the hope of playing representative rugby for their province and country.'[16]

It was the consolidation of the training hospitals in Dublin that saw something of a break in the hospitals' rugby tradition, as some of the old institutions were combined into newer affiliated hospitals and indeed the colleges had to amalgamate as well, reducing the number of teams. The introduction of a Leinster League competition for the Leinster rugby clubs in the 1971–72 season also impacted on the hospitals, as many players opted to prioritise club rugby over the Hospitals' Cup. It took a reorganisation in 1984, including playing the Hospital Cup

▲ UCD RFC game action photo, 1981 match – getting the pass away.

186

final under floodlights, to help reawaken interest and inspire interhospital and training-college rivalries again. Importantly, in the era of corporate sponsorship in a sporting context, the influx of pharmaceutical sponsors for the competition also helped. Further reorganisation with a round-robin format in the early 2000s further reinvigorated the Hospitals' Cup, ensuring more games for teams, which inspired more commitment from players.

John Robbie in action for Leinster, getting his kick away; photo from the 1980s.

Other innovative, unofficial, Leinster-based competitions included the Castle Trophy, established in 1966 by Blackrock College RFC. In the early part of the season, the club held a rugby festival open to teams from around the world who wished to compete, to help their players ease back into competitive rugby. The Oval Trophy, first organised for the 1968–69 season, was a cup for which the provincial town junior clubs could challenge. The winners of Provincial Town Cup competitions (or their equivalents) from the four provincial branches would compete for the Oval. The Unidare Trophy was another example, which was played for by the Dublin business houses. It was initially organised by seven business-based teams,[17] but it was open to any firms that had their headquarters in Dublin, including state/semi-state bodies. The rules stated that the teams were to be comprised of only full-time employees who resided in Dublin at least during the working week from Monday to Friday. Its first year was 1960, with seven teams entered, and ESB were the first winners. The Leinster Branch also acknowledged, but did not officially oversee, cup competitions by region. Thus, the McGowan Cup catered for North Leinster; the Hosie Cup catered for the North Midlands; the Midland's League was a competition for a trophy donated by Tullamore for clubs in Laois, Offaly, Westmeath and Longford; and the Southeast League was a competition for clubs in Wicklow, Wexford, Kilkenny and Carlow. This plethora of competitions emphasises rugby's growing appeal and the interest of ordinary Leinster sports fans looking for regular events in which to participate or watch.

Leinster's Schools Scene

In the four decades from 1930 through to 1969, there were forty Senior Schools Cup finals, with only seven different schools winning. Of those seven schools, Blackrock College dominated with twenty-three wins (six each in the 1930s, 1940s and 1950s, and five in the 1960s); the team were also twice runners-up. The next closest school was Castleknock, who managed to win a total of six cups and were runners-up eight times in forty years. Belvedere College won four times and lost seven finals in those four decades; St Mary's won three cups all in the 1960s (1961, 1966 and 1969); Terenure won two, the first in 1952, the second in 1958, which bookended a Blackrock five-in-a-row (1953–57) winning streak. Presentation Bray (1932) and Newbridge (1941) were the only two schools outside of Dublin to win the cup in those decades, managing one each. The Schools Cup was celebrated among a very concentrated rugby cohort in Leinster, as the evidence shows, making it the most exclusive example of how rugby in the province remained largely closed off to most of the population. It has been cited as the pinnacle of a rugby player's career time and again, often by the biggest names in Leinster rugby, yet it meant nothing to anyone unassociated with the private school system. One area where Leinster rugby still cannot deflect accusations of exclusivity is in the structures of the Schools Cup competition.

From the 1940s through to the 1990s and into the professional era, debates arose about the direction in which rugby was going. Rugby journalists like P.D. MacWeeney often despaired at the expansion of the senior competition. Under one opening season headline he claimed that there were 'Too Many Senior Rugby Clubs in Dublin'. MacWeeney argued that 'an important reason for the poor quality … of the play was the large number of senior clubs in Dublin. A city of this size cannot possibly support twelve senior teams of genuine ability, and the yearly supply of newcomers from the schools is far too thin to be spread out among so many clubs.'[18] That there was an over-reliance on the private schools for players to supply the senior ranks was recognised by MacWeeney and many others in Leinster, yet it would never be countenanced that the solution might be to expand the pool of recruits beyond fee-paying schools. For all of its progress, Leinster rugby has long retained a class-defined blind spot. Of all the things that have helped ensure this, the pedestalling of the Senior Schools Cup competition by those in control of rugby in Leinster has been the most important.

In contrast, when the area leagues were set up and the competitiveness of rugby in provincial towns inevitably increased, interest among locals who wanted to join up and play for local rugby teams grew accordingly. The recruitment drive for rugby players started in the schoolboys' section, with Carlow RFC exemplifying that in the mid-1960s. As the team regularly brought home silverware in the southeast section, they expanded and developed the club with the future in mind. Thus, Carlow reached out to the local, state-run schools to entice anyone who was interested to come down and try out at their newly constructed pavilion and improved playing fields. The success of Carlow can partly be attributed to the introduction of rugby into local schools, which influenced young boys to continue after their school days in their home-town club. It was a model of success that one might presume would inspire others, yet expanding the game among Leinster's youth outside of private schools was yet to be seriously considered by the executives within the Leinster Branch.

▲ UCD RFC 1972–3,
Metropolitan Cup
winners, 1972.

▶ Gorey's 1973–4 Towns
Cup team togged
out for a match v.
Longford.

Instead, it was decided by the Branch that there should be a competition organised to maintain the interest and motivation of privately schooled boys who did not make it onto their Schools Senior Cup team. To ensure as many 'rugby schools' boys as possible were facilitated to play the game, a Section 'B' school's competition was introduced, creating a competition for second teams. These second teams, from the strongest rugby schools, played the first teams of the schools in Section 'A', composed of the so-called weaker schools of the Senior Schools Cup. 'In the first year of the Competition, 1966–67, sixteen teams entered. It was won by Blackrock College. Since then, the number of schools entering one or more teams has increased.'[19] In 1978 an old cup was recycled and presented as a perpetual trophy for the winners of what had been named the Schools' Seconds League competition – it was an old seven-a-side competition cup called the Evening Mail Cup, dating back to 1927. Promoting the idea of reaching a wider pool of players through the national school system was not considered in any great depth by the Branch executive at this stage. Being made up primarily of ex-'rugby schools' students, the executive still retained a particular view of the pathway to senior rugby directly connected to the private school system.

▲ 11 May 2011: the Enniscorthy squad celebrate with the plate after the Provincial Towns Plate final in which they defeated Ashbourne, Naas RFC. © Barry Cregg/Sportsfile

A pass from Downes during a Blackrock schools' game. The Leinster rugby schools' competition has consistently generated large interest among its own cohort.

Ulster Schools scrum-half, Mark Hyland, gets the ball away during the interprovincial against Leinster Schools, in Donnybrook, on Saturday. — (Photograph: Paddy Whelan)

Newspaper coverage of Leinster v. Ulster schools' game. Interprovincial games at schools' level offered an incentive for rugby growth, growing interest and improvement.

Strong finish gives Leinster win

LEINSTER SCHOOLS 24
ULSTER SCHOOLS............12

SCHOOLS' RUGBY

TWELVE POINTS in the closing quarter of an hour by the Leinster Schools yielded a winning dividend against Ulster at Donnybrook on Saturday and gave the Leinster boys a 24-12 success. The win thus sets up a confrontation with Munster in Cork on Thursday week that will decide the championship reports EDMUND van ESBECK.

If, in the end, a winning margin of such conclusive proportions did not do full justice to the challenge presented by the Ulster youngsters, Leinster did thoroughly deserve to win and had a depth of skill that their opponents did not have at their command.

It was a most enjoyable match, with the smog that enveloped the ground the only unsatisfactory feature.

Leinster went into the match

warm favourites and, in the end, there was a period before the interval and in a short period after the break when Ulster threatened a surprise. But two fine tries by the Leinster boys proved decisive and they were scores worthy of winning any match.

Leinster started as if they were going to win without any element of difficulty. They scored an excellent try in the fifth minute when Dermot Finnegan, a late replacement for Stephen Butler on the Leinster left wing, got in at the left corner after a fine break by David Herman, a centre of some quality. Outside half Paul Allen converted from the touchline and Leinster looked on their way.

In the initial stages they had much the better of matters with their pack the better ball winning unit. But Ulster, to their credit, settled and after the Leinster line had a fortunate escape, outside

half Niall Malone cut through the Leinster defence to score by the posts and he converted to make it 6-6.

The Ulster pack, with a lively back row, cut down the early superiority of the home side and Malone kicked a penalty goal to give his side the lead in the 20th minute. Then Allen dropped a goal for Leinster before Malone kicked a penalty to give Ulster a 12-9 interval lead.

Victor Costello, Leinster's big second row was effectively curbed for a period in the line-out and Malone was a threat to the Leinster side.

Allen kicked a great equalising penalty from over 40 yards in the seventh minute of the second half and, thereafter, Leinster always looked the side more likely to succeed. The general level of their back line play carried more menace and in scrum half Niall Hogan, they had a player, in a key position, who showed a keen awareness of his duties to serve his back line.

The Leinster scrum was steadier even if they could not

carve out any pronounced superiority in this area, but Costello won some very good line out possession as the match entered its crucial stage and it was then that Leinster got the winning scores.

Leinster regained the lead when full back John Dunne got in at the left corner after a good movement in which Herman and left wing Finnegan played key roles. Allen made amends for missing an easy penalty by converting off a point from the touchline. That score came 15 minutes from time.

LEINSTER: J Dunne (Belvedere); N Dunlea (Belvedere), D Herman (Roscrea), M Ridge (Blackrock), D Finnegan (Clongowes); P Allen (The High School), N Hogan (Terenure) capt; D Cole (The High School), I O'Kelly (St Paul's), M Ennis (Terenure), P Tarpey (Roscrea), V Costello (Blackrock), S Rooney (Mohan's) D Widger (St Mohan's), J Mion (Blackrock). Replacement: C O'Hora (St Gerard's) for Herman (72 minutes).

ULSTER: R Davidson (R S Dungannon), G McCluskey (Portadown), J Yarr (NIAA), S Mann (Bangor), G Anderson (Bangor); N Malone (MCB), M Hyland (Campsoul), K Martin (MCB), M Kennohan (RBAI), K McCartney (Omagh), F McBride (Coleraine), K Kirkpatrick (Sullivan Upper), N Lamont (Ballyclare), L Browne (R S Dungannon), N Lamont (Ballyclare). **Referee:** R McDowell (IMR).

The Birth of Youth Rugby

Away from the private schools, during the 1970s and 1980s a general uptick in rugby interest in a Leinster context was emanating from the forthright efforts of the junior rugby scene, especially in their attempts to solidify the popularity of the game by asking its administrators to create more competitive matches. One of the more significant proposed changes in Leinster rugby was the introduction of an under-nineteens Leinster junior rugby set-up, addressing a frequent complaint about the retention of young players. Seventeen- and eighteen-year-olds were being lost to rugby because, on leaving school, they were either not physically developed enough to join adult teams straightaway, they were simply not yet good enough to play adult rugby or they were frustrated at being asked to play their way up through the ranks on the lowest teams in minor or junior rugby when they wanted to play at a higher standard. It was, then, at the behest of Judge Conroy that for the 1968–69 season a new Leinster under-nineteen trial and representative structure was put in place.[20]

After a decade of under-nineteen rugby, the Branch received a committee report in 1978–79 that began with an explanation of the need to introduce the underage section. It is worth quoting this at length to understand the realisations at which the Branch committee was arriving. In terms of the under-nineteen team:

> Those responsible for its introduction felt that the drop-out rate at this age was too great ... The under 19 section offers a smooth transition from the comparatively sheltered schools rugby to the more complex and varied situation which obtains in most clubs. Boys have often found the change rather traumatic and many became frustrated and disillusioned. They came from a scene where they were 'the seniors' and looked up to by their younger colleagues, to find themselves 'small boys' again and struggling to gain paces on lower teams in our junior competitions. Our branch ... is still convinced of the value of this grade and has set up the machinery for the smooth running of our various competitions. Under 19 matters are the concern of the junior section of the branch ...[21]

One thing that seemed important was the need for a tour for the under-nineteens – a foreign fixture to ensure enough games on the one hand but, more interestingly, as the Leinster under-nineteen committee chairman Patrick Grace freely admitted,

▲ Leinster schools rugby squad 1979-80. Interprovincial schools games become an important annual feature for the Branches in identifying talent.

'Each season … "the away match" … [was] the "carrot" which enables committee, coach and players to bring the best out of all available resources (don't say that young fellows shouldn't need a "carrot" – they do, and so do old fellows). If the constantly recurring uncertainty could be removed, attractive fixtures could be arranged against worthy opposition.'[22] As it stood, club committees relied on generous sponsorship to produce the aforementioned 'carrot'. The under-nineteen committee at provincial level wanted the Branch to ensure and guarantee the tour and the finances for it, which it believed would be achieved through willing sponsorship once the permanency of the away fixture was announced.[23]

Even before Conroy set up the under-nineteen trials, at a gathering of the Leinster Branch executive in April 1964, Skerries, Navan, Delvin, Dundalk and Carlow representatives had been lobbying not only for schoolboy teams and competitions, but also for the Branch to start investing in youth coaches. These clubs had previously asked about entering their underage teams into the Senior and Junior Schools Cups but had been unceremoniously told that those competitions were reserved for the elite schools. That being the case they demanded more efforts to be made to commence some kind of competition for club youth sides.[24] A prime example of an initiative 'from below' – where those passionate about the game at the grassroots level implemented a strategy of enticing local youth into the game,

▲ Members of the Leinster Branch Referees Association who also refereed international matches.

indicating a way forward for Leinster rugby – is Balbriggan RFC's reawakening. It started with Kerry native Brendan Griffin, who had a rugby background from his time living in Kilkenny. When he arrived in the 1960s to teach at the National School in Balrothery, a tiny village adjacent to Balbriggan, Griffin found there was little or no space in the minuscule schoolyard for the pupils to play and practise kicking games, such as GAA or soccer. However, as rugby was a handling and passing game, he recognised that it would be a feasible sport for the children to play in their limited space. Rugby was taken to with such enthusiasm by the pupils that Griffin extended the practices outside of school hours, on Saturday mornings down on the beach. Soon, children from the other schools in the area started to turn up and the numbers grew. When rugby enthusiasts in Skerries learned about the games, a member of Skerries rugby, Jack Murphy, contacted Griffin to organise an under-twelve friendly match in 1967.[25]

While Griffin did not necessarily envision re-establishing a rugby club in the town, Tom Kettle did, and when the two met, Kettle became involved in the under-twelve's rugby coaching and Balbriggan was officially resurrected. With a new set of jerseys secured from the Balbriggan textile factory Smyth & Co., which had historical ties to the old club of the 1930s, and Kettle's understanding that the town had previous history with the game, he insisted on reinstating the old Balbriggan

▲ The expansion of cup competitions to all underage levels has proven a huge boon to rugby, e.g. the McGowan, the Furlong and the O'Daly are examples of three under-13 youth cups. © Eóin Noonan/Sportsfile

club. As Judge Conroy would remember, 'From this modest start, the Youth Rugby movement began to flourish, especially in the Provincial Clubs, with an increasing number of teams participating each season. The original pioneer organisers of these [Youth] Competitions were Tom O'Brien and Pat O'Mahony (Carlow), Michael Carron (Skerries) and Tom Kettle (Balbriggan).'[26] The first full fifteen-a-side game played by the reformed Balbriggan RFC was an under-fourteen fixture against the Mountjoy Marine School in September 1968. The work and persistence to make youth rugby a success, was exemplified by the fact that Kettle turned up to Branch Schools' section meetings, even though his team wasn't affiliated to a school. Nonetheless, he managed to secure fixtures for Balbriggan youths with school teams across Dublin. Apart from the games he organised (including games against Young Munster and schools in Belfast), Kettle managed to obtain enough schoolboys' tickets to bring his young charges to international matches at Lansdowne Road throughout the 1970s, feeding their enthusiasm and love for the game.[27]

The original under-twelve teams put together in 1968 by Griffin and Kettle proved that promotion of youth rugby was a strategy needed in Leinster. A large contingent of those first boys, and those in the year immediately behind them,

▲ There are two under-15 (McCauley, Conlon) and two under-14 (Coyle, Kettle) youth cup competitions for boys, which have long been a draw to youth rugby in Leinster.

led Balbriggan not only to the final of the inaugural under-seventeen Culliton Cup final, but also to the next three finals: they were runners-up in 1975 and 1976, and victorious in 1977.[28] More importantly, Balbriggan's 1977 Culliton Cup team were the core group that constituted the adult team over the next decade of Balbriggan rugby.[29] Balbriggan was also part of an under-twelve's competition held in 1968–69, the first officially recognised underage Leinster Branch competition since rugby's introduction to Ireland. The other three teams that competed were Skerries, Drogheda and Carlow.[30] Meanwhile, Tom Kettle became the first honorary secretary of the Branch's youth subcommittee, and it was his advocacy for community rugby that led the Branch to initiate the under-seventeen Culliton Cup as the premier youth competition in the province, with the threshold later extended to under-eighteens.

Overall, the drive to cement the place of underage rugby across the province was one of the more important developments for Leinster, starting with the idea of coaching courses in the 1960s with youth teams in mind, to the commencement of mini-rugby initiatives and the idea of disseminating a booklet to all the clubs with guidance for teaching young children and teenagers the basics of rugby.[31] Mini-

▲ As well as under-13, -14, and -15 cup competitions for boys, there are also the Culliton under-17, the Tom D'Arcy under-18 and Sean Stratton under-18 competitions.

▲ In the underage girls game there are league and cup competitions at Under-14, -16 and -18 levels, including the Noleen Spain Cup, first awarded in 2019.

rugby had first appeared as early as the 1960s, through Suttonians RFC, which ran an under-nine's competition, the Cripps Trophy. While it started out for the first few years as a fifteen-a-side competition, the organisers soon realised that the teams needed to be smaller, and it became a seven-a-side game. Any club was allowed to enter a team and the idea of the minis became a grassroots initiative that was later adopted and adapted by the Branch. One of its more progressive pronouncements, from August 1977, was the junior committee's decision not just to produce a guide for starting mini rugby, but to send a copy to every single Leinster club by the end of that month.

By the time of the Branch's 1983 AGM, the momentum of youth rugby was being acknowledged and a plea to keep on developing it was made. With as many as forty-three youth teams involved in underage fixtures, the committee asked the clubs for more joined-up thinking and a readjustment of structures so as to track youth development and ensure the underage scene was a fully integrated part of all Leinster clubs.[32] Along with the growing recognition of the importance of the youth system within junior rugby, the under-eighteen Culliton Cup and under-fourteen cup competitions were proving very successful. However, there was a need to fill in the gap and orchestrate an under-sixteen competition to build on the growing momentum in the game. In March 1972, therefore, the executive committee set up a development subcommittee of eight members with Bective Rangers' Maurice Mortell acting as chairman. The tasks were laid out as follows: '(1) To study the expansion of rugby in Leinster with special reference to problems of regrading clubs and to the growth of clubs in non-Metropolitan areas. (2) To consider the development of juvenile rugby and how this can best be fostered.'[33] Nonetheless, youth rugby was relatively slow to gain full promotion by all of Leinster's teams, with senior clubs especially having to be cajoled into organising underage sides as late as the 2000s.

The Wisdom of Expansion

The emphasis on the acceptance and indeed the embrace within Leinster rugby circles of coaching and of youth rugby in the 1970s began to increase steadily. That there was no such thing as underage teams within the clubs is most revealing: it laid bare the structural reliance on the private school system to supply rugby players, as well as the sense of privilege associated with Leinster senior rugby. At the same time, the concept of a youth game was not as straightforward as we might presume. It required the knowledge to coach; thus, it makes more sense that youth rugby came into its own subsequent to the Mosney coaching camps. It also required dedicated volunteerism and community input, which often required a jostling into wakefulness. That this was more attainable in the Ireland of the 1970s is reflective of the social changes and policy realities in the country coming into effect. It is no coincidence that many schoolteachers, for example, helped ensure that Leinster rugby youth initiatives were maintained. It was barely a decade after the announcement of free secondary education when a whole new sector was created within Irish society, and soon teachers in schools all across Leinster were advocating for rugby. This brought in the new lifeblood of Leinster rugby. Contrastingly, there was a reluctance by Dublin senior clubs to follow suit, which maintained for these teams a particular set of stereotypes, as they would only incorporate privately schooled rugby players or try to entice the best players from junior clubs as their primary source of playing youth. Whatever way one looks at it, by default, the senior system deliberately retained a very exclusive attitude.

In November 1973 the Leinster Branch presented an outline of a report on the expansion of rugby across the province. It included a five-to-fifteen-year vision, aimed to address the need for growth outside Dublin, the promotion of clubs to

▲ The Under-13 McGowan Cup final in May 2015, with Mullingar playing Tullamore. © Sam Barnes/Sportsfile

▲ North Meath v. Wexford Wanderers in the Bank of Ireland Half-Time Minis during the United Rugby Championship quarter-final match between Leinster and Cell C Sharks at the Aviva Stadium in Dublin, 6 May 2023. © Harry Murphy/Sportsfile

senior level from outside the capital and the challenges of growing juvenile rugby. A pathway for provincial clubs to senior status would help stop players leaving their home clubs in search of senior rugby in Dublin; reaching out to non-rugby-playing schools by developing a competition would help expansion and retention of players; and, finally, a clear financial plan was required to achieve any or all of these goals.[34] When it came to junior rugby beyond the metropole, the Branch was lobbied by the junior committee to continue to focus on more province-wide competition. Regional sections were created with trophies for clubs to compete for creating even more competitive games. The winners of the McGowan Cup, the Hosie Cup, the Midlands League and the South East League would play in two semi-final ties and the winners of those competed for the Senior Cup.[35] With these competitive incentives for junior and provincial towns' teams, a precedent was set in the efforts to expand the rugby fraternity and acknowledge the wide-ranging interest in the game, beyond the traditional clubs.

What's more, the appointment of George Spotswood as the IRFU's first Game Development Officer (GDO) 'was to prove the prelude to changes of major consequence in this vital area of the game. There was now a new awareness that things were changing, that the old order was no longer enough.'[36] This was January 1979, some 105 years after the founding of the union. At times, the drive for change

Mini Rugby publicity shot featuring Leinster stars Robbie Henshaw, Josh van der Flier and Rhys Ruddock. The Leinster Branch has focused heavily on developing its youth rugby to broaden its base, especially since the arrival of the professional game. © David Fitzgerald/Sportsfile

in Irish rugby oddly corresponded with a thirst for new knowledge, a rejection of old conservativism and a demand for more professionalism in all aspects of life in Ireland. What was interesting was the growing acknowledgment by the Leinster Branch of some of the general public's perceptions of rugby. It was admitted that new strategies had to be put in place to address misconceptions and indeed some of the fears about rugby. One of the more obvious fears for parents was the apparent violence and dangerousness of the game. The Branch's central argument to allay fears was to explain that having suitably trained coaches, those who know how to properly supervise the games, helped avoid unnecessary injury, meaning rugby was safer than it was preconceived to be.

More concretely, the Branch put protocols in place to make sure clubs 'organize training sessions that are always very well supervised by coaches who are specially tutored to look after young children who have no experience of the game. The Under 8s play mini-rugby which is eight-a-side',[37] while the under-tens and under-twelves played ten-aside, and it was not until under-fourteen that the youths went to a full fifteen-aside game. All in all:

Time, money, effort and alteration in structures were all required to bring about the essential changes in these areas and there was a willingness on the part of ... the branches to take up the challenge embraced and the Game Development Committee ... Reports were produced on various aspects of the game. One very quick development was the establishment of an Under 20 interprovincial championship series in 1980.[38]

Nonetheless, when progress seemed to be paramount, Leinster rugby had a habit of resorting to form. For example, it seemed like the best and most talented young players in provincial towns were instructed that they should really try to attend a private school if they wanted to make it further in the game. As non-fee-paying schools took an interest in rugby, they were denied access to the Junior and Senior Schools Cup competitions. Rules were put in place to mark a clear line between private schools' rugby and everyone else. Clubs who utilised players from private schools were barred from doing so by new rules. Thus, there was to be no interference allowed with the fee-paying schools' rugby structure. These were sentiments emanating from the Branch's own committee reports, betraying an unequivocal bias.[39]

Building Broader: Widening Rugby's Base

New Structures for a New Era

In the 1970s and 1980s the Leinster Branch was beginning to change its approach to the promotion of the game, as illustrated by a letter explaining their plan to organise a Development Committee to improve the standard of Leinster rugby. Leinster experimented with structural changes to improve competitiveness and make efforts to build upon and strengthen rugby in the province, trying to improve the standards of on-field play and rugby's entertainment value. However, when they attempted to introduce things like new league structures, those progressive ideas ran into resistance. When the idea of a new Leinster-wide league structure to include the entire province of rugby clubs was floated, senior teams in Dublin dismissed any restructuring that would make them regularly have to go 'down the country' to play a match. However, these objections began to fade as time moved forward, and there was no turning back the clock of progress. As players and former players from outside the old rugby cohort added their voices to the administration side of rugby, they began to advocate for new approaches, new ideas and new structures from within the Leinster Branch executive.

Following on from lessons in the 1960s especially, as the 1980s approached it was the Branch's continued emphasis on coaching that remained fundamental. The focus on bringing rugby standards to their highest levels in Leinster was outlined in the detailed schedules of coaching courses regularly on offer. In addition, Leinster Branch coaching subcommittee reports were circulated to the presidents and committees of 'All Clubs' to advise them on various recommendations. For example, following a seminar held in Arklow in 1981, the Branch 'suggested that all Rugby organizations should consider the formation of a Rugby Committee, where one does not already exist'. The Branch's coaching subcommittee undertook the work of putting together a paper that made suggestions about how clubs might achieve that objective. As explained:

> The advent of more organized coaching, in 1964, coincided with an increase in the popularity of the game, and with a period of greater national affluence, which gave rise to the demand for better club facilities. As a result, in many cases, the playing of Rugby became the task of the Coach or Coaches. Coaching by its very nature prompted improvements not only in the skills of the game, but in the many other related matters, e.g. physical fitness, selection, first aid, treatment of injuries, match arrangements, the laws, team management, etc. Unfortunately, by seeking improvements, the coaches were often left to implement these. As a result they became 'Jack of All Trades' and, sadly, many excellent coaches, vastly overburdened, quit the game.[1]

Improvements to life in Ireland for those in the middle and upper classes began to reflect the new demands on sporting organisations – and nowhere more so, perhaps, than in rugby. Demands for better facilities diverted the administrators' time and attention away from the needs of coaching, as the committees and officials focused on finances to run a rugby club, with modern clubhouses containing the best changing facilities, showers and social areas. The result was that the resources needed on the coaching end of things became somewhat neglected.

The appointment by the IRFU of its first GDO was followed by instructions to the branches to organise their own Game Development subcommittees under the guidance of Mr Spotswood, which was realised by the Leinster Branch in May 1979.[2] A more 'modern day', more exacting approach within rugby clubs was proposed to keep up with the times. Thus, the minutiae of clubs' structures were outlined in a 'Discussion Paper' under eleven headings, each one with two subheadings outlining the functions and composition of a subcommittee for running rugby clubs in Leinster. The breakdown explained the roles of the members of the committees, and implementation procedures were further distilled in detail;[3] the specifics of the plan were exhaustive. There are several take-away insights, including the fact that there were people with the skill sets to create these guidelines in the first place, giving the sense of a more professional approach to the organisation of Leinster rugby. The fact that there were the personnel available at both club and branch level to implement this structure and execute the appurtenant actions as outlined is also telling, and highlights the working professionals long associated with overseeing Leinster rugby. Another reading is that these implementations perhaps reveal the direction that Leinster rugby was inevitably heading in, vis-à-vis professionalism – or at least the prescience apparent in devising such detailed structures, which set some of the groundwork for the eventual advent of the professional era.

Widening Rugby's Appeal

As early as 1972 it was suggested that the Branch meetings really should be attended by a representative from all twenty-seven junior and senior clubs in the province at that time. That way, any problems and issues could be discussed with all the members in mind. This widening of the net and aiming for province-wide inclusiveness were early steps that led to a positive engagement with the game by more and more people. Some of the important directives and advances for the game were, without a doubt, the emerging emphasis on the underage game. In the 1979–80 season there was a new interprovincial under-twenties championship introduced, which the branches aimed to run on the same basis as the senior interprovincial schedule, with the under-twenties playing on the same date as the seniors, just earlier in the morning. The championship proved to be a great experience for the players, although the early morning kick-offs were a stumbling block for various logistical reasons.[4]

In August 1979 the GDO, George Spotswood, gave his subcommittee report on the structures of interprovincial rugby. The concern raised was that the interprovincial series had 'produced few games of high standard and compelling interest'. This was for myriad reasons, including over-familiarity between the provinces, overcautious play to avoid losing or on an individual level so as not to be seen making mistakes and lack of incentive in the fixtures themselves.[5] However, at the same time, the games were important for Irish rugby in terms of keeping the clubs and provincial organisations in touch and on friendly terms, as well as the obvious element of being equivalent to an international trial game. Yet, it was recognised that there needed to be provincial games of higher quality to help improve players by offering them tougher tests. Foreign opposition, Spotswood's committee suggested, might help in that regard. When all four provinces were playing games more regularly against fresh opposition, then by default their game would improve. Then when the provinces came to meet each other, the theory suggested, the standards would be higher given that they would have played tougher opposition on several occasions prior. But the longest deliberations in the report were concerns around keeping young players involved and identifying talent at an early age.[6]

The senior interprovincial Leinster team of the 1980s, with Ollie Campbell and John Robbie sharing the captaincy during the 1979–80 season, achieved the Inter-pro Championship Grand Slam under coach Mick Doyle. In the next four seasons Leinster went on to win most of their matches and produced some of the standout players of that memorable era of Irish rugby. Leinster dominated the interprovincials for the first half of the 1980s and the high calibre of the players in the Blues translated into the selection of eleven Leinster players for Ireland (Duggan, Orr, MacNeil, Harbison, Campbell, Doyle, Fitzgerald, Moroney, McGrath, Murphy, Slattery). Once more, the signs of the health of rugby in the province were somewhat reflected in the ups and downs of its provincial teams that season. The under-twenties played four and won four, the under-nineteens played two and won two, but the junior side lost both of its games during the season.

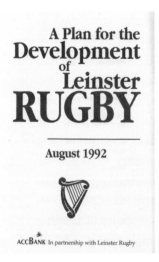

A Plan for the Development of Leinster RUGBY

August 1992

ACCBANK In partnership with Leinster Rugby

The Leinster Rugby Development Plan — *A Synopsis*

Overall Objective:
1. Establish a Leinster Identity.
2. Raise the Standard of Rugby at all levels.
3. Increase the number playing Rugby.

Areas of Action:
Coaching, Refereeing, Marketing and Facilities.

Overall Implementation:
A Chief Executive will be appointed to manage the affairs of the Branch. This position will require someone with proven management skills, and also expertise in the key areas of Leinster Rugby, namely: Rugby, Fund-raising and Finance, Marketing and Grounds.

Coaching:
Insufficient numbers and a lack of quality coaches is seen as a constraint on the development of Leinster Rugby.
- A Coaching Association has been formed with the objective of promoting and educating coaches. It has 150 members.
- A register of coaches has been created on computer.
- Coaching Meetings and Coaching Courses are being promoted and run.
- A Coaching Manual, consisting of 80 planned training sessions, will be available for Clubs.
- A Library of Videos has been set up.
- A Checklist of Equipment for every club and school has been prepared.
- Bi-Monthly meetings of Coaching Association to be held.
- Identification of all existing and potential coaches through personal contact. Further development of database is planned.
- Preparation of regular coaching news-sheet to be included in Leinster Rugby Magazine.

▲ Front cover and a synopsis of a Leinster Rugby Development Plan document, 1992. Arguably, even prior to professionalism, there was a professional approach in how the Branch ran its affairs.

As for club rugby, and how the game continued to grow, there were still twenty-one official competitions. Meanwhile, the four youth, twelve unofficial and seven seven-a-side competitions remained on the annual fixture list, underscoring Leinster rugby's popularity. By the time Leinster met Munster for their one-hundredth official interprovincial encounter on 14 November 1987, Leinster had been victors on seventy occasions to Munster's twenty-two, with eight draws having accumulated.

Leinster's record against Ulster was a mixed bag for the twenty-one games that were played between 1974–75 and the last amateur season, 1994–95. After losing to Ulster in 1974–75, Leinster won nine games in a row, before commencing a nine-in-a-row losing streak between 1984–85 and the 1992–93 season. As for the record against Munster, Leinster dominated Munster in the early 1980s, with six wins, one draw and one loss from 1979 to 1987. Munster, however, dictated their games against Leinster in the first fifteen years of the professional era, a history that the Blues subsequently began to rewrite throughout the 2010s. It is Connacht that Leinster have continued to eclipse in interprovincial rugby, winning seventeen of their twenty-one meetings in the years preceding the arrival of the professional game.

There was a period in the late 1980s and early 1990s, with the arrival of the All-Ireland League (AIL), when the Leinster squad seemed to become disinterested in the interprovincial rugby game. Some have suggested that, with the AIL, club loyalties and the competitiveness of that league became more important than the interprovincial series. Players prioritised the Leinster Senior Cup and the AIL competitions. Within the Leinster mindset the interprovincial rivalries needed a revamp, it seems.

The Leinster Branch was improving when it came to keeping an eye on the junior sections in the 1980s. Almost two-thirds of all the adult players across Leinster were playing with junior clubs and the Branch was taking notice. Opinion was beginning to shift, with the realisation that the more help on offer to junior clubs, the more benefit to Leinster rugby in general. One signal to the junior clubs and players that the Branch was paying attention was the decision to reimagine the junior interprovincial as a representative game for members of junior clubs only, and not open it to second or third team players of senior clubs. By making senior club players ineligible for the junior squad, the Branch was offering junior club players the fairest chance to play representative rugby at interprovincial level. The executive committee of the Branch praised junior players who might have opted for senior but decided that they wanted to keep playing junior, helping to retain interest in the game across the province.

▲ An action shot from a Blackrock College game.

The junior committee, in putting forward arguments for its section of Leinster rugby, explained that its motivation was a desire to see rugby improve across all counties. The simple idea the committee argued for was that play would improve universally if improvements started at underage and junior level. Thus, looking after the juniors would benefit the senior squad and raise the game in Leinster: in popularity, in skill level, in numbers playing and so on. The argument was about improving the game from the grassroots up, rather than focusing entirely on the handful of senior clubs in the province. It was also agreed in Leinster circles that there needed to be a representative-level incentive to attract non-rugby-playing schoolboys to the game. And there needed to be a careful consideration of the fixtures' schedule that didn't interfere with the club game but which also minimised costs, so provincial rugby wouldn't become too expensive.

As the 1980s came to a close, the junior committee argued for a Leinster junior tour; for games to be played at the stadium in Donnybrook as opposed to clubhouses around the province; for the avoidance of fixture clashes, so no J1 club games on the weekend of junior interprovincials; and that the junior interprovincial players needed to be looked after in a manner equal to the senior squad in terms of travel expenses, kit, accommodation, meals and welfare. As well as the voices advocating for more attention to be paid to the clubs at all levels across the province, there was a similar argument put forward in the case of underage rugby in Leinster. There was, then, a concerted effort by the junior administrators for a fairer balance in the Leinster organisation. In the end, these demands were prudent, given that within less than a decade the Leinster organisation required the entire province to be behind them as they adjusted to the new demands that professionalism would usher in.

There are continued signs of lessons being learned and waves of change to come for Leinster rugby when one delves into the development of the colleges' competition too. Players playing representative rugby with Leinster at all levels, were suddenly being sourced from Leinster's third-level colleges in the 1980s and 1990s. Caps were earned by players from Carlow RTC, Bolton Street, Dundalk RTC, the College of Commerce, the College of Catering, the Cadet School, NIHED, COMAD and Athlone RTC. Added to these over the following two seasons (1989–90 and 1990–91) were selected players from DCU, RCSI and Kevin Street. This was the kind of outreach and necessary expansion for which Leinster rugby had long cried out.

When it came to a new approach, the exemplar was the initiative to organise the Irish Colleges Rugby Union (ICRU), which came out of Dundalk, through Turlough O'Brien, Brendan Johnston and John Brown – respectively, the first ICRU chairman, treasurer and secretary. These men gave credit to UCD, with John Brown explaining that UCD played no small part in the ICRU's development, offering use of Belfield playing fields for trial matches and squad sessions. The ICRU bestowed on Leinster rugby a competitive subdivision that provided a rich vein of talent for the future, including some of the Leinster players who would emerge as the first group of young professionals in the late 1990s. As Ireland continued to modernise and the government showed the foresight to invest in third-level education, the growth in the number of colleges brought more rugby teams and more opportunities for Leinster to recruit and identify talent.

The catalyst for the ICRU was partly to do with an unarticulated 'split' when it came to third-level university and colleges' rugby. Several voices in the rugby world quite correctly pointed out the contemptible situation whereby Irish third-level rugby selection was closed off to the five so-called 'traditional' universities.[7] There was no true representative third-level Irish team. This being the situation, the ICRU went ahead under its own steam to organise and nourish rugby activities in

▲ De La Salle captain Brian Glennon lifts the Leinster Schools Cup alongside his mother, Una, after victory over Blackrock in 1985. A very, very rare occasion when a non-'traditional' rugby school took the cup. © Brendan Moran/Sportsfile

◄ Brian O'Driscoll of Blackrock College during a Leinster Schools Cup semi-final against Clongowes Wood at Lansdowne Road in March 1997. © Brendan Moran/Sportsfile

all the remaining third-level institutions across the island of Ireland. It ran its first competition, the Gleeson Cup, in the 1985–86 season and fifteen colleges entered teams, with Kevin Street College of Technology the first winners. The cup had been donated by the CEO of the City of Dublin Vocational Education Committee, a former president of UCD's rugby club, and a former UCD, Blackrock and Leinster interprovincial player, Martin Gleeson.[8]

Over the years the success of rugby in the ICRU was reflected in the over thirty colleges and five universities that were affiliated with the organisation,[9] another sign of rugby's growth and interest at the grassroots level. The games were organised during the college week, competing for four different trophies at four levels, and this mid-week structure allowed players to play with their home clubs at the weekend. The ICRU went from strength to strength, indicating how the Leinster Branch and the IRFU had been misguided in focusing only on rugby's 'traditional' educational institutes looked after by the Irish Universities Rugby Union (IURU). As an example of some of the results of a more open Leinster rugby universe, between 1987 and 1992 the Irish team produced by the ICRU consistently beat its UK rivals.[10] What's more, when the ICRU proposed matches with the IURU between 1992 and 1995, its team readily trounced the so-called traditional universities' selection, leading the IURU to make the decision to no longer play the colleges' selections. From those victorious ICRU teams, in its first ten seasons they produced at least twenty-nine interprovincial players, including eleven for Leinster, with names like Kevin Potts, Shane Byrne, Jonathan Philpott and Girvan Dempsey standing out. In its inaugural season (1987–88), the ICRU had seven colleges to choose from in its trial matches. A mere five years later, for the 1992–93 season, it had thirty-three colleges to select players from. The squad then suddenly had a pool of talent as the game of rugby was grown, nurtured and embraced by a wider swathe of the public.

Birth of the AIL

Some of the most important events during the 1980s for Leinster rugby were the debates and decisions that had to be made about the state of the club scene and the knock-on effect that was having on rugby across the province. There was a growing consciousness that there needed to be more enjoyable rugby games to entice fans to keep coming out. After a decade of discussion, a new system was proposed that would introduce a longer season with more competitive games to help improve

An action shot from a Blackrock College game in the 1990s.

Leinster and Irish rugby in general, and to increase spectator interest. The idea of the league system, with the prospect of promotion and relegation battles would, it was deemed, help ensure that the sport's following remained entertained. But the Branch had to win over the clubs and allay the traditionalists' fear of change.

Under the IRFU presidency of M.H. Carroll (1984–85), proposals by the Game Development subcommittee to inaugurate a National League competition for senior clubs were unanimously agreed. The IRFU argued that having the best rugby players from across the four provinces confront each other each season in their club games would improve the quality of Irish rugby and, imperatively, enhance the entertainment value for spectators. To determine the make-up of each division, the performance of every team in their official provincial branch competitions over five seasons prior to the commencement of the new AIL would be assessed. From there, each branch would designate which team would play in what division based on rank.

These proposals were to be sent out to the clubs for careful consideration, but the IRFU expected that all clubs would agree with the way forward, as the scheme would ensure the strengthening of Irish rugby at all levels, if and when the plans were implemented. The clubs, however, did not receive the news with the enthusiasm that the IRFU expected and there were lots of concerns and pushback, particularly from Leinster senior clubs. Despite the consensus that something new was needed, David Walsh reported in *The Sunday Press*, 'Proposals by the Irish Rugby Football Union to initiate an All-Ireland League in the Autumn of 1986 look certain to come unstuck.'[11] Walsh explained that at least twenty, almost half of the forty-seven senior clubs, would vote 'no' to the idea being proposed, and that Leinster was one of the two provinces (Munster being the other) where the majority of the clubs had an adverse reaction to the IRFU's wishes. It was in Leinster, Walsh wrote, that the most significant blow emerged when 'a decision was taken by the Branch to oppose the All-Ireland League.'[12] Even though the outcome this time around would be negative, it was becoming clearer to many observers that a rugby AIL was inevitable. As Liam Hayes of *The Sunday Press* explained:

> Since the present league system was introduced for the 1975–76 season, clubs have grumbled about its inadequacies. They argued that with a four-division programme there were too few competitive games for 15 clubs. The league season for most teams amounts to three games, and if a club loses its opening match the competitive benefits of the two remaining outings are severely diminished.[13]

Various photographs of UCD RFC, suggesting the growth and popularity of the game among young Leinster men and giving a sense of the 'before and after' of the game experience.

Among the senior clubs, then, there was much to be debated, and while everyone agreed that standards had to be improved in the game, concerns over the hard medicine involved in achieving that led to a certain level of hostility. The biggest fear for many of the clubs concerning the proposed AIL was the methodology deployed when seeding clubs. Middle and lower clubs were afraid that they would be relegated to the lowest divisions, which would be detrimental to their reputation on the one hand but would also reduce the quality of their opposition, reducing the possibilities of improving. More to the point, playing in a lower division would reduce player and spectator interest, hurting clubs both on and off the field. But at the end of the day, most clubs agreed with an All-Ireland League.

Writing in 1986, the prominent *Irish Times* rugby writer Edmund Van Esbeck led with the headline 'All-Ireland League must come some time.' In tandem with the AIL debates, the Leinster Branch was about to introduce a new league system of its own, for the 1987–88 season. The hope of this new league structure was that the best teams would emerge on their merits over the entire playing year and that it would conjure more interest in the senior club game. The purpose of the change was to try and make the game more competitive, more enjoyable to play, and to create a fan-base interested in watching exciting fixtures between top players. The article also noted that rugby's aficionados believed that there was a big Irish public waiting for a chance to see rugby matches of a high quality and that they would, indeed, attend All-Ireland League games.[14] All in all, the end of the 1980s

▲ The first Irish Colleges team, with their coach George Hook, back row, second right. The Irish Universities team shunned the 'technical' colleges rugby players, leading to the creation of an Irish Colleges team.

Irish colleges rugby

Immense contr

by Des Daly

Matches between the Combined Universities and the rest of Ireland were an annual feature on the Irish Rugby calendar from 1933 until World War Two. In 1951, the Irish Universities Rugby Union , IURU, was formed for the primary purpose of organizing a Universities XV to play against suitable opposition. When the points system for entry into third-level education was introduced in 1976 various new educational institutions started to spring up throughout Ireland, and there arose a need for an alternative body to the traditional IURU. The Irish Colleges Rugby Union. ICRU, was established in 1986 on the initiative of two Dundalk RTC men, Turlough O'Brien and Brendan Johnston, and became affiliated to the IRFU the following September. The ICRU committee set out to propagate and co-ordinate student rugby activities outside the five established University clubs. The first ICRU competition in 1986 attracted an entry of 15 Colleges. The winners, Kevin St. College of Technology, received the Gleeson Cup.

The trophy had been donated by the late Martin Gleeson, C.E.O of the City of Dublin VEC. Gleeson was a former UCD, Blackrock C. and Leinster interprovincial forward, who had been President of UCD RFC in 1967/68. Growth of the ICRU was spectacular and today, a decade later, 30 Colleges and 5 Universities (Limerick, DCU, Maynooth, UU-Coleraine and UU-Jordanstown) are affiliated to the parent body.

The ICRU organize their competitions into three divisions with the Ascent Cup (Division 1- 12 clubs), the Ascent Shield (Division 2- 10 clubs) and the Ascent Trophy (Division 3-10 clubs) all sponsored by the Bank of Ireland. Last years divisional winners were Athlone RTC, Cork College of Commerce and Portobello Institute of Education respectively. There is also an O'Boyle Cup for U20 Freshers - Waterford Institute of Technology won it in 1996/1997 - and a Heineken sponsored regional seven-a-side tournament, with the finals played in Cork. Most

matches in the ICRU competitions are played in mid-week. This enables the students to return and field with their home clubs at the weekend. The students in the University sector do not have such logistical difficulties as their clubs compete directly in IRFU and Branch competitions.

The ICRU entered the international arena in 1987/88. Following trials held at the UCD Belfield grounds a squad was selected to represent the ICRU in matches against their English, Welsh and Scottish counterparts. The Scottish Colleges were beaten 14-3, and the Welsh 34-24, both games played at Dundalk. The final match, in London on St.Patricks weekend, saw the English Colleges defeated 12-10. The Irish had won the Colleges Triple Crown. The side, captain by Leinster Interprovincial flanker, Carl Egan, (Waterford RTC/St.Marys C.)included Richard Wallace, Kevin Potts, Angus McKeen, Dan Larkin and Sean Kelly.

The Scottish Colleges were unable to field for the next two seasons so no

Irish Colleges Team, Captain Colin Varley (Limerick RTC), which defeated Irish Universities 58-8 at Castle Avenue on Wednesday 12th November, 1997.

▲ Irish Colleges rugby story by Des Daly, from the 1997 edition of the *Rugby* magazine edited and produced by Pat Fitzgerald in the 1990s.

saw a period of updates and reorganisations, but the AIL debate among clubs and
branches would soon kick off in earnest in the 1990s.

In December 1990, Van Esbeck, in his *Irish Times* column, wrote in a worried
manner about the fate of Leinster rugby. He lamented:

> [W]hen one thinks of the fine sides produced in the late seventies and early
> eighties, the spirit in those sides and their will to win, the contrast between
> now and then is both unfortunate and a cause for anxiety. Leinster is going
> through its most unproductive period in history and those who run the
> branch should set their minds to the task of bringing about some remedial
> action. While they are at it they should ponder why the largest organization at
> school level in the country has failed to beat Munster for seven years. There is
> no precedent for that, nor indeed for the province's pathetic record at senior
> level in recent years in the interprovincials.[15]

Harsh words indeed and a bleak prophecy for Leinster rugby, with the litany of
losses to Ulster and Munster, and a rare loss to Connacht in the 1988–89 season.
For Van Esbeck, the blame seems to be lie squarely with the system: 'Are too many
at the centre of power for too long?' he asked.

The Leinster Branch was not entirely on board with the AIL idea at first and
certain clubs didn't like it at all. Having enjoyed status and privilege on the basis of
tradition rather than actual performance on the field, many of the senior clubs were
now going to be judged entirely on merit. However, the troubled state of Leinster's
finances at the start of the new decade suggested that a new period of development
was becoming essential, as explained in the minutes of the Branch annual council
meeting in May 1991. Leinster's treasurer, P.J. Boyle, stated that it gave him no
pleasure to report a loss of £42,000 in the year. Gates were down and expenditures
had gone up. Something needed to change, and the AIL was proposed as the solution
to usher in an era of new fans, coaxed to watch exciting, top-class rugby.

With the apparent pressure on rugby in Leinster so suddenly visible in the 1990s,
mainly because of competition from other sporting codes, the emergence of the
rugby AIL, following on from the first Rugby World Cup in 1987, addressed rugby's
need for something fresh. Kicked off in October 1990 and sponsored by the AIB, the
new AIL format, it was hoped, would help to continue the upward trajectory of the
rugby game in Ireland. The AIL initially started off with just two divisions for senior
clubs, but was expanded to four divisions in 1993–94, with small variations in the

numbers of teams per division in subsequent seasons.[16] In the original discussions about the AIL, it had always been Leinster's position that their preference was for the expanded five-division league format.[17] But trying to find agreement across all four branches, as well as with the IRFU, at times proved tricky.

As media coverage increased and the public was enticed to the sport thanks to the popularity of the Rugby World Cups, Leinster was quicker to react than the IRFU in terms of advocating for a more inclusive game and a need to overhaul structures. In May 1992 the Branch launched a new development initiative, which at times irked the slower-moving union. For example, Leinster recognised a growing gap between the AIL and international rugby and began to reinforce the importance of the interprovincial competition, indeed advocating expanding it as a logical step up from club rugby on the road to improved international standards.[18] For Leinster, however, the 1990s initially proved problematic. Munster and Ulster were the rugby provinces of note and something was needed, and quickly, if the province was going to regain some prestige. Thus, a new Leinster development squad was brought online to help address some of the worrying trends of poor interprovincial results. The development squad had no less than fifty-four players to select from. It seems that Leinster had begun to implement a strategy with an eye to the future. Thus, in 1992–93, the Leinster senior team played five games before the interprovincials. The squad was made up of thirty-five players, interlinking with development and underage teams, all prior to the shift to the professional era. And while it is hard to dismiss the apparent sense in Leinster and Ireland of being blindsided by the professional era, at the same time there are hints that there was a new, more professional way of doing things already in place in the early 1990s.

After reports from a 1990s steering committee, a development plan had been set in train for Leinster rugby, with three strategies at the centre of that vision. The central focus articulated was the production of players of the highest calibre, who could go on to compete at an international level. The three ways of achieving that, in the Branch's plan, were to (a) increase the numbers playing rugby in the province; (b) raise the standards of Leinster club rugby; and (c) establish a much stronger Leinster identity. Arguably, achieving the third goal would be hugely aided by success in the first two strategies, but the challenge was how best to achieve these goals. The first priority, it seems, suggested that while a 'policy of identifying and developing squads of quality players' is important, 'the LONG TERM priority must be to INCREASE THE NUMBERS playing rugby i.e. broaden the base'.[19] This is a fascinating acknowledgement by Leinster of their exclusivity, despite some earlier attempts to broaden the base, which often ran into resistance from the 'traditional' rugby cohort in the senior ranks. That such resistance had, in the end, started to stunt the development of rugby and, more to the point, the quality of the game, was now being accepted.

Very tellingly, Leinster's secretary explained, 'the key to increasing numbers lies in marketing the game; however, structural support in the shape of approved coaching and refereeing must be put in place BEFORE serious marketing is undertaken. Otherwise new recruits will become disillusioned with rugby and will be lost to the game.'[20] At the end of the 1992–93 season, the proposal to appoint 'a paid Chief Executive effective immediately', was motioned; this new officer would oversee the many alterations that were needed to bring Leinster rugby back to the pinnacle of rugby in Ireland.[21] The way forward was summarised as follows: the Branch approved the recommendations and worked to obtain IRFU approval and financial support; they would next appoint a CEO and hold them responsible for overseeing and carrying through the recommendations and initiatives of the steering and development committees. There was a distinct air of professionalism to this and yet there seemed to be little awareness of what was coming down the tracks some two seasons into the future. But structures were implemented which, at the very least, would enable the Branch to muddle through until it fully grasped what was needed in the professional age.

▲ McScrum, the official Irish mascot for the 1991 Rugby World Cup. With what was only the second iteration of the Rugby World Cup in Europe, Leinster and the IRFU took the opportunity to reach out to a wider public audience and promote the game.

Professionalism on the Horizon

In the Leinster Branch's study of how best to expand and popularise the game of rugby in the province before the arrival of the professional era, undertaken by a subcommittee of experienced rugby administrators and ex-players in 1990, two main points were highlighted. First, was the need to improve skills, and second, the need to develop and market the game across the entire province. To achieve that, the report stated, the most important things to focus on were the development of coaching and

▲ Greystones RFC in action during the 1996 Metropolitan Cup final match.

increasing the numbers playing the game.[22] The study examined the geography of the province, which stretched some 140 miles north to south, and 80 miles east to west, with about 17,000 players, including youth and mini players. To help expand numbers, the Branch decided that it should target north Dublin, which then had a population of over 600,000 people, some 15 per cent of the entire country's population. Yet there were only ten rugby clubs combined within the north of the city and County Dublin, out of a total of seventy across the province. The challenges the Branch listed were: 'The difficulties being encountered in the [non-fee-paying] schools; the growth of Youth Rugby and the key problems facing their development including the "image" of the game. Much needs to be done to create a positive image in the communities to encourage parents to send their boys to play rugby.'[23]

That image of the game, we can safely assume, was the dual concern of the perceived violence of the sport and the socioeconomic exclusivity still associated with Leinster rugby. Reports about the game's catastrophic injuries turned many parents off, as did the idea that it was a sport for the wealthy, the privately schooled and the well-connected. For the vast majority of Leinster's youth, soccer and GAA were much more accessible sports. Leinster rugby players' backgrounds remained generally homogeneous on the eve of the professional era. There was a revealing geographic and cultural cachet when it came to the Leinster squad in the 1990s,

▲ An action shot from 1990s schools' game.

with representatives from just a handful of senior clubs and a small cohort of fee-paying schools. That the selectors of underage and development squads continued to search exclusively in so-called 'rugby' schools, university teams and senior clubs was plain to see. This encouraged the track that funnelled the 'traditional rugby school' players into representative rugby at underage level, which was their pathway into the senior set-up. Thus, it made sense that the youth sections needed their own representative games to forge their own pathway, until a more serious self-examination at Leinster began during the professional era.

As of yet, women's teams were nowhere mentioned in Leinster Branch records, even though it was in 1990 that women started to organise teams at Leinster rugby clubs. Undoubtedly this had to do with the exclusively male committees, where the presumption remained that rugby should be a male-only domain. Omitting the development of the women's rugby game, whether deliberately or not, reflected several realities of Irish life. That women continued to raise their voices for gender equality was clear, even in such mundane things like organising rugby teams; that men in positions of power were deaf to these demands and the changes that were needed reflected society-wide issues in Ireland. While women forged a path for themselves at club level, the rugby hierarchy turned to the question of the emergence of a men's professional rugby reality.

When the World Rugby authorities sanctioned the 'open' game, a few immediate insights can be generally agreed upon. There had been a general shift in that direction among the southern-hemisphere rugby people especially, both administrators and players, for some time. Teams were being paid to play exhibition games and there were rampant rumours of players getting under-the-table money. Rugby was 'the last major international sport to embrace professionalism. This development, though immediately attributable to the irresistible commercial power of satellite broadcasting, was ultimately the outcome of the game's internal contradictions. The principal contradiction, always in existence but more evident from the 1960s, was declared support for amateurism and clandestine toleration of abuses of the amateur code.'[24] With the massive success of televised sports, especially in the satellite-television age coming to a crescendo in the 1990s, it was difficult for rugby union to avoid what many believed was the inevitable. Irish rugby, nonetheless, seemed completely unprepared for such a scenario. And yet, there had been enough serious thought put into the way rugby was being organised and how players were being readied for games to suggest that Leinster rugby had at least put in place the foundations that allowed it to adjust.

At the same time there were great strides made by those involved in junior rugby, and they managed to make enough noise for more support and resources at the grassroots. Yet there was still a clear dichotomy of junior and senior rugby running cordially in tandem. It took the introduction of the professional game for those in charge to really begin to fully embrace the province in its totality. When everyone involved in the game at all levels was included in the readjustment needed to cater for the professional era, Leinster rugby would not merely survive, but grow to its full potential. However, it would take a few fits and starts for the Leinster, and Irish, rugby leadership to find their feet. Indeed, the IRFU was one of the strongest opponents to the professional game when it came along and publicly announced its opposition to paying players to play. As Liam O'Callaghan explained, 'the idea that an individual qualified to practice a respectable profession [like medicine] having attended a respectable [fee-paying] school … could conceivably consider rugby anything other than a pastime defied assumptions of what the function of the game was and what social cachet it should appeal to'.[25] While there were many rugby people promoting a broader umbrella, there was at the same time an entrenched mindset about 'the true nature' of rugby, about tradition and the primacy of the senior clubs, the private schools and indeed the socioeconomic clique who jealously tried to protect what they deemed was 'their' game.

▲ Leinster Branch Junior Committee 1991–2.

▲ Leinster Branch Senior Committee 1994–5.

▲ Leinster Youths squad 1991–2. Leinster were already putting in place academy-like structures prior to the professional game's arrival.

▲ Leinster Under 20s Squad 1990–1. A hierarchical (by age) youth system helped develop Leinster players for the seniors, arguably a strategy pre-empting professionalism.

▲ The Leinster team to play Munster, December 1990.

There was much angst, then, in Ireland and Leinster about the prospect of the professional game. Yet as early as 1991, the purveyors of rugby across the province presented an arguably more professional mindset. They continually highlighted the need for local clubs to do more to promote the game, and with the World Cup in 1991 coming to Irish shores, it provided a great opportunity to do so. Indeed, the IRFU further stated:

> Rugby in the provinces has survived very well for years on its own small corps of enthusiasts; the game poorly publicized below representative levels. In provincial areas it seldom enjoyed a wide appeal, partly because it was not part of the nationalist picture, partly because many clubs appeared casual about promoting it. Times have changed and with the advent of television came a new awareness of the game ... Despite considerable national coverage, rugby has still to claim 'a place' in the sporting sun beyond the cities, due in part to the failure of clubs to use the media. The ... Branches have recognized this failing, and are taking remedial steps ... to promote what is still a minority activity in most areas, one difficult to spread in regions traditionally dominated by Gaelic sports and soccer ...[26]

Within a few years of that realisation, by 1994 the major rugby clubs around Europe were calling for a European competition to be inaugurated. Arguably the era of corporate interests in sports influenced many of these aspirations. 'The late 1980s and the early 1990s, as a period, saw rugby change more abruptly, and completely, than any sport has ever changed. These [were] the revolution years, the boom years; ... The growth of interest in the sport has been remarkable ... Even at club level the situation has changed. Most British and Irish clubs are watched by substantially increased numbers.'[27] Some clubs in Ireland began to host five-figure attendances, while in England and Wales, at the bigger clubs, the numbers were reaching close to and into the tens of thousands.

It was international matches and, of course, TV interest especially that were in the lead when it came to the corporate input and the ability to stream revenue, attuned to clever marketing that began to reach out to more people and make them interested. The Five Nations, the World Cup and international tests were seeing a greater curiosity, and a new bank of players were there for the taking if rugby wanted. Also, northern-hemisphere rugby was being put under fierce pressure from their southern-hemisphere rivals in several respects. After two World Cups,

LEAGUE.

OLD BELVEDERE 3RD B XV

Versus.... AER LINGUS
at .... HOME
Kick-off.... 1 - 00 P.M.
Date.... SUN 7TH DEC K.O. / PM NB

Full-back
15 K. FARNAN

Threequarters
14 A. MULLEN
13 P. CROWLEY
12 A. MEAGHER
11 R. FANAGAN

Half-backs
10 T. BARR
9 G. GANLEY (CAPT.)

Forwards
1 E. COBB
2 B. O'CARROLL
3 G. REGAN
4 G. BEIRNE
5 S. FLEMING
6 P. CROTTY
7 B. SHAW
8 P. KAVANAGH

▲ Example of league game team sheet: Old Belvedere third B, v. Aer Lingus. This illustrates rugby's growth in Leinster and the records being kept, week-to-week, by the Branch.

▲ Two of Leinster rugby's important figures, Ham Lambert and G.P.S. Hogan.

and with a third on the way, it was apparent that the gap was widening between Australia, New Zealand and South Africa, and the European teams. The Scottish Rugby Union's Director of Rugby, Jim Telfer, was quick to raise his voice on this and was one of the loudest proponents for a European-wide club competition. In order for rugby in Europe, but also globally, to thrive and compete with soccer, for example, then a leaf out of their book was needed; a European champion's league-style competition for rugby was an imperative 'for the future of the game'.[28] As with all sports, once it was marketed and advertised properly, any code had the potential to attract a substantial fan base, and there was no reason to not be optimistic that the same would happen for a European rugby cup competition. The arguments for and the appearance of more professionalism in rugby prior to the 'shock' of 1995 becomes more apparent in hindsight, despite the mythology around the imagined 'true nature' of Leinster rugby.

The issues that Leinster rugby confronted for the 1993–94 season were expressed in the sentiment that the province needed to 'regain its proper place' at the head of Irish rugby, which it feared was slipping away, especially since Munster clubs had dominated the AIL in its first decade.[29] In response, there was a call for a vision of a Leinster uniqueness, which needed to be articulated more clearly in the run-up to what would become the professional era. Whether this was something fortuitous or inevitable or prophetic might be moot, but what was important was that the Branch had tried to invigorate that concept at this stage. More importantly, the implementation of underage development squads was a pivotal model, portentous for the future. The health of Leinster rugby was being judged by the successes and failures of the clubs at all levels, and there was much more attention being paid to movements up and down both the All-Ireland and Leinster regional leagues.

Those who had enjoyed and played the game of rugby across the province were now actually being recognised as pivotal to its success. Leinster Branch official competitions amounted to eighteen cup and league finals, alongside eighteen divisional qualifier play-offs, plus the Senior Cup qualifier, the President's Plaque and two under-nineteen league cups (the McCorry and the Gale).[30] What's more, there were four competitions for silverware in the provincial area leagues: North Midlands, South East, Midlands and North East.[31] Additionally, in the youth section there were five provincial area under-eighteen leagues (North Midlands, South East, Midlands, North East and Metropolitan) alongside the under-eighteen Culliton Cup, as well as an under-sixteens', under-fourteens', under-twelves' and under-tens' cup. Outside of the schools' competition, then, there was no shortage of rugby being played by Leinster youth across the province. The first years of the 1990s boded well, one can suggest, given the extensive number of clubs competing for a wide range of silverware across a considerable level of competition province-wide.

A Leinster Junior Interprovincial programme cover from 1984.

11

The Reinvention of Leinster Rugby, 1995–2005

Professionalism Arrives

The summer of 1995 turned the rugby world upside down. For some, what arrived was the inevitable, but for many others in Irish rugby circles, they articulated an extreme sense of shock when the International Rugby Board legalised professionalism on 27 August. As Tony Collins explained, what happened in 'the summer of 1995 [was] the culmination of a process that began in the 1960s in which amateurism gradually collapsed in on itself. The growing status and financial worth of international sport had gradually yet fatally undermined the … commitment to amateurism.'[1] The international rugby hierarchy had been awaiting a report on the game's amateur status, which had begun a year and a half earlier, in February 1994, and concluded that there was no satisfactory explanation or reason for rugby's amateurism. Collins explained this as the collapse of ideology, in that there was, of course, a reason for amateurism and that was rooted in class exclusivity. As early as 1895, the founders of rugby union called on the idea of amateurism to remain in place, mainly because they did not want to have to associate with the working classes.

Amateurism had always been about class distinction and exclusivity, and as the International Rugby Board's committee admitted, the desperate clinging on in certain circles to this idea, 'is not easily defensible as a social or moral ethic judged by the standards of today!'[2] The historical ideology at the heart of rugby's amateur

231

▲ Leinster player Chris Pim in action in the 1995 season, the year Leinster turned professional.

ethos for most, but not all, was rejected and the reality in 1995 was a lot more straightforward when it came to the reason for the professionalisation of rugby. To borrow from Collins:

> From a broader perspective, the collapse of amateur rugby union was an example of the rise of the 'free-market' in the last two decades of the twentieth century … Embracing the ideology of the market and shedding its traditional fear of organized labour – which had been the impetus for the introduction and consolidation of amateurism in rugby – the conservative sections of the middle classes that controlled rugby union no longer had use for the formal social segregation of amateurism.[3]

It was, then, in the 1995–96 season that Irish rugby had to contend with the reality of competing in the professional era and figure out the best way forward. In Leinster at the outset things continued as before, but the pressure to figure out how to organise one, or several, professional rugby teams was cumbersome. The idea that the Leinster clubs would have enough support, or enough of an identity, never mind the capital needed for a professional rugby team, seemed like an impossibility.

The provincial squads had already been signed up for the new European-wide cup competition and the scenario of regional, provincial clubs had been something suggested even before the professional era.

In broader Irish society, the mid-1990s ushered in the beginning of the Celtic Tiger economy, which was an important factor in helping to maintain professional rugby, due to additional disposable income available and people's positive reaction to the marketing of the provincial rugby teams. The IRFU had agreed to professionalism for the international squad and for the interprovincial players, which the Irish clubs, by and large, understood was a positive way to go. The pressure was on, however, because the wealthiest English clubs were already setting up a professional league across the UK. If Irish rugby was going to have any hope in the era of professionalism, then a major overhaul was going to be required. The fifteen Leinster senior clubs, all based in Dublin, called for emergency meetings with the Branch, demanding a change to the structure of the AIL, the need to allow the clubs access to their interprovincial players and the need to figure out the way the European League and the Interprovincial Championship would fit in with the domestic league structure. In some ways, the basic concerns revolved around scheduling and the availability of the

▲ Leinster player Conor O'Shea in the 1995 season.

233

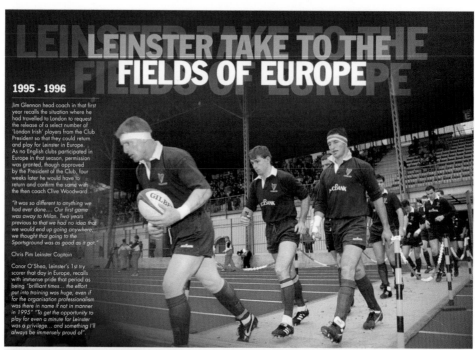

LEINSTER TAKE TO THE FIELDS OF EUROPE

1995 - 1996

Jim Glennon head coach in that first year recalls the situation where he had travelled to London to request the release of a select number of 'London Irish' players from the Club President so that they could return and play for Leinster in Europe. As no English clubs participated in Europe in that season, permission was granted, though approved by the President of the Club, four weeks later he would have to return and confirm the same with the then coach Clive Woodward.

"It was so different to anything we had ever done.... Our first game was away to Milan. Two years previous to that we had no idea that we would end up going anywhere; we thought that going to the Sportsground was as good as it got."

Chris Pim Leinster Captain

Conor O'Shea, Leinster's 1st try scorer that day in Europe, recalls with immense pride that period as being "brilliant times... the effort put into training was huge, even if for the organisation professionalism was there in name if not in manner in 1995" "To get the opportunity to play for Leinster for even a minute for Leinster was a privilege... and something I'll always be immensely proud of".

1995 - 1996

On Saturday 30th December 1995 Leinster reached their first European Semi Final at home in Lansdowne Road only to lose 23-14 to Cardiff. Jim Glennon recalls the reason for the aberration of a red jersey for that game, as it was not due to be televised but the severe weather disrupted much of the sport across Europe that weekend and hastily arranged broadcasting of the game lead to Leinster wearing red.

Leinster edging past Milan and Pontypridd hardly generated any momentum in Dublin rugby circles ahead of their 1st European Semi-Final, Leinster captain Chris Pim got over for the only Leinster try, while Alan McGowan slotted three penalties. Only 12 teams from France, Ireland, Wales, Italy and Romania were involved in the inaugural European tournament.

▲ Images from the first Leinster rugby professional era match in the European Cup, 1995.

234

professional players who, as was decreed by the IRFU, would be paid to play for their province and country only.

The implementation of the professional game had an immediate negative impact on Irish domestic rugby in terms of dealing with scheduling on the one hand, and the haemorrhaging of players, enticed by professional contracts with the largest clubs in the UK, on the other. While some Leinster clubs had a massive senior squad, allowing them to field teams without too much interruption, increasing financial pressure came to bear on the senior teams in their attempts to maintain such a scenario. The senior clubs complained that their first teams were being decimated by the number of representative matches, international and interprovincial, which saw the newly contracted professionals leave for duty. When clubs began postponing games because their pro-players were on Leinster or Ireland duty, the whole scenario became somewhat shambolic.

Another danger being highlighted was that junior rugby would get left behind altogether if the Leinster Branch didn't figure out the way forward quickly. That anxiety about the fate of junior rugby was underscored with the insight in 1996 that '[o]nce upon a time the Friday editions of the Dublin evening newspapers would devote half a page to club J1–J6 selections ... Today, Junior rugby gets little mention in the press.'[4] Rugby was in a vulnerable position, then, after 1995. The advent of professionalism had left the clubs in a difficult position, and many of them feared what the future might hold. It was clear that Ireland could not support a plethora of professional rugby teams, and the only mechanism that would work was to professionalise the provinces. Of course, this brought up its own complexities and instigated a shift in the way rugby needed to be reimagined across the island.

Jim Glennon was the first Leinster coach of the professional era (1995–96), continuing on from his position as team manager in the two previous seasons. A product of Roscrea College, Glennon had played rugby in Skerries, from underage in the late 1960s and on into the 1980s. His success as a player with Skerries was impressive. He won four PTC medals by the age of twenty-one and became the first Skerries player to win a full international cap, in 1980. He went on to earn another five Ireland caps, the last four in 1987, after a seven-year gap, at the age of thirty-three. He appeared for Ireland in the first Rugby World Cup that year also.[5] One of his standout memories of the inaugural professional season, Glennon recalled, was having to fly to London to ask for Leinster players on contract with English teams to be released to the province so they could compete in the European Cup competitions. In that first ever European Cup game in the professional era, Chris

Leinster Win
Inter-Provincial Championship

WE ARE THE CHAMPIONS!

P.J. McAllister presenting The Inter-Provincial Trophy to Leinster Captain, Chris Pim

▲ Images of Leinster winning the Interprovincial Cup in 1996. While the game is fully professional, the Interprovincial Cup was something of a legacy competition.

Pim was Leinster captain and Conor O'Shea (on loan from his club London Irish) scored the first ever Leinster try in Europe in the professional age, against Milan in Italy in November 1995.[6] This was the start of the Leinster European odyssey.

The 1990s upheaval with the introduction of professional rugby has been called the 'wild west' by those looking back at the struggles to adapt. Nonetheless, there were glimmers of positive change conceived at various levels in Leinster rugby. One of those positives was the implementation of a structure that created a 'Youths' route to success,[7] exemplified by the emerging talents of Trevor Brennan and Shane Horgan, as one newspaper snippet suggested. At the youth rugby level, Leinster rugby had forged its progressive spirit in the two decades prior, and the benefits paid off when the professional game landed:

> For so long, the Irish Schoolboys rugby team has been perceived as the pinnacle achievement for a young player, with serious aspirations to come through the system. This belief is fed by the inordinate amount of publicity given to the Leinster, Munster and Ulster Schools Cup competitions. But there is another way. Trevor Brennan (Barnhall), Tom Tierney (Richmond) … Shane Horgan (Drogheda), Mark McHugh (Drogheda) and Colin McEntee (Naas) are players that have come through what is an increasingly influential Youths system. 'Four of the Leinster Under 21 pack that play The Exiles today came

▲ Man of the Match photos: Trevor Brennan and Victor Costello, 1997–8 season. Man-of-the-match awards became increasingly prevalent for sponsors to be recognised.

▲ The Leinster Junior Executive Committee, 1995–6, tasked with facing the challenges of the professional era and how it would impact grass roots, junior rugby.

◄ Winning a Leinster professional era Cap was a moment of prestige in the pro era.

▼ Jim Glennon (right), the first Leinster coach of the professional era.

through the Youths. Noel Foxe, Trevor Hogan, Niall Breslin and Eoin Collins are all selected on merit,' said Leinster Youth coach Aidan Kenna. The message is clear. Irish Youths rugby is gathering in more players, better players.[8]

With a mini boom in underage rugby in Leinster, the provincial club organised various development and underage Leinster squads, which created a potential pathway to the professional game. Around 1998 there was something of a steadying of the ship when the vision for the professional provincial clubs was worked out, and there was a better view of the way forward.

Come April 1998, the reorganised Leinster Branch appointed as Leinster Development Manager former Leinster player Phil Lawlor, whose role was to oversee the development of rugby across the province. He was an advocate for a closer relationship between the clubs and the Branch, where clubs could reach out and ask for services, and the Branch would be willing and able to offer help where possible. The development officer job followed four main guidelines: get kids involved, thereby promoting the game at a young level; keep them involved, encouraging ongoing participation in all aspects of rugby; improve players' skills and technique; spot the elite athlete. Thus, the remit was to focus on the best players and make sure to develop their talents towards provincial and international levels. In addition to a concentration on

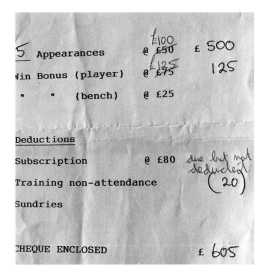

A pro-era payslip from 1995, suggesting that despite the organisation's structures, the professional era caught them a little off guard as regards paying players.

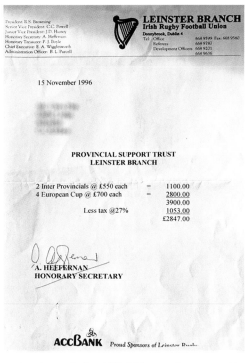

A pro-era payslip from 1996. Within a year there appeared to be a little more 'professionalism' around player payments.

▲ Leinster head coach Mike Ruddock during the interprovincial rugby match between Leinster and Connacht in Donnybrook Stadium in Dublin, August 1997. © Matt Browne/Sportsfile

schools, there was an extra focus on the general underage competitions. The Branch concluded that the most productive and efficient way of enabling these four guidelines was to work with club coaches, via a new long-term development strategy. The general philosophy was that if you can get even one coach in a club and improve their approach, then you might get between twenty to thirty young players earning a solid grounding, potentially steering them down the path towards the Leinster squad.

The Branch created a number of officer roles that focused on different aspects of promoting and improving the game. The first aim was to infiltrate the non-fee-paying schools and create links with local clubs. This was done through the organisation of clinics, coaching courses and seminars, inviting both coaches and players. A three-pronged approach to development was created via partnerships between the IRFU, the Branch and the local club in a provincial town, with each arm pledging financial input to support a club appointment of a Youth Development Officer (YDO). The YDO's job was to target local schools in a particular catchment area and introduce the game to children who had no experience of rugby. The intention was that both the school and the club would benefit from the initiative, with kids getting involved in sports for their physical and mental health helping the remit of the school, while at the same time increasing numbers in the club by bringing in new players and additional membership.

On the eve of the new millennium rugby in Ireland was reaching new heights and, as society moved into an era defined by an economic boom, it is perhaps no surprise that Leinster rugby was sowing the seeds for a brighter future. By the time Argentina came to Donnybrook in August 1999 to take on Leinster as part of the IRFU's 125th-year anniversary, the squad included such future household names as Rob Henderson, Shane Horgan, Girvan Dempsey, Denis Hickey, Reggie Corrigan, Shane Byrne, Victor Costello, Malcolm O'Kelly, Brian O'Driscoll, Trevor Brennan and Gabriel Fulcher. Felipe Contepomi was also playing that day, albeit on the Argentine side. Interestingly, eighteen of the twenty-five-man squad for this game were born in Dublin; of the other seven, only two were born in Leinster – in Wexford and Drogheda – two in Munster (Waterford and Limerick), one in New Zealand and two in the UK.[9] More work needed to be done to make Leinster rugby truly province-wide.

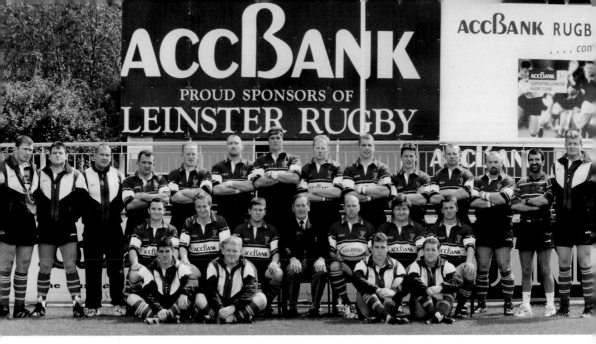

▲ Leinster squad photo, 1997–8 season. The squad was sponsored by ACC Bank and was larger than previous squads, marking a growing sense of professionalism.

'Overnight Professionals'

Interviewed in *The Irish Times* by John O'Sullivan in June 2020, twenty-five years after rugby turned professional, former Leinster captain Gabriel Fulcher and several former teammates were asked to recall the immediate outcome of the 'open game' in the minds of this first set of professional players. As Fulcher put it, for Leinster players it was a case of 'going to sleep an amateur, [and] waking up a professional'.[10] Fulcher was one of the first players to be recruited within a few months of the dawn of the open game, when he was headhunted by London Irish. He recalled:

> about half the [Irish] national squad went to English clubs within that year … The Irish pro scene was a little slower to take action in terms of paying of players, getting contracts [sorted] and recruiting players in whatever way they saw fit but they actually did a better job if you look at what happened in the next five to 10 years and beyond.[11]

It should be remembered that those overseeing Leinster were used to running the amateur game. A deep understanding of the complexities of professionalism, after it was foisted upon them, had to be learned. One of the challenges was the fact that of those involved in rugby – whether players, coaches or administrators – many had professional careers beyond their rugby commitments. Several had businesses to run or, on the younger end of the scale, were in full-time third-level education.

As one might imagine, not only were players trying to reassess their careers and balance their old lives with this new professional game, but the coaches were also struggling to adjust to the new reality. One set of teething pains came about because, in several coaches' minds, being a sports professional meant staff and players should be on the pitch or in the gym five days a week. As ex-player Darragh O'Mahony remembered, for the first several years of professionalism 'it was a case of more, more, more; you are being paid so why aren't you doing something Monday morning, afternoon and evening. There were days when you would come back in and wouldn't be able to walk [after] training on a Monday, Tuesday and Wednesday, you are so physically drained.'[12] Luckily calmer heads prevailed and began to look more closely at the models already in place. The contrast between today and the first five years of professional rugby couldn't be starker. O'Mahony's description certainly invoked the disparity when he recalled there was 'no great science to it, be as big as you can, be as strong as you can, keep going as long as you can ... it had become a pressure environment'.[13] Sentiments of being treated like a piece of meat were at times iterated by early professionals, as the rugby union world made the transition from its amateur past.

In the first year that the game had gone professional, there was almost a tone of defeat in the end-of-season report from Leinster. At the 1995–96 Branch AGM there was certainly a tone of frustration. The Branch was trying 'to foresee the changes that would be necessary to plan for the years ahead. However even the best laid plans were thrown into confusion following the meeting of the International Board last August and the adoption of the principle of the "Open Game" to be administered individually by each Union in its own fashion.'[14] The committee was quick to express its annoyance at the fact that the media seemed to report something new emerging from the International Rugby Board on a weekly basis, thus constantly putting Leinster's plans in jeopardy. The one positive that offered them a glimmer of hope, at least, was the arrival of European Cup rugby.[15]

To the relief of the Leinster Branch, the IRFU decided to introduce a grant-aid scheme of £100,000 for each province for the development of rugby. But now there was a whole new challenge facing the Branch management team. With financial pressures and problems already identified in league structures, the Branch had to conceive a new approach to the competitive structure of the AIL and a programme had to be agreed for the 1996–97 season.[16] Local initiatives to keep players interested in rugby at all levels led to the committee giving approvals for rugby 'sevens', for ten-a-side games and for pre-season tournaments, which were

▲ An example of an interprovincial match-day programme from 1996, dominated by sponsorship front and back.

also touted as a way of bringing players back early to ensure fitness was addressed in advance of the season. Additionally, the regeneration of Donnybrook was begun, with the widening of the pitch, improvement to the playing surface and expansion of the terraces at either end for increased capacity, as well as the installation of new floodlights either completed or in train. The next stage was the redevelopment of the big stand, earmarked as a long-term project. Also at Donnybrook, advertising signage space inside and outside the ground was increased to maximise income. Murphy Breweries, via the Heineken Brand, agreed to sponsor the Metropolitan Cup and the J1 League for three years, and they ploughed money into national media coverage too, with the *Evening Herald* and the *Star* newspaper covering games. More sponsorship than ever before was going to be needed going forward, and marketing was to be ramped up.

Despite these positive steps, the uncertainty of the future was expressed in the hesitation by Irish rugby bosses to decide on how best to implement a pay-for-play system. 'Following the decision arrived at [by] the International Board

▲ The Leinster Under-20s 1995 squad, winners of two trophies. Back row, sixth from the left, a certain Leo Cullen (current head coach 2023) stands tall.

in August 1995 that the game become "Open" the IRFU made a decision not to pay players below National Squad Level … it was subsequently decided to make a match fee available to Senior Provincial players for European Cup games and the Interprovincial Championship.'[17] But even this was rolled out on such an ad hoc basis, that players like Chris Pim recalled receiving payslips where the amount of money received for a game was often crossed out with a pen and rewritten alongside improvised bonuses. As many of the first generation of professional players also had full-time jobs, Leinster could somewhat get away with 'winging it', at least for a time. However, the one central concern that all the clubs were raising was the approaches being made to Irish players by clubs from England. In response, the IRFU realised, albeit slowly, that going forward it would need to negotiate full-time contracts early, in order to keep the top players in Ireland. That aside, the success of the Leinster senior team in the inaugural professional season was noteworthy. Under manager Jim Glennon and coach Ciaran Callan, alongside selector Paul Dean, and with the use of a thirty-eight-player squad, the

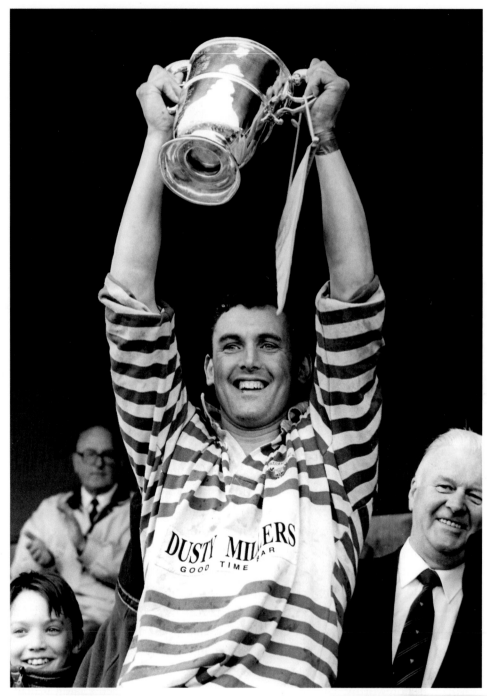

▲ Greystones win the 1996 Metropolitan Cup.

team won the Interprovincial Championship; they also reached the semi-final of the inaugural European Cup, but lost out to Cardiff at Lansdowne Road, in front of an attendance of 7,350.[18]

Elsewhere, youth club teams were still increasing and the clubs finally seemed to have grasped that the underage set-up was essential to their own future success. That said, the Leinster Branch continued to place a central focus on the private school tradition. Indeed, end-of-year Branch reports continued to reiterate what had almost become year in, year out, boiler-plate contentions about the centrality of the fee-paying schools: 'The strength of Leinster Schools Rugby is crucial to our continued success as a Province at all levels of representative and A.I.L. Club rugby.'[19] In 1999 the *Irish Times*' rugby correspondent, Gerry Thornley, flagged a couple of glaring realities with the schools' set-up. Under the headline, 'Debunking the myth of schools' rugby', Thornley highlighted the excessive focus that the Leinster Schools Cup seemed to attract from the doyens of the provincial set-up, which in turn created an almost cult-like obsession. Thornley admitted, 'This writer, like others, will dutifully attend and wax lyrical about the purity/glorified escapism (dilute to taste) of schools' cup rugby'.[20] Thornley had been admonished by a particular private school's head coach for being too critical in his reportage of the games and the players. It was this that initiated in him a sense of reflection, leading him to raise some concerns to which Leinster rugby were apparently oblivious. He spotlighted the whole dynamic around this competition, not least in the schools themselves:

> They're the ones who train the kids upwards of five times a week (to the detriment of schooling?) They're the ones who prepare for the Leinster Schools' Senior Cup as if it's the biggest competition in the world. They're the ones, in at least one if not two cases, who reportedly prescribe creatine as part of the players' diet. In short, they're the ones applying the pressure as much as anyone else.[21]

Because schools' rugby in Leinster meant a competition between a handful of privileged schools, an obscene amount of money was piled into the boys' rugby programmes in order to attract a particular cohort of student and, indeed, fee-paying parent. That the system, as it has stood for so many years, produced a 'closed shop' was highlighted by Thornley:

... generally, it is the same elite within an elite which wins the competition year after year. Sporadically, the likes of CBC Monkstown (winners in '76 and finalists in '84) or De La Salle Churchtown (winners in '83 and '84) upset the cosy cartel. But ... [usually] it's been the same four schools who have won the Leinster Schools' Senior Cup ... Most pertinently of all, even some within the IRFU will privately admit that the elitist schools' game contributed to the Union abrogating their responsibilities when it came to spreading the Gospel. Arguably, the likes of Barnhall ... with their extensive under-age rugby network in non-schools' rugby areas, do more, far more, for the long-term betterment of Irish rugby. When the Leinster Schools' Senior Cup starts producing players from non-traditional bases, then truly they can claim to be doing something for Irish rugby. For the moment, it remains ... something of a closed shop and a sacred cow for all that.[22]

Apart from the Leinster Branch's privileging of the fee-paying schools, their 'sacred cow', elsewhere they continued to support grassroots rugby, and while there was a need to readjust at all levels in the professional era, at least many of the club-orientated structures in place were enabling the game to thrive.

In spite of early teething problems, the fact remained there was growth in interest in rugby and a desire for high-quality professional sports among the Leinster public. The honorary secretary's tone in the end-of-year summation for the 1996–97 season was much less angst-ridden than the previous year's. The professional-era realities were 'now accepted facts of life. Nonetheless, the three-tier policy of the IRFU, namely country, province, clubs, has caused anxiety both for the Branch and the Leinster Clubs which has been compounded by the departure of many of our more talented players to play what they see as more financially rewarding and challenging rugby in the United Kingdom.'[23] This reality led to some legitimate criticism, in terms of the lack of urgency to adjust to the change, and certainly the bizarre fantasy of an amateur ethos still hanging around Irish rugby while it had long been put out of its misery elsewhere. One thing that was immediately recognised was that the presence and the success of the now expanded European Cup was essential to the survival of Leinster in the professional era.

The appointment of a director of coaching was also a pressing new priority. As Sandy Heffernan wrote, 'Contracts will be offered to a panel of 30 players for the forthcoming season ... With the creation of Provincial contracts, allied to the National contracts, it is hoped that some of our overseas players will return to Leinster.'[24]

▲ Terenure, Leinster Senior League Cup winners 1996. As Leinster adjusted to the professional era, pro players were still affiliated with and allowed to play with their clubs.

With a determination to make Leinster rugby a success, the Branch reported to the IRFU in 1997 its concerns around 'the issues involved in accommodating full-time professionalism in Leinster, the exodus of Leinster players to overseas clubs and the creation of a playing and professional environment necessary to attract back those Leinster players contracted overseas'.[25] With the dust somewhat settling in 1996–97, the Branch asked for the clubs' support in the transition to the 'open game', while it tackled the numerous problems thrown at it vis-à-vis professionalism.

Ostensibly, what the administration needed to get their minds around was the reinvention of a Provincial Leinster Rugby Club. That required a whole new dimension of thinking about the province as its own entity and what that meant in terms of creating a fan base, a sense of club loyalty therein and the relationship with *all* of Leinster going forward. As the turn of the millennium approached, despite the professional players retaining an affiliation with club sides, once they had become a senior Leinster player they were essentially a Leinster rugby team employee and not likely to play much, if any, club rugby. In the meantime, the priority for the Branch was to stop those professional players departing en masse to the UK. Thus, contract issues needed to be sorted out much more efficiently.[26] Three seasons in

▲ Leinster Schools 1997 squad. Earning a place in the Leinster schools team and entering the system in this manner would become a central route to the professional game.

and Leinster rugby was adjusting expeditiously. Problems, of course, arose along the way, and when the amateur clubs began to pay players as well, some began to find themselves in financial trouble. There were still adjustments required and a need for calibration as the professional era settled in.

On the ground, the work of development officers in the rest of the province continued to try to pair up local clubs with whatever ordinary schools were close by, making pathways between school and club players. This led to an increase in the numbers of secondary schools newly affiliated to the Branch.[27] Some of the most noticeable success of the work being done was in southeast Leinster. It was quite striking that seven Wexford schools came into rugby in 1997, the same year that a young Clongowes Wood rugby player and Wexford native, Gordon D'Arcy, was togging out with the Leinster senior squad and had been called up to play for Ireland. In addition, the first ever full-time CEO of Leinster rugby, Eddie Wigglesworth, was tasked with setting the professional Leinster rugby outfit on the right path in the new era. He was joined by full-time employees Brian Purcell, Valerie Keogh and Catriona Muldowney running the Branch itself, and Marion Horan running the Association of Referees.[28] The transition was ongoing, but the Leinster outfit was finding its feet as an organisation for the new rugby age.

On the domestic level, the AIL introduced play-offs to decide the champions of each division for the first time, a proposition that envisioned not only exciting competitive games, but an increase in fan interest and hopefully bigger gates for play-off games. However, there still seemed to be a slow-moving approach in the professional era, which hindered Leinster's success. For example, the squad that competed in the 1997–98 season only had eight full-time, contracted players and the other twenty-two were all part-timers. The next season, 1998–99, signalled some greater urgency perhaps, when twenty-one full-time contracts were offered to squad players and another nine part-time contracts. In terms of facilities, nonetheless, it would soon become apparent that Leinster, as yet, lagged far behind in terms of what was needed. The Branch was still trying to navigate the unchartered waters of professional rugby and sensitive to every change and alteration that the era was delivering. Thus, when the 1998–99 season saw 'the number of teams competing in the Metropolitan Area … halved', as well as a slight fall-off outside of Dublin too, the Branch rang the alarm bells and foretold of worrying trends.[29] But the levelling off was part and parcel of the new professional era. Clubs amalgamated as the professional Leinster rugby outfit emerged, and youth and development squads were implemented in order to ensure a persistent conveyor belt of talent.

Further Developments in the Pro Era

The post-1995 rugby scene in Leinster invited in a preponderance of players and coaches from the southern hemisphere across all the clubs at all levels. One could not frequent a town across the province during a rugby weekend without hearing a Kiwi, Aussie or South African brogue in the bars and nightclubs of provincial centres. As *Ireland on Sunday*'s Mark Jones reflected, 'From junior levels right to the very top, the men from down under have cast their spell.'[30] There was, then, a trend across the northern rugby world, where Australian, New Zealand and South African influence was the new norm. The motivation was the need to quickly adjust to the high standards of rugby needed to compete in an era when there was now a professional league. The required rise in standards went from the top to the bottom. It was common sense, then, that clubs, the provinces and the IRFU itself looked to their southern-hemisphere brethren for guidance. The New Zealand, Australian and South African game of rugby had for many years been streets ahead of rugby in Europe. Facilities, preparation, coaching and management more broadly were verging on the professional level already. Thus, when opportunities to hire from 'down under' arose, many clubs took full advantage.

This did cause some tension, however, and something of a backlash amongst a few involved in Irish rugby. For home-grown coaches who attended the Leinster Branch seminars, lectures and courses, and earned their requisite accreditations only to be told that there was an Aussie, Kiwi or South African being flown in to try out something new in club coaching, there was sometimes a feeling of being skipped in the queue. However, in the first decades of the professional era, the expertise of those who had more professional experience (and were happy and willing to offer it to Irish rugby) was badly needed. In the end, one of the main problems was the danger of the expenses that such recruitment was causing for clubs, with the temptation of trying to buy success on the pitch – a strategy that would ultimately hurt rugby if it was allowed to persist in the club game without oversight.[31] These were the kinds of omens being predicted by pundits and observers of the game at club level at least.

At the junior level there were now sixty-four Leinster clubs, although there were a few ongoing issues for the junior section with reports of clubs apparently struggling to field teams and enter competitions due to players often going AWOL.[32] Despite concerns about losing Irish players from the game at the recreational

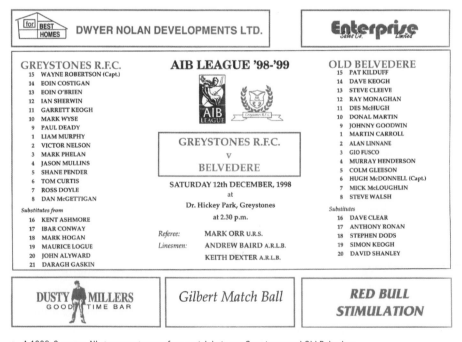

▲ A 1998-9 season AIL game programme for a match between Greystones and Old Belvedere.

level, the number of overseas players and coaches continued to increase in the junior section. There were many positive elements to this, such as foreign players introducing new ideas and unfamiliar elements of play from their home countries, and of course helping to fill some of the gaps in terms of player and coaching numbers. The IRFU and the Leinster Branch had been careful to ensure the amateur clubs would receive grant money to ensure grassroots rugby progressed positively, despite the professional team taking up much of the administration's focus. These awards were to be supplemented with an increase in prize money also, with Leinster League Division One-winners who made it through to compete in the round-robin for the AIL Division Four promotion game awarded £1,000 for winning their Leinster Division, and £1,500 if they won the round robin to help them adjust to their newly achieved senior status as an AIL club.[33]

The public's appetite for Leinster rugby came into its own in the new millennium, with season tickets exploding from a mere 7,000 in 1999 up to 22,000 in 2000.[34] For the forthcoming season the Branch awarded twenty-nine contracts to professional players, with a number of part-time contracts also. With the under-twenty-one team undefeated for the season, the foundations for a future successful team were certainly there. The under-eighteens won the provincial trophy again that year, for two in a row, and defeated a Scottish Borders team both home and away.[35] It was now a matter for the senior

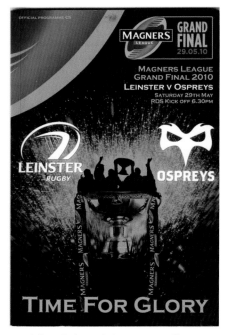

▲ ▼ Leinster Rugby match-day programmes: Magners League final 2010 front cover and a pre-season friendly between Leinster Lions and Bristol Shoguns, 2002, at Longford RFC.

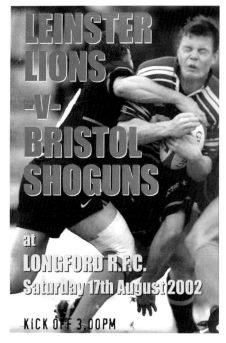

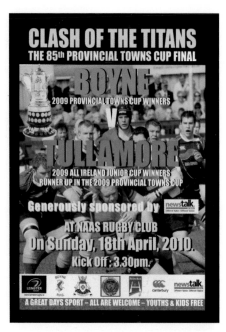

▲ ▼ Leinster club rugby match-day programmes, Boyne v. Tullamore in the 2010 Provincial Towns Cup final, and Old Belvedere v. Blackrock College in the 1999–2000 season Senior Cup final.

squad to achieve their full potential. In the 2001–02 Branch handbook there were sixty-five rugby clubs affiliated, which should have given the administrators a sense of positivity given the amount of adult and youth teams playing the game.

The handbook also listed women's teams affiliated – there were only a handful at that stage, including Clane, Guinness, Ashbourne, Blackrock, Portlaoise, Mullingar, Carlow and Old Belvedere. While the women's game was becoming more forthright about its importance for sportswomen and girls, its growing popularity, and the support it deserved and needed from the Branch, it was still relatively young in an Irish context. When efforts were made to create women's teams within clubs, schools, colleges and universities, these were welcomed, although some men in the organisation may have seen the women's game as a mere novelty. For others, it was received as a wholly positive endeavour to see young women with a passion for the rugby game. It would take a few years and a little bit more enlightenment – and indeed a cold, hard sense of economic opportunity – to entice Leinster rugby to embrace and absorb the idea of women's rugby more fully.

Aside from the first signs of real progress in the women's game, the men's senior team saw Jim Glennon step down as manager at the end of the 1997–98 season. Mike Ruddock was already acting as head coach, and continued in that role until the end of the 1999–2000 season. Looking back, both men admitted that although rugby had entered a professional

Cashel woman stars in the world of rugby

■ International XV to face England at the weekend

by John Donohoe

While the sport of women's gaelic football has been gaining an increasingly high profile in recent years, one game which has not yet received as much prominence is women's rugby.

And while Longford has had some fairly successful women footballers, one young woman to watch out for on the rugby scene is Toni Brennan from Newtowncashel.

Twenty-six year old Toni is a member of the Irish woman's rugby team, and has played against Wales and France.

She plays club rugby with Corinthians in Galway, where she is teaching in the Holy Rosary College in Mountbellew. Corinthians are playing Division 1 in Galway and Toni has been playing with them for three years.

"My next game with Ireland is against England at Stradbrook, the Blackrock RFC grounds," Toni explains. The Irish women met the French side in Dublin too, and travelled over to Llaneli to meet Wales.

Toni took up rugby at college in the University of Limerick.

"I've been playing on the left wing at number 11 position, but my usual posi-tion would be second centre," she explains.

However, one thing which is of great concern to Toni and the Irish Womens Rugby Football Union is the fact that there is no sponsorship of the Irish women's team, as there is with the men's side, or indeed, many other sports.

"The Welsh, French and English women's teams are all sponsored, and they have fantastic gear. We had to pay to go over to Wales - pay to play, so to speak," Toni says.

The IRFU are currently in discussion with the women's union over the funding issue, and Toni is appealing to any business in the Leader region which would be interested in lending support to the women's team, to contact the union.

▲ The *Longford Leader*, 5 March 1999, with a story that underscores the growth of Irish women's rugby.

reality, Leinster was far, far away from being a fully professional outfit, without any real facilities in place to cater for a professional sports squad. It was the inception of the three-nations tournament known as the Celtic League in 2001, with all games played from August to December, that allowed the coaches, players and managers to demand more from the Branch, laying the foundations that would transform Leinster into the world-class rugby organisation it would become. After Ruddock left, Australian Matt Williams took over at a pivotal moment, when the Celtic League in particular demanded the Leinster organisation step up another gear in how it conducted itself as a professional sporting outfit. Williams believed that winning the Celtic League in December 2001 instilled a sense of belief into a group of players who had not tasted silverware in their first five seasons of professional rugby. Seeds had been sown and higher expectations were demanded. However, Munster were also excelling and had in their midst some of Ireland's best-ever rugby players, who would lead the southern province to great success in the early 2000s.

On the positive side for Leinster rugby more generally, the rise of the Celtic Tiger era in Ireland coincided with an uptick in spectatorship, which one might safely deduce helped ensure regular crowds for Leinster rugby matches. Increased interest in Leinster in 2000–01 was mirrored across the other European nations who had teams involved in the Heineken Cup, which had been running from the inception of the professional era in 1995. The cup facilitated

the lure of watching world stars playing in Europe's premier club tournament … [it] pulled in over a quarter of a million spectators through the turnstiles at the 36 matches [in 2000-01]. Eight matches … attracted crowds of over 10,000

... to help take the overall figure to 255,376 compared to the 1999/2000 three rounds total of 205,406. ... [And] the good news does not end there – the tournament is just as popular with armchair viewers.[36]

When Leinster faced Munster in the Celtic League final at Lansdowne Road for the 2001 championship, it heightened the sense of provincial rivalry for the professional era. Leinster were crowned the first winners of the league in front of an attendance estimated at about 25,500, making that competition a major success in its inaugural year. While so much focus was generally aimed at the pan-European Heineken Cup, this initial success in the Celtic League was a pivotal moment for Leinster. In terms of running a professional sports team, in a regular professional league – ensuring a fit, conditioned and skilful squad of players – it suggested that the Leinster organisation was moving in the right direction.

Having secured his team the first ever Celtic League win and coming close to a European Cup final in the 2002–03 season, Matt Williams, as a standout coach, was headhunted by Scotland in 2003, and an offer of an international rugby job was one he felt he couldn't, at that moment in his career, turn down. The subsequent story of the appointment and dismissal in 2003–04 of his replacement, Gary Ella, alongside the poaching of coach Declan Kidney (first by Leinster and then by Munster) in

▲ Action shot from a Leinster club rugby match in the 1990s.

2004–05 arguably upset the momentum that Williams had conjured. Ella's dismissal was somewhat acrimonious. For all intents and purposes there seemed to be a clash of personalities between him and some of the bigger-named players in his squad. Ella felt that certain figures came to the club with an over-inflated sense of privilege and not enough respect for the squad. Frustrated at the lack of success on the pitch, Ella partially blamed poor results on the internationals in his team, suggesting their priorities were focused on the green jersey first and not on their club. There were, then, some differences of opinion with the IRFU and with Branch officials at Leinster, and in the end Ella's contract was ended. The acrimony came when Ella aired his criticisms in the press of the players, as well as the Branch and the IRFU after they delayed paying him his termination-of-contract fees, in what seemed to be a rather uncomfortable ending.

▲ Lansdowne Cup winning senior side in the 1990s – Leinster professional players still togged out for their clubs.

▲ Enniscorthy Towns' Cup finalists 1995.

▲ Leinster Branch Executive Committee, 2002.

After the relatively poor previous season under Ella's stewardship, new coach Declan Kidney had managed to somewhat restore winning ways for Leinster, as they went on a run of fifteen games undefeated in Dublin and finished third of the eleven teams competing in the Celtic League. They won five out of six games against the other Irish provinces also, but the perennial defeat to Munster continued to haunt Leinster, as they went on to lose three out of the next four games in that campaign. Nonetheless, Leinster fared well in the European competition, having won all six pool matches in the Heineken Cup only to be defeated in the quarter-finals by Leicester; it was after that defeat that Kidney resigned under somewhat controversial circumstances and there was a sense of betrayal when he announced, after less than a season, that he was leaving Leinster to coach Munster. Gerry Murphy, who had been one of Kidney's assistants, took over as interim coach just to finish out the last two months of the 2004–05 season, until the appointment of Michael Cheika in the summer of 2005. Kidney returned to his native province of Munster, and very quickly led that squad to rugby success.

Despite Kidney's departure, Leinster looked a formidable side when, at times, eleven of the starting fifteen were of international calibre. Regardless, when the New Year of that 2004–05 season rolled around, the first result perhaps summed up what many identified as a perennial problem when Leinster suffered another loss to provincial rivals Munster. The accusation persisted that the Leinster team were not really a team at all, but a conglomerate of spoiled individuals without any passion or grit. That the vast majority of the players were rich boys from the

Leinster

Donnybrook
Dublin 4
Eire
T +353 (0)1 6689599
F +353 (0)1 6689580
E irfulb@iol.ie
w www.leinster-rugby.com

Media contact

Tom McCormack
T +353 (0)1 2303015
F +353 (0)1 2303014
M +353 (0)86 2454215
E tommcc@indigo.ie

Executive Staff and Team contacts

President	Team Manager
John West	Ken Ging
Chief Executive	Head Coach
Barry O'Sullivan	Matt Williams
Hon Secretary	Assistant Coach
Sandy Heffernan	Alan Gaffney

Club details
Ground: Donnybrook
Capacity: 7,500
Floodlights: Yes

Colours
Home: Blue/White/Yellow
Away: White/Blue/Yellow

Main sponsor: Bank of Scotland

Irish Interprovincial Championship 2000-2001
3rd Place

Update

Leinster coach Matt Williams reports an excellent start to Leinster's preparations for the forthcoming Celtic League. "So far all our fitness, strength and ballwork sessions have gone very well. Lions' Brian O' Driscoll and Malcolm O'Kelly are on a well deserved break until August 10th but they and all rest of the players are really looking forward to doing well in what is a new competition for us. New signings Keith Gleeson, Adam Magro, Nathan Spooner and Ben Willis are in good shape and Paul Wallace is enjoying being back with Leinster (from Saracens) and his ankle rehabilitation is on schedule for the start of the Celtic League. Roll on August 17th!" he said.

Surname	Christian name	Position	Height	Weight	Date of Birth	Honours
Barretto	Steve	Prop	1.78m/5'10"	113kg/17st 11lb	15.06.78	
Blaney	Dave	Hooker	1.83m/6'0"	94kg/14st 11lb	03.03.79	
Breslin	Niall	Flanker	1.88m/6'2"	100kg/15st 10lb	22.10.80	
Brennan	Trevor	Flanker	1.96m/6'5"	109kg/17st 0lb	22.09.73	Ireland
Byrne	Emmett	Prop	1.83m/6'0"	107kg/16st 12lb	04.04.73	Ireland
Byrne	Shane	Hooker	1.78m/5'10"	98kg/15st 6lb	18.07.71	Ireland
Casey	Bob	Lock	1.96m/6'5"	120kg/18st 12lb	18.07.78	Ireland
Corrigan	Reg	Prop	1.88m/6'2"	113kg/17st 0lb	19.11.70	Ireland
Costello	Victor	No 8	1.96m/6'5"	119kg/18st 10lb	23.10.70	Ireland
Coyle	Peter	Prop	1.83m/6'0"	108kg/17st 0lb	18.11.75	
Cullen	Leo	Lock	2.03m/6'8"	108kg/17st 0lb	09.01.78	
D'arcy	Gordon	Full Back/Wing	1.78m/5'10"	89kg/14st 0lb	10.02.80	Ireland
Dempsey	Girvan	Full Back	1.83m/6'0"	90kg/14st 2lb	02.10.75	Ireland
Dunne	Andrew	Outside Half	1.73m/5'8"	79kg/12st 6lb	18.10.79	
Farrell	Emmet	Outside Half	1.78m/5'10"	90kg/14st 2lb	06.03.77	
Gleeson	Keith	Flanker	1.85m/6'1"	96kg/15st 0lb		
Hickie	Denis	Wing	1.81m/5'11"	92kg/14st 7lb	13.02.76	Ireland
Hickie	Gavin	Hooker	1.81m/5'11"	96kg/15st 0lb	24.04.80	
Horgan	Shane	Centre/Wing	1.93m/6'4"	101kg/15st 12lb	18.07.78	Ireland
Jennings	Shane	Flanker	1.83m/6'0"	96kg/15st 0lb		
Keogh	Simon	Scrum Half/Wing	1.71m/5'7"	80kg/12st 9lb	05.09.75	
Magro	Adam	Centre	1.83m/6'0"	87kg/13st 10lb	14.04.71	Australia
McCullen	Aidan	Flanker	1.93m/6'4"	106kg/16st 10lb	15.01.77	
McKenna	Peter	F Back/Wg/Cen	1.81m/5'11"	86kg/13st 7lb	24.11.73	Ireland
McWeeney	John	Wing	1.91m/6'3"	92kg/14st 7lb	26.05.76	Ireland
Miller	Eric	Flanker	1.88m/6'2"	104kg/16st 5lb	23.09.75	Ireland/Lions
Norton	James	Wing	1.75m/5'9"	85kg/13st 5lb	18.05.81	
O'Brien	Declan	Flanker	1.91m/6'3"	108kg/17st 0lb	25.11.73	
O'Driscoll	Brian	Centre	1.75m/5'9"	92kg/14st 7lb	21.01.79	Ireland/Lions
O'Kelly	Malcolm	Lock	2.03m/6'8"	109kg/17st 2lb	19.07.74	Ireland/Lions
O'Meara	Brian	Scrum Half	1.75m/5'9"	86kg/13st 7lb	05.04.76	Ireland
Quinlan	David	Centre	1.93m/6'4"	98kg/15st 6lb		
Spooner	Nathan	Outside Half	1.81m/5'11"	88kg/13st 12lb	07.11.75	Australia
Treston	Niall	Prop	1.81m/5'11"	104kg/16st 5lb	06.02.80	
Wallace	Paul	Prop	1.85m/6'1"	107kg/16st 12lb	30.12.71	Ireland/Lions
Willis	Ben	Scrum Half	1.71m/5'7"	86kg/13st 7lb	08.10.76	

▲ *Celtic League Media Guide 2001-02*, Leinster Rugby Club details.

posh parts of Dublin echoed throughout the province and, indeed, further afield. On the day that Leinster lost to Munster in Cork, the team that lined out had such names as Girvan Dempsey (Terenure), Eric Miller (Terenure), Shane Horgan (Lansdowne), Reggie Corrigan (Lansdowne), Brian O'Driscoll (UCD), Gordon D'Arcy (Lansdowne), Victor Costello (St Mary's), Shane Jennings (St Mary's), Denis Hickie (St Mary's), Guy Easterby (Blackrock), Shane Byrne (Blackrock), Leo Cullen (Blackrock), Emmet Byrne (Wanderers) and David Holwell (a New Zealander). Twelve internationals started that day, yet they were still defeated. The conundrum remained of how to solve the so-called Leinster identity problem.

The frustration of Leinster rugby followers was manifest when the team were knocked out of the Heineken Cup at the quarter-final stage in 2005. Their

▲ Leinster v. Argentina match to mark the 125th anniversary of the Branch. Felipe Contepomi on the run for the Pumas.

disappointment, at least temporarily, is evident in the fact that at a subsequent quarter-final game of the Celtic League at Lansdowne Road, a paltry turnout of 3,100 spectators came to watch. This was not even half the number required to break even once the stadium was opened for any game. To rub salt into the wounds, Declan Kidney went on to win the Heineken Cup final with his Munster charges in 2006, while Leinster remained a club in need of a serious self-re-evaluation. The end of 2004–05 required something of a clear-out, with several players moving on and the start of a veritable overhaul of Leinster rugby's approach to the professional game. Perhaps the criticisms at times manifest in the low gate receipts spurred on a sense that something new was needed, a fresh approach for Leinster Rugby to fully realise itself in the professional era. Records suggest they invested in the right person to help lead that change at the club, as Leinster entered another new phase in its evolution with the appointment of Michael Cheika.

2001 - 2002

INAUGURAL CELTIC LEAGUE FINAL

The League season started on the 17th August with a 39-11 win over Glasgow. The inaugural Celtic League final was held on 15th December 2001, Leinster faced Munster in a dramatic game the impact of which was to be the birth of a terrible beauty... in the form of a fierce rivalry, one that would dominate the Irish rugby landscape, both in the League and Europe for the decade that followed.

▲ Leinster in the inaugural Celtic League final (top), and Leinster players after defeat in the final.

▲ Blackrock College RFC yearbook for the start of the club season 2000-01, with a young Brian O'Driscoll on the cover.

12

Creating Club Leinster

Creating Club Leinster

Leinster Branch CEO Michael Dawson, who was appointed to the role in November 2001 from Davy Stockbrokers, came with a background as a former player, first team coach and director with the Lansdowne club. In April 2004 Dawson was interviewed for the business supplement of *The Sunday Times*, giving a frank insight into the Leinster rugby enterprise. As an introduction, business writer Ciaran Hancock explained that while the playing season might be coming to a close and 'while the players take a rest, the rugby province continues its quest to bring commercial success in the form of a new home'.[1] Almost a decade into the professional rugby world, Leinster had come a long way and, as a business, the focus for those at the top had to be the ledgers. Thus, Leinster's early departure in the group stages of the Heineken Cup was one of the first subjects broached. That 'early exit from the competition cost the club about €500,000 in lost revenue. In the brave new world of professionalism, where Leinster's running costs are more than €4m annually, it's a sum of money that would have come in useful.'[2]

The way that the professional game worked was that players were actually contracted to the IRFU, so a wage bill at the time of €2.5 million was picked up by the Irish rugby head office, but the Branch had to create the other €2 million plus needed to make ends meet. In his role as CEO, Dawson had a perpetually upbeat perspective, highlighting the fact that in the previous year's Heineken Cup quarter-final against Biarritz, Leinster broke the record for a European rugby crowd

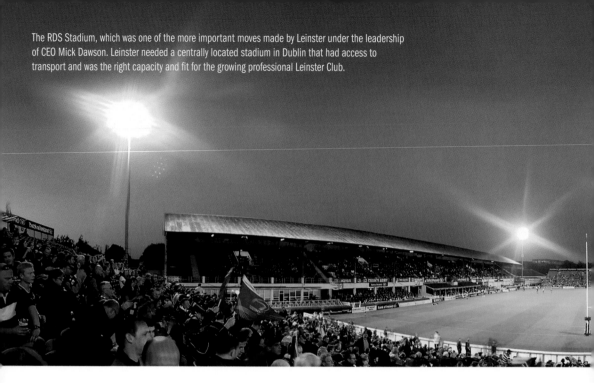

at that stage of the tournament, with over 44,000 coming out to Lansdowne Road. The Donnybrook ground, at this stage of the Leinster journey, was still the team's primary home, but its limited capacity meant that the much larger Lansdowne Road stadium was the venue of choice for the biggest games in the schedule. The CEO also highlighted how securing a sponsorship deal with the Bank of Scotland for €2.5 million over three years gave him much optimism for the future.[3]

That Dawson spoke frankly about the long-term plans for the professional aspect at Leinster heralded the focus and desire within the organisation to achieve the highest standards in professional rugby union. What's more, it was during the 2003–04 season of the Celtic League that a home-and-away format was introduced for the first time for competing teams. The Celtic League became an important centrepiece to the rugby season as the Heineken Cup was only guaranteeing six matches – a team had to qualify from its pool into the play-offs if they were going to have more than this. So the Celtic League was important for keeping players sharp and for match practice, as well as creating competition for places and providing live, first-rate professional rugby matches for the fans throughout the entire season.

It was well recognised in 2004, to use Dawson's phrasing, that the strength of the Leinster brand was growing, with over 12,000 Leinster jerseys being sold in 2003 alone. However, the reality for professional rugby in Leinster was that it was a far cry from being a truly province-wide game. When confronted by a comparison with Munster and the issue of rugby being merely 'a D4 game', Dawson claimed,

'Clearly our support is primarily Dublin-based, but we'd draw fans from all parts of the city and not just the environs of D4', if a bigger and more accessible stadium than the ground in Donnybrook could be secured. As he explained, 'if you live outside Dublin, accessibility is a problem especially with games being played on Friday nights and traffic the way it is'.[4] Dawson was clear in his focus on how to make the Leinster team appeal to not just everyone across the city of Dublin, but further afield in Leinster as well. That is, he strongly believed that if Leinster's wider fan base had a stadium that they felt was more accessible, in terms of a larger capacity and more convenient location, then they would come.

In the final assessment of the progress of Leinster's professional arm in 2004, there was an acknowledgement that provincial support needed to be nurtured and expanded, largely because of the historical exclusiveness ingrained in the way senior and thus provincial rugby had maintained itself. Dawson's own assessment was forthright about the realities of a club in the professional era, and the three main challenges then facing the organisation were a proper stadium, the growth of revenue to meet the demands of funding the team, and the widening of the fan base beyond the D4 catchment area, which was, at that point, essentially the Leinster footprint.[5] That Leinster needed to do a better job of developing its market throughout the entire province was further articulated by various business commentators who were asked to offer their assessments of Leinster's progress in the pro era. One said:

> Leinster are perceived by most … as being a south Dublin phenomenon. While the club has received nationwide media coverage, it has largely failed to make the break with that Dublin dependence. Clubs such as Carlow and Barnhall have shown that there is potential in the rest of the province but these new markets have yet to be developed by Leinster. The club needs to select key population areas with existing rugby infrastructure and target clubs and schools there.[6]

This sentiment was echoed by several of the commentators, who were tasked with rating the progress and challenges facing the professional sports team of Leinster rugby. One commentator offered up the idea that whenever there were games at Lansdowne, due to its excess capacity on any given Leinster game day, the organisation should offer free tickets to schoolchildren, which would in turn boost adult ticket sales because parents would need to accompany their kids. It was likely that this would also lead to an increase in merchandising sales, because it was most often children's demands that drove purchases.[7]

While these were some of the off-field issues that informed the evolution of the Leinster rugby outfit, on the field there was much to be positive about. The team were improving season on season under Cheika, and the structures that fostered young talent were leaving those who watched the pitch-related progress feeling upbeat. Aside from the Leinster senior team's positive diagnosis in terms of the talent on the pitch, the domestic Leinster league was not doing so well and there was an abundance of pessimism in the ether when it came to the challenges for the amateur club game. In the words of Eddie Wigglesworth, who had become the IRFU's director of rugby development, 'The game has gone through dramatic, catastrophic change since it went professional and a very significant spend spiral came into club rugby in Ireland at the time. We have fiscal turmoil now, we have player loss at junior level, volunteer haemorrhage, foreign coach and foreign player importation.'[8] Clearly, then, the state of rugby in Ireland and in Leinster was not all peachy, despite the professional team's more positive progress.

More specifically, there was a lot of angst among the clubs. The local rugby scene was beginning to lose its volunteer base, it seemed, with people becoming disillusioned at the way clubs were spending money and who they were spending it on. In response to this particular sense of crisis, a new AIL format was proposed and debated in the spring of 2004 to try and resuscitate rugby at club level. The new format was as follows: 'There will be a 10-week provincial league beginning

▲ Leinster junior club action, Old Kilcullen & Ashbourne, early 2000s. As the pro-era advanced the clubs struggled at times to adjust, but rugby interest kept growing.

in September 2005 organized by the provincial branches. Based on the results of the provincial leagues, three AIL leagues will be formed for the second half of the season … It is the province that wins or loses an AIL divisional slot and not the club.'[9] So, regardless of how well a senior one team in the AIL was doing, if they did not have structures in place that would bring success in the provincial leagues, then that club would lose its spot in the AIL. As well as the proposed new league format, a Leinster Branch subcommittee met regularly with the IRFU to ensure that the proper investments were being channelled into the domestic game. Its arguments had a familiar ring about them: with a strong domestic league as the foundation, especially through investment in youth sections, then the success of the game in Ireland should continue. Without retaining focus on the grassroots, rugby at the upper levels would begin to struggle.[10]

In that regard, the junior committee reported some worrying trends, with a noticeable decline in numbers playing junior rugby and teams struggling to fulfil fixtures on certain weekends during the year. As the Branch's junior secretary disdainfully pointed out, 'Rugby is now competing against skiing holidays and stag weekends home and abroad. As our society had become more affluent, we

LEINSTER YOUTH COMMITTEE IN FOCUS

The Leinster Youths Committee was established in the late 1970's following the development of youth rugby by Tom Kettle, Balbriggan RFC and Dave O'Daly, Navan RFC. Youths Rugby was in its infancy in the Province with Balbriggan very much at the forefront of its development in Leinster. The purpose of the Youth Committee was to develop rugby and regulate competitions within the sector. The early competitions were for mini's, U13's, 15's, and 17's with five under age Provincial Cups, the Kettle, McGowan, Coyle, Culleton and McAuley Cups, competed for each year at these levels. Competitions have now extended to girls and boys at all age grade levels as well as festivals for the mini's.

During the mid-1990's the registration and card system was developed and headed up by Hugh Woodhouse, Mullingar RFC a long established member of the Youth Committee with over 40 years' service to youth rugby. The registration system was brought in to ensure that players were playing at the correct grade. Speaking with Hugh he remembers in the early days of the system clubs submitted a birth cert and photo into the branch and the details were put onto card, stamped on the back and laminated. Today technology has made the process less arduous and more efficient for everyone. The registration system was formally adopted by the IRFU in 2000.

In addition to the establishment of the Youth Committee there were two other key dates; the establishment of the Schools Youth competitions which enables players that attend non-exempt schools (rugby schools) to continue playing rugby for their clubs. The third key date was in 2008 when Girls Rugby came under the wing of the Youth Committee.

The development of girl's rugby has been growing exponentially over the past decade and is testament to the commitment by Leinster and the Youth Committee to this sector of the game. The girls compete in 2 competitions a league and a cup as well as representative rugby for their areas.

Over the decades this committee has grown from strength to strength and is undoubtedly the backbone of the success of youth rugby in Leinster. With the growth of youth rugby came the necessity to extend the youth committee to deal with the extra work load this brought with it.

Currently the Youth Committee is made up of 25 members including Chairperson, outgoing Chairperson, Secretary, IRFU registrar, reps from each of the provincial areas, 5 Metro, 2 from the North East, South East, Midlands and North Midlands. Additionally there are representatives from the Schools, Referees, Girls and PR Committees. All of these members are volunteers.

A word from the Chairperson of the Youth Committee – Paul Power.

"It is a privilege to Chair the Leinster Youth Committee for the 2019/20 season and to work alongside the members of the committee who work tirelessly to provide rugby for boys and girls from the start of their rugby journey through to the senior ranks.

I am particularly delighted with the increase in the number of girls playing rugby, a huge debt of gratitude is owed to the club volunteers who continually give of their time freely to promote and development our game for all to enjoy"

▲ Leinster Youth Committee document from 2019, underscoring Leinster rugby's shift in nurturing youth rugby.

need to examine urgently how we will deal in the future with the increasing counter attractions to the game of rugby football.'[11] If ever there was a sign of Celtic Tigerism, then surely this was it. Losing players to winter skiing trips was simply unheard of pre-Celtic Tiger era. Nonetheless, as of the 2003–04 season there were still twenty-eight official Branch competitions and a grand total of sixty-five clubs officially affiliated with the Branch. Greencore were the main sponsors of the Leinster League, the PTC and the Leinster junior squad.

Additionally, the women's game was growing more and more important. It was in the early 2000s, as women's rugby had come more to the fore, that the Leinster Branch had fully begun to factor in the women's game. This was indicated by the positive disbursement of money to the female squad, which appeared in print for the first time on an official Leinster Branch finance report under 'women's expenses', albeit for a paltry amount when viewed in the overall expenditure. Nonetheless, the total had jumped to €19,000 from a minuscule €2,000 in the previous year.[12] That women's rugby was finally being taken a little more seriously was an important sign of positive change.

Irish Rugby Football Union
Junior Interprovincial Championship 2001/2002
Leinster v. Munster, at Edenderry R.F.C., Saturday September 15th 2001.

LEINSTER XV

15	Hugh Martin	(Coolmine)
14	Bernie White	(Enniscorthy)
13	Gary Brennan	(Wicklow)
12	John Ward	(Navan)
11	Mark Higgins	(Enniscorthy)
10	Alan Kingsley	(Portlaoise)
9	Ciaran Reilly	(Navan)
1	Kenny Dorian	(Dundalk)
2	Paul Deering	(Tullamore)
3	Anthony O'Donnell	(Arklow)
4	Nicholas Crawford	(Coolmine)
5	Kevin Quinn	(Ashbourne)
6	Chris Moore	(Cill Dara)
7	Nigel Peavoy	(Portlaoise)
8	Jeff Mahon (Capt.)	(Ashbourne)
16	Alan Tynan	(Roscrea)
17	John O'Toole	(Arklow)
18	Alan Gee	(Portlaoise)
19	Ivor O'Brien	(Kilkenny)
20	Gary Clarke	(Coolmine)
21	Willie Duggan	(Kilkenny)
22	Greg Jacob	(Enniscorthy)

Officials

Referee:
Gary Greene
Ulster Branch

Touchjudges:
Gerry McFadden
Billy Payne

4th Official:
Donal Byrne

MUNSTER XV

15	Liam Delaney	(Nenagh Ormond)
14	Joey Lawlor	(Youghal)
13	Eoin Cahill	(Bruff)
12	Willie Schubert	(Ballincollig)
11	Tommy O'Callaghan	(Presentation)
10	Kevin McKillican	(St. Senans)
9	Noel Dunne (Capt.)	(Cobh Pirates)
1	Roy McArdle	(Youghal)
2	Donagh Murphy	(Crosshaven)
3	Mark Mulhaire	(Thurles)
4	Brian McMahon	(Bruff)
5	Pat O'Donoghue	(Cashel)
6	Barry O'Sullivan	(Bandon)
7	Merle O'Connell	(Crosshaven)
8	Martin O'Rourke	(Bruff)
16	Tommy Ellard	(Clanwilliam)
17	Robbie Doyle	(Old Christians)
18	D.J. O'Leary	(Muskerry)
19	David Lee	(St. Senans)
20	Stephen Ryan	(St. Senans)
21	Ian Dunne	(Cobh Pirates)
22	Edwin Thompson	(Cashel)
23	Colm Hurley	(Bandon)

Welcome to Edenderry R.F.C., celebrating 50 years (1951 to 2001)

Programme giving Leinster Junior XV selection v. Munster Junior XV selection for a game to celebrate fifty years of Edenderry RFC in 2001.

The Rise of the Women's Game

One of the factors around the promotion of and recommendation to participate in sports, throughout history, from childhood through to adulthood, was the growing understanding of the necessity for exercise. The onset of the Industrial Revolution brought, for some, if not a sedentary life, certainly a monotonous existence in terms of the type of repetitious labour that 'modern-day' workers carried out. It didn't take long for doctors, intellectuals and, indeed, businessmen to realise that this was a pattern that needed modification. Exercise and recreation became central to the fabric of society quite rapidly. Thus, gymnasiums, swimming pools, athletic and football clubs began to fill the need for exercise, entertainment, identity and for variety and stimulation in daily life. Of course, at the outset,

> these new football clubs constituted an entirely masculine kingdom. They provided a respite from the new world of Victorian middle-class domesticity, offering young men a haven from women, children and family duty, while giving them the opportunity to display an overtly masculine physicality in defiance of contemporary fears of softness or effeminacy. Football was not only fashionable, it also had become, perhaps more importantly, respectable.[13]

Sport was important, but sport was an activity reserved by and large for men.

To illustrate that particular belief in an Irish context, one just has to explore the relationship that the Catholic Church in Ireland had with sport:

> In 1934 John Charles McQuaid later to become archbishop of Dublin and then president of Blackrock College, learned that the National Athletic and Cycling Association (NACA) was allowing women to compete in track and field events at the same meetings as men. McQuaid declared that this was 'un-Catholic and un-Irish' and said that 'no boy from my college will take part in any athletic meeting controlled by your organization at which women will compete, no matter what attire they may adopt.'[14]

This should not be read as merely the view of the Catholic Church, nor necessarily the cantankerous McQuaid, when it was, in fact, the view of most men and echoed society's views. McQuaid represented Irish patriarchal condescension towards women when he started a campaign against the entire NACA and lobbied the nation to join in. 'Mixed athletics McQuaid pointed out, was "a social abuse outraging our rightful Irish tradition." What's more, he opined, it was a moral abuse and "… the Christian modesty of girls must be, in a special way safeguarded, for it is supremely unbecoming that they should flaunt themselves and display themselves before the eyes of all."[15] There was a relatively uniform perception throughout the twentieth century of masculinity and femininity when it came to sports in Ireland. If Irish society was suspect about women even appearing on the sporting field (the exceptions, interestingly, included camogie for the ordinary classes, and hockey and racquet sports for the well-heeled), there was certainly no worldview that countenanced women's presence, never mind abilities, on a rugby field.

Rugby was deemed not suitable for women, women deemed not suitable for rugby. For example, the 'French rugby union federation only opened its doors to women in 1989'. Prior to that, throughout the 1970s, the French sports ministry proclaimed that rugby was not appropriate for girls or women because it was 'dangerous, both physically and morally'.[16] The point was that, universally, rugby was jealously guarded by the male world, and for many men it would be deemed a travesty if women were allowed participate. Thus, it may be no surprise that when women began to organise teams on a more permanent ground from the 1970s on, they were, at times, either highly ridiculed or determinedly ignored. As succinctly explained by social critics Helene Joncheray and Haïfa Tlili:

In Defence of Mixed Rugby !

4 New Street,
Longford.
2/5/'75.

Dear Editor,

Having read the article in your paper entitled "Mixed Rugby Mess," I would like to inform the writer that if he himself was present at the match he might not have misjudged, as he did, the whole point of the game.

The ladies togged out with the intention of proving to the males that as members of the "physically" weaker sex, they could endure 80 long minutes of a really man's game. I would like to think we succeeded admirably in our aim and I would also like to state that no girl suffered any serious injury.

I am quite sure that the spectators who did attend the game did not expect to see the ladies playing the role of the 'delicate' female, modelling her hot pants while chasing after the little egg-shaped ball in all directions.

I think the writer's comments on the season's results of Longford RFC unfair, for as any sportsman knows, the winning is not the sole objective of the players who participate in the game.

Finally, I would like to add that the rugby teams satisfied quite well their interested supporters during the season, perhaps they did not bring back any trophies to Longford but by their performances on and off the pitch they made quite a reputation for themselves among visiting clubs throughout the length and breadth of the country.

Yours Sincerely,
TERESA OWENS.

▲ *Longford Leader*, 1975 letter to the editor defending women's rugby.

▶ *Westmeath Examiner*, 30 March 1996, Mullingar women's rugby notes.

▼ Irish Women's Rugby Football Union becomes affiliated to the Irish Rugby Football Union, 12 February 2001. Pictured at the announcement are President of the IWRFU Carole Ann Byrne and President of the IRFU Eddie Coleman. © Brendan Moran/Sportsfile

Women's sports have had an eventful history composed of rejections, struggles, prejudice and then slow recognition. For a long time, men had a stronghold on the sports sphere and women were kept out of sports. The chaotic history of how women got into sports and how they were accepted as sportswomen in their own right can obviously be compared to the way women's status in society has evolved.[17]

What made rugby an outlier in becoming one of the later sports to be viewed as acceptable were the cultural and social constructs of the female image, which too often mattered more to the male-dominated media than the skills and the competition displayed in women's rugby.

Despite the fact that the first officially recorded female rugby player, Emily Valentine, played a match for Portora Royal School in Enniskillen in 1887 and scored a try, the uptake of women's rugby in Ireland was slow. While women's games were played and female rugby teams appeared more concretely in the 1970s and 1980s across the globe, it wasn't until the 1990s that women's rugby was pushed forward in Ireland. And even in the 1990s, for girls and women, 'exposure to formal sports was still uncommon … This was … a consequence of widely held societal beliefs that excessive sporting or physical activity was damaging to a woman's health and diminished her capacity to procreate.'[18] With more and more opportunities for Irish men and women to complete secondary, and eventually third-level, education, such attitudes were being recalibrated, but undoubtedly, in an Irish context, this was extremely slow going. While at various points throughout history it was acceptable for young girls to compete in young boys' teams, as pre-teens of course, it was not inclusion because, as soon as they left primary school, there was no pathway to continue in rugby for teenage girls. There was the novelty of the odd women's game played for charity or as a fundraiser, but certainly there were no girls' or women's teams with regular fixtures and competitions in Leinster.

In Leinster, support and enthusiasm for the game would be translated onto the field in the 1990s when Irish women sought to play rugby at the clubs they had been affiliated to, via their connections to men. Where once women were the backbone of clubs as volunteers and supportive mothers, daughters, wives and/or girlfriends, as more and more women raised their voices for equality in Ireland more generally, this was reflected in rugby.[19] Thus, in the 1990s, women in Leinster began to better organise themselves into teams and lobby their clubs for inclusion. Clubs were now being asked for the use of facilities and a reciprocation of the

▲ DUFC women's rugby on College Park, highlighting the progress and continued growth of the women's game.

▲ Leinster Women's team win 2018 interprovincial title. The Leinster women have become a formidable force in Irish and European rugby.

support women had long shown for the men's game. It was 1992 when a clearer opportunity arose, allowing rugby women to take their game that step further forward. 'A physiotherapist with her local club Blackrock College, [Mary] O'Beirne played host for the inaugural meeting of the Ireland Women's Rugby Football Union (IWRFU). O'Beirne was to be the first President of this independent body …'[20] Once they were up and running, the first task was to organise the clubs into leagues based on ability and strength, ensuring continuity as well as what Carole Ann Clarke, future IWRFU president and Leinster captain, described as 'safety in the game', by streaming the women's clubs.[21]

The women's organisation got off to a relatively positive start, establishing the women's AIL in January 1993,[22] and, with a first Irish international game played against Scotland that year, solid roots had been set. However, the distraction of 1995's big change in world rugby indicated that the ladies' game was going to have to fight its corner. As explained succinctly by Irish ex-rugby player Katie Liston, when recalling the establishment of the first Irish women's rugby organisation:

> Those [first women] players established their own strength and conditioning programmes, trained with male club players for a greater physical challenge … En route, many women's rugby players were stigmatized, personally and as a group, for playing a 'man's game'. The general attitude was that women had no place in the local rugby club as board members or as coaches and certainly not as players. This was not unusual in that sportswomen who participated in other traditional 'male' sports were regarded as some sort of sexual deviants. Rugby was the worst however. Not only was the social stigma greater and arguably more potent, but the women's game was chronically underfunded and its representatives were typically treated as a noisy interloper in a male preserve.[23]

Unsurprisingly, women's rugby was not showing up on the agendas of Leinster meetings, until one of the issues up for discussion, in October 1992, was the shortage of referees. In deliberations towards the end of Branch meeting, it was duly noted that there was 'also a need for women referees'.[24] The women's game in Leinster began to grow once there were signs of acceptance and, more to the point, support, albeit halting at first. The success in schools helped trigger success in local clubs, as Boyne, Wicklow, Gorey, Naas, Blackrock and Wexford all established girls' youths and eventually women's teams. There were not much more than 200 players and about ten women's rugby teams, however, as the decade rolled on, and more

▲ 30 March 2019: Enniscorthy celebrate winning the Leinster Rugby U16 Girls Cup final. © Matt Browne/Sportsfile

▲ Vodafone Women's Interprovincial Championship final, 2 September 2023, in which Leinster beat Munster. © Eóin Noonan/ Sportsfile.

needed to be done. In order to put in place a more concrete plan of development, it was decided among several of the women involved that it was up to themselves to drive the expansion of women's rugby.

When Ireland competed in their first ever women's Rugby World Cup in 1998, the IRFU found its better nature and 'a sense that the voices of those within the IWRFU were finally being heard and that, for the first time, women's rugby was close to getting a place at the top table' was achieved.[25] Unfortunately, at the close of 2021, there seemed to have been a backslide in that progress along with a resurgence of male chauvinism within the male-dominated IRFU, and women rugby players and officials, yet again, had to raise their voices over the lack of fair and equal treatment by the national body. Looking at the rugby-playing numbers in Leinster in 2005, there were 550 adult women playing in the province (in contrast to over 7,000 adult males). There were 291 adult teams, of which twenty-two were women's,[26] suggesting slow progress. For women in Irish sports to find full and equal recognition to men's sports has required efforts to induce something of a social paradigm shift.

Arguably huge strides were made in the 2010s, at least in normalising women's interest and participation in sports. Popular culture and society at large no longer necessarily depicted women's interest in sports as an aberration. The skill and competitiveness of the modern women's rugby game have generally earned deserved credit, which must be maintained by those at the upper levels in control of the game. The movement towards a more inclusive game in Leinster and Irish rugby in the 1990s required women to redefine categories from the stereotypical and socially mandated roles of wives, girlfriends, mothers and sisters. One space that allowed that to manifest, thus allowing women's rugby to develop, was the universities' and colleges' women's rugby scene.[27] Reports from the IRFU in 1999 noted that women's rugby at these institutions had vast potential. While that fact, in itself, was recognised, the report did not go on and try to address the structures of women's rugby. Whether it was not in its remit to study that, or whether this was because of natural bias is not clear; of course, if the former were true, it confirms the latter anyway. All the report really did was give a nod to the good work women were doing and left it at that. Regardless, the foundations of a strong Leinster women's rugby scene were laid from 1990 through to 2010. Leinster has gone from strength to strength, but no doubt that is down to the hard work women have had to undertake in Irish society and in sports' arenas more broadly, to maintain any semblance of equality.

Building Momentum, 2005–9

The year 2005 seemed to mark a new era in the long history of rugby in Leinster, commencing with the appointment of a new coaching and management team for the Leinster senior squad. In the summer of that year Leinster announced the arrival of Michael Cheika and David Knox. Cheika presented himself as a man with a plan, and an impressive-looking Leinster squad had enticed him to come to try to ensure the team achieved its full potential. In an interview in July 2005 Cheika set out his and Knox's stall, stating, 'One thing I'm very committed to is achieving … We bring a certain skill set to the table. We work on making the small parts of the players' game better. Fine detail so that they can perform under pressure. Not just hope that it happens. I want to teach everyone in the squad something new.'[28] This was a pertinent insight into the mentality that Cheika would instil across the board at Leinster. He implemented a culture of consistency from inside the boardroom to the groundspeople, the office staff and the players. The Leinster players all agreed that the first pre-season they had under Cheika was the toughest they had ever had. His style was described as:

> Controlled. Measured. Personalised. Building blocks. Workloads. Phases. It's easy to become a rugby geek these days. Cheika is applying his system moulding the players in his shape … 'I need to know the personalities and the bodies, the physical possibilities of everyone. I need to know where players need help, where they are good and can give help to others. And definitely a lot more responsibility and onus.'[29]

Cheika's arrival is sometimes positioned in a timeline of forward-moving parts, as the moment that Leinster truly became holistic, universally professional and subsequently set on a path to success.

The attitude and vision of an all-inclusive buy-in, mandated by a voice not of or from Leinster, helped clear the slate and transform the Leinster mindset. What Leinster began to implement was the pinnacle of 'rugby science … an emerging field of research that is used to inform the practice, performance, health, well-being, and development of rugby players and coaches at all standards'.[30] The key topics that rugby science addressed included physical and psychological preparation for rugby; planning and monitoring training; managing fatigue, recovery and nutrition; the effects of environmental conditions and travel on performance; the mechanics of rugby techniques and injury; and young players and talent identification. In modern rugby the professional game has ushered in a precise science to the sport, which modern coaches must manage and direct correctly to get the best results for a team. The unknown factors of luck and personality, or a player's psychology at any one given moment, are factors that might make a slight difference, but the honing of basic skills is the controllable factor that coaches demand from the outset.[31] With the arrival of what one might label the 'Cheika era', arguably rugby science became more prominent, reflecting a pinnacle in the evolution of rugby in Leinster.

In the IRFU report of 2005–06, ten years after professionalisation began, it was highlighted that a fresh approach was needed in Ireland to ensure that the professional provincial teams were sustained. Given that the history of the rugby provinces started with a view to selecting players for the national team, there has always been an intertwining of the provincial branches and the national body. Undoubtedly, this relationship has undergone substantial change with the onset of the professional era, with the provinces ostensibly becoming much more autonomous, subsidiary entities to the parent body. Yet, there remains a symbiotic relationship between the IRFU and the provincial branches in terms of promoting rugby and establishing a strong playing base. Thus:

> The current wellbeing of the professional game begins with the heightened profile of rugby, a profile that could not have been imagined ten years ago but it has the potential to mask the growing concerns of how to sustain the levels of performance we have come to expect as the norm. The need to use our collective resources from schools, clubs and the provincial teams to develop the next generation of professional rugby players is paramount and it is crucial that each unit of our game understands the role it plays in the process and the benefits that flow from success at each level.[32]

These IRFU sentiments speak directly to the direction that the branches took in their development of rugby at various points in the game's history. When the IRFU explained that '[w]e do not want rugby to be simply a spectator sport, its roots and strengths are as a participation sport',[33] it was through the increase of playing numbers and in making the game competitive enough for all those who play that the rugby world would be sustained.

But the reality of the professional game meant that there were large and ever-present financial challenges to be met. Paying professionals while ensuring that the club game had the right kinds of financial support proved a difficult balancing act. In that 2005–06 report, the model that was set out asked the provincial clubs to wean themselves off IRFU grant aid and to become financially independent in their operational costs. That same year the IRFU's introduction of a High-Performance Unit was part of the plan to introduce to Ireland, province by province, structures, systems and programmes resourced by the best of the best to produce quality players, not by chance but by design, in order to ensure the sustainability of the four professional Irish clubs. With professionalism, the more obvious edge between teams in a scientific rugby age was often the availability of top athletes to a particular team at a particular time, so the question of injuries and missing players or, more honestly, the quality of the replacement players became a more and more important element. Thus, developmental teams and an underage system helped to create a more contented squad of talented players, who had to understand their importance within a hierarchical, rotation system as pivotal actors, whether they played or not.

It was generally agreed that the preparation of elite athletes was now paramount, their strength and conditioning and their skill acquisition implemented by a head coach whose management and motivational qualities were as much about a season-long process as they were about game-day influence. Scrutinising data recorded by digital devices informed the best coaching approaches, which 'use a combination of traditional conditioning and game-based training to develop physical qualities and promote the transfer of the physical qualities to the high pressure and fatiguing environments of competition'.[34] The professional game adopted a new approach that included an entire off-field management structure. Therefore:

> Whilst the head coach is responsible for the overall performance of the team, different staff within the team work with the coach and the players in order to develop physical qualities and the transfer of skill … Equally, assistant coaches (and skill acquisition specialists) are responsible for identifying the factors (e.g. fatigue, pressure) that might influence the execution of skill, and developing training scenarios that regularly expose players to these demands. The goal is to maximise transfer of learning from the training environment into the high-pressure environment of competition.[35]

For the coaches, another element of this new approach utilising sports science was not just physical but also mental preparation for games. Players get pushed to their limit in training, allowing modern-day professional players to be identified during training sessions – those players who appear unsuited to the toughness of training are marked as not suitable for competition. Anecdotes of Michael Cheika's methods as a coach, and the way he tried and tested his squad of players during these sessions, evidence such approaches. Stories of incessant goading to work harder, run faster, tackle more – all the while not making basic handling, passing or kicking errors with the ball – tell of the new scientific approach that arguably became much starker from 2005 onwards.

In the 2005–06 season, positive signs of Leinster's progress were manifested in a strong presence on the Irish international team, with ten players winning caps.[36] Another sign of the strength and depth of the Leinster organisation and player-focused approach was the different levels of representative teams being organised. There was a twenty-nine-man Leinster Schools under-nineteen squad; a thirty-one-man Leinster Schools under-eighteen squad; a twenty-three-man Leinster Section 'A' Schools squad; and a twenty-five-man Leinster under-eighteen clubs/youth team, which won the Interprovincial Championship. Leinster also won a first ever under-nineteen Interprovincial Championship, with a Grand Slam over the other

▲ Leinster coach Michael Cheika during squad training in 2008. © Pat Murphy/Sportsfile

three provinces, and the under-twenty-one Interprovincial Championship, in a play-off format, beating Munster in the final, only the second time Leinster had won this competition at the under-twenty-one level. All these successes exemplified the huge amount of progress that Leinster rugby had made in the new millennium, as a much more professional organisation. At the same time the game of rugby in the province had also gained newer support in terms of a fan base for the professional team, which in turn led to the growing popularity of the club game across Leinster as clubs grew their playing membership in all age groups, and more and more schools began to allow rugby teams to emerge.

The senior squad utilised a total of thirty players, of which sixteen were internationals (fourteen Irish, one Argentinian, one English) during the Heineken Cup, playing a total of eight matches. For the Celtic League, the squad was broadened to a total of thirty-nine players used for twenty matches.[37] In that league,

▲ Scenes from Leinster's first European Cup win.

although they finished runners-up, nonetheless Leinster had the best home record (nine wins, one loss), scored the most points overall (545), the most tries (59) and collected the most bonus points for tries scored. Unfortunately, they were knocked out in the semi-final of the Heineken Cup by Munster, a team that continued to prove something of a bugbear for a few seasons to come. It was clear that talent was being produced at Leinster – alongside exciting, high-scoring rugby – and while silverware was not achieved, it was coming closer.

A scientific approach, coupled with a professional interconnectedness throughout the Leinster organisation saw the Branch begin to focus more seriously on province-wide rugby needs. Two new Regional Development Officers (RDOs) and a new club development manager position were created, and Leinster called for more consistent regulations to be made throughout Irish rugby when it came to the underage game.[38] For example, in 2005 the Branch drafted a proposal to be submitted to the IRFU that stopped under-eighteens from playing adult rugby. The intention was to prevent injury/burn-out in young players and to help maintain the numbers playing within the underage structure. The focus on maintaining an approach of inclusivity was embraced in Leinster, as one officer noted: 'There are a

▲ Australian Leinster player Rocky Elsom, who was seen as one of the pivotal additions that got Leinster over the line to European glory.

285

▲ Argentinian Leinster player Felipe Contepomi shows the importance of overseas players to help get Leinster to the highest grade in 2009, as the academy at home developed.

lot of non-nationals in the country and we should try to get them to begin playing rugby. Initiatives such as the Tallaght initiative should be brought to people who are interested.'[39] The recognition of non-nationals in Ireland reflects the booming economy Ireland experienced in the late 1990s and early 2000s, one of the results of which was an inward migration of jobseekers. Given Ireland's long history of sending people outwards, the new phenomenon produced many and varying challenges for Irish society.

That Leinster rugby reflected social and cultural complexities in this regard is echoed in the sentiments that explain how, '[t]he modern game of rugby union operates within … [a] global, mediated and professional environment. As the world becomes more compressed … rapid globalisation highlights and impacts the speed at which the complexity of national identities in sport has increased and is a useful lens through which to understand identity issues in the contemporary world.'[40] Professional rugby brought with it all of these complexities about identity and belonging, especially given the complicated nature of identity politics on the island of Ireland in general. With new rules for foreign players playing for the Irish provincial clubs creating a pathway to Irish citizenship and to potentially becoming a rugby international, more players from the southern hemisphere had their interest piqued. This phenomenon created by the world of professional sports raises all sorts of fascinating questions about national identity in the modern age. The presence of 'non-nationals' has been very much part and parcel of the professional era's contradictions and negotiations within the sport of rugby.

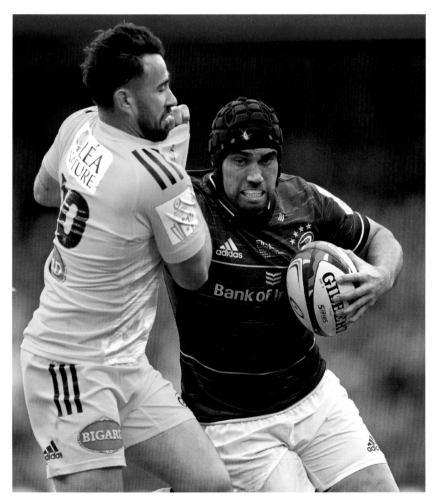

▲ New Zealand-born Charlie Ngatai of Leinster during the Heineken Champions Cup final between Leinster and La Rochelle at the Aviva Stadium in Dublin. © Brendan Moran/Sportsfile

Consolidating a Professional Leinster Rugby FC

Things Fall into Place

At amateur club level, between 2000 and 2020, more players were attracted to rugby and some new clubs created, while older ones became more inclusive – all of which elicited financial pressures when it came to finding pitches, having a suitable pavilion, organising jerseys and even the general overheads of light, heat and hot water, for instance. The amateur clubs partook in innovative fundraising schemes throughout the year to meet the costs of running a club, as the game grew in popularity. The first stop was membership subscription fees, of course, and most clubs initiated a club lotto. Income from a club bar was a big help and the general recruitment of sponsors was crucial. But the community efforts are also important to recall: bake sales, bingo, fashion shows, talent shows, the pub quiz, poker nights, race nights and raffles. There was even a sheep-shearing fundraiser where wool was sold to raise cash for a club, or another that allowed the grass on the pitches to grow over the summer with proceeds raised from the hay that was baled and sold at the start of autumn. In the media, the *Evening Herald* provided a weekly Leinster rugby section, which did wonders for rugby in the province, although the Branch complained that the clubs needed to do more to tap into this massive opportunity to promote themselves. To try to light a fire under the clubs, there were ongoing meetings with public relations officers (PROs) and the Leinster marketing committee.

All of this illustrated the progression of the game across the province, reflecting a change in the world of rugby as well as the factors of modernity that were brought to bear in the twenty-first century. In the 2006–07 season there were 7,653 newly registered players across the province alone, bringing the total number of players in Leinster to 41,643. The credit must start with the Community Development Officers (CDOs), Regional Development Officers (RDOs) and the Youth and Schools committee members.[1] In addition, women's rugby in Leinster was now under the umbrella of the Branch and was growing year on year. What's more, Dorothy Collins was the Branch honorary secretary for the 2006–07 season, her fifth year in that role. The organisation had a strong set of structures in place to deal with all the responsibilities of the Branch: alongside the executive board, the various committees consisted of groups overseeing the domestic game, with the junior, youths, schools and senior clubs subcommittees; a competitions committee; a sponsorship committee; and a professional game committee, with the provincial team management, the academy, the commercial and marketing, the finance and the administration committees. Under the administration there were also the international ticket, disciplinary, appeals, strategic review and stadium

▲ Leinster star players Brian O'Driscoll, Gordon D'Arcy and Jamie Heaslip in 2011.

subcommittees.[2] Grant and loan schemes were rolled out and advice offered around finances, as well as workshops organised to help increase clubs' volunteer bases, coaching courses and player development programmes. There was also an increase in the number of ordinary schools playing rugby in 2007, with the development of new cup and league competitions for which non-fee-paying schools could challenge. Indeed, there were up to 300 teams from non-'rugby schools' taking part, while the number of youth teams in Leinster clubs was also increasing.[3]

At club level, the progress of rugby in Leinster during the Celtic Tiger era saw an upsurge in teams affiliating and the organisation had become a much broader church. For example, the International Gay Rugby (IGR) was formed in 2000, when rugby teams from across the world came together to promote an all-inclusive non-discriminatory sport, regardless of sexuality. The goal of the IGR was to promote equality and diversity in rugby, specifically working towards eliminating discrimination because of sexual orientation and to provide opportunities for members of the LGBTQ+ community to compete in rugby, where once there had been great hostility.[4]

In Leinster that cause was taken up by the Emerald Warriors when they were founded in 2003 by Richie Whyte, among others. As Whyte explained, while the IGR's remit precipitated the club, it also came from the simple fact that he had wanted to organise a social activity in Ireland that did not revolve around the stereotypical Irish penchant for going to the pub. Whyte had found generally few outdoor or sporting options in Irish society in which social gatherings, outside of an advocacy context, for gay men were common. As a rugby player during his school days, therefore, it made perfect sense to set up a rugby club for gay men who were looking for a sporting pastime as a conduit for building a sense of community, as well as friendships. After a year of training at the War Memorial Park, Islandbridge, Dublin, fundraising and organising, the Warriors managed to play a few games in 2004, including competing in the Bingham Cup competition, an LGBTQ+ tournament, in London that year. Over the next few seasons, the club went from strength to strength, before reaching out to the Leinster Branch and petitioning for official recognition. If perhaps not proactive, the Branch was very supportive and, in September 2007, the Emerald Warriors became the first LGBTQ+ rugby club to join the Leinster Metropolitan League. The club's success was demonstrated when they hosted the Bingham Cup tournament in 2008 in Dublin.[5] While gaining many victories in LGBTQ+ competitive tournaments and challenge matches, the Warriors initially struggled to earn a win in their own

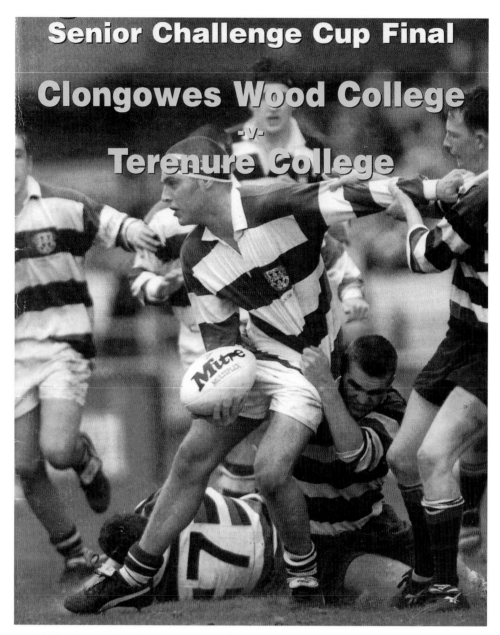

▲ Senior Schools Cup programme cover, early 2000s.

▲ Leinster Branch Executive Committee, 2006.

domestic league. The historic victory eventually arrived in 2011, when the Warriors won their first official Leinster league match over DUFC. If the history of Leinster rugby reflected something of an evolution in both the game itself and in Irish society more broadly, perhaps the Emerald Warriors' success as a club speaks to that postulation.

Elsewhere, in the middle of the 'noughties', key initiatives and marketing plans were outlined in a

> Market Research Project on all aspects of the Domestic Game. The goal of this project is to unlock growth and retention opportunities for Domestic Rugby in Ireland via breakthrough strategic marketing initiatives. The research will explore a wide range of issues such as Key Triggers & Barriers of Growing and Holding interest in Rugby, Attitudes to Structure of Season and Competitions, Facilities, Communications Model and more.[6]

The research programme was aimed specifically at domestic participants and its most pertinent outcome was to understand how to retain eighteen- to twenty-three-year-old players. Also, in the early 2000s, it was recognised that the professional team needed to find the right stadium in order to bring together all the necessary elements that would see Leinster thrive. For various reasons, not least because of

the playing surface's overuse, the Donnybrook venue was no longer fit for purpose. Thus, the Branch began negotiating with the Royal Dublin Showgrounds (RDS) in 2006 to make that venue a permanent home, with its 18,800-seater capacity stadium. Alongside the proposal for increased capacity at the RDS, the Branch advocated for a new layout, a pitch refurbishment and new lights going in, to be ready by September 2007.[7]

Professional-era rugby was very much organised with marketing in mind, prioritising the importance of youth interest, mainly those at the optimal entry-level playing age for adult rugby. The Branch explained:

Emerald Warriors pose for a team photo in 2023. © Ryan Byrne/INPHO

[A]s part of our drive as a sport to develop closer links between Clubs, School and Community contact, meetings and presentations have been held with a number of Councils … and in particular with Dublin City Council. City and County councils are now in receipt of considerable capital funding for investment in sport and leisure activities and we are keen in Leinster to develop, in a partnership manner, opportunities for Domestic Rugby to benefit from this source of funding.[8]

One of the biggest successes was the *Evening Herald*'s Leinster club rugby section, which appeared in the paper every Friday evening, generating great interest in club games. These weekly supplements not only offered fixtures and results but also allowed rugby clubs to present their latest news, advertise events and present stories and insights on all aspects of the club, from the playing side of the game to fundraising and the social side. In many ways this kind of one-stop-shop for all things club rugby epitomised how Leinster rugby had evolved into a much more celebratory community sport for the Leinster populace.

In terms of progress, when the Leinster Branch celebrated its centenary in 1979, the number of schools affiliated with it was a mere forty-four: thirty-three from Dublin (only six of which were north of the Liffey), four in Wicklow, two in Kildare, and one each from Kilkenny, Louth, Carlow, Westmeath and Roscrea in Tipperary. Thirty years later, in 2009, the number of schools connected to the Branch had almost trebled and came from across the entire province. In order to deal with such success, the Branch had to quickly generate a new suite of competitions and create a suitably competitive playing environment for all the school teams. As provincial development manager Philip Lawlor aptly illustrated, 'the number of competitions now [2009] run by the schools committee is over 25 and the winner and runners-up … [of those] competitions reads like a roadmap of schools throughout the province; St Mel's Longford, Naas CBS, *Colaiste Lorcain*

▲ Leinster Branch messaging 'from the ground up', referencing the grassroots of Leinster rugby.

Castledermot … Kilkenny CBS, East Glendalough Wicklow, Tallaght Community School, Dundalk Grammar Louth, Enniscorthy CBS Wexford.'[9] The Branch's policy was also to introduce tag rugby to as many primary schools as possible, complemented by organising blitzes at local clubs and inviting local primary schools to compete. This was done through the YDO programme, which focused on attracting young people to rugby. It began by reaching out to as many primary and secondary schools as possible, and the scheme proved so successful from the outset that by 2009 there were as many as forty YDOs working across Leinster with over 120 schools affiliated to the Branch. In addition, there was an explosion of mini rugby across Leinster. With progress so apparent, the IRFU committed €9.5 million in funding to the provincial clubs and schools, recognising the success and, more to the point, the sustainability of the system of youth development that linked schools' rugby with local clubs, helping maintain a stream of players across the entire province into the game.

Although Leinster rugby had clearly broadened its approach, there was still nonetheless a tendency for most professional players to come into the pro-game through the so-called traditional routes. As an ex-Leinster player and a former rugby coach, Conor O'Shea explained, 'The potential and the catchment area of Leinster was always unfulfilled … To the credit of Leinster Rugby and all involved, this is changing, the face and perception of the team is no longer one of a specific Dublin postal code but one that is representative and reflective of all of the peoples of the 12 counties.'[10] However, in 2008, when one examines the senior Leinster squad, it was not as all-encompassing as O'Shea had suggested, even as the popularity of rugby soared, with a broadening of the fan base and an increase in the numbers playing. Despite the relative lack of any real change in terms of Leinster rugby players' backgrounds, with the influence of Michael Cheika on the team, Leinster became 'a province with the feel of a club … the standard bearers for how professional clubs should be run. Leinster … developed and evolved but still retained the traditional style that we all grew up recognizing as Leinster.'[11] Describing Leinster rugby today, those involved in driving the club onwards to bigger and better achievements do so in the language of its professional characteristics. Thus, the Leinster organisation is self-assured when explaining:

> Our brand is our reputation. It is all of the thoughts, feelings and perceptions that people hold about Leinster Rugby. Our brand defines what Leinster Rugby stands for. It describes what we want to achieve and how we want to achieve it. Our brand guides all aspects of our behaviour, from stadium and match

MASCOTS

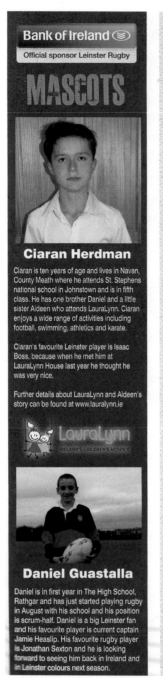

Ciaran Herdman

Ciaran is ten years of age and lives in Navan, County Meath where he attends St. Stephens national school in Johnstown and is in fifth class. He has one brother Daniel and a little sister Aideen who attends LauraLynn. Ciaran enjoys a wide range of activities including football, swimming, athletics and karate.

Ciaran's favourite Leinster player is Isaac Boss, because when he met him at LauraLynn House last year he thought he was very nice.

Further details about LauraLynn and Aideen's story can be found at www.lauralynn.ie

Daniel Guastalla

Daniel is in first year in The High School, Rathgar and has just started playing rugby in August with his school and his position is scrum-half. Daniel is a big Leinster fan and his favourite player is current captain Jamie Heaslip. His favourite rugby player is Jonathan Sexton and he is looking forward to seeing him back in Ireland and in Leinster colours next season.

MINI RUGBY

MALAHIDE RFC

Max Reid, Cian Murphy, Dan O'Leary, Cian Russell, Jack O'Dwyer, Jed Tormey, Sean Caddle, Colm Nicholl, Aaron Connolly, Oisin Daly, Robert Mahon, Noah Pedersen, John Ryan, Liam Walsh, Harvey Coffey, Daragh Fitzpatrick, Daniel Guerrini, Maxim Muraviev.

WESTMANSTOWN RFC

Niall Henry (2nd Coach), Sean McMahon, Sean O'Grady, Daniel Whooley, Oisin Kehoe, Dominic Ukandu, Conor Henry, Jack Maher, Gavin Cameron, Calum Oliphant, Patrick Reeves Smith, Liam Phelan, Shane Henry (Coach) Missing from Image: Oisin O'Neill, Jude Sloan, Michael Ryan.

ARKLOW RFC

Back LEFT to RIGHT: Coach Ian Gavigan, Chris Mitchell, Paddy O Gorman, Ryan Byrne, Kealan Delaney, Ryan Hallam, Evan Doyle, Eoin Gavigan, Darragh Ó Murchú, Coach Michael Byrne

Front LEFT to RIGHT: Alain Gordet, Jack O Gorman, Chris O Brien, Sean McCarthy, Jonathan Collins, Evan Fogarty, Rian Downes

Missing from Image: William Byrne, Ethan Allen & Tiernan McDonald.

ST MARY'S RFC

Coaches: Steve Tracey, Michael McGill.

Conor Tracey, Jake McGill, Leon Potts, Darragh Gilbourne, Rory Dillon, Tom McEniff, Alexander Shortle, Mark McHugh, Darragh Farrell, Robert Keenan, Liam Colleran, Elliott Daly, Hugh Gerathy, Matthew O'Shea, Jamie Grace, Tristan Groenwald, Daniel Patterson, Ronan Kelleher Gaillott.

▲ Mini Rugby, Leinster club-level work highlighted in match-day programmes.

experience to putting a rugby ball in the hands of an eight-year-old for the first time in Tullamore. Our brand influences our marketing, communications, merchandising and more; ultimately it guides everything we do, on and off the pitch … Brand Values … Pursuit of excellence … Quiet confidence.[12]

This is a fascinating insight into the clockwork mechanisms behind the sheen of the watch-face, relating the precise engineering that has helped Leinster Rugby reach the pinnacles of European rugby. It has done so through a reinvention of a culture within the province that embraced community and melded with precise organisation and unashamed, business-like ambition. Indeed, that has been articulated in terms that boldly assert:

> Leinster Rugby doesn't belong to the IRFU, the Board, staff, players or supporters, it belongs to all of us in the 12 counties of Leinster. It belongs to the people of Leinster who love and support rugby and as such we are a club of everyone. We will be open and welcoming (supporters old and new, young and old, families and friends to all who care about Leinster Rugby) and want the province to succeed and be the best it can … We will strive to create memorable moments that exemplify elite rugby through outstanding performance … [we] will be open, transparent, fair and honest in everything we do.[13]

In the scheme of Leinster rugby's evolution these sentiments are far, far removed from rugby's nineteenth-century origins, and even from the late twentieth-century version, illustrating Leinster's adjustment to the first years of professionalism.

Oh, How Far You've Come

In the 1996–97 season Leinster had, at first, just two full-time professionals, while the rest of the squad were trying to balance their work, college or family and rugby life. Where once interprovincial games struggled to attract a few thousand to matches, even in the earliest years of the professional game, by the time of the inaugural Celtic League final in December 2001, there were 27,000 rugby supporters at Lansdowne Road to watch Leinster defeat Munster 24–20. In 2007 Leinster CEO Michael Dawson outlined the new responsibilities that the Leinster Branch had taken on, as the IRFU continued to decentralise and empower the provinces to control their own affairs in the professional era. That season, the

◀ Images from Leinster's clash with Ulster in the Magners League at Lansdowne Road, 31 December 2006. © Oliver McVeigh/Sportsfile

Leinster organisation had over 130 people employed by the Branch, which included about sixty professional players from senior down to academy. The back-up staff for the playing side were twenty full-time employees with another forty-three in the rugby department, including those responsible for retention and developing the domestic game in the province. Dawson's prognosis for the future of Leinster rugby was positive if very business-like, as is the prerogative of the twenty-first-century sporting world, and Leinster secured record sponsorship deals and record gates.

That Leinster was turning a corner was evidenced in the 2006–07 season, when they were celebrated as

> Magners League best supported team of the season based on the highest average gate. This is a remarkable increase given the growth of the game across both the province and the country in recent times and great credit must go to the team and the Branch for all their hard work that went into this area … The website had also proved to be a very important tool for Leinster Rugby and the figures again show that there has been a serious increase in the number of people now logging on …[14]

The academy teams continued to have under-nineteen and under-twenty success, which was pivotal to the model that the Branch had set up to ensure future success. In the end, while all clubs required 'a bit of good luck and a lot of hard work [to] continue to develop', the Leinster Branch could celebrate the modern demeanour of its team, its brand and its status. It was a testament to those involved in allowing the game of rugby to shake off many of its older traditions and foibles.[15]

Part of the marketing strategy that was deployed by the Branch revealed some of the predilections of modern Irish society. For example, the creation of family season tickets, and the running of family days at certain games, as well as providing elements of family entertainment on site on match days, all aimed to attract this most lucrative of consumer groups. Indeed, a dedicated children's supporter's club was launched in 2006–07, which was explained as an important initiative to strengthen the brand by enticing families to become involved.[16] The exacting nature of marketing is somewhat laid bare in these examples. Leinster began 'the practice of offering the non-Dublin clubs discounted tickets [which] was expanded and formalized with the "One Province" ticketing initiative. This involved making stand tickets available to clubs and schools at a heavily discounted rate, enabling clubs and schools to offset the saving against travel expenses.'[17] All of these things opened

▲ Young Leinster fans ahead of a Celtic League match against Ospreys in Dublin, 14 September 2013. © Paul Mohan/Sportsfile

up Leinster rugby to the entire province, addressing the criticisms of the age-old exclusivity associated with the sport.

In the digital age, new media required new strategies as the Leinster organisation worked to create a sense of transparency and access to the professional team. This came about in such simple measures during the season as weekly briefings at noon on Wednesdays for print, TV, radio and digital media. The main area of expansion from about 2005 onwards was in digital media, via email, digital social platforms and podcasts – all of which helped create a sense that there was more of a connection between the supporters and the team. There were, for example, over 40,000 subscribers to the Leinster e-zine for the 2006–07 season. There were also over 3,100 people signed up for a free text service. The website over the last two decades had been afforded much investment, with regular updates and redesigns. From the beginning it proved a massive success, with an average of 221,615 hits per day in 2006–07. The communications manager's report for that season suggested that 'complacency is the only barrier to expansion and we are committed to broadening as much positive publicity for each and every facet of Leinster' in the season ahead.[18] Leinster maintained all of its programmes and ambitions throughout

▲ Participants during the Bank of Ireland Leinster Rugby Summer Camp at Greystones RFC in 2017. © Piaras Ó Mídheach/ Sportsfile

the decade and a half from 2005 to 2020. Even with the downturn in the Irish economy, Leinster Rugby insisted on maintaining its developmental structures, exhibiting a long-term view that has proven to be part of its great success.

Sports lovers in counties across Leinster became vociferous fans of the very successful Leinster organisation. Leinster Rugby never had as high a profile, as large a fan base or as extensive a participation as they had in the 2010s. This was thanks to the success and strength of Ireland's professional teams, who competed to a top four level, year in, year out, in Europe and in the Celtic League, as well as the national team's prowess. The Celtic League had consolidated its existence with the advent of significant sponsorship, when it became known as the Magners League, and 'moved on to a new level … [with] a genuine level of increased support and interest in the competition … In particular, the interprovincial fixtures produced high quality intense rugby fuelled by local pride. Attendances at these matches were significantly increased … with peak attendances in Lansdowne Road where Leinster v. Munster achieved 22,500 spectators and Leinster v. Ulster … 48,000.'[19] There were over 100,000 bodies playing rugby across the country in 2007 and annual figures suggested that about a third of those were in Leinster, somewhere around 35,000.[20]

▲ Tullamore RFC players after the Bank of Ireland Paul Flood Plate final, 2021. © Michael P. Ryan/Sportsfile

▲ Tullamore players lifting the cup after the Leinster Rugby Under-14 Cup match between Tullamore and Wexford, 2019.
© Eóin Noonan/Sportsfile

Arguably one of the most important events in the history of Leinster was one of a very contemporary nature, spurred by the decision to redevelop the Lansdowne Road stadium. It was fitting that Leinster were the team that closed the old stadium, when they played and won a Celtic League match against Ulster on New Year's Eve 2006, to a then record crowd for an interprovincial Celtic League match. The old Lansdowne stadium was demolished starting in May 2007 and, from beginning to end, reconstruction took three years, with the stadium reopened to the public in May 2010. But it was what happened during this hiatus, the need to 'borrow' another stadium, which marked an event that undoubtedly stands out in the history of rugby in the province.

Back at Jones' Road

Undoubtedly, there was a deep suspicion and lack of clarity about the history of rugby in Ireland, which was dramatically played out when it was learned that the home of Gaelic games, Croke Park, would be opened to 'foreign' sports, namely rugby and soccer, in 2008. There is no need to rehash the myriad issues that surfaced vis-à-vis the controversies of the day, many of them having to do with international fixtures and the complex history of British colonial rule in Ireland. But that this was a return of rugby to Jones' Road might be a surprise to some. Indeed, prior to the development of the Croke Park venue and its environs as we know them today, Jones' Road housed playing fields for athletics in general. It hosted rugby games, as well as Gaelic football and hurling. One game of rugby in particular that Leinster played at Croke Park cannot be overlooked in its importance. The professional era of Irish rugby took on an entirely new complexion in 2009 with the coming together of two of Ireland's most prominent professional rugby outfits, Munster and Leinster, in the Heineken Cup semi-final at the GAA headquarters. The significance of the fact that 82,208 fans showed up to watch that match, should not be diminished. This record-breaking number of attendees for any club rugby union match in history across the world demonstrates the centrality of rugby in a Leinster sporting context and that the code, in many senses, was born again at this moment when it returned to Jones' Road. As the Leinster Rugby team became more and more successful and professional, clearly interest increased in both the professional club as well as in the game itself.

As Paul Rouse identified, 'The phenomenal growth of rugby in Ireland over the [2000s] is a tribute to rugby's administrators and their capacity to extend rugby into areas where the game previously had no meaningful support. This is particularly

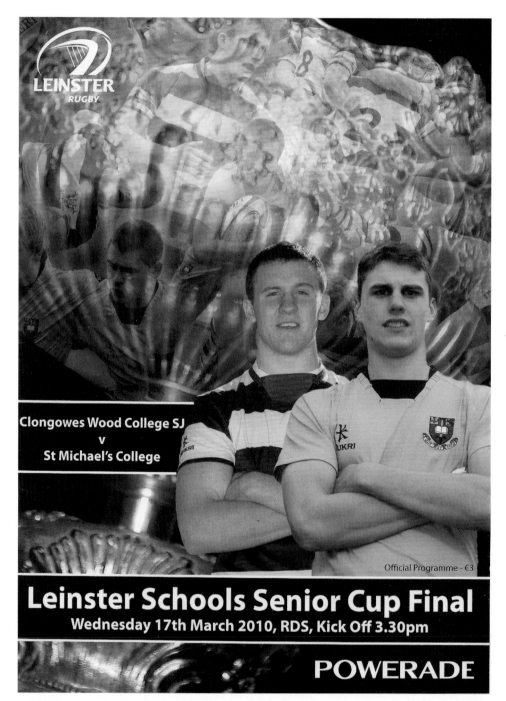

▲ Cover of Leinster Schools Senior Cup final (sponsored by Powerade) programme, Clongowes Wood College v. St Michael's College.

▲ Isa Nacewa, Leinster, goes over to score his side's fourth try against Biarritz in the Amlin Challenge Cup semi-final at the RDS, Ballsbridge, 27 April 2013. © Stephen McCarthy/Sportsfile

true of Leinster.'[21] In spite of ongoing negative feelings and mutual hostility between certain factions within both the rugby and GAA camps, this event normalised relations among the majority. But even more significantly, for Leinster Rugby this became the match that laid to rest those questions from many quarters, both within and without, about commitment, character and cutthroatedness. Comments and reports about Munster's professional-era successes were regularly framed in the media, and by the public, next to Leinster's failures. Those failures were put down to an apparent Leinster weakness and a question of character. In reply to those taunts, former Leinster player turned pundit Reggie Corrigan, ahead of the 2009 Heineken Cup semi-final, reprimanded rugby fans who lived in Leinster but who supported Munster, for being 'Lunster' fans. This was a quite clever ruse designed to tap into, to paraphrase Marcus Free, a romantic narrative of Leinster collective endeavour driven by a 'classless' spectrum of supporters from 'dockers to doctors' that additionally bridged the divide between D4 and the rest of Leinster, not to mention D4 and the rest of Dublin. Despite the long history of Leinster rugby's class, religious and political exclusivities, Corrigan and his 'Lunster' sentiments were successful at facilitating the notion of playing for 'the parish' and 'the jersey', representing family and community, which Leinster rugby now frequently invokes.[22]

SEISMIC
SEMI FINAL
MUNSTER V LEINSTER IN CROKE PARK 82,208 (6-25)

"We worked on a number of plays
especially for that particular match
and they pretty well all came
off which is unusual"

Rocky Elsom

Munster Rugby v Leinster Rugby
FT score 6-25
Heineken Cup Semi-Final
02.05.2009
Croke Park

Attendence
82,208

Leinster v. Munster in Croke Park 2008, the biggest attendance at a club rugby match in world rugby.

With such an emotive and high-octane spectatorship at this match, one can argue that something was harnessed that day that has helped define Leinster's pre-eminence in European rugby ever since. For many rugby observers, beating Munster was the proverbial ridding of the monkey on Leinster's back that proved the backbone of the organisation, silenced many naysayers and critics, and of course gave the fans something to shout loudly about. From the success of the Leinster team in 2009, a marker was laid down for both the progress that had been made up to that point and the expectations for the club ever since then. Writing in the programme for the 2009 Heineken Cup Final, Felipe Contepomi recalled that under Michael Cheika's reign:

Leinster have been the club that has grown most in Europe if you look at the increase in supporters, the infrastructure. When I first arrived, our gym was not even a portacabin. It was a shed with holes, like a Second World War shed. Now, we don't envy any other team in Europe for facilities. The gym, the pitch, the stadium. As a club it's grown. And it will keep growing. I started playing in front of 400 people and now we have an average of 12–13,000. I know now that it is the supporters' team and we are just passing through, that's what I really enjoyed, seeing the club grow like that.[23]

▲ Michael Cheika as coach was credited with bringing Leinster great success and helping them reach their full potential through his high standards of professionalism and dedication. © Pat Murphy/Sportsfile

With the team winning relatively consistently ever since, the redefinition of a sporting identity was complete, with Leinster rugby enshrined as 'just another Irish sport' in which all sports fans can partake. The professional era has helped reinvent a tradition and create an imagined community across Leinster, with a newly conceived provincial identity and provincial pride thanks to the strategies deployed in the context of a global sporting model, tied to a winning rugby team.

Leinster rugby recalibrated its identity and 'grafted onto an existing, broader narrative based on a popular perception' about the common interests of the people across the province, regardless of their backgrounds.[24] The players performed

▲ Leinster celebrate with the Heineken Cup, after the final v. Leicester Tigers on 23 May 2009. © Ray McManus/Sportsfile

unerringly on the day of the Heineken Cup semi-final in Croke Park, producing the win that has since encouraged Leinster supporters to identify with the team as a representation of the province and its people. To some extent it may also have provided the ability to purge the rugby team of the fact of its origins. The prism through which this effort could be viewed is one of inclusion – that is, Leinster rugby can only be commended in its effort to create a distinctive club, which has managed to draw on the many different strands of identity and culture that were 'of' and from a broadly tented Leinster.[25] The accomplishments of Leinster Rugby in general around raising awareness, and the triumphs on the pitch of the professional team, have given supporters, old and new, a strong sense of commonality in the club and around the sport.[26] The organisation, via a successful team, has achieved the ambition of creating 'a powerful and inclusive story of rugby success that everybody who feels a connection to [Leinster] can be part of and enjoy. In practical terms, this mean[t] making a connection with people in [and across Leinster] as the sporting entity that represents them.'[27] At the end of the day, what Leinster did

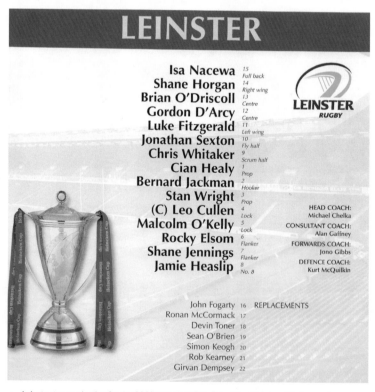

LEINSTER

Isa Nacewa	15	Full back
Shane Horgan	14	Right wing
Brian O'Driscoll	13	Centre
Gordon D'Arcy	12	Centre
Luke Fitzgerald	11	Left wing
Jonathan Sexton	10	Fly half
Chris Whitaker	9	Scrum half
Cian Healy	1	Prop
Bernard Jackman	2	Hooker
Stan Wright	3	Prop
(C) Leo Cullen	4	Lock
Malcolm O'Kelly	5	Lock
Rocky Elsom	6	Flanker
Shane Jennings	7	Flanker
Jamie Heaslip	8	No. 8

LEINSTER RUGBY

HEAD COACH:
Michael Chelka

CONSULTANT COACH:
Alan Gaffney

FORWARDS COACH:
Jono Gibbs

DEFENCE COACH:
Kurt McQuilkin

John Fogarty 16 REPLACEMENTS
Ronan McCormack 17
Devin Toner 18
Sean O'Brien 19
Simon Keogh 20
Rob Kearney 21
Girvan Dempsey 22

▲ Leinster team selection for the 2009 Heineken Cup, from the official match-day programme.

312

was become a high-achieving sporting outfit that has seen support for the game of rugby grow exponentially, since 2009 especially.

As the 2010s progressed and Leinster was gaining momentum, the numbers playing the game confirmed that rugby was continuing to expand. One of the areas that saw sustained enthusiasm was the women's game. The IRFU included a new strategy explicitly aimed at increasing women's participation, which was published in its 2008–2012 strategic review. From that review, the union learned that 'Development and increased Participation within Women's rugby at adult and age grade levels continues to grow with 19 active Adult teams and 1,140 participants. Seven active teams are also involved at Age Grade levels.'[28] Speaking of the vision for the future of Leinster rugby specifically, the report confidently proclaimed, 'growth and success at all levels and in all sections of the Domestic Game in Leinster continues to grow, as an example participation numbers in season 2006/07 were 41,295 which has grown to over 60,000 in season 2009/10 an increase of over 45%'.[29] Of course there was massive investment in time and money in order to achieve this outcome, as well as a focus on the promotion of province-wide rugby, with an emphasis on participation.

▲ Kilkenny Women's RFC winners of the Division 5 cup, 23 April 2022 v. Tallaght at Ollie Campbell Park (Old Belvedere), final score 35-14.

▲ Members of Navan RFC – from left: Joseph Dunne, Luke Caffrey and Harry Staunton – with the Challenge Cup, Pro12 trophy and the British and Irish Cup in 2014. © Stephen McCarthy/Sportsfile

As Branch Secretary Des Kavanagh highlighted in May 2010, 'The main body of work undertaken by Leinster Rugby involves the putting of a rugby ball in as many hands as possible in a fun, healthy, safe and sustainable environment.'[30] At the onset of a global financial crisis that decimated Ireland, the Leinster Branch made a brave decision when the IRFU cut the funding to the YDO scheme. In contrast, the Leinster committee insisted its own organisation keep funding that programme in the province. It put forty officers into eighty-eight secondary schools, coaching over 3,500 players and helping to put 148 teams onto rugby fields at the weekend. It was also involved in some 260 primary schools for tag rugby, in which some 20,000 schoolchildren participated. New partnerships with local area county councils meant that development officers could work to bring rugby to areas where it was not otherwise played. All of this was maintained regardless of the era of austerity that severely damaged the country upon the collapse of the Celtic Tiger economy.

Those overseeing Leinster rugby understood how essential it was for the sport in the province to keep widening its base. As for women's club rugby, this had forged on since the establishment in 2004–05 of the Leinster Women's Committee by Su Carty. That first decade of the 2000s, Carty admitted, had been a steep learning curve, with support from the IRFU and the Leinster Branch, as yet, still tacit rather than proactive. However, the strides that had been made within women's rugby were not now going to be turned back. There were twenty-one Leinster AIL women's teams, with the total participation in women's rugby at 1,478 players by 2010. One concern was that 'few women attended coaching courses during this season, however a recent appeal to clubs to up skill their female players/coaches has been met with an excellent response'.[31] Indeed, during the 2009–10 season there was a need to run additional foundation courses for women. There was still a serious lack of female referees, however, so the Branch planned referees' courses aimed at recruiting women. Women's and girl's teams were being encouraged, but it

▲ Naas RFC captain Emily McKeown and her teammates celebrate winning the Leinster Rugby Women's Division 4 Cup final against Portlaoise RFC in Naas, Kildare, 23 March 2019.

was still a challenge to get enough young girls involved. In order to accommodate the underage female game, there was a flexibility within the age groups so as to ensure that there would always be sufficient numbers to field underage teams for matches. The YDOs were working with girls' schools, and the women's game was going from strength to strength, in spite of general cutbacks.[32]

Advocating in schools and in clubs and, almost as importantly, with the media to highlight female sporting heroes who could be role models for future generations of rugby players saw coverage of the women's game slowly increase. Its success culminated in 2013 Grand Slam success for Ireland (the Women's Six Nations having started in 2007), as well as hosting the 2017 Women's Rugby World Cup in Dublin and Belfast. It was people like Su Carty who helped shape women's rugby's successes, steering the IWRFU to amalgamate with the IRFU. Carty explained that the IWRFU 'was a voluntary group, with very little resources and, really, the future couldn't be in isolation from the IRFU, we needed to strive forward and become properly looked after as part of the family'.[33] That translated into more support for the Leinster rugby scene as well, and, with the continued success of the province in the women's game, it become a self-perpetuating policy whereby young kids emulate their sporting heroes, following them into the game and justifying the investment from the top down.

▲ World rugby council member Su Carty during the IRFU Women in Rugby report media conference at the Aviva Stadium in Dublin. © Eóin Noonan/Sportsfile

Women's clubs in Leinster continue to grow and go from strength to strength. There are eight teams in both Division One and Two of the Leinster women's leagues; seven in Division Three; and five in both Divisions Four and Five, making a total of thirty-three women's teams from thirty-one different clubs (MU-Barnhall and CYM/Garda clubs have two women's teams competing in two different divisions). That the

▲ Under-18 Girls Interprovincial match between Ulster and Leinster at Newforge Country Club in Belfast. © John Dickson/ Sportsfile

momentum behind the women's game is as yet relatively young suggests that, in spite of the 2020 pandemic interruption, the game should continue to grow if it is given the proper support by the leadership across Irish rugby. In contrast to the controversy over the IRFU's mistreatment of the women's international side, at Leinster Branch level, in May 2021 the executive

> voted to bestow senior status on clubs participating in the Women's All Ireland League at its AGM. The decision was a victory for Dublin club Railway Union RFC, the holders of the All Ireland League title, which has been bidding to have equal status … for seven years … It means the players will now be recognised as senior players, while it will also mean that clubs driving the women's game will have a say at committee level.[34]

Not for the first time in the history of Leinster rugby, the Branch have led the way – something from which the IRFU should be humble enough to learn.

14

Leinster Conquering Europe

The Next Step in the Process

The 2009–2010 season was one of near misses for Leinster, being knocked out of the European Cup at the semi-final stage and also losing the Magners League final. A lot of players retired at the end of that season, which also saw the departure of Michael Cheika as head coach. The Australian has been much lauded as an important figure in Leinster rugby's history for changing the mindset of many of Leinster's players and, more importantly, Leinster rugby people, bringing in a particular vision of what a professional outfit and playing culture needed to be. Winning the 2009 Heineken Cup announced the arrival of Leinster as the European rugby team to beat. Gates were growing (they had doubled in five seasons) and standards of play were rising. All this boded well for the future of professional rugby and Leinster was hitting its superlative era, just as the professional game was too. Leinster won the Heineken Cup for the second time in 2010–11 and retained it in 2011–12 under coach Joe Schmidt. At the end of the 2011–12 season, the Branch, according to one report, vowed to keep ploughing money into underage structures to find new talent, to ensure there was never a return to the dark days when they were not as competitive in Europe or, perhaps more to the point, the days of playing second fiddle to Munster.[1]

In the annual report for that season, the culture and vision of a province-wide Leinster rugby organisation was articulated by the president's assertion that rugby in Leinster is a team game made up by all of its constituent parts both on and off the field, and whether it is … our dedicated groundsman in Donnybrook … or whichever member of the professional and support team you engage with, all are on the same team and the 'blue magic' is everywhere and with everyone in Leinster Rugby … I would like also to refer to the wonderful support for the Leinster team from all parts of the Province, and through the 'One Province' initiative the droves of buses which travel to the RDS or Aviva Stadium is hugely impressive and appreciated.[2]

In an Irish context there are some other uniquely telling glimpses of the national story in the running of the organisation. The business of Leinster's professional rugby outfit, that Venn diagram of enterprise and sport, meant that somewhere down the food chain there were youth teams and towns' clubs surviving by and large on the patience and dedication of a volunteer group. This was the model adopted in the late 1990s as rugby in Ireland laboured to figure out how best to approach the professional era. The lowliest clubs in this model relied upon, if truth be told, the monetary leftovers from the parent organisation, after the professional side was administered to first and foremost. In that regard the enterprise was always contingent upon what was happening in broader society. Thus, Des Kavanagh revealed in the 2011–12 report, the economic downturn did significantly impact on the game, with clubs unable to field teams at some of the junior rugby levels, while the loss of volunteers within the province, especially to emigration, was hurting grassroots clubs. Anecdotally, it was also believed players left the game for fear that injuries that might mean (unpaid) time off work, which could jeopardise their careers during the recession.

In a rugby context, the national and provincial organisations needed to fill the gaps that austerity-era policies created. Leinster pledged to maintain youth rugby supports, with the Branch's treasurer's report in 2012 stating:

Our game continues to grow at an astounding rate throughout our province and the demands on our club and community programmes are continuous. … The success and the depth of our schools and youths is astounding … A contingency fund was set up this season to assist clubs with temporary cash flow issues and a number of applications were dealt with … We have achieved outstanding success over the last four years.[3]

Even as sports defunding was implemented, clubhouses across all the football codes were one of the few places of refuge left during the recession. Starting with the 2011–12 Leinster rugby report, one of the central components of the Leinster organisation was the effort to ensure 'far greater engagement between school, club personnel and Leinster Rugby'.[4] Growing the numbers participating, improving the quality of the game and retaining the coaches and the players were all recognised as essential components.[5]

Numerically, it was junior rugby where most teams and adult players competed, underscoring the popularity of rugby as recreation. Support for club and youth rugby followed a report that showed 'almost 20% of our [Leinster's] population indicate that Rugby is their game of preference and our sport enjoying unparalleled popularity, it is time for ourselves to review with clarity what direction our non-

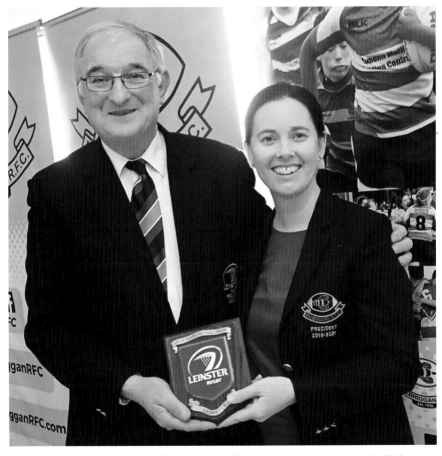

▲ Balbriggan RFC Club President Leigh O'Toole, incoming 2022, with Leinster Branch President John Walsh.

AIL rugby is heading to and bring recommendations and fresh thought to provide the infrastructure to support additional growth of our game throughout the province'.[6] The women's rugby report recorded some changes at this time as well, including a new competition, the Leinster Plate, and a reorganisation of the league to accommodate a Third Division for the 2012–13 season. The women's provincial team won the interprovincial title for the first time in five years and, all in all, the women's game was progressing, with sixteen clubs that had underage girls' teams, seven of which were new teams. Inroads were made with girls' mini teams starting to grow, which it was hoped would lead to further additions of teams within the clubs to continue to feed the women's game in Leinster.

With continual talent being produced, exciting and high-scoring rugby being played, and silverware adorning the trophy cabinets, Leinster rugby continued to evolve on the ground and the fan base became central to the organisation's identity. With the RDS secured as a home venue, coupled with regular access to the Aviva Stadium for the biggest league and European rugby games, a generation of avid fandom was secured. With the move to the RDS as permanent tenants, the commercial department focused their efforts on ensuring attendances, with new ideas to create full houses for home games. The strategy was to reach out even further into the province with the help of sponsors, Bank of Ireland, to strengthen and broaden the Leinster brand. The 'blue' branding that has focused Leinster supporters on their team creates a colourful, carnivalesque atmosphere as Leinster continue to bring success on the field. The club provide elements of family entertainment on site on match days catering for young, old and in-between. The cultural centrality of sports as entertainment is more than profit and loss for supporters, fans and families seeking a fun day out. From hiring train carriages to take fans from Tullamore RF, through the Phoenix Park tunnel direct to Lansdowne Road,[7] to busloads from provincial town rugby clubs coming up to the RDS, to the multitudes on the DART on Friday evenings from the Dublin suburbs, north as well as south, all descending for a Leinster match, the rugby season has become a staple sporting outing for many in the province. The streets of Dublin bustle when Leinster are at home to play, whether in the league competition or the European Cup.

Since 2007 Leinster have regularly filled their home ground at the RDS weekly and can entice 30–40,000 fans for the more important and high-profile games at the Aviva. Leinster schemes for season-ticket holders extended to 'Blue Benefits', which includes discounts and deals with select sponsors, as well as events like themed matches, with previous examples including Spring Fling, Ladies' Night and Kids'

Takeover. And finally, community and club ticketing schemes allow large groups of supporters from across the entire province to become familiar sights at Leinster rugby matches. For example, the 'traditional half time mini rugby … [allows] clubs [to] get a run out on the hallowed turf',[8] and has helped elicit the permanency of a wide fan base, following Leinster's professional team. In all of this, it is interesting to note how quickly things become a 'tradition'. For example, half-time mini rugby appeared in the 2000s and became a popular expectation and added incentive for clubs to develop their underage systems.

Throughout the 2010s the Leinster supporters club worked on an initiative called the 'Blue Planet' to reach a Leinster diaspora. This was entirely aimed at Celtic Tiger crash migrants, the youth of Ireland who found their way to New Zealand, Australia, Canada, the Middle East and elsewhere. In the digital age, the diaspora was to be reached using social media platforms in particular. These new migrants, a twenty-first century brain drain, were not only well educated or well trained in their professions but were also, by and large, well exposed to the various social media digital platforms. Leinster rugby benefited from this 'brave new world', and the connectivity to the 'Blue Planet' meant the game could attract a fan base not just in the twelve counties of Leinster but worldwide. The obvious benefits include a wider market available to financially support the organisation, through

323

▲ Leinster supporters cheer on their side during the Challenge Cup final against Stade Français, 17 May 2013. © Brendan Moran/Sportsfile

things like merchandising, membership subscriptions and an extended viewership. It is a veritable sea change, from a sport that at times struggled to recognise the rest of Leinster outside its dominant domicile of D4 to one that reached into the other counties where rugby was a poor third in terms of popular sports and now represents a self-identified Leinster rugby diaspora. The impact of social media was one of the important elements in the rapid rise of Leinster rugby, with its power to reach so many people in relatively easy ways, utilising the World Wide Web.[9]

In terms of the population embracing new technologies, the arrival of big tech companies into the economy and the desire to engage online markets and consume are all clearly traits of Irish twenty-first-century culture, a reality reflected in, and to the benefit of, the Leinster Rugby organisation.

The CEO report for the 2012–13 season noted that 'the flagship and financial engine of Leinster Rugby is the senior team who have once again managed to attract both supporters and sponsors which manages to fund the game throughout the province'.[10] The centrality of the holistic process remained the foundation of the province's entire rugby approach and its realisation. Nonetheless, the game ebbed and flowed in the immediate years of the Celtic Tiger crash, acting as something of a barometer for Irish society more broadly. For example, in spite of the positivity in the women's game, some clubs reported the loss of players to emigration and, more tellingly, women's teams reported the loss of their players because of job losses. This might remind the more enlightened among us of the gender bias in Irish society, where a patriarchal culture still perhaps deems men's jobs as more important than those of women. It is a telling moment that when financial pressures became a factor in the ability to participate in sports, it was women's teams that were impacted harder in terms of player losses, largely through unemployment, familial responsibilities and emigration, to the extent that it became a big concern for the Leinster Branch women's section.[11] On the positive side, new initiatives were undertaken in the schools' section to retain support for that competition, while a new open-draw format for Senior and Junior Cup competitions was also implemented.

During Joe Schmidt's reign (2010–13), Leinster played some of their best rugby and won the Heineken Cup twice. In fact, a record four trophies from six finals in three years made Schmidt a fan favourite across the province. In the first season, despite a shaky start with some losses in the league, Leinster would face off against Northampton Saints in the Heineken Cup final at season's end. They trailed by sixteen points at half-time in that game before coming back to defeat the English side by thirty-three points to twenty-two, erasing any historical criticisms about Leinster's lack of commitment or courage. In the 2011–12 season Leinster again reached the Heineken Cup final and roundly trounced Ulster. But they were beaten in the final of the Pro12 League in 2012, as they had been in 2011. The 2012–13 season saw Leinster eliminated from the Heineken

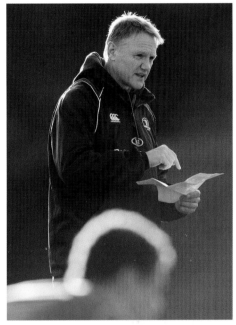

▲ Leinster head coach Joe Schmidt. Celtic League 2012-13, Round 22, Leinster v. Ospreys, RDS, Ballsbridge, Dublin. © Stephen McCarthy/Sportsfile

Cup during the early rounds, automatically joining the newly organised secondary European competition, the European Challenge Cup, as a result. The club proceeded to win both the European Challenge Cup and the Pro12 League final, thus finishing the season with a double in May 2013. With those successes behind them at the start of the 2013–14 season, Schmidt was enticed to take over as Ireland head coach. Having brought Leinster a further step forward after the success of Michael Cheika, it was always going to be a tough ask to replace the popular Schmidt.

It fell to Australian Matt O'Connor to bear that burden and, despite winning the Pro12 League competition in his first season, O'Connor left his role as coach at

▲ Leinster players celebrate with the Challenge Cup following their victory. © Stephen McCarthy/ Sportsfile

◄ Departing Leinster head coach Joe Schmidt with Isa Nacewa and Jonathan Sexton following their Pro12 victory over Ulster, 25 May 2013. © Stephen McCarthy/Sportsfile

the end of his second year in charge. A misstep by him in response to questions about his team's poor performances came when he criticised the control the IRFU and the Ireland coach exercised over his use of Leinster players. With Schmidt being so popular in Leinster and, more to the point, refuting O'Connor's accusations, the Australian didn't see out his Leinster contract. Leinster's high expectations throughout the 2010s and O'Connor's lack of results in the 2014–15 season opened the way for Leo Cullen to take over as head coach in the 2015–16 season. Over the decade of the 2010s, Leinster has come to a stage where winning has become a culture within the professional rugby club and the team has become dominant in Irish rugby.

Towards a Conclusion

Leo Cullen has been credited with further advancing Leinster, gaining the most out of the structures that have been put in place across the entire organisation, especially among the various coaching and playing groups, not just the senior team. Having won so much with Leinster and jumped into coaching not long after hanging up his boots, Cullen did not have to demand the respect of all involved in Leinster; it was already ingrained from working with him. He has been regularly referred to, by those who have played and coached with him, as a rugby perfectionist with an unparalleled knowledge of the intricacies of the game. In 2018 Cullen became the first man to have won a European Champions Cup title as a player and a head coach, both for Leinster. With his coaching team, he has been known for

Leinster Rugby Official Media Partnership with the *Irish Independent* every Friday, as advertised on game-day programmes. Newspapers continue to be important conduits for generating sports followers/fans.

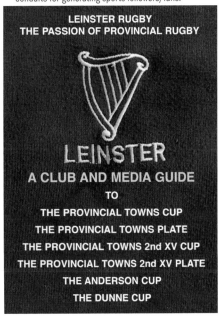

Leinster Rugby Club and Media Guide to the provincial cup competitions (Towns Cup, Towns Plate, Towns 2nd XV Cup, Towns 2nd XV Plate, Anderson Cup and Dunne Cup).

▲ The Leinster team celebrate following the European Rugby Champions Cup final win over Racing 92 at the San Mames Stadium in Bilbao, Spain, 12 May 2018. © Ramsey Cardy/Sportsfile

▲ Leinster head coach Leo Cullen and captain Isa Nacewa, during their homecoming in Dublin, May 2018, following their victory in the European Champions Cup final. © Ramsey Cardy/Sportsfile

discipline, honesty and, above all, hard graft in order to bring success. Cullen has been credited with not only promoting and protecting Leinster's 'from the ground up' ethos, but for that ethos thriving under his leadership as more and more development and academy players came through the Leinster ranks every season and won senior caps under his stewardship.

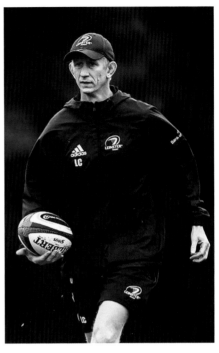

Leinster's on-field success, alongside the extensive careers and number of games professionals play today, plus the obvious investment in promoting the game and the frequent television coverage, has created celebrity for professional Leinster players. What's more, when their playing days are curtailed, ex-players regularly become rugby pundits on TV, on the radio, in newspapers and in the digital realm – or perhaps they step into coaching roles, remaining prominent around rugby games. Given the media focus on Leinster's European-wide success, there are several players in the last decade whose names are known worldwide, with their club accolades

▲ Leinster head coach Leo Cullen at work. The former Leinster captain took the reigns in 2015 and continues in the role in 2023, the longest-serving Leinster coach in the pro era. © Ramsey Cardy/ Sportsfile

reflected in international selection too. Leinster players who retired in the 2010s – such as Jamie Heaslip, Rob Kearney and Brian O'Driscoll – remain well known around the province and indeed the country, and are idols for many young sportsmen. These players have won every trophy available to win with Leinster and have gained individual recognition, with high-profile 'man of the match' recognitions, memorable and frequent scoring accolades, and European or World player awards along their journeys. More recently, the persistently competitive Jonathan Sexton; the prevailing James Ryan, who held Leinster and Ireland captaincies at a relatively young age; and the star centre who cannot get away from comparisons with Brian O'Driscoll, Garry Ringrose, are all recognisable faces in Dublin and Leinster, and internationally as they continue to achieve Leinster success in the 2020s.

More conspicuously, the focus on players from non-traditional rugby schools has been at the forefront of marketing in the professional age, despite the fact that the vast majority of the star players, even today, come from the private school

2013
League Champion

2012
European Champion

2014
League Champion

▲ Brian O'Driscoll montage. O'Driscoll epitomises the rise and evolution of rugby in Leinster, having played from 1999 to 2014 with the club, through the 'lean years' and on to great success.

set-up in Leinster. The emphasis on domestic stars from non-Dublin backgrounds aims to provide a narrative that highlights county diversity and the popularity of the code province-wide. Examples of exemplary Branch success stories in terms of coming through all levels and grades, and not via the usual privately schooled route, are Seán O'Brien and Tadhg Furlong. O'Brien, as a young sports enthusiast, played all the football codes and excelled as much in GAA as rugby. His father had been a recreational rugby player with the Tullow club and O'Brien took to the game with verve. When asked why he took up rugby, he jokingly explained that he finally discovered a game that would allow him to put his head down and push. Playing with the Tullow Community School in Carlow, it was there that his rugby potential was recognised. He was earmarked for the Leinster farm system and played his way up through Schools, Youths, U18s, U20s, U21s, Leinster 'A's and then the Senior teams. If ever there was an example of the pathway to success in the professional game for young men and women around the province, it was the road that O'Brien travelled.

As well as O'Brien, the Leinster organisation have continuously highlighted the stories of Tadhg Furlong and Shane Horgan. Indeed, probably one of the standout and most memorable television ads for rugby in Ireland was one in which Furlong was imagined as a young boy in a field on a farm tackling an enormous tractor tube and rolling a gigantic tractor wheel across a yard, juxtaposed with him lining out in the tunnel about to step into the biggest professional rugby venue for any Irish player. Furlong followed a somewhat similar path to O'Brien, with his GAA hurling and football background. He talks about having to bide his time to find a welcome into the Leinster squad. Journalist Peter Breen wrote of him early on:

> [I]t is clear that Furlong holds great stock on the path that he has made. Having progressed through the Under-18 Clubs (youths) system through to Leinster Under-20 and the Academy, he is attempting to blaze the same kind of trail which players like Shane Horgan and Sean O'Brien have done. 'I'm very proud to have represented the Leinster Youths,' he says. 'Even though the likes of Shane and Seanie have come up through the club game, I think that we're hopefully going to see a strong generation of Youth players. There are more and more players coming through this system to complement the established schools and that's going to make for a stronger Leinster hopefully for years to come.'[12]

▲ Shane Horgan on his way to scoring a try against Llanelli Scarlets in the Heineken Cup in 2009. © Matt Browne/Sportsfile

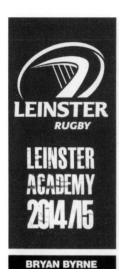

LEINSTER RUGBY

LEINSTER ACADEMY 2014/15

TADHG BEIRNE

DOB	8th Jan 1992
Birthplace	Co.Kildare
Height	1.98 m (6' 6")
Weight	104 kg (16 st 5 lb)
Position	Lock
Club	Lansdowne FC

HARRISON BREWER

DOB	22nd Mar 1995
Birthplace	Christchurch, New Zealand
Height	1.93 m (6' 4")
Weight	104 kg (16 st 5 lb)
Position	Centre
Club	Terenure College RFC

ADAM BYRNE

DOB	10th Apr 1994
Birthplace	
Height	1.91 m (6' 3")
Weight	95 kg (14 st 13 lb)
Position	Wing / Full Back
Club	UCD RFC

BRYAN BYRNE

DOB	9th Sep 1993
Birthplace	
Height	1.78 m (5' 10")
Weight	103 kg (16 st 3 lb)
Position	Hooker
Club	Clontarf FC

EDWARD BYRNE

DOB	9th Sep 1993
Birthplace	
Height	1.81 m (5' 11")
Weight	106 kg (16 st 9 lb)
Position	Prop
Club	UCD RFC

ROSS BYRNE

DOB	8th April 1995
Birthplace	Dublin
Height	1.89 m (6' 2")
Weight	93 kg (14 st 9 lb)
Position	Out-Half
Club	UCD RFC

JORDAN COGHLAN

DOB	30th Oct 1992
Birthplace	Dublin
Height	1.93 m (6' 4")
Weight	108 kg (17 st 0 lb)
Position	Centre
Club	UCD RFC

STEVE CROSBIE

DOB	10th Feb 1993
Birthplace	
Height	1.85 m (6' 1")
Weight	92 kg (14 st 6 lb)
Position	Fly Half
Club	Old Belvedere RFC

TOM DALY

DOB	31st Jul 1993
Birthplace	
Height	1.91 m (6' 3")
Weight	100 kg (15 st 10 lb)
Position	Centre
Club	Lansdowne FC

BILLY DARDIS

DOB	31st Jan 1995
Birthplace	Dublin
Height	1.77 m (5' 10")
Weight	85 kg (13 st 5 lb)
Position	Full Back
Club	UCD RFC

PETER DOOLEY

DOB	4th Aug 1994
Birthplace	
Height	1.85 m (6' 1")
Weight	113 kg (17 st 11 lb)
Position	Prop
Club	Lansdowne FC

THOMAS FARRELL

DOB	1st Oct 1993
Birthplace	
Height	1.88 m (6' 2")
Weight	97 kg (15 st 3 lb)
Position	Centre
Club	Lansdowne FC

IAN FITZPATRICK

DOB	25 August 1994
Birthplace	Co. Meath
Height	1.83 m (6' 0")
Weight	87 kg (13 st 8 lb)
Position	Back three
Club	Lansdowne FC

CIAN KELLEHER

DOB	7th Aug 1994
Birthplace	Sandymount
Height	1.73 m (5' 8")
Weight	94 kg (14 st 10 lb)
Position	Wing / Full Back
Club	

DAN LEAVY

DOB	23rd May 1994
Birthplace	Dublin
Height	1.91 m (6' 3")
Weight	101 kg (15 st 12 lb)
Position	Flanker
Club	UCD RFC

NICK McCARTHY

DOB	25th Mar 1995
Birthplace	Michigan, USA
Height	1.82 m (5' 11")
Weight	83 kg (13 st 0 lb)
Position	Scrum Half
Club	UCD RFC

CATHAL MARSH

DOB	1st Oct 1992
Birthplace	Dublin
Height	1.78 m (5' 10")
Weight	84 kg (13 st 2 lb)
Position	Fly Half
Club	St. Mary's College RFC

ROSS MOLONY

DOB	11th May 1994
Birthplace	Dublin
Height	1.98 m (6' 6")
Weight	107 kg (16 st 11 lb)
Position	Lock
Club	UCD RFC

RORY O'LOUGHLIN

DOB	January 21st 1994
Birthplace	Dublin
Height	1.88 m (6' 2")
Weight	93 kg (14 st 6 lb)
Position	Centre
Club	Old Belvedere

GARRY RINGROSE

DOB	26th Jan 1995
Birthplace	Co. Dublin
Height	1.87 m (6' 2")
Weight	91 kg (14 st 5 lb)
Position	Centre
Club	UCD RFC

GAVIN THORNBURY

DOB	19th Oct 1993
Birthplace	Dublin
Height	2.01 m (6' 7")
Weight	108 kg (17 st 0 lb)
Position	Second Row
Club	UCD RFC

PEADAR TIMMINS

DOB	8th Jan 1994
Birthplace	Co. Wicklow
Height	1.90 m (6' 3")
Weight	101 kg (16 st 0 lb)
Position	Back Row
Club	UCD

JOSH VAN DER FLIER

DOB	25th Apr 1993
Birthplace	Dublin
Height	1.85 m (6' 1")
Weight	98 kg (15 st 6 lb)
Position	Flanker
Club	UCD RFC

▲ Leinster Academy Squad 2014–15, listed in match-day programmes.

Stories of Leinster's star players from rural backgrounds aim to portray the idea of the local, the communal and the 'from the ground up' mantra that forge a connection with the province-wide fan base. Amidst the image of an internationally standout and proficient club, one that can dominate Europe, the highlighting of Furlong's, O'Brien's, and, earlier, Horgan's success with Leinster speaks to the idea that

> Irish success in international club-rugby in the 2000s has generated sporting heroes whose success is traced to amateur commitment to place and community despite rugby's professionalization … This attribution offered a vision of a nationally sustainable professional game where player professionalism was driven by local rootedness, despite the provinces' regional rather than traditional club status. Journalists and other commentators in the Irish media depicted rugby's crossing of amateur/professional, middle/working-class, urban/rural, and North/South divides as the successful national integration of multiple masculinities …[13]

For example, the Tullow Tank, Seán O'Brien, was fundamentally associated with his Carlow rootedness as the epitome of the Leinster rugby player. The constant focus by fans and the organisation on these players specifically has somewhat helped Leinster shed the history of its own exclusivity. It is no accident that the emphasis on O'Brien's

▲ Leinster legend and current contact skills coach Seán O'Brien.

and, in particular, Furlong's farming background are conspicuously advertised. Leinster rugby has been able to create this phenomenal growth and popularity of the game with an outstanding degree of success in the pro era by being more rounded and inclusive. The 'popularization of the new identity of province-as-club, embodying the bridging of amateur and professional eras and motivations by stressing, in various media interviews, its roots in locality and the provincial jersey as symbolically representing "friends and family … probably something I was born into"'[14] has seen rugby compete with the other football codes where it had not done so before. The Branch's move to broaden the game to players and clubs beyond the traditional schools and clubs in Dublin shows an acknowledgement of the wider

Leinster player Tadhg Furlong having lots of fun with participants during the Bank of Ireland Leinster Rugby Summer Camp at Gorey RFC in Wexford, 2018. © Eóin Noonan/Sportsfile

▲ 12 May 2018: Leinster players celebrate following the European Rugby Champions Cup final between Leinster and Racing 92 at San Mames Stadium in Bilbao, Spain. © Stephen McCarthy/Sportsfile

pool of talent that might be interested in playing the game. The fact that in today's professional landscape the players are recognisable sporting celebrities probably adds a dash of incentive for young sporting hopefuls to boot.

One of Leinster's newest clubs perhaps signals the contemporary standpoint of Leinster rugby in quite a telling fashion. As Ireland adjusted to a newfound multiculturalism, a team calling themselves the Southern Cross Dogos affiliated to the Leinster Branch in December 2016. The club, composed entirely of expatriates, was organised by a group of Argentinian players based in Dublin. Their motivation was more than just competing in one of the strongest amateur rugby leagues in the world – they wanted to do so in style, akin to the expressive rugby associated with the Barbarians. Moreover, one of the stated goals of the Dogos is to offer the immigrant community an opportunity to come together around the common bond of love of rugby, to aid integration, help people adapt and to promote multiculturalism in an Irish context.

Perhaps even more interestingly, the foundation of the Dogos was motivated by the onset of Brexit and an awareness of the growing forces of right-wing politics and their negative policies rooted in xenophobia, racism, homophobia and privileged entitlement. As a team open to both immigrants and Irish players, they are very deliberately a club with a point to make in reaction to the negative forces growing across Europe and also evident in Ireland. In many ways the appearance of the club epitomises so much about the progress of Leinster rugby and the historical road that it has taken to become a more open sport. Affiliated with Dublin City University (DCU) – with players from Argentina, South Africa, Kenya, Canada,

Belgium and France, supplemented by a few Irish locals – the club, whose motto is 'rugby without walls', start training in July each year, with sessions in the mountains of Wicklow and on the beaches of County Louth, before participating in the Tullamore sevens. 'John Arlott wrote in his *Pageantry of Sport* (1968) that games are truly part of the history of a nation and reflect the social life of the people and the changes in economy, religion and politics ...'[15] Leinster rugby, one might agree, has certainly evolved to reflect some of the perpetual changes that have shaped this province's, as well as Ireland's, historical trajectories.

Leinster rugby's success had its source in the decades of building clubs, like the youth teams that were organised and pushed onwards from the 1970s. In the 1980s and 1990s the struggle was the need to improve skills, to become more consistently competitive and to retain interest and playing numbers to continue to field teams at all levels. Fierce competition with other sports was one factor rugby had to contend with, in the 1990s especially. In the new millennium, however, the number of children following and playing rugby increased substantially, portending a positive future. Thanks to the massive success of Leinster's senior team on the field, the organisation managed to create a 'culture that ignited Leinster's ascension to greatness ... from the coaches and players ... [to] the administrators who have forged structural changes off the pitch to put in place the building blocks of change'.[16] As the club game across Leinster continues to attract followers in all counties, and as all counties have managed to maintain a fan base that follows the Leinster senior team, Leinster rugby's history certainly depicts an evolution that mirrors social and cultural progress in Ireland's easternmost province.

▲ The Southern Cross Dogos affiliated to the Leinster Branch in December 2016. The club, composed entirely of expatriates, was organised by a group of Argentinian players based in Dublin.

EPILOGUE

Leinster Rugby's Pandemic Pivot

The rich history of rugby in Leinster is recorded in a plethora of repositories: people's memories, official documents, newspapers, photographs, video and audio recordings, match results, team sheets and stories of administrators, players, clubs, schools, venues and games. From all these narratives and records the hope here was to unveil Leinster rugby's idiosyncrasies, which make it an identifiable history for those who already know the game and an eye-opening tale for those who are discovering Leinster rugby for the first time. There is, of course, a temptation to write much more about the recent past of Leinster's progress (and success!) in the last decade, from 2010 to 2020. However, the danger for any historian is that the more contemporary the topic becomes, the more subjective the final outcome appears. What's more, with the triumphs and popularity of Leinster rugby, there are not only official records and copious amounts of hardcopy materials available about that period, but, with the explosion of digital platforms pertaining to both amateur club rugby and the Leinster professional team, there exists a rabbit warren of information that would elicit a stand-alone, encyclopedic volume.

Nonetheless, as this study has progressed towards a conclusion in the spring of 2022, this present moment, as most people recognise, has been one of historic significance. The onset of a global pandemic, it goes without saying, has been a major factor in the story of Leinster rugby. The challenging and difficult prospect for the management of the senior team in its entirety (players, coaches, administrators, etc.) has been multifold. For professional players to individually maintain fitness, focus and motivation, not to mention keeping everyone paid and ensuring the entire organisation stayed afloat financially while everything was brought to a halt, required new thinking. How to keep connected to the fans was also key. Additionally, there was also the Branch's responsibility to the amateur game. Keeping the province's club game in focus, in the midst of almost two years of crisis, undoubtedly has brought to light further insights for consideration. With the initial cancellation of all rugby – the professional competitions as well as amateur club rugby – communities had to rally together and come up with innovative ways to respond to the needs of clubs and their general membership. Committees, parents, supporters, alickadoos, referees, coaches, various volunteers and the players were all badly affected by the shutdown of rugby across the nation. But it is the response of these people that has become the most significant element of these trying times.

The digital era was to a large extent a major factor in enabling the world of rugby to work through those exasperating months. Clubs organised various online digital initiatives for fundraising and to raise spirits, keeping everyone – players, coaches, administrators and all members – connected in various ways, often through social media or new online meeting platforms. The level of inventiveness and determination to keep the clubs connected underscored the level of volunteerism and community support at the heart of Leinster rugby across all levels. On the

▲ Judge Conroy (and friend) eating breakfast at Butlin's, Mosney, during a rugby coaching camp in the 1960s. From the first 'official' coaching camps, the game has come a long, long way!

▲ Leinster club rugby women's teams' collage, International Women's Day, March 2022. During and since the pandemic the strength of women's rugby in Leinster has proven invaluable to the community.

community side, everything from interviews with current and former players and coaches, old photos and stories, throwbacks to old team successes, online Zoom quizzes and competitions, online movies of mascots getting up to mischief and examples of members undertaking daily swims or 5k-a-day walks and runs were used to retain connections and inspire the club members to keep going through the most stringent lockdown measures imposed on any nation in Europe as a result of Covid-19. What's more, for the youth and the playing members in particular, the roll-out of Zoom training sessions, from strength and fitness to basic skills videos, coupled with incentives like passing and kicking challenges, all revealed the level of commitment and the importance of local Leinster rugby clubs, indeed sports clubs in general, to the health of the nation in more ways than mere physical fitness.

If ever the centrality of sports to society was evident, undoubtedly it has been in the midst of the Covid situation in Ireland. Without the community, volunteerism and innovation of those involved in the club-rugby world and all sporting clubs, the outcome, as bad as it has been, would have been ingloriously worse. As restrictions began to be eased back, members of sporting clubs organised fundraisers to help fill the financial gaps that lockdown caused, through initiatives like GoFundMe pages. Club AGMs were held online and the people at the heart of their clubs looked for opportunities as a community during this particular emergency, such as addressing badly needed clubhouse renovations. When games resumed and crowds were absent, or few people could travel to games, clubs live-streamed or recorded their matches for same-day viewing. Talk about the rugby-club 'family' emerged more potently and the importance of the game to many, many people came to the forefront.

Of course, for the professional Leinster team and club there were even more troubling challenges and difficulties to contend with, not least the financial implications for the entire organisation. While sponsorship is probably the biggest factor, with gate receipts second in terms of maintaining revenues to keep a professional rugby team going, the fact that so many different elements of society have been unduly hit by what the pandemic wrought put Leinster in an arduous position. Having a season cancelled and another season played behind closed doors, or with severely restricted numbers, not only erased gate revenues, but put sponsorship deals in jeopardy. Other knock-on effects, like the loss of merchandising sales, meant rugby clubs and the Leinster Branch itself suffered a big financial loss. The Branch lost staff and those remaining, including players, volunteered to take pay cuts during a crisis that initially saw all games halted. Even as the restrictions loosened, attendance capacities for games remained truncated, leaving the professional body in a precarious state. Uncertainty about how games would proceed saw the loss of season-ticket revenue, for instance, and the organisation needed to pivot to deal with the situation.

That said, the story coming out of the sporting world has not just revealed something more positive in those two dark years of 2020–21, but also rendered plain for all to see the centrality of clubs and organisations to daily life across the entire province. A Leinster Rugby Covid subcommittee put together resources for players and members to look after their mental health during lockdown, for example. The message was to stay in touch with teammates and clubs, and keep an eye out for one another, just as one would on the pitch. Reciprocally, as Leinster Branch's Kevin Quinn explained, the loyalty of the Leinster fan base came through when the Branch offered an innovative membership programme that relied on digital platforms to offer product to those subscribers. Interviews, podcasts and feature videos were all organised and made available, alongside an online quarterly magazine for members only. When games resumed without crowds, members got a digital match-day programme of high quality in terms of content and presentation, innovations that will remain post-pandemic.

The connection, then, between the amateur game of club rugby and the professional organisation are what have given the Leinster Branch staying power throughout the crisis. Pivoting to digital content has meant continuity: for example, virtual match-day mascots allowed Leinster to solicit input by having followers nominate young Leinster fans to be beamed onto viewers screens from their homes, virtually recreating the ball-carriers who led the team onto a pitch at the beginning of a match. This underscored efforts by the club to keep including the Leinster faithful on match days, despite empty stadia. Or there was the virtual 'sea of blue', where crowds could connect to in-stadium video screens while watching live. Importantly, the pause offered a chance to negotiate new broadcasting rights as Leinster renewed partnerships with RTÉ and TG4, intended to reach a wider audience than ever before – a recognition, no doubt, of the importance of the inclusivity that rugby has had to foster and the power of a larger communal backing to ensure survival in moments of crisis. Indeed, the centrality of sport and the depth of rugby interest across the province could be assessed when summer camps reopened for children with more subscribers than ever before in the history of that programme, while initiatives such as tag rugby for mothers and fathers were commenced or reinvigorated in the summer of 2021.[1]

As the province emerged, tentatively, from two years of Covid restrictions and as sports cautiously resumed, Leinster rugby uncovered a healthy network of common support within communities across all counties that were mutually essential to each others' survival. In the first two decades of the twenty-first century, it is fair to say that Leinster rugby has been an entirely different proposition across all of Dublin city and in Leinster more broadly. Rugby today is recognisable not just through its professional players but by its camaraderie, a palpable familiarity and by its saving grace in a time of crisis. Leinster Rugby have undergone comprehensive changes to make them more accessible, attractive and popular in the eleven counties outside their particular Dublin stronghold. They have pivoted when needed and the payoff is illustrated in the support structures, the broader communality and the survival of all associated with Leinster Rugby, and with rugby in Leinster.

The Leinster team line-up at the start of the Heineken Cup semi-final v. Munster, Croke Park, Dublin, 2 May 2009.
This Leinster victory proved a huge turning point in the future dominance of Leinster rugby in Ireland and indeed Europe.

Endnotes

Introduction

1 J.C. Conroy (ed.), *Rugby in Leinster, 1879–1979* (Dublin, 1979); Tony Collins, *How Football Began: A Global History of How the World's Football Codes Were Born* (London and New York, 2019); Tony Collins, *A Social History of English Rugby Union* (London and New York, 2009); Tony Collins, *Rugby's Great Split: Class, Culture and the Origins of Rugby League Football,* (London and Portland, 1999); Paul Rouse, *Sport and Ireland: A History* (Oxford, 2015); Edmund Van Esbeck, *One Hundred Years of Irish Rugby: The Official History of the Irish Rugby Football Union, 1874–1974* (Dublin, 1974).

2 Richard M. Peter, *The Origins and Development of Football in Ireland: Being a Reprint of R.M. Peter's Irish Football Annual 1880 with an introduction by Neal Garnham* (Belfast, 1999), p. 1.

3 Trevor West, *The Bold Collegians: The Development of Sport in Trinity College, Dublin* (Dublin, 1991).

4 Liam O'Callaghan, *Rugby in Munster: A Social and Cultural History* (Cork, 2019), p. 23.

5 Greg Ryan, 'The Paradox of Māori Rugby 1870–1914' in idem (ed.), *Tackling Rugby Myths: Rugby and New Zealand Society 1854–2004* (Otago, 2005), p. 89.

6 Rouse, *Sport and Ireland*, p. 205.

7 Ibid., p. 4.

8 Ibid., p. 216.

9 Van Esbeck, *One Hundred Years of Irish Rugby*, p. 5.

10 Steven A. Riess, *Sport in Industrial America, 1850–1920* (Wheeling, Illinois, 1995), pp. 18–19.

11 Collins, *A Social History of English Rugby Union*, p. 82.

12 Ibid.,p.26.

13 Brendan Behan, *Borstal Boy* (London, 1990), p. 352.

14 Ibid., pp. 251–2.

15 Ibid., p. 252.

Chapter 1

1 TCDA, MUN/CLUB/RUGBY/F/21.

2 Rouse, *Sport and Ireland*, p. 130.

3 Collins, *A Social History of English Rugby Union*, p. 5.

4 TCDA, MUN/CLUB/RUGBY/F/1.

5 Ibid.

6 Ibid.

7 Ibid. The first reports of rugby games appeared in *The Dublin Warder* as early as 22 and 29 November 1856.

8 TCDA, MUN/CLUB/RUGBY/F/38/50.

9 Ibid.

10 Ibid.

11 TCDA, MUN/CLUB/RUGBY/F/46.

12 Ibid.

13 TCDA, MUN/CLUB/RUGBY/F/38/16.

14 www.ria.ie/ga/node/98320 (29 July 2020).

15 TCDA, MUN/CLUB/RUGBY/F/23.

16 TCDA, MUN/CLUB/RUGBY/F/1.

17 O'Callaghan, *Rugby in Munster*, p. 76.

18 Mike Cronin, '"Trinity Mysteries": responding to a chaotic reading of Irish history', *The International Journal of the History of Sport*, 28:18 (2011), p. 2757.

19 TCDA, MUN/CLUB/RUGBY/F/1.

20 Tom Hunt, *Sport and Society in Victorian Ireland: The Case of Westmeath* (Cork, 2007), p. 174.

21 '… almost one-third of 389 Irishmen capped before 1914 were medics.' Huw Richards, *A Game for Hooligans: The History of Rugby Union* (Edinburgh and London, 2007), p. 41.

22 *Wanderers Football Club 1870–1920: Celebrating 150 Years*, p. 164.

23 From 1875 to 1945 there were 146 games between the clubs: Trinity winning 92, Wanderers 39, with 15 draws. TCDA, MUN/CLUB/RUGBY/F/23.

24 Garry Redmond (ed.), *Lansdowne Football Club, Centenary 1872–1972: A Club History* (Dublin, 1972), p. 3.

25 Rev. Dermot Murray and Michael O'Dea (eds), *1902–2002: Association of Referees, Leinster Branch IRFU* (Dublin, 2002), p. 14.

26 TCDA, MUN/CLUB/RUGBY/F/25.

27 Van Esbeck, *One Hundred Years of Irish Rugby*, p. 38.

28 Ibid., p. 39.

29 Conleth Feighery, Michael Farrell and Morgan Crowe, *The Hospital Pass: 140 Years of Dublin Hospitals Rugby* (Dublin 2021), p. 10.

30 MUN/CLUB/RUGBY/F/22.

31 Thomas J. O'Brien (ed.), *County Carlow Football Club Rugby History, 1873–1977* (Carlow, 1977).

32 Ibid., p. 21.

33 Ibid.

34 Ibid., p. 23.

35 M.J. Tutty, 'Clontarf', *Dublin Historical Record*, Vol. 21, No. 1 (March–May 1966), pp. 2–13.

36 www.clontarfrugby.com/club-history/ (19 June 2020).

37 Clontarf FC annual report for season 1879–80, courtesy of Brendan Smith CFC.

38 www.dundalkrfc.ie/about (1 February 2021).

39 O'Brien, *County Carlow Football Club Rugby History*, p. 29.

Chapter 2

1 Keith A.P. Sandiford, 'The Victorians at Play: Problems in Historiographical Methodology', *Journal of Social History*, Vol. 15, No. 2 (Winter, 1981), 271–88.

2 Richard McElligott, '"A Youth Tainted with the Deadly Poison of Anglicism"? Sport and childhood in the Irish Independence period', in Boylan and Gallagher (eds), *Constructions of the Irish Child in the Independence Period, 1910–1940* (Palgrave Macmillan: Oxford, 2018), p. 280.

3 www.wesleycollege.ie/About/History/ (12 May 2021).

4 Richard Lee Cole, *Wesley College, Dublin: an historical summary 1845-1962* (Dublin, 1963), p. 14.

5 Examples include Kilkenny College (est. 1538); The King's Hospital (est. 1669); Wilson's Hospital (est. 1761); St Columba's College, Dublin (est. 1843); Wesley College (est. 1845); The High School, Dublin (est. 1870); St Andrew's College, Dublin (est. 1894); and Sandford Park School (est. 1922).

6 Lesley Whiteside, *A History of the King's Hospital* (Dublin, 1985).

7 Ibid., p. 151.

8 Ibid., p. 153.

9 W.J.R. Wallace, *Faithful to Our Trust: A History of the Erasmus Smith Trust and the High School, Dublin* (Dublin, 2004), p. 136.

10 Ibid., p. 247.

11 Georgina Fitzpatrick, *St. Andrew's College 1894–1994: Ardens Sed Virens* (Dublin, 1994), p. 26–7.

12 Ibid., p. 27.

13 Lesley Whiteside with Andrew Whitside, *Where Swift and Berkeley Learnt: A History of Kilkenny College* (Dublin, 2009).

14 Ibid., p. 78.

15 G.K. White, *A History of Columba's College, 1843–1974* (Dublin, 1981), p. 131.

16 McElligott, '"A Youth Tainted with the Deadly Poison of Anglicism?"', p. 282.

17 Anon., *1881–1981 Bective Rangers Football Club Centenary* (Dublin, 1981), p. 103.

18 Ibid.

19 www.castleknockcollege.ie/co-curricular/rugby/ (10 May 2021).

20 Anon., *CUS 1867–1967, A Centenary Record* (Dublin, 1967).

21 Ibid., pp. 69–70.

22 Thus, Newbridge College (est. 1852), C.B.C. Monkstown (est. 1856), Terenure College

(est. 1860), St Mary's College, Dublin (est. 1890 & 1926), and the Cistercian College, Roscrea, Co. Offaly (est. 1905), all adopted rugby football. In the twentieth century more Catholic fee-paying schools in Leinster followed suit: St Gerard's School, Bray (1918), Presentation College Bray (est. 1921), St Conleth's College (1939), St Michael's College, Dublin (1944), and Gonzaga College (1950).

23 Conroy, *Rugby in Leinster*, p. 76.

24 www.newbridge-college.ie/About-the-College/History (11 May 2021).

25 McElligott, "'A Youth Tainted with the Deadly Poison of Anglicism?'", p. 283.

26 This is out of a possible 134. Their nearest rivals are Belvedere College with twelve (DDPC).

27 Sandiford, 'The Victorians at Play', pp. 271–88.

28 Sean P. Farragher, *The French College Blackrock, 1860–1890* (Dublin, 2011), p. 203.

29 O'Callaghan, *Rugby in Munster*, p. 76.

30 Farragher, *The French College Blackrock*, pp. 416–17.

Chapter 3

1 In attendance were A. Morell (DUFC), E.A. McCarthy (Kingston), F. Kennedy (Wanderers), G. Drougut (Phoenix), C.B. Croker (Lansdowne) and R.M. Paten (Dundalk). All teams entering had to guarantee at least £2.2.0 to the challenge cup fund. MUN/CLUB/RUGBY/F/15.

2 DUFC, Phoenix, Wanderers, Kingstown and Lansdowne. Conroy, *Rugby in Leinster*, p. 53.

3 Trinity's first XV that 1881–82 season: Atkinson, Browne, Brut, Buchanan, Cassidy, Downing, Frith, Johnston, King, MacCarthy, MacLean, Morell (capt.), A.C. O'Sullivan, A.W. O'Sullivan, Vincent. TCDA, MUN/CLUB/RUGBY/F/15.

4 Conroy, *Rugby in Leinster*, p. 54.

5 Edmund Van Esbeck, *Irish Rugby 1874–1999: A History* (Dublin, 1999), p. 12.

6 *The Irish Times*, 23 September 1882.

7 *The Irish Times*, 3 October 1882.

8 Anon., *1881–1981 Bective Rangers Football Club Centenary*, p. 25.

9 Ibid., p. 27.

10 Ibid., p. 27.

11 Ibid., p. 37.

12 *The Irish Field*, 21 December 1882.

13 www.monkstownfc.ie/about-monkstown-fc/the-monkstown-story/ (1 October 2020).

14 Conroy, *Rugby in Leinster*, p. 62.

15 John Walsh, *The Provincial Towns Cup: For Generations It's The Spirit of Rugby* (Naas, 2020).

16 Conroy, *Rugby in Leinster*, p. 64.

17 Ibid.

18 Ibid.

19 UCD Archives, Leinster Branch, P280/01.

20 *Midland Counties Advertiser*, 18 October 1883.

21 *Midland Counties Advertiser*, 15 November 1883.

22 O'Brien, *County Carlow Football Club Rugby History*, p. 33.

23 Conroy, *Rugby in Leinster*, p. 30.

24 Cited in ibid., p. 31.

25 Ibid.

26 UCD Archives, Leinster Branch, P280/01.

27 https://www.dib.ie/biography/bulger-law rence-quinlivan-larry-a9796#co-subject-B (accessed 1 March 2023).

28 https://www.dib.ie/biography/magee-aloy sius-mary-louis-a5330 (accessed 22 February 2021).

29 UCD Archives, Leinster Branch, P280/01.

Chapter 4

1 Diarmaid Ferriter, *The Transformation of Ireland, 1900-2000* (London, 2005), p. 80.

2 Ibid., p. 53.

3 Ibid.

4 Kurt Kullmann, *Rugby Town: The Sporting History of D4* (Dublin, 2016), p. 11.

5 Neal Garnham, 'Football and National Identity in Pre-Great War Ireland', *Irish Economic and Social History*, XXVIII (2001), p. 29.

6 National Archives of Ireland, DFA/5/301/65 I.

7   Collins, *A Social History of English Rugby Union*, p. 107.

8   Rouse, *Sport and Ireland*, p. 242.

9   Wanderers FC, Lansdowne FC, Bective FC, Monkstown FC, Old Wesley RFC and Railway Union RFC; while UCD was initially located at Earlsford Terrace off St Stephen's Green on the south side of Dublin, today the rugby club and university are firmly ensconced in D4; another three are on the edges – namely Blackrock, St Mary's College and Parkmore – while a fourth, Palmerstown (today's DLSP), is based a little further south in Dublin, at Kilternan.

10   William A. Maher, CSSP, *A History of St Mary's College, Rathmines, Dublin, 1890–1990* (Dublin, 1994), pp. 49–50.

11   1904/5, 06/07, 07/08 St Mary's won the Junior Cup (runners-up in 01/02, 02/03 and 05/06); Junior League winners, 08/09, 09/10 and Junior Cup winners again in 1910/11. Promoted to senior in 1911/12.

12   A number of newly affiliated clubs were dropped within a few months of their founding: Rathmines P&P, CUS, Catholic University P&P, Dundalk, Santry and Ceclia Street. CUS, Catholic University (i.e. UCD) and Dundalk would later re-affiliate. UCD Archives, Leinster Branch, P280/1.

13   Kullmann, *Rugby Town,* p. 17.

14   Ibid., p. 46.

15   http://web.archive.org/web/201170430154135/ http://www.dublinmaccabi.com/history/rugby (27 January 2021).

16   Terry Goodwin, *The Complete Who's Who of International Rugby* (England, 1987). Also see Bethel Solomons player profile on www.scrum.com; Edmund Van Esbeck, *The Story of Irish Rugby* (London, 1986), p. 253.

17   In the fourteen years and fifteen finals from 1900 to 1914, the winners of the junior cup were: Old St Mary's (four wins 1905, 1907, 1908, 1911 and four losses 1902, 1903, 1906, 1909); RIC (three times 1902, 1903, 1906);

Carlow (three wins 1904, 1912, 1913); Clontarf (once 1900); Santry (once 1901); Dundalk (once 1909, and lost the next year in 1910); Merrion (once in 1910, and lost one in 1914); UCD (once in 1914 and lost one in 1912).

18   O'Brien, *County Carlow Football Club Rugby History*, p. 55.

19   At the October 1901 AGM proposals were raised for consideration (postponed for the present) to start a competition for the third teams of senior clubs and the second teams of junior clubs. UCD Archives, Leinster Branch, P280/1.

20   In the first season of the new format, the teams in Section A were: Bective, Civil Service, DUFC, Lansdowne, Palmerstown, St Mary's College and Wanderers. Section B were Railway Union, Blackrock College, Clontarf, Monkstown, Sandford and the Veterinary College. Of these clubs, Veterinary, Palmerstown, Civil Service, St Mary's and Railway Union were junior clubs and entered second teams. Sandford College was designated a Minor team, and only had a starting fifteen to its name. All the other clubs were entering third XVs, which shows the strength of the game in the metropole in 1907–08.

21   *Evening Herald*, 3 June 1959.

22   Ibid.

23   UCD Archives, Leinster Branch, P280/1-3.

24   Rugby 'pals' regiments specifically made up of players from Irish rugby clubs were organised and facilitated by the IRFU during the war.

25   Neal Garnham, 'Rugby and Empire in Ireland: Irish reactions to colonial rugby tours before 1914', Sport in History, 23:1 (2003), p. 111.

26   Ibid., p. 108.

27   Simon Glassock, 'Good Sports? Scotland, Empire and Rugby c.1924–1928', *Sports History*, Vol. 36, No. 3 (2016), p. 350.

28   Stephen Cooper, *After the Final Whistle: The First Rugby World Cup and the First World War* (Cheltenham, 2016), p. 128.

29   Neal Garnham, 'Football and National

Identity in Pre-Great War Ireland', *Irish Economic and Social History*, XXVIII (2001), pp. 28–9.

30 UCD Archives, Leinster Branch P280/02.

31 Redmond, *Lansdowne Football Club*, p. 49.

32 Fitzpatrick, *St. Andrew's College*, pp. 36–7.

33 Nigel McCrery, *Into Touch: Rugby Internationals Killed in The Great War* (Barnsley, 2014), p. 109.

34 TCDA, MUN CLUB RUGBYF/47/9.

35 Liam O'Callaghan, 'Irish Rugby and the First World War', *Sport in Society* Vol. 19, No. 1 (2016), p. 98.

36 Ibid., p. 97.

37 See Cooper, *After the Final Whistle*.

38 Ibid., p. 106.

39 *Irish Independent*, 8 January 1906.

40 UCD Archives, Leinster Branch, P280/1.

41 The Interprovincial Leinster team was selected from just seven clubs, with seven DUFC players, two each from Wesley and Lansdowne, and one each from Monkstown, Wanderers, Blackrock and Blackheath (England). See the *Irish Independent*, 8 January 1906.

42 Jan. 1903, Leinster Branch Exec. Meeting. Accounts showed gate money was the biggest earner, with the 1903 LSC bringing in £222-10-6. The interprovincials were next, and then the schools, junior league, and junior cup. UCD Archives, Leinster Branch, P280/1.

Chapter 5

1 National Archives of Ireland, 2006/149/37.

2 Liam O'Callaghan, 'Rugby Football and Identity Politics in Free State Ireland', *Éire-Ireland*, Vol. 48, Iss. 1&2 (Spring/Summer 2013), p. 149.

3 TCDA, MUN CLUB RUGBYF/47/9.

4 TCDA, MUN CLUB RUGBYF/47/9.

5 Old Belvedere, initially founded in 1918, came to an abrupt halt during the War of Independence, but reformed in 1930 and have been in perpetual existence since then – hence 1980 marked the golden jubilee.

6 Edmund Van Esbeck, 'Ten out of fifty': A *Chronicle of Old Belvedere Football Club, 1930–1980* (Dublin, 1980), p. 1.

7 Oliver Murphy, *Belvedere's Rugby Heroes* (Dublin, 2006).

8 https://oldbelvedere.ie/content_page/283187/ClubHistory/ (accessed 27 April 2021).

9 O'Callaghan, 'Rugby Football and Identity Politics in Free State Ireland', p. 150.

10 National Archives of Ireland, DFA/1/GR/1489; National Archives of Ireland, DFA/5/301/65 I.

11 O'Callaghan, 'Rugby Football and Identity Politics in Free State Ireland', p. 148.

12 *Mullingar Presidents Selected XV v Wolfhounds Official Opening of Grounds and Clubhouse Souvenir Handbook, 1977.*

13 https://digital.ucd.ie/view/ucdlib:38697 (17 March 2023).

14 https://doi.org/10.7925/drs1.ucdlib_38721 (17 March 2023).

15 Anon., *1881–1981 Bective Rangers Football Club Centenary*, p. 43.

16 Ibid.

17 Rouse, *Sport and Ireland*, p. 279.

18 UCD Archives, Leinster Branch P280/26.

19 O'Callaghan, *Rugby in Munster*, p. 53.

20 'The Intermediate Education Act of 1921 took the first steps to establish local government scholarships, which helped the gifted few …'. Incorporated Society Schools offered scholarships to Protestant children to attend The King's Hospital, based on ability and financial situation. Whiteside with Whitside, *Where Swift and Berkeley Learnt*, p. 94.

21 UCD Archives, Leinster Branch P280/25.

22 UCD Archives, Leinster Branch, P280/03.

23 O'Brien, *County Carlow Football Club Rugby History*, p. 56.

24 *Leinster Branch EGM report*, 13 September 1920 (DDPC).

25 Murray and O'Dea, *1902–2002: Association of Referees*, p. 19.

26 Ibid., p. 20.

27 Ibid., p. 18.

28 Ibid., p. 22.

Chapter 6

1   McElligott, '"A Youth Tainted with the Deadly Poison of Anglicism?"', p. 295.

2   O'Callaghan, 'Rugby Football and Identity Politics in Free State Ireland', p. 156.

3   Ibid., p. 157.

4   Ibid.

5   Ibid., p. 161.

6   UCD Archive, Leinster Branch P280/25.

7   Walsh, *The Provincial Towns Cup.*

8   Letter from Harry Gale written to all in the IRFU and Leinster Branch rugby. Email courtesy of John Walsh, Leinster Branch president, May 2021.

9   Anon., *1881–1981 Bective Rangers Football Club Centenary*, p. 43.

10 Ibid.

11 *Leinster Branch EGM report*, 13 September 1920 (DDPC).

12 UCD Archives, Leinster Branch P280/03.

13 UCD Archives, Leinster Branch, P280/35 and P280/36.

14 Ian d'Alton and Ida Milne (eds), *Protestant and Irish: The minority's search for place in independent Ireland* (Cork, 2019), 175.

15 Ian d'Alton, '"A Vestigial Population?": Perspectives on Southern Irish Protestants', *Eire-Ireland*, Vol. 44, Nos 3 & 4 (Fall/Winter, 2009).

16 O'Brien, *County Carlow Football Club Rugby History*, p. 62.

17 Conroy, *Rugby in Leinster*, pp. 64–5.

18 UCD Archives, Leinster Branch P280/25.

19 O'Callaghan, 'Rugby Football and Identity Politics in Free State Ireland', p. 162.

20 UCD Archives, Leinster Branch P280/03.

21 Van Esbeck, *One Hundred Years of Irish Rugby*, pp. 106–7.

22 UCD Archives, Leinster Branch, P280/37 and P280/40.

23 O'Callaghan, 'Rugby Football and Identity Politics in Free State Ireland', p. 163.

24 Ibid., p. 164.

25 UCD Archives, Leinster Branch, P280/35 and P280/36; Van Esbeck, *One Hundred Years of Irish Rugby*, pp. 106–7.

26 Van Esbeck, *One Hundred Years of Irish Rugby*, pp. 108–9.

27 UCD Archive, Leinster Branch, P280/03.

28 UCD Archives, Leinster Branch, P280/04.

29 Ibid.

30 Caroline McFadden, *From Rope Walk to Bowhill: A History of Rugby in Balbriggan* (Balbriggan RFC: Balbriggan, 2015), p. 54.

31 Ibid., p. 49.

32 Redmond, *Lansdowne Football Club*, p. 54.

33 'U.C.D. Rugby Club 75th Anniversary Programme: University College Dublin V The Wolfhounds, Sunday October 27, 1985, Donnybrook' (DDPC).

34 Des Daly Private Collection, uncatalogued records (DDPC).

35 https://offalyhistoryblog.wordpress.com/2017/04/08/p-h-egan-of-tullamore-1852-1968-by-david-egan/ (6 October 2020).

36 www.independent.ie/sport/rugby/leinster-rugby/club-focus-tulliers-continue-to-make-strides-35014014.html (21 October 2020).

37 www.greystonesrfc.ie/home/grfc-club-history/ (1 February 2021).

38 Ibid.

39 Sean F. Allan, *Seapoint RFC: A History* (1978).

40 Ibid.

41 UCD Archives, Leinster Branch, P280/05.

42 UCD Archives, Leinster Branch, P280/04.

43 https://lansdownerugby.com/about-the-club/ (11 December 2021).

44 https://www.dib.ie/biography/clinch-james-daniel-jammie-a1753 (21 December 2020).

45 Ibid.

46 Leinster Branch Honorary Secretary's Report 1934–1935, 1 October 1935 (DDPC).

47 Ibid.

Chapter 7

1   Brian Girvan, 'Forgotten Volunteers of World War II', *History Ireland*, Vol. 6, Iss. 1 (Spring 1998).

2   Executive Meeting, April 1927 – the Players Club cigarette company had been playing since about 1925 and there was a Mills cigarette company team too; they amalgamated to become the Imperial Tobacco Company RFC in 1927. UCD Archives, Leinster Branch, P280/1.

3   UCD Archives, Leinster Branch, P280/05.

4   UCD Archives, Leinster Branch, P280/26.

5   *Sunday Independent*, 16 November 1941.

6   *Honorary Secretary's Report of the Leinster Branch Junior Section*, 7 October 1941, (DDPC)

7   Ibid.

8   UCD Archives, Leinster Branch, P280/48 and P280/49.

9   Uncatalogued records 1938–1945 (DDPC).

10 Metropolitan selection: Clontarf, Old Belvedere (2), DUFC, CYMS (2), Wanderers (2), Lansdowne (2), Old Wesley, St Mary's, UCD, RSPU, and Blackrock. Provincial town selection: Wexford Wanderers (2), Dundalk (2), Skerries (1), Athy (4), Carlow (2), Shannon Buccaneers (1), Kilkenny (1), Drogheda (1), Tullamore (1).

11 Uncatalogued records 1938–1945 (DDPC).

12 In the junior interprovincial set-up, the 1980–81 season was the first season that the new rule about eligibility was applied to Leinster specifically, which stated that junior players who were playing for senior clubs' second teams must not be selected for the junior interprovincial team. The motivation behind the new rule was a request from the Union Development Committee.

13 Uncatalogued records 1938–1945 (DDPC).

14 *The Irish Press*, no day, October 1941 (DDPC).

15 Uncatalogued records 1938–1945 (DDPC).

16 *The Field*, 13 December 1941.

17 Newspaper (unknown) snippet, 6 October 1943, headlined: 'Rugby Standard in Leinster "Not Satisfactory"', uncatalogued records (DDPC).

18 *Irish Independent,* 3 November 1943.

19 Uncatalogued records (DDPC).

20 Uncatalogued records (DDPC).

21 www.guinnessrugby.ie/the-club.html   (30 June 2021).

22 'Terenure College – humble beginnings?' *Rugby Ireland: International*, Vol. 1, No. 9 (January 1999).

23 https://tcrfc.ie/club-history/ (1 February 2021).

24 UCD Archives, Leinster Branch, P280/07.

25 UCD Archives, Leinster Branch, P280/26.

26 www.swordsrfc.com/club-history/ (22 February 2021).

27 Private email correspondence, the president of Roscrea RFC.

28 Mary Fay and Seamus Rafferty, *50 Years On: Edenderry RFC 1951–2001* (Edenderry, 2002), p. 7.

29 Ibid., p. 15.

30 Ibid., p. 18.

31 1963–4 ERFC topped the League winning their first title, remaining unbeaten all season. Fay and Raferty, *50 Years On*, p. 20.

32 Winners 1949 to 1970 were: Mary's, Mary's, UCD, Old Belvedere, Old Belvedere, Clontarf, UCD, Old Belvedere, Palmerston, Lansdowne, Bective, Old Belvedere, Wanderers, Lansdowne, Old Belvedere, Clontarf, Lansdowne, Blackrock, Wanderers, Palmerston, Lansdowne and Wanderers. Conroy, *Rugby in Leinster*, p. 68.

33 Harry Gale document, email from Jim Walsh, May 2021.

34 Conroy, *Rugby in Leinster*, p. 67.

35 Jason Tuck, 'Making Sense of Emerald Commotion: Rugby Union, National Identity and Ireland', *Identities: Global Studies in Culture and Power*, Vol. 10, No. 4 (2003), pp. 502–3.

36 Joseph Maguire and Jason Tuck, 'Global sports and patriot games: Rugby union and national identity in a united sporting kingdom since 1945', *Immigrants & Minorities,* Vol. 17, No. 1 (1998), p. 114.

37 UCD Archive, Leinster Branch, P280/06.

38   UCD Archives, Leinster Branch, P280/07.

39   UCD Archives, Leinster Branch, P280/26.

40   Conroy, *Rugby in Leinster*, p. 59.

41   'Terenure College – humble beginnings?', *Rugby Ireland: International*, no date (DDPC).

42   Gale correspondence courtesy of president Leinster Branch, email from Jim Walsh.

43   https://www.dib.ie/biography/oflanagan-kevin-patrick-a9423 (4 February 2021).

44   Ibid.

45   'Great rugby man Seamus won five caps for Ireland', *Enniscorthy Guardian*, 16 September 2012.

46   *The Irish Times*, 30 April 1996.

Chapter 8

1   O'Brien, *County Carlow Football Club Rugby History*, p. 129.

2   Ibid.

3   UCD Archives, Leinster Branch, P280/27.

4   Winters Cup, 1962–63, for Metropolitan Junior 4 sides, third B teams of senior clubs, third A teams of junior clubs, the third teams of minor clubs and second teams of a growing club that were not yet graded. Fifty-seven consecutive finals staged up to 2019. Fifteen different winning clubs. Conroy, *Rugby in Leinster*, p. 71.

5   First Provincial Town's Plate winners were Navan in March 1963. The 1963/64 Spencer Cup was presented by Suttonians for the Metropolitan Junior Clubs. See Walsh, *The Provincial Towns Cup*.

6   West, *The Bold Collegians*, p. 109.

7   Ibid.

8   UCD Archives, Leinster Branch, P280/28.

9   Anon., *1881–1981 Bective Rangers Football Club Centenary*, p. 79.

10   Van Esbeck, *One Hundred Years of Irish Rugby*, p. 158.

11   'Leinster Branch IRFU Coaching Course for Players and Coaches at Butlin's Holiday Camp Mosney 28th August to 4th September 1965' (DDPC).

12   On Mon.–Thurs., 9.30 breakfast; practical on the field, 10.30 until 1 p.m.; lunch 1.30 p.m.; 2.30 p.m. until 5 p.m., evening of practical coaching each day. Lectures each evening from 5/5.15 to 6/6.15 p.m. Dinner 6.45 p.m. [at] 7.30 p.m., every evening, a lecture with time for discussion or for watching a video. 'Leinster Branch IRFU Coaching Course for Players and Coaches'.

13   Conroy, *Rugby in Leinster*, p. 94.

14   For example, London-Irish, Queens' Belfast, Waterloo, Cork Con., Portadown, Ballymena, Dungannon, Cobh, Derry, Dolphin, NIFC. From the provincial towns and junior clubs there were: Guinness, Navan, Portlaoise, Civil Service, Newbridge, Athlone and Carlow. 'Leinster Branch IRFU Coaching Course for Players and Coaches'.

15   Conference of Referees, Leinster Branch, September 1968 (DDPC).

16   Van Esbeck, *One Hundred Years of Irish Rugby*, p. x.

17   Murray and O'Dea, *1902–2002: Association of Referees*, p. 42.

18   Ibid. p. 43.

19   Longford RFC, 'Official Opening of new clubhouse', programme for a match between Wolfhounds and Longford President's XV in 1978/79 season. Courtesy of Derick Turner.

20   Ibid.

21   Ibid.

22   Ibid.

23   See *Gorey Rugby Football Club: 50 Great Years, 1968–2018* (club publication).

24   Ibid.

25   https://wicklowrfc.ie/history/ (1 February 2021).

26   UCD Archive, Leinster Branch, P280/08.

27   UCD Archive, Leinster Branch, P280/09.

28   Ibid.

29   National Archives of Ireland, 2006/149/37; see also, DFA/5/340/12/132/1.

30   Conroy, *Rugby in Leinster*, p. 39.

31   'Terenure College – humble beginnings?', *Rugby Ireland: International*, Vol. 1, No. 9 (January 1999).

Chapter 9

1   Conroy, *Rugby in Leinster*, pp. 23–4. Working subcommittees that were being prepared to facilitate the Leinster Branch were: (1) The Administration Groups [comprising] '(a) The Fixtures Sub-Committee. (b) Match Sub-Committee. (c) Public Relations Sub-Committee. (d) Advisory Sub-Committee.' [In addition, there were:] '(2) The Financial Group … composed of: (a) The Property and Grounds Sub-Committee. (b) The Tickets Sub-Committee. (c) The Planning Sub-Committee. (3) The Playing Group Committee [which initially meant:] the selection committees … Senior, Junior, Under 19 and Schools Sub-Committees. The Disciplinary Sub-Committee. The Donnybrook Grounds Sub-Committee. The Finance Sub-Committee. The International Tickets Sub-Committee. The Medical Sub-Committee. The Publicity Sub-Committee. The Youth Sub-Committee.'

2   Ibid., Appendix 2.

3   Ibid., p. 20.

4   Ibid., pp. 20–1.

5   Ibid.

6   Conroy, *Rugby in Leinster*, p. 59.

7   UCD Archives, Leinster Branch, P280/11.

8   TCDA, MUC/CLUB/DUCAC/19.

9   UCD Archives, Leinster Branch, P280/13.

10 TCDA, MUC/CLUB/DUCAC/19.

11 UCD Archives, Leinster Branch, P280/13.

12 UCD Archives, Leinster Branch P280/29.

13 The hospitals were: Richmond, Mercers, Jervis Street, Meath, Sir Patrick Dun's, Adelaide, Steevens' and the Royal Dublin Hospital.

14 Feighery, Farrell and Crowe, *The Hospital Pass*, p. 2.

15 Ibid., p. 11.

16 Ibid., p. 79.

17 Unidare Ltd, Guinness & Co., Insurance Corporation of Ireland, Arnott & Company, B. & I. Steam Packet Company, Crescent Trust, and Irish Dunlop Company Ltd. Conroy, *Rugby in Leinster*, pp. 84–5.

18 'Too Many Senior Rugby Clubs in Dublin', *The Irish Times,* September 1943.

19 Conroy, *Rugby in Leinster*, p. 79.

20 Against Cardiff and District Youths, Connacht Under 19 XV, London Counties Youth X, Munster U19 XV, Llanelli and District Youth XV, Ulster U19 XV, Irish Schoolboys XV, Rest of Leinster XV, Lancashire Colts, Connacht Youth XV and Lancashire.

21 *Leinster Branch Under 19 committee report for the season 1978–79* (DDPC).

22 Ibid.

23 UCD Archives, Leinster Branch, P280/28.

24 UCD Archives, Leinster Branch, P280/27.

25 McFadden, *From Rope Walk to Bowhill*, p. 84.

26 Conroy, *Rugby in Leinster*, p. 102.

27 McFadden, *From Rope Walk to Bowhill*, pp. 95–6.

28 Ibid., pp. 90–1.

29 Ibid., pp. 99–100.

30 Ibid., p. 83.

31 UCD Archives, Leinster Branch, P280/29.

32 UCD Archives, Leinster Branch, P280/30.

33 Conroy, *Rugby in Leinster*, p. 20.

34 UCD Archives, Leinster Branch, P280/10.

35 Conroy, *Rugby in Leinster,* pp. 56–7.

36 Van Esbeck, *Irish Rugby 1874–1999*, p. 139.

37 *Navan RFC 75th Souvenir Programme,* 23 (DDPC).

38 Van Esbeck, *Irish Rugby 1874–1999*, p. 139.

39 UCD Archives, Leinster Branch, P280/10.

Chapter 10

1   Letter from Branch Coaching subcommittee to all Leinster rugby clubs, 1981 (DDPC).

2   UCD Archives, Leinster Branch, P280/12.

3   'Team Committee; Club Selection Committee; Coaching Coordinators Committee; Physical Education Coordinators Committee; Medical Committee; Referees Committee; Fixture Committee; Team Selection Committee; Coaching Committee; Physical Education Committee; and a Club Rugby Committee.' Letter from Branch Coaching subcommittee to all Leinster rugby clubs, 1981 (DDPC).

4   Early-morning starts were not good for player fitness or availability, and not many fans were turning up at early-morning games. But it was the economic factor, the cost, that saw early-morning games scrapped.

5   G.C. Spotswood, *IRFU Report of the Game Development Sub-Committee on Structure of Interprovincial Rugby, August 1979* (DDPC)

6   Ibid.

7   UCC, UCG, QUB, TCD, UCD.

8   www.leinsterrugby.ie/action-hots-up-for-gleeson-cup/ (8 December 2020).

9   Limerick University, LU; Dublin City University, DCU; Maynooth University, MU; Ulster University, UU-Jordanstown, and UU-Coleraine.

10   In its first ten seasons playing, the ICRU played thirty matches, winning twenty-three of them and holding a 100 per cent winning record over all the English opposition they faced. *ICRU Rugby Tour to South Africa in June/July 1999 Commemorative Programme* (DDPC).

11   *The Sunday Press*, 17 February 1985.

12   Ibid.

13   *The Sunday Press*, 30 March 1986.

14   *The Irish Times*, 16 December 1986.

15   *The Irish Times*, 18 December 1990.

16   *Sunday Independent*, 10 April 1994; *Irish Examiner*, 3 April 1995; and *Sunday Independent,* 28 April 1996.

17   UCD Archives, Leinster Branch, P280/14.

18   UCD Archives, Leinster Branch, P280/17.

19   Capitals in original. *Leinster Branch Honorary Secretary Report 1992–1993* (DDPC).

20   Ibid.

21   Ibid.

22   Ibid.

23   Ibid.

24   O'Callaghan, *Rugby in Munster*, p. 210.

25   Ibid., p. 211.

26   *IRFU Newsletter*, May 1991 (DDPC).

27   Stephen Jones, *Endless Winter: The Inside Story of the Rugby Revolution* (Edinburgh and London, 1994), p. 13.

28   *Scotland on Sunday*, no date, 1994 (DDPC).

29   *Leinster Branch Committee Meeting Minutes,* 1 December 1992 (DDPC).

30   Terenure were the Aluset-sponsored Senior Cup winners; the Metropolitan Cup, St Mary's; J2 O'Connell Cup, Lansdowne; J3 Moran Cup, St Mary's; J4 Winters Cup, Old Wesley; J5 O'Connor Cup, and J6 Fox Cup, both St Mary's; Spencer Cup, Suttonians; Provincial Towns Cup, Carlow. The other four provincial town trophies were won by Dundalk, Enniscorthy, Edenderry and Naas.

31   The club winners included Curragh, Portarlington, Athy, Naas, Gorey, Carlow, Longford, Mullingar, Tullamore, Dundalk, Balbriggan and Navan.

Chapter 11

1   Collins, *A Social History of English Rugby Union*, pp. 203–4.

2   Ibid., p. 205.

3   Ibid.

4   *Lansdowne Star*, 5 April 1996 (DDPC).

5   *Fingal Independent,* 26 January 2019.

6   Fitzgerald, *Ecstasy and Agony*, pp. 32–3.

7   Des Daly Private Collection, newspaper cutting, no date or title.

8   Newspaper cutting, no date or title (DDPC).

9   There were seven players who attended Blackrock College; three St Mary's College; two each from Terenure College and The King's Hospital; then one each from Clongowes (Gordon D'Arcy), CBC Monkstown (Reggie Corrigan), Pres. Bray (Declan O'Brien), Wexford ES (Malcolm O'Kelly) and Leixlip (Trevor Brennan).

10   www.irishtimes.com/sport/rugby/bridging-the-gap-a-lot-of-what-i-loved-about-rugby-got-lost-in-the-end-1.4274972 (28 July 2020).

11   Ibid.

12   Ibid.

13   Ibid.

14   *Leinster Branch Honorary Secretary Report 1995/1996* (DDPC).

15   Ibid.

16 Ibid.

17 Ibid.

18 Ibid.

19 Ibid.

20 *The Irish Times*, 26 January 1999.

21 Ibid.

22 Ibid.

23 *Leinster Branch Honorary Secretary Report 1996–1997* (DDPC).

24 Ibid.

25 Ibid.

26 *Rugby Ireland: International*, Vol. 1, No. 9 (January 1999), p. 28.

27 For 1997–8 these included the Good Counsel College, New Ross; New Ross, VEC; St Mel's, Longford; Scoil Eoin, Athy; Mary's CBC, Enniscorthy; Enniscorthy, VEC; St Peter's College, Wexford; Wexford CBS; and Mary's Diocesan School Drogheda. *Leinster Branch Honorary Secretary Report 1996-1997* (DDPC).

28 Ibid.

29 Ibid.

30 *Navan RFC 75th Souvenir Programme* (DDPC). Navan were seventy-five years old in 1999.

31 Ibid.

32 *Leinster Branch Junior Honorary Secretary Report 1998–1999* (DDPC).

33 Ibid.

34 *Leinster Branch Financial Statements, year ended 30 April 2000* (DDPC).

35 *Leinster Branch Honorary Secretary Report 1999–2000* (DDPC).

36 *Celtic Call*, Issue 8 (DDPC).

Chapter 12

1 *The Sunday Times*, 25 April 2004.

2 Ibid.

3 Ibid.

4 Ibid.

5 Ibid.

6 Ibid.

7 Ibid.

8 *The Sunday Times*, 29 February 2004.

9 *Leinster Branch Honorary Secretary Report 2003–2004* (DDPC).

10 Ibid.

11 *Leinster Branch Junior Honorary Secretary Report 2003–2004* (DDPC).

12 *Leinster Branch Financial Statements, year ended 30 April 2004* (DDPC).

13 Collins, *How Football Began*, p. 20.

14 *Sunday Independent: Sport*, 24 May 2009.

15 Ibid.

16 Helene Joncheray and Haïfa Tlili, 'Are there still social barriers to women's rugby?', *Sport in Society 16(6) (2013)*.

17 Ibid.

18 McElligott, '"A Youth Tainted with the Deadly Poison of Anglicism?"', p. 286.

19 *Irish Examiner*, 2 April 2021.

20 www.the42.ie/trailblazers-irish-womens-rugby-1-5404690-Apr2021/ (1 December 2020).

21 Ibid.

22 www.leinsterrugby.ie/blackrocks-women-celebrate-30-years/ (11 April 2022).

23 *Irish Independent*, 6 August 2017.

24 *Leinster Branch Committee Meeting Minutes, October 1992* (DDPC).

25 Ibid.

26 For comparison, the numbers of rugby players in secondary schools reached 8,800; youth players were 3,600; minis were 2,700, while primary school tag-rugby players hit 11,815! The total number of Leinster players registered through the Leinster Branch came to 33,990 (in Ireland the number was 100,974). There were 440 secondary school teams, 144 youth teams and 225 mini teams. *IRFU Annual Report, 2005–2006* (DDPC).

27 J.S. Waldron and D.C. Glass, 'Review of Rugby Football at Universities and Colleges in Ireland for the IRFU, July 1999' (DDPC).

28 *The Irish Times: Sports Supplement*, 30 July 2005.

29 Ibid.

30 Craig Twist and Paul Worsfold (eds), *The Science of Rugby* (London and New York, 2015). See Introduction, no page number.

31 Ibid.

32 *IRFU report 2005–2006* (DDPC).

33 Ibid.

34 Twist and Worsfold, *The Science of Rugby*, p. 10.

35 Ibid.

36 Reggie Corrigan, Leo Cullen, Gordan D'Arcy, Girvan Dempsey, Shane Horgan, Keran Lewis, Eric Miller, Brian O'Driscoll, Malcolm O'Kelly and David Quinlan. Ireland played a two-game tour to Japan, three autumn test games, the Six Nations and three games during the summer tour to New Zealand and Australia.

37 Ten clubs were represented: St Mary's (9), Lansdowne (8), UCD (7), Blackrock (4), Clontarf (4), Terenure (3), Barnhall (1), Carlow (1), Greystones (1) and Old Belvedere (1). The captains during the season were Felipe Contepomi (4 HC and 13 CL), Brian O' Driscoll (4 HC and 6 CL) and Keith Gleeson (1 CL).

38 Note: the Leinster Branch comprised approximately 180 delegates – four from each of the nineteen senior clubs in the province and one or two from each of the fifty-five junior clubs, depending on their status. *Leinster Branch Committee Meeting Minutes*, 7 November 2006 (DDPC).

39 Ibid.

40 Gabriel Carroll and Alan Bairner, 'In from the side: exile international rugby union players in Britain, blood ties and national identities', *National Identities*, Vol. 21, No. 4 (2019), p. 417.

Chapter 13

1 *Leinster Branch Annual Report, 2006–2007* (DDPC).

2 Ibid.

3 Ibid.

4 www.binghamcup.com/about (25 February 2021). The Bingham Cup was named after a rugby player who was pivotal in promoting rugby among and for gay men, who died on one of the planes that was crashed by hijackers in the USA on 11 September 2001.

5 www.binghamcup.com/about (25 February 2021).

6 *Leinster Branch Annual Report, 2006–2007* (DDPC).

7 *Leinster Branch Committee Meeting Minutes,* 7 November 2006 (DDPC).

8 *Leinster Branch Annual Report, 2006–2007* (DDPC).

9 'School's Senior Cup Final Programme, 2009' (DDPC).

10 Alan Fitzgerald (ed.), *The Ecstasy and the Agony of Leinster Rugby: 20 Years of Professional Club Rugby* (Dublin, 2015), p. 2.

11 Ibid., p. 3.

12 Ibid., p. 8.

13 Ibid., pp. 11–12.

14 'Leinster had over 112,000 spectators at their home games in Donnybrook and Lansdowne Road this season at an average of just over 12,500. This represents an increase of 115% from season 05/06.' *Leinster Branch Annual Report, 2006–2007* (DDPC).

15 Ibid.

16 Bank of Ireland were secured as the new sponsors alongside REMAX, Kenilworth Motors, Powerade, Cellular World, Canterbury. Ground advertising had been sold out and extra space was being sought for the demand to advertise inside the province's rugby stadium. Season tickets had a dramatic rise: sales grew 50 per cent. *Leinster Branch Annual Report, 2006–2007* (DDPC).

17 Ibid.

18 Ibid.

19 *IRFU Annual Report, 2006–2007* (DDPC).

20 Ibid.

21 Paul Rouse, 'The Impact of Pay-TV on Sport', *Series Working Papers in History and Policy*, UCD History Hub, 2012, http://historyhub.ie/the-impact-of-pay-tv-on-sport.

22 Marcus Free, 'Diaspora and Rootedness, Amateurism and Professionalism in Media Discourses of Irish Soccer and Rugby in the 1990s and 2000s', *Éire-Ireland*, Vol. 48, Iss. 1&2 (spring/summer 2013).

23 *Programme, Heineken Cup Final 2009. Leicester Tigers V Leinster,* 23 May 2009 (DDPC).

24 Ruadhán Cooke and Éamon Ó Cofaigh, 'IRF Off: Connacht's Fight for Survival and the Foundation Myth of a Rugby Identity', *The International Journal of the History of Sport,* Vol. 34, Nos 3–4 (2017), p. 209.

25 Ibid., p. 212.

26 May 2009, Leinster won their first Heineken Cup by beating Leicester Tigers in Edinburgh.

27 Cooke and Ó Cofaigh, 'IRF Off', p. 213.

28 *IRFU Annual Report, 2007–2008* (DDPC).

29 Ibid.

30 *Leinster Branch Annual Report, 2009–2010* (DDPC).

31 Ibid.

32 Ibid.

33 www.the42.ie/growth-of-womens-rugby-su-carty-3528007-Aug2017/ (8 May 2021).

34 *Irish Independent,* 28 May 2021.

Chapter 14

1 *Leinster Branch Annual Report, 2011–2012* (DDPC).

2 Ibid.

3 *Leinster Branch Annual Report, 2011–2012* (DDPC).

4 Ibid. Over 380 primary schools (28,000 children, of which over 10,000 girls were involved) and over 160 secondary schools (over 8,000 students, of which about 2,000 female rugby players), reflecting the CROs and CCROs work across the province.

5 Ibid. 270 adult teams and 255 youth teams (about 72 clubs); 138 schools affiliated. Competitions: 30 schools', 41 provincial-youth's and 28 youth local area competitions, plus 48 adult competitions, made up of 32 leagues and 16 cups.

6 *Leinster Branch Annual Report, 2011–2012* (DDPC).

7 'Noticeboard', *The Evening Herald,* 26 November 2010.

8 *Leinster Rugby Annual Report, 2011–12* (DDPC).

9 Ibid.

10 Ibid.

11 Ibid.

12 *The Herald,* 7 February 2014.

13 Marcus Free, 'Diaspora and Rootedness, Amateurism and Professionalism in Media Discourses of Irish Soccer and Rugby in the 1990s and 2000s', *Éire-Ireland,* Vol. 48, Iss. 1&2 (Spring/Summer 2013), pp. 211–29.

14 Ibid.

15 Tony Collins, John Martin, Wray Vamplew, John Burnett and Emma Lile (eds), *Encyclopaedia of Traditional British Rural Sports* (London and New York, 2005), p. 6.

16 Fitzgerald, *The Ecstasy and the Agony of Leinster Rugby,* p. 143.

Epilogue

1 https://sportforbusiness.com/kevin-quinn-of-leinster-rugby-in-conversation/ (21 November 2021).

Bibliography

PRIMARY SOURCES

Archives

National Archives of Ireland (NAI)
    Reference: 2005/3/116
    Reference: 2006/149/37
    Reference: DFA/5/340/12/132/1
    Reference: DFA/2/1/38
    Reference: DFA/5/301/65 I
    Reference: TSCH/3/S2950
    Reference: 2011/39/40
    Reference: 2011/17/1234
    Reference: 2011/39/38

Trinity College Dublin Archives (TCDA)
    MUN/CLUB/RUGBY/F/1–58.
    MUN/CLUB/DUCAC/1–19.

University College Dublin, UCD Archives (UCDA)
    Archives of the Leinster Branch of the Irish Rugby Football Union, P280/1–84.

Private and Club Collections

Courtesy of Brendan Smith, Clontarf Football Club
    Clontarf FC, annual report for season 1886–87.
    Clontarf RFC, First General Meeting, 4 October 1892.
    Clontarf RFC meeting minutes, 1 October 1907.
    Clontarf RFC, General Meeting, 22 November 1892.
    Clontarf RFC, General Meeting, 29 November 1892.
    Clontarf RFC, General Meeting, 13 December 1892.

Courtesy of Derick Turner, Longford RFC
    Longford RFC, 'Official Opening of new clubhouse' programme for a match between
        Wolfhounds and Longford President's XV in 1978–79 season.

Courtesy of John Walsh, Leinster Branch President, 2020
    Letter from Harry Gale written to all in the IRFU and Leinster Branch rugby.

Courtesy of Pat Fitzgerald private collection
    Alan Fitzgerald (ed.), *The Ecstasy & The Agony of Leinster Rugby: 20 Years of Professional Club*
        Rugby, internal publication produced by Leinster Rugby.
    Rugby Ireland: International, Vol. 1, No. 8, November 1998.

Des Daly Private Collection (DDPC), uncatalogued
Various Leinster Branch and IRFU documents

Letter from Leinster Branch coaching sub-committee to all Branch rugby clubs, 1981.

Leinster Branch official circular, May 1988.

Leinster Branch IRFU EGM report, 13 September 1920.

Leinster Branch IRFU Junior Section, Honorary Secretary's report, 7 October 1941.

Leinster Branch IRFU, Conference of Referees General Meeting, September 1968.

Leinster Branch IRFU, Under 19 committee report for the season, 1978–79.

Leinster Branch IRFU, Honorary Secretary's report, AGM, 1989–90.

Leinster Branch IRFU, Executive Committee Meeting, 1 December 1992.

Leinster Branch IRFU, Honorary Secretary's report, AGM, 1992–93.

Leinster Branch IRFU, Honorary Treasurer's report, 1994–95.

Leinster Branch IRFU, Junior Committee General Meeting, October 1992.

Leinster Branch IRFU, Executive Committee Meeting, 1 December 1992.

Leinster Branch IRFU, Honorary Secretary's report, AGM, 1995–1996.

Leinster Branch IRFU, Honorary Secretary's report, AGM, 1996–1997.

Leinster Branch IRFU, Honorary Secretary's report, AGM, 1997–1998.

Leinster Branch IRFU, Honorary Secretary's report, AGM, 1998–1999.

Leinster Branch IRFU, Honorary Secretary's report, AGM, 1999–2000.

Leinster Branch IRFU, financial statements for the year ended 30 April 2000.

Leinster Branch IRFU, Junior Section, Honorary Secretary's report, 2003–04.

Leinster Branch IRFU, Honorary Secretary's report, AGM, 2003–04.

Leinster Branch IRFU, financial statements for the year ended April 2004.

Leinster Branch IRFU, Executive Committee Meeting, 7 November 2006.

Leinster Branch IRFU, annual report, 2006–07.

Leinster Branch IRFU, Junior Rugby annual report, 2006–07.

Leinster Branch IRFU, Honorary Secretary's report, AGM, 2009–2010.

Leinster Branch IRFU, President's annual report, 2011–12.

Leinster Branch IRFU, President's annual report, 2012–13.

Leinster Branch IRFU, President's annual report, 2013–14.

IRFU annual report, 2000–2001.

IRFU annual report, 2005–2006.

IRFU annual report, 2006–2007.

IRFU annual report, 2007–2008.

J.S. Waldron and D.C. Glass, 'IRFU Review of Rugby Football at Universities and Colleges in Ireland' report, July 1999.

DDPC Miscellaneous Documents (uncatalogued)

Celtic Call, issue 8.

'Football in Ireland', cutting from untitled newspaper, March 1941.

'IRFU Ulster Branch, Club Coaching', August 1971.

IRFU Newsletter, May 1991.

'Leinster Branch IRFU Coaching Course for Players and Coaches at Butlin's Holiday Camp, Mosney, 28th August to 4th September 1965'.

'Leinster Branch IRFU Coaching Course for Players and Coaches at Butlin's Holiday Camp, Mosney, 23rd August to 30th August 1967'.

'Leinster Branch IRFU Coaching Course for Players and Coaches at Butlin's Holiday Camp, Mosney, 24th August to 31st August 1968'.

'Leinster Branch IRFU Coaching Course for Players and Coaches at Butlin's Holiday Camp, Mosney, 23rd August to 30th August 1969'.

'Leinster Branch IRFU Coaching Course for Players and Coaches at Butlin's Holiday Camp, Mosney, 22nd to 29th August 1970'.

'Leinster Branch IRFU Coaching Course for Players and Coaches at Butlin's Holiday Camp, Mosney, 21st to 28th August 1971'.

'Leinster Branch IRFU Coaching Course, August 27 & 28 at Donnybrook, 1983'.

New Zealand Rugby News, 13 November 1974.

The Lansdowne Star, April 1996.

DDPC Match Programmes (uncatalogued)

Commemorative Programme: ICRU rugby tour to South Africa in June/July 1999.

Commemorative Programme: IURU, Irish Universities tour of Korea and Japan, 1987.

Commemorative Programme: UCD Rugby Club, 75th Anniversary, University College Dublin v The Wolfhounds, Sunday 27 October 1985, Donnybrook.

Programme: University College Dublin, Dublin University Annual Colours Match 1962.

Programme: The Senior School's Cup Final programme for the 1997–98 season.

Programme: School's Senior Cup Final 2009.

Programme: Heineken Cup Final 2009, Leicester Tigers v Leinster, Murrayfield, Edinburgh, 23 May 2009.

Souvenir Programme: Navan RFC 75th Souvenir Programme, 1999.

Newspapers

Dublin Daily Nation	*Irish Press, The*	*Sunday Dispatch*
Evening Herald	*Irish Times, The*	*Sunday Independent*
Fingal Independent	*Leinster Reporter*	*Sunday Press, The*
Irish Daily Mail	*Midland Counties Advertiser*	*Sunday Times, The*
Irish Examiner	*Midland Tribune*	*Times, The*
Irish Field, The	*Scotland on Sunday*	*Sunday Times, The* (London), Irish edition
Irish Independent	*Sport*	

SECONDARY SOURCES

Books

Anon., *1881–1981 Bective Rangers Football Club Centenary: A Commemorative Journal* (Bective Rangers Club: Dublin, 1981).

Anon., *CUS 1867–1967: A Centenary Record* (Catholic University School: Dublin, 1967).

Bairner, Alan (ed.), *Sport and the Irish: Histories, Identities, Issues* (University College Dublin Press: Dublin, 2005).

Behan, Brendan, *Borstal Boy* (Arrow Books: London, 1990).

Burton, Mike, *Have Balls Will Travel: The Story of a Rugby Tour* (Futura Macdonald & Co.: London, 1984).

Carter, Neil, *Medicine, Sport and the Body: A Historical Perspective* (Bloomsbury Academic: London, 2012).

Cashmore, Ellis, *Making Sense of Sports* (3rd edition; Routledge: New York, 2000).

Cogley, Fred, *St. Mary's College Rugby Football Club 1900–2000: A Centenary Celebration* (St Mary's College RFC: Dublin, 2000).

Cole, Richard Lee, *Wesley College, Dublin: An Historical Summary 1845–1962* (Dublin University Press: Dublin, 1963).

Collins, Tony, *Rugby's Great Split: Class, Culture and the Origins of Rugby League Football* (Frank Cass: London and Portland, 1999).

Collins, Tony, *A Social History of English Rugby Union* (Routledge: London and New York, 2009).

Collins, Tony, *How Football Began: A Global History of How the World's Football Codes Were Born* (Routledge: London and New York, 2019).

Collins, Tony, John Martin, Wray Vamplew, John Burnett and Emma Lile (eds), *Encyclopedia of Traditional British Rural Sports* (Routledge: London and New York, 2005).

Conroy, J.C. (ed.), *Rugby in Leinster, 1879–1979* (Leinster Branch IRFU: Dublin, 1979).

Coolahan, John, *Irish Education: Its History and Structure* (Institute of Public Administration: Dublin, 1981).

Cooper, Stephen, *After the Final Whistle: The First Rugby World Cup and the First World War* (The History Press: Cheltenham, 2016).

Cronin, Mike, Mark Durcan and Paul Rouse (eds), *The GAA: A People's History* (The Collins Press: Cork, 2009).

Cronin, Mike, William Murphy and Paul Rouse (eds), *The Gaelic Athletic Association, 1884–2009* (Irish Academic Press: Dublin and Portland, OR, 2009).

d'Alton, Ian, and Ida Milne (eds), *Protestant and Irish: The Minority's Search for Place in Independent Ireland* (Cork University Press: Cork, 2019).

Diffley, Sean, *Blackrock College RFC, 1882–83–1982–83: The Official History* (Printset & Design Limited: Dublin, 1982).

Dooley, Terence, and Christopher Ridgeway (eds), *Sport and Leisure in the Irish and British Country House* (Four Courts Press: Dublin, 2019).

Downs, Declan, *Leinster Schools Senior Rugby Cup, 1886–1986* (Director Publications: Dublin, 1986).

Dunning, Eric, Dominic Malcolm and Ivan Waddington (eds), *Sport Histories: Figurational Studies of the Development of Modern Sports* (Routledge: London and New York, 2004).

Farmar, Tony, *Privileged Lives: A Social History of Middle-Class Ireland, 1882–1989* (A.&A. Famar Ltd: Dublin, 2010).

Farragher, Sean P., *The French College Blackrock, 1860–1890* (Paraclete Press: Dublin, 2011).

Fay, Mary, and Seamus Rafferty, *50 Years On: Edenderry RFC 1951–2001* (Edenderry Rugby Football Club: Edenderry, 2002).

Ferriter, Diarmaid, *The Transformation of Ireland 1900–2000* (Profile Books: London, 2005).

Fitzmaurice, Gabriel, *In Praise of Football* (Mercier Press: Cork, 2009).

Fitzpatrick, Georgina, *St. Andrew's College 1894–1994: Ardens Sed Virens* (St Andrews College: Dublin, 1994).

Goodwin, Terry, *The Complete Who's Who of International Rugby* (Blandford Press: England, 1987).

Harris, John, and Nicholas Wise (eds), *Rugby in Global Perspective: Playing on the Periphery* (Routledge: London, 2020).

Hughes, Brian, and Connor Morrissey (ed), *Southern Irish Loyalism, 1912–1949* (Liverpool University Press: Liverpool, 2020).

Hunt, Tom, *Sport and Society in Victorian Ireland: The Case of Westmeath* (Cork University Press: Cork, 2007).

Jackson, Alvin, *Ireland 1798–1998: War, Peace and Beyond* (Wiley Blackwell: West Sussex, 2010).

Johnes, Martin, *A History of Sport in Wales* (University of Wales Press: Cardiff, 2005).

Jones, Stephen, *Endless Winter: The Inside Story of the Rugby Revolution* (Mainstream Publishing: Edinburgh and London, 1994).

Keogh, Dermot, *Jews in Twentieth-Century Ireland: Refugees, Anti-Semitism and the Holocaust* (Cork University Press: Cork, 1998).

Kiberd, Declan, *Inventing Ireland* (Harvard University Press: Cambridge, MA, 1996).

Kullmann, Kurt, *Rugby Town: The Sporting History of D4* (The History Press Ireland: Dublin, 2016).

Maher, William A., CSSP, *A History of St Mary's College, Rathmines, Dublin, 1890–1990* (Paraclete Press: Dublin, 1994).

McCrery, Nigel, *Into Touch: Rugby Internationals Killed in the Great War* (Pen & Sword Military: Barnsley, 2014).

McFadden, Caroline, *From Rope Walk to Bowhill: A History of Rugby in Balbriggan* (Balbriggan RFC: Balbriggan, 2015).

McKenna, Peter, *Rugby Explained: A Guide to Understanding the Game* (Blackwater Press: Dublin, 2007).

McKinney, Stewart, *Voices from the Back of the Bus: Tall Tales and Hoary Stories from Rugby's Real Heroes* (Mainstream Publishing: Edinburgh and London, 2009).

Moody, T.W., and F.X. Martin (eds), *The Course of Irish History* (fourth edition; Roberts Rinehart Publishers: Lanham, MD, 2001).

Moynihan, Jer, David Hasslacher and George Copeland (eds), *Enniscorthy Rugby Football Club, 1912–2012* (Enniscorthy RFC: Enniscorthy, 2012).

Murphy, Brian P., *St. Gerard's School Bray* (Kestrel Books: Bray, 1999).

Murphy, Geordan, *The Outsider* (Penguin Ireland: Dublin, 2012).

Murphy, Oliver (ed.), *Belvedere's Rugby Heroes: The History of Rugby in Belvedere College and the Thirty-two Belvederians Who Played Senior Rugby for Ireland* (The Belvedere Museum: Dublin, 2006).

Murray, Rev. Dermot, and Michael O'Dea (eds), *1902–2002: Association of Referees* (Leinster Branch IRFU: Dublin, 2002).

O'Brien, Seán, *Fuel: The Autobiography* (Penguin Ireland: Dublin, 2020).

O'Brien, Thomas J. (ed.), *County Carlow Football Club Rugby History, 1873–1977* (privately published: Carlow, 1977).

O'Callaghan, Liam, *Rugby in Munster: A Social and Cultural History* (Cork University Press: Cork, 2011).

O'Herlihy, Donal *et al.* (eds), *To the Cause of Liberality: A History of the O'Connell Schools and the Christian Brothers, North Richmond Street* (The Allen Library Project: Dublin, 1995).

O'Sullivan, John, *Wanderers Football Club 1870–1920: Celebrating 150 Years* (Wanderers F.C.: Dublin, 2020).

Oughton, Adrian G., *Wilson's Hospital School: Church of Ireland Centre of Education, 1761–2011* (Wilson's Hospital School Limited: Westmeath, 2011).

Peter, Richard M., *The Origins and Development of Football in Ireland: Being a Reprint of R.M. Peter's Irish Football Annual 1880 with an introduction by Neal Garnham* (Ulster Historical Foundation: Belfast, 1999).

Porter, Dilwyn, and Adrian Smith (eds), *Sport and National Identity in the Post-War World* (Routledge: London, 2004).

Ramshaw, Gregory, *Heritage and Sport: An Introduction* (Channel View Publications: Bristol, 2020).

Rayner, Mike, *Rugby Union and Professionalisation: Elite Player Perspectives* (Routledge: New York, 2018).

Redmond, Garry (ed.), *Lansdowne Football Club, Centenary 1872–1972: A Club History* (Lansdowne FC: Dublin, 1972).

Reyburn, Wallace, *A History of Rugby* (Arthur Barker Ltd: London, 1971).

Rhys, Chris, *The Guinness Rugby Union Fact Book* (Guinness Publishing: Middlesex, 1992).

Richards, Huw, *A Game for Hooligans: The History of Rugby Union* (Mainstream Publishing: Edinburgh and London, 2007).

Riess, Steven A., *Sport in Industrial America, 1850–1920* (Harlan Davidson Inc.: Wheeling, Illinois, 1995).

Rouse, Paul, *Sport & Ireland: A History* (Oxford University Press: Oxford, 2015).

Rouse, Paul, *The Hurlers: The First All-Ireland Championship and the Making of Modern Hurling* (Penguin Books: Dublin, 2018).

Twist, Craig, and Paul Worsfold (eds), *The Science of Rugby* (Routledge: London and New York, 2015).

Van Esbeck, Edmund, *One Hundred Years of Irish Rugby: The Official History of the Irish Rugby Football Union, 1874–1974* (Gill & Macmillan: Dublin, 1974).

Van Esbeck, Edmund, *'Ten Out of Fifty': A Chronicle of Old Belvedere Football Club, 1930–1980* (Dublin Print and Paper: Dublin, 1980).

Van Esbeck, Edmund, *The Story of Irish Rugby* (Stanley Paul: London, 1986).

Van Esbeck, Edmund, *Irish Rugby, 1874–1999: A History* (Gill & Macmillan: Dublin, 1999).

Walker, Stephen, *Ireland's Call: Irish Sporting Heroes Who Fell in the Great War* (Merrion Press: Dublin, 2015).

Wallace, W.J.R., *Faithful to Our Trust: A History of the Erasmus Smith Trust and the High School, Dublin* (The Columba Press: Dublin, 2004).

Walsh, John, *The Provincial Towns Cup: For Generations It's the Spirit of Rugby* (Millbrook Press Ltd: Naas, 2020).

West, Trevor, *The Bold Collegians: The Development of Sport in Trinity College, Dublin* (The Lilliput Press: Dublin, 1991).

West, Trevor (ed.), *Dublin University Football Club, 1854–2004: 150 Years of Trinity Rugby* (Wordwell: Bray, 2004).

Whannel, Garry, *Media Sports Stars: Masculinities and Moralities* (Routledge: London & New York, 2002).

White, G.K., *A History of Columba's College, 1843–1974* (Dublin University Press: Dublin, 1981).

Whiteside, Lesley, *A History of the King's Hospital* (The King's Hospital: Dublin, 1985).

Whiteside, Lesley, with Andrew Whitside, *Where Swift and Berkeley Learnt: A History of Kilkenny College* (The Columba Press: Dublin, 2009).

Wyse Jackson, Patrick, *A Portrait of St Columba's College, 1843–1993* (Old Columban Society: Dublin, 1993).

Articles and Book Chapters

Andrews, David L., 'Welsh Indigenous! and British Imperial? – Welsh rugby, culture, and society 1890–1914', *Journal of Sport History*, Vol. 18, No. 3 (Winter 1991).

Baker, William J., 'William Webb Ellis and the Origins of Rugby Football: The life and death of a Victorian myth', *Albion: A Quarterly Journal Concerned with British Studies*, Vol. 13, No. 2 (Summer 1981).

Carroll, Gabriel and Alan Bairner, 'In from the Side: Exile international rugby union players in Britain, blood ties and national identities', *National Identities*, Vol. 21, No. 4 (2019).

Collins, Tony, 'The Oval World: A global history of rugby', *The International Journal of the History of Sport*, 32:16 (2015).

Cooke, Ruadhán and Éamon Ó Cofaigh, 'IRF Off: Connacht's fight for survival and the foundation myth of a rugby identity', *The International Journal of the History of Sport*, 34:3–4 (2017).

Crawford, Heather K., 'Southern Irish Protestants and "Irishness"', *Oral History*, Vol. 39, No. 1 (Spring 2011).

Cronin, Mike, 'What Went Wrong with Counting? Thinking about sports and class in Britain and Ireland', *Sport in History*, 29:3 (2009).

Cronin, Mike, '"Trinity Mysteries": Responding to a chaotic reading of Irish history', *The International Journal of the History of Sport*, 28:18 (2011).

Cronin, Mike, 'Not Quite Free? Irish postcoloniality and the career of Pat O'Callaghan', *The International Journal of the History of Sport*, 32:7 (2015).

Cronin, Mike, David Doyle and Liam O'Callaghan, 'Foreign Fields and Foreigners on the Field: Irish sport, inclusion and assimilation', *The International Journal of the History of Sport*, 25:8 (2008).

Crossan, Seán and Philip Dine, 'Sport and the Media in Ireland', *Media History*, 17:2 (2011).

D'Alton, Ian, '"A Vestigial Population"?: Perspectives on Southern Irish Protestants', *Éire-Ireland*, 44:3 & 4 (Fall/Winter 2009).

Dann, Jeff, 'The Representation of British Sports in Late Nineteenth and Early Twentieth Century Elite Irish School Publications', *Media History*, 17:2 (2011).

Free, Marcus, 'Diaspora and Rootedness, Amateurism and Professionalism in Media Discourses of Irish Soccer and Rugby in the 1990s and 2000s', *Éire-Ireland*, Vol. 48, Iss. 1&2 (Spring/Summer 2013).

Garnham, Neal, 'Rugby and Empire in Ireland: Irish reactions to colonial rugby tours before 1914', *Sport in History*, 23:1 (2003).

Garnham, Neal, 'Football and National Identity in Pre-Great War Ireland', *Irish Economic and Social History*, XXVIII (2001).

Girvan, Brian, 'Forgotten Volunteers of World War II', *History Ireland*, Iss. 1, Vol. 6 (Spring 1998).

Glassock, Simon, 'Good Sports? Scotland, Empire and rugby c.1924–1928', *Sports History*, Vol. 36, No. 3 (2016).

Griffin, Brian, '"The More Sport the Merrier, Say We": Sport in Ireland during the Great Famine', *Irish Economic and Social History*, Vol. 45(1) (2018).

Griffin, Brian, and John Strachan, 'Introduction: Sport in Ireland from the 1880s to the 1920s', *Irish Studies Review*, Vol. 27:3 (2019).

Howe, David, 'Women's Rugby and the Nexus Between Embodiment, Professionalism and Sexuality: An ethnographic account', *Football Studies* 4, no. 2 (2001).

Huggins, Mike J., 'More Sinful Pleasures? Leisure, respectability and the male middle classes in Victorian England', *Journal of Social History*, Vol. 33, No. 3 (Spring, 2000).

Huggins, Mike J., 'Second-class citizens? English middle-class culture and sport, 1850–1910: a reconsideration', *The International Journal of the History of Sport*, 17:1 (2000).

Joncheray, Helene and Haïfa Tlili, 'Are There Still Social Barriers to Women's Rugby?', *Sport in Society*, 16(6) (2013).

Lincoln, Allison, and Rusty MacLean, 'There's a Deathless Myth on the Close Tonight: Re-assessing rugby's place in the history of sport', *The International Journal of the History of Sport*, Vol. 29, No. 13 (September 2012).

Maguire, Joseph, and Jason Tuck, 'Global Sports and Patriot Games: Rugby union and national identity in a united sporting kingdom since 1945', *Immigrants & Minorities*, 17:1 (1998).

McElligott, Richard, '"A Youth Tainted with the Deadly Poison of Anglicism"? Sport and childhood in the Irish Independence period', in Ciara Boylan and Ciara Gallagher (eds), *Constructions of the Irish Child in the Independence Period, 1910–1940* (Palgrave Macmillan: Oxford, 2018).

O'Callaghan, Liam, 'Rugby Football and Identity Politics in Free State Ireland', *Éire-Ireland*, Vol. 48, Iss. 1&2 (Spring/Summer 2013).

O'Callaghan, Liam, 'Irish Rugby and the First World War', *Sport in Society*, 19:1 (2016).

Ó Conchubhair, Brian, 'Trying Irish in the Free State,' *Éire-Ireland*, Vol. 48, Iss. 1&2, (Spring/Summer 2013).

O'Connor, Anne V., 'Education in Nineteenth-Century Ireland', in Angela Bourke, Siobhán Kilfeather, Maria Luddy, Margaret Mac Curtain, Gerardine Meaney, Máirín Ni Dhonnchadha, Mary O'Dowd and Clair Wills (eds), *The Field Day Anthology of Irish Writing, Volume V: Irish Women's Writings and Traditions* (Cork University Press: Cork, 2002).

O'Donnell, Hugh, 'Mapping the Mythical: A geopolitics of national sporting stereotypes', *Discourse and Society*, Vol. 5, No. 3 (1994).

O'Halloran, Philip, 'The Dublin Hospitals Rugby Cup – the Oldest Trophy in World Rugby,' *RCSI on the Inside*, Vol. 1, No. 1 (2008).

Rouse, Paul, 'The Impact of Pay-TV on Sport,' *Series Working Papers in History and Policy*, UCD History Hub (2012).

Rouse, Paul, 'The Sporting World and the Human Heart,' *Irish Studies Review*, Vol. 27, Iss. 3 (July 2019).

Ryan, Greg, 'The Paradox of Maori Rugby 1870–1914' in Greg Ryan (ed.), *Tackling Rugby Myths: Rugby and New Zealand Society 1854–2004* (University of Otago Press: Otago, 2005).

Sandiford, Keith A.P., 'The Victorians at Play: Problems in Historiographical Methodology' *Journal of Social History*, Vol. 15, No. 2 (Winter 1981).

Sandiford, Keith A.P., 'Cricket and the Victorian Society,' *Journal of Social History*, Vol. 17, No. 2 (Winter 1983).

Stoddart, Brian, 'Sport and Society 1890–1940: A Foray,' *Sport in Society*, 9:5 (2006).

Stoddart, Brian, 'Sport, Cultural Imperialism and Colonial Response in the British Empire,' *Sport in Society*, 9:5 (2006).

'Terenure College – Humble Beginnings?', *Rugby Ireland: International*, Vol. 1, No. 9 (January 1999).

Tuck, Jason, 'Making Sense of Emerald Commotion: Rugby Union, National Identity and Ireland', *Identities: Global Studies in Culture and Power*, 10:4 (2003).

Tutty, M.J., 'Clontarf,' *Dublin Historical Record*, Vol. 21, No. 1 (March–May 1966).

Van Esbeck, Edmund, 'Lansdowne – A Superb Contribution,' *Rugby Ireland: International*, Vol. 1 No. 3 (December 1997).

Vincent, Geoffrey T., '"To Uphold the Honour of the Province": Football in Canterbury c.1854–1890' in Greg Ryan (ed.), *Tackling Rugby Myths: Rugby and New Zealand Society 1854–2004* (University of Otago Press: Otago, 2005).

Websites and Electronic Resources

Email Correspondence:

Ardee RFC, email from Ian Stewart, Ardee RFC CCRO, 27 Jan. 2021.

Ashbourne RFC, email from Bill Duggan, 19 Mar. 2021.

Birr RFC, email from Padraig Burns, Honorary Secretary, 20 Feb. 2021.

CYM RFC, email from Bernard Murray, President, 26 Jan. 2021.

Dublin Dogos RFC, email from Gonzalo Saenz, club founder, 9 Apr. 2021.

Dundalk, Navan and North Meath, emails from Gerald Williamson, various dates Feb. 2021.

Emerald Warriors timeline and history, email from Richie Fagan, 5 Mar. 2021.

Mullingar RFC, email from Ita Murphy, 28 Jan.2021, and from Terry Short, 1 Feb. 2021.

Naas RFC, email from John Walsh.

Newbridge RFC, email from Oliver Delaney, 5 Feb. 2021.

North Meath RFC, email from Jack Kenny, 8 Feb. 2021.

Parkmore RFC, email from Shane Quigley, 27 Jan. 2021.

Portarlington RFC, email from David Hainsworth, 1 Feb. 2021.

Roscrea RFC, email from Terry Farrelly, President, 8 Mar. 2021.

Seapoint RFC, Mick O'Toole, President, 27 Jan. 2021.

Tallaght RFC, email from Emma Louise Doyle, 17 Feb. 2021.

Terenure College RFC, email from Colm Jenkinson, 3 Feb. 2021.

Tullow RFC, email from Cora Browne, 19 Feb. 2021.

Websites:

http://bgfravens.com/node/7

http://enniscorthyathenaeum.com/

https://athyrugbyclub.com/history

https://junior.cus.ie/school-sports-2/

https://offalyhistoryblog.wordpress.com/2017/04/08/p-h-egan-of-tullamore-1852-1968-by-david-egan/

https://tcrfc.ie/club-history/

http://web.archive.org/web/20170430154135/

https://wicklowrfc.ie/history/

www.balbriggan.net/balbriggans

www.binghamcup.com/about

www.castleknockcollege.ie/co-curricular/rugby/

www.census.nationalarchives.ie/exhibition/dublin/short_history.html

www.clongowes.net/about-clongowes/history/

www.clontarfrugby.com/club-history/
www.dlspfc.ie/club-info/one-of-dublins-earliest-rugby-clubs.86.html
www.dublinmaccabi.com/history/rugby
www.dundalkrfc.ie/about
www.greystonesrfc.ie/home/grfc-club-history/
www.guinnessrugby.ie/the-club.html
www.intouchrugby.com/magazine/derek-mcgrath-departs-erc/
www.leinsterrugby.ie/action-hots-up-for-gleeson-cup/
www.monkstownfc.ie/about-monkstown-fc/the-monkstown-story/
www.newbridge-college.ie/About-the-College/History
www.ria.ie/ga/node/98320
www.sac.ie/page/?title=Rugby&pid=76
www.Scrum.com
www.swordsrfc.com/club-history/
www.the42.ie/trailblazers-irish-womens-rugby-1-5404690-Apr2021/
www.the42.ie/growth-of-womens-rugby-su-carty-3528007-Aug2017/
www.tullamorerugby.com/about-the-club/club-history
www.wesleycollege.ie/About/History/

Online Newspaper Articles

www.independent.ie/regionals/droghedaindependent/news/dr-dolan-served-adopted-county-well-27155018.html
www.independent.ie/sport/rugby/leinster-rugby/club-focus-tulliers-continue-to-make-strides-35014014.html
www.irishexaminer.com/sport/rugby/arid-30971711.html
www.irishtimes.com/sport/rugby/bridging-the-gap-a-lot-of-what-i-loved-about-rugby-got-lost-in-the-end-1.4274972
www.irishtimes.com/sport/rugby/punches-kicks-and-mass-brawls-the-1977-colours-match-had-it-all-1.3716115

LIST OF ILLUSTRATIONS

p. 37: Early sketch of Belvedere College, https://belvederecollege.ie/about/college-history/

p. 38: St Columba's College in the news, celebrating its centenary. *The Times*, 5 June 1949.

p. 39: Castleknock College, https://commons.wikimedia.org/wiki/File:Castleknock_ College_2020_b.jpg.

p. 40: Leinster Schools Cup rugby in the news, *The Freeman's Journal*, 1895; Rush v. the Grammar School, Past and Present report, *The Cork Examiner*, 1893.

p. 42: A Leinster Senior Schools Cup medal. From DDPC.

p. 43: The Blackrock College team that won the first Leinster Schools Cup, 1887–8, taken from J.C. Conroy (ed.), *Rugby in Leinster, 1879–1979* (Dublin, 1979).

p. 44: 9 February 2023. Bank of Ireland Leinster Rugby Schools Junior Cup first round match between St Mary's College and Gonzaga College at Energia Park in Dublin. © Daire Brennan/Sportsfile.

p. 45: Mark Hernan of St Michael's College leads his side out for the Leinster Schools Senior Cup final v. Gonzaga, 2019. © Ramsey Cardy/Sportsfile.

Chapter 3

p. 49: The Leinster Schools Senior trophy. © Daire Brennan/Sportsfile; DUFC/Trinity College, the first winners of the Leinster Senior Cup, 1882, from J.C. Conroy (ed.), *Rugby in Leinster, 1879–1979* (Dublin, 1979).

pp. 51–3: Miscellaneous early photos of rugby, including a New Zealand team, from the early 1900s. From DDPC.

p. 54: Blackrock P&P Senior Cup winning team 1887. From DDPC.

p. 56: Leinster Junior Schools Cup. © Ben McShane/Sportsfile.

p. 57: Lansdowne FC, winners of the Leinster Senior Cup 1891, from DDPC; 1880s team sheet, Clontarf FC records, courtesy of Brendan Smith.

p. 58: Leinster Metropolitan Cup, 2022. © Seb Daly/Sportsfile

p. 60: Athy Rugby Club in the *Nationalist and Leinster Times*, 1894.

p. 63: The 1884 Leinster team that played Ulster that season, taken from J.C. Conroy (ed.), *Rugby in Leinster, 1879–1979* (Dublin, 1979).

p. 64: Ulster v. Leinster match report in the *Evening Herald*, 1899.

Chapter 4

p. 66: Cropped photograph of the imprisoned Éamon de Valera, in 1916. Courtesy of Kilmainham Gaol Archives.

p. 68: Donnybrook village in the 1920s, from *1881–1981 Bective Rangers Football Club Centenary: A Commemorative Journal* (Bective Rangers Club: Dublin, 1981); inner-city Dublin slums, taken from www.census.nationalarchives.ie/exhibition/dublin/poverty_ health/Em3Faithful_Place_TyroneSt_7.044.html

p. 73: Some Railway Union RFC representatives, probably taken in the 1970s or 1980s. From DDPC.

p. 75: The County Carlow FC winners of the 1913 Junior Cup, taken from Thomas O'Brien (ed.), *County Carlow Football Club History, 1873–1977* (Carlow, 1977).

p. 78: Two university rugby teams from the 1910s pose together for pre-game picture. From DDPC.

p. 79: The Irish 'pals' rugby players at Lansdowne Road who were recruited into the British

p. 111: Railway Union's Harry Gale's introduction letter to his essay indicating his criticism towards Leinster rugby and the plight of Junior Rugby. Courtesy of John Walsh, Naas RFC.

p. 112: Enniscorthy RFC members on the steps of the Hibernian Hotel, Dublin, after winning the Provincial Town Cup, taken from *Enniscorthy Rugby Football Club, 1912–2012, Centenary Book*, p. 14, courtesy of Rory Fanning.

p. 114: Rugby action, Carlow v. Balbriggan at Lansdowne Road in the 1931 Provincial Towns Cup final, taken from Thomas O'Brien (ed.), *County Carlow Football Club History, 1873–1977* (Carlow, 1977).

p. 116: Provincial Towns Cup final, 1927. Team photo taken in Donnybrook in front of the Bective Club House, photo courtesy of Hugh Cumiskey; Carlow FC Provincial Town Cup winners in 1929, taken from Thomas O'Brien (ed.), *County Carlow Football Club History, 1873–1977* (Carlow, 1977).

p. 119: Judge Cahir Davitt, public domain; Mrs Davitt, wife of Leinster Branch President Cahir Davitt, presents the Towns Cup to the Carlow captain W.J. Duggan, taken from Thomas O'Brien (ed.), *County Carlow Football Club History, 1873–1977* (Carlow, 1977).

p. 121: An early example of a rugby injury story in the *Leinster Leader*, 1930s (exact date unknown).

p. 122: Homemade flyer for a cake sale to raise money for St Mary's RFC; Leinster trial teams, 'Whites XV v. Blues XV'; early photo of rugby on tour. All from DDPC.

p. 123: Action from an Athy RFC game, sometime in the 1930s. From DDPC.

p. 124: UCD RFC beating London University, 1932. From DDPC.

p. 126: International trial match report from the *Irish Independent* of 29 January 1934, from DDPC; Leinster Branch Junior Section circular of December 1930 inviting clubs to select players for a junior interprovincial trial match in 1931, LRFU Archive at the UCDA.

Chapter 7

p. 130: Examples of 'Emergency'-era ration books from the Second World War, https://skehana.galwaycommunityheritage.org/content/topics/events/emergency-rationing

p. 131: 1945 Leinster v. New Zealand action shot. From DDPC.

p. 134: A 1946 poster advertising a Dublin v. Wexford selection, a match organised to help reawaken rugby across the province after the Second World War. From DDPC.

p. 135: Leinster Senior Cup final 1949 action shot. From DDPC.

p. 141: Two Gorey RFC teams, both from 1954, taken from *Gorey Rugby Football Club, 50 Great Years, 1968–2018*, courtesy of Trysh Sullivan.

p. 144: Newspaper coverage of the Midland Towns Cup competition, the Ryan Cup, created to promote rugby in Leinster outside of Dublin 4. From DDPC.

p. 145: Leinster Senior Cup winners 1953, Lansdowne FC. From DDPC.

p. 146: Invite sent to clubs and schools to a meeting to discuss the rules and laws of the game, prior to the season's start, from Association of Referees, 1954. From LRFU Archive at the UCDA.

p. 148: The 1949 Leinster team that played Connacht. From DDPC.

p. 150: Example programme line-up for Ireland trials, whites v. blues, which includes Bill Mulcahy and Tony O'Reilly on the whites, from the early 1960s. From DDPC.

p. 151: Dr Kevin O'Flanagan, the oldest player still living to be capped for Ireland. O'Flanagan played both soccer and rugby to international level.

p. 195: Members of the Leinster Branch Referees Association who also refereed international matches taken from J.C. Conroy (ed.), *Rugby in Leinster, 1879–1979* (Dublin, 1979).

p. 196: Youth Underage Cups, Leinster Rugby, © Eóin Noonan/Sportsfile

p. 197: Youth Underage Cups, Leinster Rugby, www.leinsterrugby.ie/history-of-the-leinster-rugby-youths-cups/

p. 198: Youth Underage Cups, Leinster Rugby, www.leinsterrugby.ie/history-of-the-leinster-rugby-youths-cups/

p. 200: The Under-13 McGowan Cup final in May 2015, with Mullingar playing Tullamore. © Sam Barnes/Sportsfile

p. 201: North Meath v. Wexford Wanderers in the Bank of Ireland Half-Time Minis during the United Rugby Championship quarter-final match between Leinster and Cell C Sharks at the Aviva Stadium in Dublin, 6 May 2023. © Harry Murphy/Sportsfile

pp. 202–3: Mini Rugby Publicity Shot, **featuring Leinster stars Robbie Henshaw, Josh van der Flier and Rhys Ruddock.** The Leinster Branch has focused heavily on developing its youth rugby to broaden its base, especially since the arrival of the professional game. © **David Fitzgerald/Sportsfile.**

Chapter 10

p. 208: Front cover and synopsis of the Leinster Rugby Development Plan document, 1992. From DDPC.

p. 210: An action shot from a Blackrock College game. From DDPC.

p. 212: De La Salle captain Brian Glennon lifts the Leinster Schools Cup alongside his mother, Una, after victory over Blackrock in 1985. © Ray McManus/Sportsfile; Brian O'Driscoll of Blackrock College during a Leinster Schools Cup semi-final against Clongowes Wood at Lansdowne Road in March 1997. © Brendan Moran/Sportsfile.

p. 214 An action shot from a Blackrock College game in the 1990s. From DDPC.

p. 216: Various photographs of UCD RFC. From DDPC.

p. 217: The first Irish Colleges team, with their coach George Hook. From DDPC.

p. 218: Irish Colleges rugby story, by Des Daly, from the 1997 edition of *Rugby* magazine, edited and produced by Pat Fitzgerald in the 1990s. From DDPC.

p. 221: McScrum, the official Irish mascot for the 1991 Rugby World Cup. From DDPC.

p. 222: Greystones RFC in action during the 1996 Metro Cup final match. From DDPC.

p. 223: An action shot from a 1990s schools' game. From DDPC.

p. 225: Leinster Branch Junior Committee 1991–2; Leinster Branch Senior Committee 1994–5, both photographs courtesy of Pat Fitzgerald private collection.

p. 226: Leinster Youths Squad 1991–2; Leinster Under 20s Squad 1990–1; the Leinster team to play Munster, December 1990, all photographs courtesy of Pat Fitzgerald private collection.

p. 228: Example of league game team sheet: Old Belvedere third B team v. Aer Lingus; Ham Lambert and G.P.S. Hogan, both from DDPC.

p. 229: A Leinster Junior Interprovincial programme cover from 1984. Courtesy of Pat Fitzgerald private collection.

Chapter 11

p. 261: 23 April 2006: Cameron Jowitt, Leinster, leaves the field after being substituted. Heineken Cup 2005–06 semi-final, Leinster v. Munster, Lansdowne Road, Dublin. © Brendan Moran/Sportsfile.

p. 262: Leinster in the inaugural Celtic League final (top), and Leinster players after defeat in the final, from *The Ecstasy & The Agony of Leinster Rugby: 20 Years of Professional Club Rugby*, internal Leinster Rugby publication. Copy courtesy of Pat Fitzgerald private collection.

p. 263: Blackrock College RFC yearbook for the start of the club season 2000–01, with a young Brian O'Driscoll on the cover. From DDPC.

Chapter 12

pp. 266–7: The RDS Stadium, https://upload.wikimedia.org/wikipedia/commons/e/e5/RDS_Panoramic.jpg

p. 269: Leinster junior club action, Old Kilcullen v. Ashbourne, early 2000s. From DDPC.

p. 270: Leinster Youth Committee document from 2019, underscoring Leinster rugby's shift in nurturing youth rugby. From DDPC.

p. 271: Programme giving Leinster Junior XV selection v. Munster Junior XV selection for a game to celebrate fifty years of Edenderry RFC in 2001. From DDPC.

p. 273: *Longford Leader,* 1975 letter to the editor defending women's rugby.

p. 274: *Westmeath Examiner*, 30 March 1996, Mullingar women's rugby notes; Irish Women's Rugby Football Union becomes affiliated to the Irish Rugby Football Union, 12 February 2001. Pictured at the announcement are President of the IWRFU Carole Ann Byrne and President of the IRFU Eddie Coleman. © Brendan Moran/Sportsfile.

p. 276: DUFC women's rugby on College Green, https://www.tcd.ie/Sport/facilities/college-outdoor/; Leinster Women's team win 2018 interprovincial title, www.scrumqueens.com/news/leinster-claim-irish-title

p. 278: 30 March 2019: Enniscorthy celebrate winning the Leinster Rugby U16 Girls Cup final, © Matt Browne/Sportsfile; Vodafone Women's Interprovincial Championship final, 2 September 2023, in which Leinster beat Munster, © Eóin Noonan/Sportsfile.

p. 283: Leinster coach Michael Cheika during squad training in 2008. © Pat Murphy/Sportsfile.

p. 284: Scenes from Leinster's first European Cup win, from *The Ecstasy & The Agony of Leinster Rugby: 20 Years of Professional Club Rugby*, internal Leinster Rugby publication. Copy courtesy of Pat Fitzgerald private collection.

p. 285: Australian Leinster player Rocky Elsom, from *The Ecstasy & The Agony of Leinster Rugby: 20 Years of Professional Club Rugby*, internal Leinster Rugby publication. Copy courtesy of Pat Fitzgerald private collection.

p. 286: Argentinian Leinster player Felipe Contepomi, from *The Ecstasy & The Agony of Leinster Rugby: 20 Years of Professional Club Rugby*, internal Leinster Rugby publication. Copy courtesy of Pat Fitzgerald private collection.

p. 287: New Zealand-born Charlie Ngatai of Leinster during the Heineken Champions Cup final between Leinster and La Rochelle at Aviva Stadium in Dublin. © Brendan Moran/Sportsfile.

Chapter 13

Chapter 14

p. 321: Balbriggan RFC Club President Leigh O'Toole, incoming 2022, with Leinster Branch President John Walsh.

p. 323: Jonathan Sexton during the Leinster Rugby captain's run at the RDS Arena, 15 November 2019. © Ramsey Cardy/Sportsfile.

p. 324: Leinster supporters cheer on their side during the Challenge Cup final against Stade Français, 17 May 2013. © Brendan Moran/Sportsfile.

p. 325: Leinster head coach Joe Schmidt. Celtic League 2012–13, Round 22, Leinster v. Ospreys, RDS, Ballsbridge, Dublin. © Stephen McCarthy/Sportsfile.

p. 326: Leinster players celebrate with the Challenge Cup following their victory. © Stephen McCarthy/Sportsfile; Departing Leinster head coach Joe Schmidt with Isa Nacewa and Jonathan Sexton following their Pro12 victory over Ulster, 25 May 2013. © Stephen McCarthy/Sportsfile.

p. 327: Leinster Rugby Official Media Partnership with the *Irish Independent* every Friday, as advertised on game-day programmes, from DDPC; Leinster Rugby Club and Media Guide to the provincial cup competitions (Towns Cup, Towns Plate, Towns 2nd XV Cup, Towns 2nd XV Plate, Anderson Cup and Dunne Cup). Courtesy of Pat Fitzgerald, private collection.

p. 328: The Leinster team celebrate following the European Rugby Champions Cup final win over Racing 92 at the San Mames Stadium in Bilbao, Spain, 12 May 2018; Leinster head coach Leo Cullen and captain Isa Nacewa during their homecoming in Dublin, May 2018, following their victory in the European Champions Cup final. Both images © Ramsey Cardy/Sportsfile.

p. 329: Leinster head coach Leo Cullen. © Ramsey Cardy/Sportsfile.

p. 330: Brian O'Driscoll montage from *The Ecstasy & The Agony of Leinster Rugby: 20 Years of Professional Club Rugby*, internal Leinster Rugby publication. Copy courtesy of Pat Fitzgerald private collection.

p. 331: Shane Horgan on his way to scoring a try against Llanelli Scarlets in the Heineken Cup in 2009. © Matt Browne/Sportsfile.

pp. 332–3: Leinster Academy Squad 2014–15, listed in match-day programmes. From DDPC.

p. 334: Leinster legend and current contact skills coach Seán O'Brien.

p. 335: Leinster player Tadhg Furlong with having lots of fun with participants during the Bank of Ireland Leinster Rugby Summer Camp at Gorey RFC in Wexford, 2018. © Eóin Noonan/Sportsfile.

pp. 336–7: 12 May 2018; Leinster players celebrate following the European Rugby Champions Cup final match between Leinster and Racing 92 at San Mames Stadium in Bilbao, Spain. © Stephen McCarthy/Sportsfile.

p. 338: Leinster players celebrate with the cup after the Vodafone Women's Interprovincial Championship final, 2023. © Eóin Noonan/Sportsfile.

p. 339: The Southern Cross Dogos affiliated to the Leinster Branch in December 2016. The club, composed entirely of expatriates, was organised by a group of Argentinian players based in Dublin.

Epilogue

INDEX